S0-BDG-575

Man's Struggle for Shelter
in an Urbanizing World

This book is one of a series published under the auspices of the Joint Center for Urban Studies, a cooperative venture of the Massachusetts Institute of Technology and Harvard University. The Joint Center was founded in 1959 to organize and encourage research on urban and regional problems. Participants have included scholars from the fields of anthropology, architecture, business, city planning, economics, education, engineering, history, law, philosophy, political science, and sociology.

The findings and conclusions of this book are, as with all Joint Center publications, solely the responsibility of the author.

Man's Struggle for Shelter

in an Urbanizing World

CHARLES ABRAMS

THE M.I.T. PRESS

MASSACHUSETTS INSTITUTE OF TECHNOLOGY

CAMBRIDGE, MASSACHUSETTS, AND LONDON, ENGLAND

Third M.I.T. Press Paperback Printing, March 1970

Copyright © 1964
by
The Massachusetts Institute of Technology
and the President and Fellows of Harvard College
All Rights Reserved

ISBN 0 262 010100 (paperback)
ISBN 0 262 510014 (hardcover)

Library of Congress Catalog Card Number: 64-16506
Printed in the United States of America

Foreword

In 1952, thirteen years after the publication of my study on the American land problem,[1] Ernest Weissmann, director of the United Nations Housing, Building and Planning Branch, persuaded me to undertake a survey of the world's urban land problems and policies. The study[2] sparked my interest in the evolving problems of the less developed nations and widened a focus that until then had been concentrated mainly on the American scene. During the ten years that followed, I was sent to India as a U.N. consultant and subsequently served on U.N. missions to Ghana, Turkey, the Philippines, Pakistan, Nigeria, Ireland, Jamaica, Japan, Singapore, and Bolivia. Thereafter my interest and information broadened with additional assignments for the governments of Venezuela, Barbados, and Puerto Rico, an assignment to Jamaica for the International Cooperation Administration, another to Colombia for the Pan-American Union, and attendance at numerous seminars and conferences of world experts convened by the United Nations. The findings and recommendations of these missions are embraced in fourteen separate reports.

In 1961, the Joint Center for Urban Studies of the Massachusetts Institute of Technology and Harvard University asked me to put the findings of my reports into a book. Irrespective of the number of countries one visits, to write a book that involves a world of nations with varying problems, backgrounds, and stages of development carries a greater risk for an author than merely to publish his case studies preceded by a brief essay.

Yet because a few dominant themes of almost universal relevance had impressed themselves upon me during the missions, I felt that a more comprehensive book was authorized and that a few general theories could be advanced. Virtually all the nations I visited have been experiencing an urbanization that is perhaps the most dynamic revolution in man's history. In the next forty years, the population growth in the world's cities will probably be double the entire population growth that the world has experienced in the last 6000 years. The less developed nations are feeling the impact not only of torrential population in-migrations to their cities but of mutations in their economies and in ways of life that have remained unaltered for centuries. While the European transformation to industrialization and urbanization had been far less rapid, the less developed countries have been experiencing their changes almost simultaneously. Yet neither in Europe nor in North America have

---

[1] *Revolution in Land* (New York: Harper, 1939).

[2] *Urban Land Problems and Policies, Housing and Town and Country Planning, Bulletin # 7* (New York: United Nations, 1953).

there been many revolutionary advances in housing production or in city planning from which the developing countries might benefit materially. This lag has evidenced itself in the vast problems of slum life, squatting, and homelessness, which are having political, social, and economic repercussions almost everywhere.

Although the book highlights housing as an important component of the urbanizing process, its discussion cannot be separated from numerous other aspects of the development process. A book about housing must be a book about cities as well, and a book on housing and cities must also deal with the implications of the urban land problem. Housing is not only shelter but part of the fabric of neighborhood life and of the whole social milieu; it also touches upon many facets of industrialization, economic activity, and development. The social aspects of change, the immaturity of the legal, political, and administrative devices, as well as the need for training and education are only a few of the challenges to the emerging societies. The place of private and public investment in building and in materials production, together with the unsettled and often primitive financing, tax, land, savings, and transportation policies, is another.

If one permits his hopes to condition his speculations, he may even conclude that a universal urbanization will modify man's eternal drives for space by diverting them from a centrifugal competition for tillable land to an intensive competition for the compact spaces in and around cities within each nation. In that event, it is even possible that in the urban world of a half century hence, both the vulnerability of urban nations and the inner drives toward urban land may at last lay to rest the *Lebensraum* concept that has perennially arisen to threaten world peace.[3]

Although it deserves an eminent place in our current thinking, the shelter problem has been subordinated in most studies of growth as well as in international aid programs. Less than $200,000, or about 0.1 per cent of United States technical assistance, went for housing to all countries outside Latin America in 1962. In Latin America, on the other hand, hundreds of millions of aid dollars have been hastily poured into housing programs before the essential theories of urban development and housing have even been framed.

Yet the need is not only for general theories but for practical proposals. The answers, moreover, suggest themselves only after one has

[3] In 1897, an article cited in the *Encyclopedia of Social Reform* (New York and London: Funk, Wagnall & Co., p. 547), stated that "A hundred years hence we shall almost certainly be flying. . . . As one result of the flying machine . . . we shall probably be delivered from the institution of war, since such terrible destruction will be possible with a corps of fighting aeroplanes that no nation will dare to risk it." The writer was as much off his mark regarding the day when man would be flying as he was in his prediction that wars would end with the event. But three quarters of a century later, the prediction no longer seems so remote.

visited the country and talked to the people as well as the officials and experts. The examples that I have given of the roof-loan scheme in Ghana and of core housing and installment construction in Asia and in Latin America are only a few of the experimental ideas that have come out of observations at the scene. Taxation to force unused land into use, the "planned inevitability" concept, planning for "urban renewability," planned squatting, and devices for inducing savings are other proposals appearing in the reports of the missions. So too, the drafting of a housing and planning statute on a mission to a developing country such as Pakistan is more than a legal exercise—it also sets in motion a political formula for the relationship between government, the individual, and his property.

After studying and reporting on the housing problems of fourteen nations in four continents, I have identified no panaceas for the housing problem in the developing countries. Often not even a start can be made without establishing the training for the many interrelated disciplines that touch upon the development process. This was dramatically illustrated for me in Turkey. During my experience there, I concluded that little headway would be made until architects, engineers, and social scientists could be trained for the multiple tasks that lay ahead. The establishment of the Middle East Technical University, which in 1964 was training 2100 people in a whole range of sciences, will do more in the long run, I believe, in preparing Turkey and perhaps several other countries in the Middle East for meeting their housing and urbanization problems than any other single recommendation I might have proffered.

The book lays claim to no universal or lasting truths. What is applicable to Bolivia may not be so in Nigeria. In fact, each country within Africa, South America, and Asia will present special problems of its own. Some countries are less industrialized than others; some are advanced industrially but suffer from lack of institutional development. Each may change for the better or worse as the years go by. At a time when theories must be tested as well as formulated, an author's conclusions cannot always be expected to be enduring or infallible.

Because of the almost complete lack of research on housing and urbanization in the underdeveloped areas, I am hopeful that this study of shelter, urban land, and urbanization problems may provide a series of hypotheses that others will challenge and evaluate. If it succeeds in casting a stronger light on the importance of housing, urban land, and urbanization in the developing areas, and if it also inspires greater attention to these problems in aid programs, it will have more than served its purpose.

A few words are required about the type of reader for whom the book is intended. Most of the chapters can, I believe, be read by the layman as well as the expert. But to have excluded some of the more technical aspects such as the discussion of financing programs and planning would not have done the subject full justice, for this type of information is often the key to the more difficult aspects of the problem. While the layman can skip over the more technical chapters, the specialist may be interested in reading the individual reports of the missions, from which most of the factual material in this study is drawn. For the benefit of those who wish to study the individual cases in their own context, I have made available the reports on Ghana, Turkey, Pakistan, the Philippines, Venezuela, Jamaica, Ireland, Barbados, and Bolivia at the planning libraries of Harvard University, the Massachusetts Institute of Technology, the University of California in Berkeley, and the University of Pennsylvania. The studies on Nigeria and Singapore (as well as any subsequent studies I may make) will, I trust, be added to the list by the United Nations or other agencies when the reports have received government clearance. For those interested in comparing the problems of a developing area in the United States, I have also made available my reports on Puerto Rico, my report for the Governor's Advisory Commission on Housing Problems in California, and the research studies of others on which it is based.

I am indebted to a number of people who have helped make this a better book: Lloyd Rodwin and Martin Meyerson, codirectors of the Joint Center for Urban Studies of the Massachusetts Institute of Technology and Harvard University, encouraged me to write it and provided the grant through the Center that made it possible. I am deeply grateful to Alexander L. Crosby for his editorial suggestions and to Charles M. Haar, Aaron Fleisher, Catherine Bauer Wurster, and Yehuda Tamir, who read the manuscript in draft and provided valuable criticisms in both form and content. I am grateful also to Under-Secretary of State W. Averell Harriman for his reading of Chapter 17 and for his valuable suggestions. The United Nations photographic library, George Nez, and Donald Hansen generously contributed some of the photographs.

I owe a particular debt to Otto Koenigsberger, who was associated with me on missions to Ghana, Pakistan, the Philippines, Nigeria, and Singapore. I have had many valuable exchanges of ideas with him, and both of us learned much during the earlier assignments when very little was known about either the problems or their implications. To Peggy Andre, Joanne Josephson, and Fred Gluck, I owe thanks for their clerical assistance. Finally, to my wife, Ruth Abrams, I owe much more than I can express for her tolerance during the missions and during the many months when I was writing and rewriting this book.

Charles Abrams

New York, New York
January 2, 1964

Contents

*To the many hundreds of good people in the nations
I visited who made this book possible by the gracious gift of
their time, their thoughts, and their counsel.*

1

Population Inflation and
Urban Invasion

Despite man's unprecedented progress in industry, education, and the sciences, the simple refuge affording privacy and protection against the elements is still beyond the reach of most members of the human race. The unevenness of man's advance from the lower species is best illustrated in his struggle for shelter. Here, more than in any other aspect of living, people of more primitive cultures have shown a greater capacity for coping with nature's challenges than urban man.

One reason for this lag is the population surge that has more than doubled the world's numbers in a century. Thanks to modern medicine, sanitation, and food production, the years are being extended for an ever-increasing number of people who once would have died before they could proliferate. A population that remained virtually steady during the first eighteen hundred years of Christendom is rising by fifty to sixty million annually. Less than forty years hence, an estimated six to seven billion people will somehow have to be housed, fed, and clothed.[1]

With the frittered farmlands no longer yielding enough food for the growing number of mouths, and with escape to frontier countries shut off, the cities within each country have become the most obvious prospect for distributing the human surplus.[2] The first problem for the peo-

[1] United Nations Population Commission, *World Population Situation and Prospects*, memorandum submitted by the Secretary-General, December 22, 1958, p. 2.
[2] Between 1900 and 1950, the population living in cities of 100,000 or more in Asia rose from an estimated 19.4 million to 105.6 million (a gain of 444 per cent), and in Africa from 1.1 million to 10.2 million (a gain of 827 per cent). World

ple who swarm into the cities is to get a roof over their heads; land and housing are therefore assuming a new importance in the struggle for subsistence.

LAND AND HOUSING IN THE NEW URBAN SCENE

Ever since the dawn of civilization, man's effort to keep alive has been involved with the land. He has looked to the land for his food and clothing, and for the space to cook, wash, spend his leisure time, and sleep. Land has played an important part in the building of his house too, for from it he has extracted the mud, stones, wood, grass, or bamboo that he could put together with his own hands. The enclosure he managed to erect met his simple needs, i.e., a place for mating, a repository for his few possessions, and a protection against weather. He had access to the field and to sunshine, proximity to work and family, and the relatively ample space in which to move about.

As masses of people head cityward today, they find the land staked out into small lots, to be bought or rented. Even if they can buy the land, they no longer can build homes with their own tools and talents. Nor have they the time to build. In many instances their meager diet provides them with too little energy after their daily exertions and their long, tiring journeys from work.[3] Materials must now be bought from manufacturers or middlemen. Moreover, laws prescribe how and where people can build. To buy or rent a home, there must be a constant flow of money from a steady job. In short, the house has become a commodity, like bread. The individual no longer initiates or controls its production and, worse still, is seldom able to buy or rent what he needs.[4]

---

population living in cities with 20,000 or more inhabitants mounted from about 21.7 million in 1800 to 502.2 million in 1950, expanding 23 times in 150 years, while the total world population expanded about 2.6 times in the same period. In 1800, 2.4 per cent of the world's population lived in urban centers of 20,000 or more; in 1950, 20.9 per cent. From United Nations Economic and Social Council, *Report on the World Social Situation* (New York, 1957), Ch. VII. See also United Nations Economic and Social Council, *Report on the World Social Situation* (New York, April 1961).

[3] In India, for example, the calorie intake in the mid-1950's was 1700, while the estimated requirements were 2250; in the Philippines, 1960 as against 2230; and in French North Africa, 1920 as against 2430. Douglas H. K. Lee, *Climate and Economic Development in the Tropics* (New York: Harper, 1957).

[4] From rough data, the estimate has been made that only about 10 to 30 per cent of urban households in Asia had incomes of the $50 to $70 per month required in the mid-1950's to support a house costing $1000, the rental or purchase cost of which would be about $10 a month. See United Nations Economic and Social Council, *Financing of Housing and Community Improvement Programmes* (New York, March 7, 1955), pp. 17, 18.

The problem has been complicated, moreover, by the fact that people have been pouring into the cities much faster than the emerging industries can absorb them. Between 1960 and 1970, 200 million people are expected to move into the cities of Asia, Africa, and Latin America.[5] The ever-growing horde descending upon the cities has intensified and will continue to intensify the demand for housing, and it has heightened the competition for wages to pay for homes. The migrant generally arrives without income or skills and often continues to live on a marginal level for most of his stay. As a result, street sleeping, slums, overcrowding, and squatting have produced a new human predicament in the burgeoning cities. The first three problems are described in this chapter. Squatting is discussed in more detail in Chapter 2.

STREET SLEEPING

A street sleeper is a mobile squatter without a house. If the climate and the authorities are clement, the street sleeper continues bedding down in the streets until he can find a better cover and the means to pay for it. Others accept the pavement as their established abode.

While there was considerable street sleeping in Europe in the early stages of industrialization, it has been eliminated there except for derelicts and vagrants. But in Calcutta, some 600,000 people sleep in the streets. Census figures for Bombay made public in 1963 showed that 1 in every 66 persons was homeless, while another 77,000 people lived under stairways, in cattle sheds, on landings, or in similar spaces.[6] Though many workers in the cities can afford to pay for minimum shelter, the means for producing it have not yet been developed. Some people have therefore put up bamboo and burlap lean-tos on the cement walks, where the women cook over smoky fire pots using cow dung as fuel. Ten or more people in India share these tiny bustees. In Hong Kong, it

[5] Estimates of housing needs are precarious. Descriptions of housing conditions in Asiatic cities may be more informative than statistical estimates, which, even where accurate, obsolesce in a few months. One estimate in 1951 was that from 100 to 150 million rural and urban families in Asia lived in overcrowded, insanitary, and substandard shelter. See United Nations Report of Mission of Experts, *Low Cost Housing in South and South-East Asia* (New York, March 12, 1951), p. 3. Another estimate is that in Asia, Africa, and Latin America, half the population either is homeless or lives under unsafe or grossly overcrowded housing conditions. See United Nations Meeting of Experts, February 7–21, 1962, Working Paper 4, *The Role of Housing and Urban Development in National Development Programs* (New York, 1962), pp. 9, 10.

[6] Thomas F. Brady, "India's 'Big Town,'" *New York Times*, November 2, 1963. According to the *Manchester Guardian*, December 13, 1963, there were about 1700 adults and 50 children sleeping in the streets of London in 1904, compared with 129 adults on one cold November night in 1963 and 120 on another night in the same year.

has not been unusual for street cleaners to find forsaken carcasses, which they remove on their morning rounds.[7]

In Lagos, Nigeria, a street sleeper will watch a shop at night and keep away other street sleepers in return for the nightly use of a threshold. A few thousand homeless will seek a spot on the piers in the rat-ridden lagoon or scout around for an unguarded space on which to lay a straw mat.

Street sleeping permits no family life, no privacy, no relief from heat, no escape from cold or rain, and no decent means for disposing of human waste. It is the way of the stray animal, the lowest form of urban life.

TYPES OF SLUMS

More commonly workers have swarmed into city slums. The word "slum" is a catchall for poor housing of every kind as well as a label for the environment. The same word denotes a Chicago mansion turned into furnished rooms and a cardboard carton sheltering a human being in Lima.

Because of its inclusiveness, the word too often obscures the vast differences between one type of slum and another. Slums may be either rented or owner-occupied, either legal or illegal. They include cabins, shanties, dens, dugouts, sheds, stalls, and other manifestations of poverty. Some are single-family shelters converted into several smaller compartments; some are one-story and others six-story tenements. Although most slums are in the industrial cities, many are found in mining towns and farm areas. Others line the back alleys of mansions.

Some slums are new and some the abandoned houses of those who have moved up in the economic scale. The new slum is built because it has a use at the price, while the old slum survives because there is nothing cheaper and more serviceable to replace it. The new huts built of scavenged scrap by in-migrants to Asian or South American cities are often worse than the old ones.

Slums flourish in many environments. They emerge from marshes, hillsides, or war ruins in the Philippines; they are built within old forts or on swamps in Puerto Rico and India; and they line the hills in Latin America. Punctuating the cemeteries and the side roads near new apartment houses in Karachi, slums also appear as holes in ancient caves near Rawalpindi and in southern Spain. They abound in the Casbah of Tunis

[7] Harold Ingrams, *Hong Kong* (London: Her Majesty's Stationery Offices, 1952), p. 81. When I was in Hong Kong in 1963, J. F. Fraser, director of housing in the colony, told me that after the massive housing program and the curtailment of illegal immigration, this manifestation of suffering and homelessness is no longer as frequent as before.

and in the resort centers of Havana and the West Indies; they are the thousands of dark single rooms of Ahmedabad, Cawnpore, and Nagpur.

Slum life is not always the symbol of retrogression. It may in fact be the first advance from homelessness into shelter, or the way station on the road from abject poverty to hope. The slum exists because no nation is able to produce adequate housing at a cost that workers can afford. It is the shelter that the industrial age provides for its rank and file. Housing has remained the Cinderella of the Industrial Revolution, and the slum the humble cover to which she has been indefinitely assigned.

WASTE DISPOSAL IN SLUMS

One of the most troublesome aspects of slum life continues to be the simple disposal of human excrement, which may be discharged into a ditch shared by dozens of families or left to decompose between shacks. Skyscrapers may shoot up side by side with colonies of slum dwellers whose only latrine is a rarely cleaned trench shared sometimes by hundreds of families. In the age of the atom, the disposal of human feces remains one of the stubbornly persistent problems of urban man.

Absence of a system for removing excrement from living areas continually exposes the healthy to the contaminated wastes of the ill and the disease carrier. In the crowded urban communities that have mushroomed in recent years, such pollution is accepted as part of the way of life. For example, in Lagos, Nigeria, out of 4759 schoolchildren whose stools were examined, 85 per cent were infected with parasites, roundworm and hookworm being the most common forms. Dysentery and diarrhea accounted for 10.1 per cent of all deaths in 1960. In the same year, 54.5 per cent of all the deaths in Nigeria's capital city occurred among children under five years of age. Although pail collection is common in undeveloped areas, it is far from being the most sanitary form of waste disposal. Yet in many areas even this primitive service is absent or haphazard; often night soil is allowed to accumulate for weeks or months before it is removed. Sometimes it is left to decompose.

OVERCROWDING IN SLUMS

The afflictions of slum living are intensified by crowding and lack of privacy. If there were an adequate supply of urban slums for everyone who needed shelter, their baneful effects might be confined to squalor, darkness, and decrepitude. But the general shortage of slums means that those that exist are also packed with people. "Crowding" in these instances means that the houses are crowded onto almost all available space; it also refers to crowding within the house itself. For example, the number of people per room in Guatemala averages more than three, compared with a little less than one person per room in Australia, the United States, the United Kingdom, and Switzerland.[8]

Lack of privacy, exposure to contagion, and social disintegration are only a few of the by-products of a life with almost no room to breathe, ail, or die. In the single-room tenements of Bombay, occupancy in 1948 already ranged from six to nine persons per room with an over-all average of seven, while crowding ten persons into a space 10 by 15 feet was common.[9] Average floor space per person was about 27 square feet. In such tenements, one occupant could not see another in the dark passages or rooms. Sickly complexions, emaciated bodies, and the drawn faces of the children tell their tale.

In Panama, where shelters bulge at the seams with as many as twenty individuals living in a room 15 by 15 feet, sleeping is done in relays. In Kingston, Jamaica, nine persons occupy tiny huts 6 by 10 feet. In Accra, Ghana, occupancy per single house in 1960 was 19.3 persons; the occupancy was even higher in Kumasi. In Lagos, Nigeria, which has three migrants to every natural birth, as many as eighty people share a small house on a site scheduled for clearance, and even in the fringe areas, sixteen to twenty persons per house is not unusual.

In-migration into some cities of the Far East has created living conditions without any vestige of privacy or room for motion. In Hong Kong, five or six human beings share cubicles measuring 40 square feet. Density is as high as 2000 persons per acre in one-story hutments in which there is no water, sanitation, or organized system of refuse disposal. Fowl or pigs share some of the huts or the tiny open spaces around them.

In a single shophouse in Singapore, I saw families of six to eight people facing life in airless, windowless rooms 7 by 10 feet, with as many as five children sleeping on the roach-ridden floor beneath the bed. About a third of the occupants in the average shophouse have no window at all; the rest have either one window (which is usually shuttered) or only access to a light shaft. Frequently the occupant uses his rented space not only for sleeping but as a "farm" for growing bean sprouts or as a shop. The illness of a child or a parent means that the whole family must share the discomforts, if not the disease as well. Yet this is the way of life for tens of thousands of people in Singapore and elsewhere.[10]

[8] United Nations, *Technical Assistance Newsletter,* Vol. II, No. 2 (New York, May 1961).

[9] National Planning Commission of India, *National Housing* (Bombay: Vora & Co., February 1948).

[10] Charles Abrams, Susumu Kobe, and Otto Koenigsberger, *Report for the Government of Singapore,* prepared by an Expert Mission appointed under the United Nations Technical Assistance Programme (min., Singapore, August 1963).

Both Hong Kong and Singapore have undertaken extensive rehousing programs, but the demand for space is so intense and the size of the average household so large that it is not unusual to see five and sometimes as many as ten people sharing one of the new rooms. In Singapore, of 10,125 applications to the Housing and Redevelopment Board, the family size of nearly half was listed as seven persons or more. Many of these families would be assigned single rooms. In Hong Kong's new housing projects, I saw families of ten sharing a single room for their shelter, and often it was also the workshop from which they were trying to eke out a living.

It is virtually impossible, particularly in tropical areas, to keep water clean when it must be carried long distances and retained for hours or days in exposed tubs or cans. Often the water is contaminated at the source. In one slum area I inspected in Kingston, Jamaica, a single tap serves seven hundred persons; in another, occupied by eight thousand people, there was no water at all.

The housing situation is no better in many villages. In fourteen villages of Upper and Lower Egypt, for example, 27.5 per cent of the shelters have no roofs at all. These settlements are usually clusters of cramped, drafty, dark mud huts crowded together to avoid encroaching on the farmland.[11] Conditions such as these, coupled with average peasant income of $11.50 a year per person, accelerate the move to the cities, where the housing conditions are most often worse.

The magnitude of the problem in the underdeveloped world may be gleaned from the fact that more than a billion people in Africa, Asia, and Latin America, or roughly half the population of these continents, are homeless or live in housing that is described by the United Nations as a menace to health and an affront to human dignity.[12] Worse still, in almost all the developing areas, housing conditions are steadily deteriorating. Many families pay so much for the privilege of bedding down on a floor or other space that little is left for the bare essentials of life. And as the surge to the cities goes on, the competition for space will become keener, rents will rise further, squatting and overcrowding will increase, and the effort to carry on some semblance of family life will become less and less hopeful.

SOME SOCIAL BY-PRODUCTS

In the more developed areas whose slums might be viewed in Asia as châteaux, overcrowded slums have been found to yield a high juvenile

[11] Hassan Fathy, "Rural Self-Help Housing," *International Labor Review*, January 1962.

[12] United Nations, *The United Nations Development Decade*, Proposals for Action, Report of the Secretary-General (New York, 1962).

delinquency rate; high rates of family dependence on public assistance; high proportions of illiteracy; high proportions of employed women; more unemployment, poverty, and divorce; more nonsupport cases and alcoholism; a high incidence of mental disorders and mental deficiency; low marriage rates; a low average educational level; and high residential mobility.

It would be a mistake, however, to view the slum's impact as the same everywhere, or to see poor housing as the only cause of social abnormality. Although bad housing contributes to juvenile delinquency and crime, its influence may in some cases be mitigated by compensating elements, such as strong parental influences, constructive discipline in the school or community, good associations, and counteracting ethical values. Environment is more than physical environment; it is a combination of physical, social, and personal factors that influence parents and children. Yet the change in a normal boy from rural Puerto Rico when he moves into a slum in New York City is often appalling—despite New York's well-organized educational and social services.

Many aspects of the shelter problem need further study. Though much has been written on slum life in Europe and the United States, less is known about slums in the underdeveloped countries. We understand even less about the effects of overcrowding and of poor housing on the emotions. What, for example, is the child's response to sexual intimacy between adults in a jammed household?

Little is known also of the destruction of human dignity when the home and community in which the family once had a place no longer exist. In the tribal communities or in those in which housing was built as part of a compound, the job of keeping the common grounds clean was often assigned to particular members. In the shift to crowded cities, this responsibility has either been passed on to governments that are unable to cope with it, or has been left to the people themselves. In Africa, for example, the collective accountability of tribal life is being replaced by individuation, self-interest, and self-preservation. The Indian village, which for all its hardships offered community life and access to the open field, has no compensatory alternative in the herding and the disunity of the new urban agglomerations. The working father is no longer near home, and the working mother hurries toward the factory or the crowded marketplace to help pay the landlord. The child, seeing its parents only at evening, quickens to outside forces more readily than ever before. The females left behind in the villages find the opportunities for marriage diminishing as the young males emigrate.

From the earliest days of civilization, man had been able to create a home with his own hands. Now, for the first time, this is no longer within his competence. The hovels he lives in are worse than those he

built when he emerged from the cave. Indeed, th
often sounder shelters with better roofs and more
of some Asian cities.

THE STREET, THE NEIGHBORHOOD, AND THE

A large group of houses can make a "neighborhood" if the peop
live there bring to it the elements of intimate association and a unity
interest. The neighborhood is a place where children meet and influence each other and where the residents have a feeling of belonging.
But often the big city is merely the aggregate of heterogeneous clusters of
hovels, plus shops, factories, streets, and public services. This mass of
makeshifts in the teeming cities has provided no substitute for the village institutions that bestow relative equality of status, humble as it may
be. The new city formations are saturated, impersonal, tentative, and
without the mellowed traditions or folkways of the older way of life.
Restraints and sanctions are absent, and the lack of living space undermines family discipline by driving the child into the streets.

The inhuman densities inside the shelter might be relieved by adequate space outside, but too often the only outside space is a narrow,
rutted path that must provide room for movement of people, the carrying off of waste and rain water, cooking, peddling one's wares, and sometimes space for draft animals as well. Where streets are paved and wide
enough, however, the street has assumed some of the functions that the
home unit lacks. In Asia, the street is often the mass dining room for the
family and the place where one gets his oxygen amid the miscellaneous
odors of culinary activity. It is the market, the display room for wares,
the social meeting place and the recreational outlet, the source of livelihood for the peddler, the rickshaw or trishaw man, as well as the theater
of action in which every child, visitor, tradesman, and hawker among
the thousands converging on the street are the players. The street is
often convulsive, yet exciting. To share it with the automobile is hard.
It is inefficient for its many new tasks, but still vital; it is exasperating,
but a way of life—a slumscape of the turbulent cities. Here and in their
cubicles, the family demonstrates that remarkable genius of the human
species which has been responsible for survival through its centuries of
trial.

The growing city, with all its faults, is the crucible in which man's
destiny will be determined. The slum may be with us always, and for
many people it may be the only escape from famine and stagnation, the
temporary anchorage of struggling mankind slowly moving toward
something better. But the prospect of something better should be there,
however remote.

iest history, the city has been linked with man's freedoms[13]
ge in the days of Cain and Joshua, the hub of a vigorous political
n Greece, the impetus to law in Rome. When man's mind roamed
e in Utopian dreams, it was the city that was so often closest to his
onception of heaven—the "Celestial City," the "Heavenly City," the
"New Jerusalem," the "Holy City," and the "City of God." Moreover, it
was the city of trade, commerce, and property that helped undermine
serfdom and that ushered in other freedoms in the process. Though industrialization posed a threat in the cities of Europe, more freedoms
somehow emerged in cities, and more freedoms survived in them. The
story may, if given time, repeat itself even in the cankerous formations
of the more recently industrialized areas. For despite its changes and
challenges, the city still contains the raw ingredients of freedom. The
city still harbors the hope, in an increasingly hazardous and complex
society, that the social and economic fluidity which was its historic at-
tribute can be maintained against the chaotic forces that challenge it. It
is still the marketplace for goods and ideas, the locus of a contractual
society, the mirror for emulation, the meeting place for diversities, the
center of culture. In the European cities that once also felt the first
shocks of industrialization, parliamentary government ultimately established its political validity, encrusted its precedents with a heavy layer
of protective traditions, and constructed the essential devices for mini-
mizing violent changes. Perhaps in the troubled cities of the developing
world, the same values too may emerge and grow.

The swelling cities of the East may indeed be reliving some of the
history of the Western cities. They have become the haven of the refugee,
the hungry, the politically oppressed. The Filipino hinterlanders fleeing
the Huks pour into Manila, the Hindus escaping the Moslems head into
Old Delhi, and the victims of Chinese communism drift into Hong Kong.
When his miserable two acres no longer yield enough grain for the
Indian peasant, or the floods drown the Pakistani's meager crop, he
moves toward the teeming city. As the desert wind blows over the
drought-ridden land, the Arab whips his camel toward the bustling new
human settlements.

[13] The word "freedom" is an abstraction that is symbolic, controversial, and fluc-
tuating in its meanings. It embraces a variety of "freedoms from" and "freedoms to."
Without elaborating on its complexities, I have used the word here in a circular
sense in which man, given a tolerable environment, has tended to evolve institutions
and devices that allow him greater social and economic mobility and a larger variety
of personal options. The institutions he helps create in turn tend to fortify such
options. The urban scene, I believe, has in the past provided this opportunity
better than any other way of life that man has yet devised. The city is also a setting
where he has been better able to acquire the knowledge essential to identify more
electives, and where he is allowed to strive for their attainment free of unreasonable
restraints.

But in too many of the developing cities, the older customs and institutions of value are weakening before the newer ones have taken root. The building of a stable life is thwarted by housing famine and the frustrations of crowded living. Unfortunately, those with the talent and vision to reform the social pattern are rare, and trained civil servants few. Hopes and fears for freedom and opportunity rise and fall with each crisis and with the disillusionments linked with it.

By 1950, one in every five of the world's people lived in cities of more than 20,000. With fifty to sixty million new mouths to feed annually, the push to the city gains impetus. In Asia, Africa, and Latin America, the total population is expected to increase by two fifths in the fifteen years between 1961 and 1975, and urban populations are expected to double. Thus the urban housing stock must be increased four times in that period (without making allowance for dilapidation and decay).[14] The average income per person of only fifty cents a day in 90 per cent of the world's countries has not kept the birth rate from rising. In fact, it is rising more sharply in the very areas that can least afford to accommodate more children. Yet for many, if not ultimately for most, the city is becoming the only alternative to hunger and despair.

With rates of urban growth in Asia 400 per cent higher than in the West, and the movement to the cities only beginning, it is idle to speculate on what might have been the better life. The die has been cast. The irrepressible forces of urbanization are forging ahead, and in the long run there appears to be no other option. The question is only whether human endurance will persist in these settlements until better patterns emerge.

[14] United Nations Meeting of Experts, February 7–21, 1962, Working Paper 4, *The Role of Housing and Urban Development in National Development Programs*, *op. cit.*, p. 9. This figure includes relief of existing shortages.

2

Squatting and Squatters

Human history has been an endless struggle for control of the earth's surface; and conquest, or the acquisition of property by force, has been one of its more ruthless expedients. With the surge of population from the rural lands to the cities, a new type of conquest has been manifesting itself in the cities of the developing world. Its form is squatting, and it is evidencing itself in the forcible preemption of land by landless and homeless people in search of a haven. Unlike other forms of conquest that were propelled by the pursuit of glory, trade routes, or revenues, squatting is part of a desperate contest for shelter and land. Of all forms of illegal seizure, squatting is the most condonable.

The old frontier areas of the more developed nations were once also the scenes of squatting, but in time titles were established, the land was often granted or sold to the squatters, and the law of force was supplanted by the force of law. Squatting, however, was rarely carried over into the cities of America[1] or Europe, because law and property rights

---

[1] Occasional squatting occurs in the more developed nations on newly irrigated lands or in forests opened by roads. More than 29,000 acres along the Colorado River, closed to homesteading in the early part of the century, are occupied by squatters who during the last two decades have infiltrated into the area and stayed there. Business thrives and property turnover occurs, with one large plot bringing as much as $125,000. There are squatter trailer courts, gas stations, stores, and boating facilities. The squatters have become politically strong by organizing for the protection of their "rights," and the government has seemingly condoned their presence by establishing a post office and negotiating for rental arrangements. Such squatting, however, is rare in the United States though common during frontier days. Daniel M. Burnham, *The Wall Street Journal*, June 14, 1961.

in cities were too firmly rooted. Members of the British privileged classes who had acquiesced in rural squatting until the time of the enclosures would not long allow the same indulgences for urban property. The urban slum, not the squatter's shack, became the mark of industrialization in Europe and later in America.

Squatting in the cities of the underdeveloped world today is usually open and defiant, tempting more squatting by its successes. It has affected not only government-owned land but private land as well, including tracts provided with costly facilities. When squatting is prevalent, orderly development and expansion are impeded, investment in greatly needed urban enterprises may be discouraged, and the political stabilization of governments may be delayed.

The squatting problem exists in many parts of Asia, Latin America, and Africa—in fact, wherever there has been a mass movement of people to cities and insufficient shelter. There are now some 240,000 squatter units (*gececondu*) in Turkey. Squatters make up about 45 per cent of the population of Ankara, where some land has had to be turned over to them. They are 21 per cent of Istanbul's population and 18 per cent of Izmir's.[2] In 1951, they numbered sixty thousand in Baghdad and twenty thousand in Basra, Iraq;[3] in Karachi, squatters represented about a third of the population. Squatters account for at least 20 per cent of Manila's population, and in Davao squatters have taken possession of the whole parkway area running from the city hall to the retail center.[4] Urban centers in South America are also experiencing a flood of migrant squatters. In Venezuela the proportion of squatters (rural and urban) is more than 65 per cent of the total population, with a 35 per cent rate for Caracas and 50 per cent for Maracaibo. Cali, Colombia, has a squatter population that makes up about 30 per cent of the total figure.[5] In Santiago, Chile, squatters represent an estimated 25 per cent of the population. They constitute 15 per cent in Singapore and 12 per cent in Kingston, Jamaica.[6]

Though usually primitive, the appearance of squatting colonies varies

[2] *First Five-Year Development Plan, 1963–1967* (Ankara, 1963).

[3] International Bank for Reconstruction and Development, *The Economic Development of Iraq* (Baltimore, 1952), p. 55.

[4] Charles Abrams and Otto Koenigsberger, *Report on Housing in the Philippine Islands* (New York: United Nations, 1959).

[5] Estimates of the squatter population are never precise. Those given here are based either on the statements of officials or on official documents. In most cases they are conservative. Many squatters now call themselves tenants because they may have paid a nominal sum to the owner, who most often had no choice but to accept what was offered.

[6] Squatters are known by various names—"parachutists" (Mexico), *"favelos"* (Brazil), *"rancheros"* or *"conqueros"* (Venezuela). Their colonies are called, among other things, "witch-towns," *"barrios piratas," "callampas," "bidonvilles,"* and *"arrabales."*

somewhat according to the availability of building materials, the financial status of the squatters, and the prospects of continued possession. Little one-room shacks built of adobe and scrap are cropping up in Medellín, Barranquilla, and Cali, Colombia, and in fact throughout Latin America. The colonies lack paved streets, a sewerage system, and a water supply. Havana has a profusion of rude huts without sanitary facilities. In Algiers, tin-can towns, or *bidonvilles,* stand just five minutes away from the center of the city in almost any direction. The tightly packed shanties with only narrow alleys for passage are built of old oil drums, scrap metal, tin cans, and odd boards. Each hut, about 10 by 10 feet, houses an average of four or more persons and often a goat. In Tunis, the squatters live in caves dug out of hillsides.[7] Around the edges of Johannesburg, South Africa, sprawl squatter colonies that are a chaos of shacks and hovels pieced together by the homeless and destitute. In India's larger cities, squatters can be found hanging on to their precarious hovels in old forts or wherever they can acquire a foothold. They include not only the unemployed but also construction workers, some 250,000 of whom move from zone to zone as they finish one job and start another.[8] Their tin and rag shanties remain long after they have left for other places. Almost 150,000 squatters live in Delhi, about 90,000 of whom are on public land.

Squatting is triggered by many factors—enforced migration of refugees because of fear, hunger, or rural depression, the quest for subsistence in the burgeoning urban areas, and simple opportunism. Usually it is the by-product of urban landlessness and housing famine. Surplus rural labor and the need for labor in the towns combine to speed migrations. When there is no housing for the migrants, they do the only thing they can—they appropriate land, more often publicly owned land, from which there is less fear of being dislodged. Sympathy with the squatters' movements or lack of a consistent official policy encourages further squatting. Existing settlements spread, and new settlements mushroom. Many of Delhi's squatters put up shacks during the 1962 political campaign when they thought that politicians had assured them they would not be harassed.[9] Their shacks were demolished after the election.

SQUATTING IN PAKISTAN

In Pakistan the pattern has varied from major aggregations in well-defined areas (as in Karachi, Lyallpur, Hyderabad, and Dacca) to a

[7] From unpublished material available in the Library of the Housing and Home Finance Agency, Washington, D.C.

[8] Sharokh Sabavala, "India Counts Its Heads," *New Leader* (New York), February 27, 1961, p. 17.

[9] *New York Times,* April 8, 1962, p. 4.

few scattered colonies (as in Lahore, Rawalpindi, Peshawar, and Chittagong). Some squatters' settlements stand on costly land ripe for improvement. In Lyallpur, for example, squatters held land valued in 1957 at $1000 an acre. Squatters line the public avenues in Karachi and have moved into cemeteries and behind sacred old mosques. When construction workers erected temporary barracks abutting on the land where apartment houses were being built, the workers' colony remained long after the apartments were completed. Then the barracks were sold or extended until the area became a bustling shacktown.

The squatter movement began in Pakistan with the partition of India, which caused millions of Moslems to cross the new border in quest of a haven. By the end of 1948 some 6.6 million Moslems had entered Pakistan, while some 5.6 million non-Moslems had moved to India. The influx was resumed when violence broke out again. Fleeing for their lives, the Moslems settled where they could. A major housing program begun in the late fifties following a United Nations report, and a grant of $50 million in United States counterpart funds has succeeded in rehousing a large number of the squatters,[10] but the problem is far from solved.

SQUATTING IN THE PHILIPPINES

In the Philippines, before the smoke and dust of World War II devastation had cleared, thousands of Philippine families had already moved into the ruins. They put makeshift roofs over the naked columns and raised partitions of ragged cloth or old tin to separate family groups. Others settled on private land and have stayed there. Tondo, the so-called Casbah, and the Intramuros section are typical of squatter concentrations in Manila. The long rows of shacks near Cebu's piers and the thousands of families entrenched on the park-site area of Davao are examples in other provinces. There are also squatters on the shores of fishponds who are polluting the water, squatters in market areas, street squatters who have been evicted from their homes, shop squatters, and even wagon squatters who curl up for the night in their Coca-Cola carts. The variety is never-ending—a somber tribute to human ingenuity in the face of privation.

The sites marked for bombing and those chosen for squatting in Manila were often identical. They were at the city's core, the waterfront, and the centers of work. An anchorage downtown affords the squatter access to the city's hub and shortens his journey to work. The squatter has learned how to hang on—he has reduced the hazard of eviction by combining with others to resist it by force. A landowner who summarily removes a squatter may not wake up the morning after.

[10] See recommendations in Charles Abrams and Otto Koenigsberger, *Report on Housing in Pakistan* (New York: United Nations, 1957).

At first, the townspeople felt sympathy for the squatters in their ruins. But as time wore on and the justification for further indulgence faded, the squatters dug in deeper. Other squatters began to arrive en masse. Private property owners, fearing for their lives if they took summary action, often compromised by accepting a nominal rent, or actually paid a ransom to regain possession. The squatters could then move to another piece of property, hoping to repeat the profitable experience. Thus squatting became a business as well as a way of getting shelter in the Philippines. Some squatters have sublet their quarters; others have even sold them.

Seeing the squatters firm in their footholds, others have come, enlarging the colonies or creating new ones. As in a military campaign, some would bivouac during the night with their stock of materials behind a newly placed billboard. Next day, the horizon would be dotted with new rows of hovels, to which others would be added shack by shack, until the expansion was checked by a road, by a canal, or by an owner prepared to spill blood.

The public and political attitudes toward squatting vary. A brave mayor may challenge the colonists and sometimes gain more for his courage than he loses in squatters' votes. More often, however, the number of votes may be too formidable, in which event the public and private rights are gradually forfeited to the squatters. In Davao, the squatters are so firmly entrenched that a number are building costly houses. Lawyers, physicians, dentists, and managers of clinics and well-financed enterprises have boldly hung out their signs.

Squatting has grown into an enterprise in which poverty, guile, and opportunism compete for the prizes of lawlessness. The owner's fear makes him less disposed to protect his holdings. Traders encourage new ventures by guaranteeing protection to the venturers in return for a share in the prize. Some lawyers act for a fee or as direct entrepreneurs. Local squatters' associations as well as a national squatters' group have been organized to lobby for their rights. A squatters' congressman protects their interests in the legislature. Although a few officials occasionally speak up for the law, most have yielded to cynicism or futility.

When the squatters feel greater security, optimism replaces despair, odd evidences of affluence blossom amid the squalor, and speculation and turnover increase. The fact of possession commands a cash price adjusted to the probabilities of the owner's capitulation. In Manila, both the price of the foothold and the value of the owner's land fluctuated with the ups and downs of the late Mayor Lacson's anti-squatting campaign. In the City of Davao, where the mayor was less resolute, the signs on houses indicated not only an upward shift in squatter status, but increasing confidence in the uninterrupted enjoyment of possession. The signs on the houses in one area read:

"For Sale"
"For Rent"
"Dental Clinic"
"Physicians and Surgeons"
"Room for Rent"
"Master Plumber—Licensed"
"Abogado—Notary Public"
"House for Rent or for Sale"
"Wanted: House-maid"
"Dublin Enterprises"
"Milano Fencers' Guild"

While the squatters will violate private rights and resist eviction by force, they are usually law-abiding in other respects. A local law compelling the numbering of all houses, for example, is scrupulously observed. And while some of the shacks are used by criminals and prostitutes, most squatters are hardworking citizens who have either bought in or dug in.

SQUATTING IN VENEZUELA

In chronically troubled Caracas, Venezuela's capital city, squatters' colonies dominate the scene both inside the city and on its outskirts. The "ranchos" are perched on the mountain ranges. They are close to the shopping areas and in the city center. They also adjoin the housing superblocks built by the government.

Traveling by automobile from Caracas along the sea to the Macuto area, one never loses sight of growing rancho colonies carved out of niches or built on the mountainside. When the crags become sharp and steep, the ranchos fade, only to reappear on the first gentler incline.

The population of metropolitan Caracas has spurted from 694,000 in 1950 to 1.3 million in 1961, and now public services cannot keep pace with rancho expansion. When the rains come, a lava of human excrement is washed down on the roads below.

In contrast to other cities, whose suburban sprawl is the spread of middle-class families to the outskirts, the suburbs of Caracas blend mansions with ranchos. The mansions are on the flatlands and are provided with ample water and utilities. The ranchos are high up, depending on water hauled in oil cans. In the Caracas suburbs, squatter shacks have appeared wherever there is a new private development, as for example the stylish La Carabelleda Golf and Yacht Club, with its $75,000 mansions. The shacks also abut on the Puerto Azau, which is one of the larger beach apartment developments. The availability of water and utilities for a new development becomes the signal for a new rancho settlement close by. It then grows rapidly until the mountainside no longer yields usable space for settlers.

The type of rancho construction varies from house to house. Earth, cardboard, old boxes, tin, scrap, stucco, and brick tile are common materials. Most are one-story, but there is also a well-built four-story rancho for tenants.

Ranchos are rented and sold like legitimate real estate. One rancho occupant in the Caracas central superblock area told me that her husband, a telegraph worker, had sold his last rancho because it was too far from work. He had bought his present rancho for $1200. It had four small rooms with an old tin roof, and a container for night soil, which the city's garbage collector picked up intermittently. Water came from a common tap a good distance away. The house was on a narrow undrained dirt road, standing almost back to back with another in a long row that stretched out as far as the eye could see.[11]

A local survey of two rancho colonies showed that from 93 to 96 per cent of the ranchos were owner-occupied. The rest were rented for about $15 a month. The average stay of rancho occupants was thirteen years. From 18 to 25 per cent of the family heads were unemployed. Data on 18 per cent of the residents in the Pinto Salinas area showed the average income was $170 a month. More than 30 per cent were *oficios del hogar* (tailors and similar homeworkers), but almost every occupation was represented, including policemen.

Since about 30 per cent of the rancho families have television sets, about 32 to 35 per cent have refrigerators, and some 15 per cent own automobiles, it is evident that rancho living is more often the result of land and housing hunger than of poverty.

The ranchos exist in other Venezuelan cities and are numerous in rural areas as well. Some twenty thousand squatters in 1962 lived in the projected steel city of Ciudad Guayana, even while it was being planned and when the steel mill was providing only a thousand jobs. The 1950 census of agriculture and livestock placed the number of rural squatters at 35.8 per cent of the total of 248,738 agricultural workers. Squatting is the second most widespread form of tenure. One estimate is that 65 per cent of the country's population have no legal title to their land. Rural squatters may be found on private, state, and municipal lands. They till the soil with their hands and primitive tools and drift from one parcel of eroded land to another. The Institute of Inter-American Affairs describes the system in Valencia as "a black spot on the agriculture of this region."[12] A land reform program initiated by former President Rómulo Betancourt succeeded in giving land to 42,100 families in three

[11] Memorandum of Charles Abrams to Banco Obrero (mim., New York, July 1, 1960).

[12] *The Lake Valencia Region in Venezuela* (Washington, D.C., 1948), p. 7.

years, but acute unemployment and very low incomes for the bulk of the people continued a major problem. With the population growing at the rate of 3.6 per cent a year, a swelling inventory of potential migrant-squatters waits at the door of crowded Caracas and other Venezuelan cities.

In the interests of health, the government has also provided a few urban squatting colonies with electricity and some sanitary services, but living in the ranchos is still primitive.

SQUATTING IN JAMAICA, BRITISH WEST INDIES

Squatter areas dot Jamaica's cities and rural areas, but the two most prominent colonies are in Trenchtown, with some eight thousand squatters in 1961 and Kingston Penn, with some two thousand. Both are in Kingston, Jamaica's capital, which had a population of 123,000 in 1960. The Kingston area, with 400,000 people, is annually increased by some twenty thousand, half of whom pour into it from the island's hinterlands, while the other half represent the natural increase.[13]

The island has inherited the British legal tradition. Officially it must either act against lawlessness or deny that it exists. When two thousand squatters took over the privately owned Kingston Penn area, Kingston's police summarily hosed them out. The squatters bided their time and moved right back. Because the much-hated police seldom make return visits, the squatters remain, unmolested.

If there is defiance of law and violence, the environment in which these people live is much to blame. Conditions in the squatter areas beggar description. Hordes of small children roam the filthy roads barefoot, some of them completely naked.[14]

Most of the squatter shelters are makeshifts of wood findings, tin scrap, or cardboard, set up in crowded clusters of single-room hovels. I visited one where eight persons lived in a room 7 by 10 feet. The occupant was a cobbler, one of many jobless craftsmen, whose only customers were his squatter neighbors.

Some of the squatters are eccentric, but most are normal people who lack a chance to emerge from their depressed position. The areas where they live are out of bounds for other Jamaicans. The squatters complain that they are turned down for jobs when they reveal their addresses.

[13] Charles Abrams, James G. Banks, J. Robert Dodge, Marvin S. Gilman, and Dr. Kalervo Oberg, *Report of Housing Team of the International Cooperation Administration to the United States Operations Mission* (Jamaica, April 1961).

[14] One of the more constructive elements in the Trenchtown colony is a playfield supervised by the Reverend Hugh B. Sherlock, who has succeeded in reducing tensions in part of the area by a tenacious eighteen-year effort. A cricket field set up on the outskirts affords relief from the nearby squalor. Despite the scarcity of water, the suits and shoes of the cricketers are spotlessly white.

The squatters fend for themselves. Since pit latrines are illegal, human waste is deposited in makeshift boreholes between the shacks. The city carts will not collect the rubbish, which therefore is also deposited between the shacks, in a gully, or in an ever-rising dump. Rats, lice, and roaches share the holes and crevices in the squatters' huts. But worst of all, there was no water in Kingston Penn and just one tap for every 700 people in Trenchtown.

In this atmosphere, discontent and violence have been intensified by the rise of the Ras Tafari movement, a militant "Back to Africa" cult, some of whose members openly advocate violence. The movement has grown into one of the most volatile aspects of Jamaica's political life. Despite the lack of a concerted leadership, the Ras Tafari movement was still flourishing in 1963, primarily in the squatter areas. It has been able to draw more and more followers because of economic depression, ignorance, and hopelessness. The Ras Tafari brethren numbered ten to fifteen thousand in Kingston with an equal number of active sympathizers and still more potential supporters.[15]

It is obvious that conditions in the colonies are hardly conducive to social stability and respect for law. Unemployment, overcrowding, and desolation have increased resentments. Thus manipulation by troublemakers is made easy. If a single strong leader were to emerge, violence would be more frequent. The danger of explosion is always present, however. In 1963, a band of Ras Tafari killed eight people in cold blood in Montego Bay.

Aware of the need for social and economic assistance, the government in 1961 proposed, among other things, to repatriate those Ras Tafari who wished to go to Africa. The government has recently begun to recognize that the majority of Ras Tafari and their sympathizers are good citizens, willing to work if given the chance. Following the recommendations of a mission sent by the International Cooperation Administration of the United States in 1961, provision of water and better housing began to receive a higher priority along with social services and economic programs.

Squatter areas breed many things in many parts of the world: sullenness, hatred of authority, and violation of law are only a few. The Ras Tafari movement and the many sympathizers it has garnered happen to

---

[15] Some of the Ras Tafari brethren want repatriation. Many only seek some outlet for their frustrations or relief from their distress. To a simple people, fresh from the fields and bewildered by urban life, the cult gives emotional satisfaction as well as hope for escape to a promised land. Not all Ras Tafari wear beards and long locks. Some have a deep sense of morality and oppose crime and violence. Among the "extremist" leaders to whom I spoke were coherent men with beliefs not very different from those which have marked other cults in America and Europe, with perhaps more romantic or more explosive variations.

Figure 1. A street sleeper in Hong Kong—one of a million Chinese refugees.

Figure 2. Refugee children in Hong Kong—a "dwelling unit."

Figure 3. A typical trench for waste disposal in a Moroccan slum. (*Courtesy of Laboratoire Photographique du Service de l'Urbanisme du Maroc.*)

Figure 4. Moroccan slum area after the installation of a drain. (*Courtesy of Laboratoire Photographique du Service de l'Urbanisme du Maroc.*)

Figure 5. A cave dwelling in Pakistan on the way to Rawalpindi.

Figure 6. A play space in Singapore.

Figure 7.   An extensive squatter settlement in Morocco.

Figure 8.   Roof squatters' shacks in Hong Kong.

be the particular manifestation in Jamaica. The creation of a decent environment, the provision of better housing, as well as work and hope, could do much to stem the tide of discontent that surges in the squatter colonies of Kingston and elsewhere.

TYPES OF SQUATTERS

The types of buildings erected by squatters vary with the materials available, but most are one-story makeshifts made of mud, scrap lumber, or tin. Sometimes there are substantial houses. In Lima, Peru, squatter groups have even been said to hire surveyors to lay out sites. Some houses are built so that the owners can take them to other sites if officials or private owners persevere in harassing them.

The types of squatter tenure are not uniform and may generally be classified as follows:

The *owner squatter* owns his shack, though not the land; he erects the shack on any vacant plot he can find. Public lands and those of absentee owners are the most prized. The owner squatter is the most common variety.

The *squatter tenant* is in the poorest class, does not own or build a shack, but pays rent to another squatter. Many new in-migrants start as squatter tenants, hoping to advance to squatter ownership.

The *squatter holdover* is a former tenant who has ceased paying rent and whom the landlord fears to evict.

The *squatter landlord* is usually a squatter of long standing who has rooms or huts to rent, often at exorbitant profit.

The *speculator squatter* is usually a professional to whom squatting is a sound business venture. He squats for the tribute he expects the government or the private owner to grant him sooner or later. He is often the most eloquent in his protests and the most stubborn in resisting eviction.

The *store squatter or occupational squatter* establishes his small lockup store on land he does not own, and he may do a thriving business without paying rent or taxes. Sometimes his family sleeps in the shop. A citizen of Davao, in the Philippines, can get a dental cavity filled by a squatter dentist, his appendix removed by a squatter surgeon, or his soul sent on to a more enduring tenure by a squatter clergyman.

The *semi-squatter* has surreptitiously built his hut on private land and subsequently come to terms with the owner. The semi-squatter, strictly speaking, has ceased to be a squatter and has become a tenant. In constructing his house, he usually flouts the building codes.

The *floating squatter* lives in an old hulk or junk which is floated or sailed into the city's harbor. It serves as the family home and often the workshop. It may be owned or rented, and the stay may be temporary or permanent. In Hong Kong, there are so many thousands of junks and sampans in one area that one is no longer aware of the water on which they rest.

The *squatter "cooperator"* is part of the group that shares the common foothold and protects it against intruders, public and private. The members may be from the same village, family, or tribe or may share a common trade, as in the case of groups of weavers on evacuee land in Pakistan.

Although there have been admirable attempts by squatters to build clean houses and to rear their children properly, squatter colonies are generally safety and health hazards. Many of the foundations are unsafe; most of the shacks are overcrowded. The criminal, the prostitute, and the derelict make the colonies their retreats. Most often fires are accidental, but there has also been suspicion of arson committed by an owner, the value of whose land would soar with the elimination of the squatter occupants. More than 70 per cent of the fires in Manila are said to originate in the squatters' sheds. In Hong Kong, where there were over 300,000 squatters in January 1950 out of a total population of 2,360,000, one fire in Kowloon City rendered some 20,000 persons homeless. In another fire on Christmas day of 1953, 50,000 lost their homes, and in July 1954, another fire displaced 24,000. The squatters set up houses on the public streets, where they cooked their meals and dropped their daily excrement, and no sooner was the government able to find accommodations for the victims of one disaster than it was beset with the frustrations of another. In 1963, despite an extensive resettlement and rehousing program, squatters still lined the hillsides or colonized the ravines and slopes where fire or typhoons threaten constantly to carry away their pathetic huts and belongings.

In Singapore, 130,000 people live in squalid and insanitary *attap kampongs* throughout the municipal area. They have standpipe water and the most primitive sanitation. "It is a physical impossibility to eject these people; they have nowhere else to go. Although the municipality does excellent work in trying to keep these areas properly drained and free from disease, nevertheless they constitute a menace to the general health of the whole city."[16] Singapore squatters demand fantastic prices for possession; a parcel of land free of squatters is three times as expensive as land that is squatter-occupied. When a fire ousted 16,000 persons from a squatter area, the government acquired the land for a housing project. Because it would have had to pay the value of the land as a cleared site, it passed a law fixing the price at one third of the value. When acquiring squatter-occupied land, it often compensates the squatter for his "rights."

Part of the blame for the intense squatter traffic in Singapore is ascribed to speculators who are aware of the physical difficulties obstructing demolition. "The Land Inspectors are intimidated in the execution of their duties and enforcement of instructions becomes a dangerous process." The effort to enforce orders by constables has proved insufficient to prevent "a disturbance of the peace."[17]

THE THREAT TO SOVEREIGNTY

Attempts to end squatting have most often proved futile. The report of the City Improvement Committee of Rangoon, Burma, says squatters are "defying the corporation to eject them from the places over which they considered they had established certain rights," and "since the corporation has no power to order anyone out of the buildings or sites occupied, the Committee finds itself impotent to effect measures for the benefits of the citizens." The Committee has been forced to rely on "the method of persuasion" only.[18]

In Pakistan, the U.N. mission was told by officials in 1957 that the squatters' political strength has tied government hands. In one area a "King of the Squatters" had set himself up to fix the price of land, collecting a tribute from each squatter family for protection. In Manila, the squatters have openly threatened bloodshed if any effort is made to remove them. In the face of official impuissance and public indifference, there is emerging a general cynicism about obedience to law, honesty in government, and respect for property rights.

Even courts are powerless to enforce their orders, and frequently, as in Turkey and the Philippines, squatters have had to be given legal title to government lands. Disrespect for law and government has become epidemic in a growing number of countries. The dangers are intensified by the fact that squatters have usually headed into the nation's capitals and other political nerve centers.

The political impact of squatting has been felt not only in Asia but in the sensitive areas of Central and South America. In Cali, Colombia, squatter violence precipitated an emigration of industry. As unemployment increased, the situation became so threatening that a major program to rehouse the squatters had to be undertaken as an emergency.

[17] *Annual Report of the Singapore Improvement Trust* (Singapore, 1958), p. 35.
[18] Charles Abrams, *Urban Land Problems and Policies, Housing and Town and Country Planning, Bulletin* #7 (New York: United Nations, 1953), p. 14.

In India, after Nehru's election, when the squatters' area in Delhi was cleared after two previous fruitless efforts, the Communist party organized a mass demonstration and demanded new land. It may be no more than a coincidence that 75 of the 256 seats in the West Bengal Assembly were Communist, but certainly homelessness has never kept people from listening to a Communist speaker.[19]

To look upon all the squatters, or even the majority of them, as lawbreakers, is to misjudge the problem completely. Had land been made available to him, the squatter would not have appropriated it. A land policy that would have granted him a site, however small and humble, might have prevented a critical challenge to social and political equilibrium in the underdeveloped areas. But this obligation has never been accepted by the more developed nations of the world as a charge upon their consciences.

[19] An article by Paul Grimes in the *New York Times* of July 31, 1961, p. 7, says: "Communism has fed on the discontent of the refugees, the 900,000 other persons who sleep on sidewalks or are jammed in hovels, the 100,000 farmers who move to Calcutta yearly from overcrowded agricultural land and the tens of thousands of educated unemployed."

3

The Urban Land Problem

LAND DEARTH AMID LAND PLENTY

Squatting is only one aspect of the world struggle for shelter, though one of its more dramatic manifestations. It is also one of the aspects of the land problem—a problem that has troubled economists and political philosophers for some two hundred years. Written against the background of agricultural economies, the nineteenth-century classical economic tracts reflected the fear that a stubborn earth would not yield enough food for the ever-growing number of people. Private ownership of land, previously affirmed as a natural right, began to be considered a new type of robbery. The laborer toiled for his wage; the capitalist, though an exploiter, staked his money and brains; but the landowner simply bided his time as he watched nature's gifts fill his coffers, and, as the population grew, so did his unmerited gains. Something drastic had to be done before rent swallowed up all the profits of agriculture and industry and the landlords came to own the world. Even Karl Marx, whose primary target was the industrialist rather than the landlord, thought the latter the worse culprit, since he just sat on his land and made no contribution to wealth at all.

By now, many facts should have modified this fear of land shortage and the morbid outlook for humanity that it forecast. On the same limited earth, agricultural production is today increasing far beyond Malthusian expectations. In fact, on a global basis (excluding mainland China) it is rising about 1 per cent faster than population, a margin that

holds true for Asia and the Near East.¹ Though half the world is still
underfed and the contrast in diets between the more and the less developed areas is as striking as ever, only 10 per cent of the world's surface is being farmed, but another 40 per cent may be added with the
extension of irrigation and other modern techniques. Nevertheless, Herbert Spencer's fear that men would soon have "no room for the soles of
their feet" and that "landless men might equitably be expelled from the
earth altogether"² continues to reecho. The fear is still expressed in some
quarters that in sixty years or so the population will be so large that it
will ultimately be "squeezed to death."³

The foray against rural landlordism was first carried over to the urban
scene by Henry George, who had seen the stock range "succeeded by
the farm; the farm of extensive culture by the farm of intensive culture;
the grain field by the market garden; and the market garden, in its turn,
is cut up into city lots."⁴ Why, he asked, must cities be overcrowded?
"Simply because of private ownership of land. . . . Before anybody can
build a house a blackmail price must be paid to some dog in the
manger."⁵

George's agitations in Europe and America seemed to make ethical
sense at the time, but as the years wore on and as improved transportation opened new lands to urban use, his theories, at least as they applied
to cities, lapsed into oblivion. Yet today, as population swells in the
developing areas, and the contest for urban land freshens, the injustice
of the urban landownership pattern is again being exposed.

Landownership in most developing areas is still the major source of
wealth, inheriting some of the emotional characteristics it once possessed
in the rural economy. The title to land often gives prestige, as it once
did in Europe. In countries offering few alternatives for investment of
cash, land increment is as profitable a reward as any competing investment can offer. In Israel, for example, land prices in the Tel Aviv area
rose 200 per cent in the two years preceding 1963. Sometimes rising land

¹ United Nations, *Technical Assistance Newsletter,* Vol. II, No. 2 (New York,
May 1961). The ratio of food to population in Asia, however, is 3 per cent behind
prewar figures. In Latin America the gain is somewhat less than 1 per cent, while
African food production is not quite keeping pace with population.

² Herbert Spencer, *Social Statics* (New York: Appleton, 1873), p. 132.

³ "A physicist at the University of Illinois, using his own mathematical formula,
recently predicted that in only 65 years—in the year 2026—the population of the
world will have increased to a figure approaching infinity, a number too large to
count." Quoted in United Nations, *Technical Assistance Newsletter, op. cit.*

⁴ Quoted in R. M. Robbins, *Our Landed Heritage* (New York: Peter Smith,
1950), p. 275.

⁵ Henry George, "The Crime of Poverty," *Our Land and Land Policy* (New
York: Doubleday, 1911), p. 215.

costs simply correspond to the rise in the general price level.[6] More often roads and other public improvements, coupled with population increase, boom the value of land outside the central sections far beyond commodity prices. Lack of an effective mortgage system and high interest rates for borrowing money prevent a diffusion of landownership among the rank and file even in areas where land is plentiful. Population increase accentuates land value, and the landless view with envy and often with bitterness the lucky few who are protected by law in their possession of land and enriched in fact by the surging demand for it. It is no surprise therefore that squatting is so often viewed by the squatter as a form of constructive justice.

Despite the pressures on urban land, few developing countries have as yet challenged the withholding of land from use, and few have thought of tapping the increment by taxation. But in some nations, the cries for land reform of one sort or another are being heard as the prevailing competition for urban land highlights the disparity between wealth and poverty.

A number of methods have been adopted to curb rising prices.[7] In Jamaica all real estate taxes have been removed from buildings and placed only on land, in the expectation that land will thereby be forced into improvement and speculation will diminish. Zoning, price control, subdivision controls, and other devices have been imported by other underdeveloped countries, but few of these devices have been able to offset the effects of population growth and the clamor for building sites.

In the more developed areas, there has been a shift in the nature of landownership during the past century. Here the rich have put most of their capital into manufacture, trade, and banking, or have invested in such personal property as stocks, bonds, savings, inventories, and patents rather than land. The middle class and even some in the poorer class have become owners of dwellings that they inhabit themselves or rent to others. These groups are no longer considered prosperous simply because they own their homes or operate small boarding houses. But even in these more developed countries, the rise in land prices due to population increase has brought a demand for more drastic taxation to curb land profits.[8]

[6] It is argued, however, that the fall in the value of money in India during 1950–1960 was not more than 2.1 per cent per annum while the increase in urban land values was many times that amount. "Recent Events in the Value of Money, An International Comparison," *Economic Review*, Vol. XIII, No. 19 (May 8, 1961), p. 324.

[7] These are listed in Charles Abrams, *Urban Land Problems and Policies, Housing and Town and Country Planning, Bulletin* #7 (New York: United Nations, 1953).

[8] See for example, Sherman Maisel, "Background Information on Costs of Land

In the developing areas, ownership of land by the less prosperous is still a primary aspiration but a distant hope. Yet, though the descent of people upon urban land has created the appearance of land dearth, there is actually enough land to accommodate industrial man with space for living and working, for mobility and recreation. City dwellers take up little room, either standing up or lying down. The developing areas have skipped the steam age, with its requirements for locating industry and homes near the beltline. Moreover, the machines that men run, though not yet numerous in these areas, are becoming increasingly compact.

With greater efficiency in transport and with new sources of power, man is no longer enslaved by the tyranny of distance. Thousands can be accommodated within a relatively small space, as in the cities of Europe or America. For example, the entire population of the world could be housed at about fifty persons to the acre within present-day West Germany, whose recent Führer immolated millions of people in his quest for *Lebensraum*. In 1940, Germany was far less densely populated than England, Wales, or New Jersey. Illustrating the paradox in land use, Barbados has been described as the most crowded space in the world, except for some of the provinces of China. Yet, although 240,000 people inhabit its 166 square miles, its largest city has no high-rise buildings, and suburbanization has hardly begun.

Surprisingly, densities in some parts of the United States are higher than those in Europe. Although Japan is one of the most crowded nations in the world, it was less crowded per square mile at the time of Pearl Harbor than Massachusetts or Rhode Island. Tokyo, with more people than any other city, has land within a twenty-minute ride from its center that is still used as paddy fields. Moreover, the vast open spaces of Hokkaido could accommodate many times Japan's present population. As for the future of our planet, although the space frontier has been pierced as far as the moon, man has hardly settled more than forty feet above the earth's surface.[9]

Yet such calculations do not tell the whole story, since they fail to explain the shortage of land within particular tracts carved out as working units or living areas. Neither do they recognize the transport needs of man and industry in the new age of mobility; nor the need for roads, water, public facilities, airports, and recreation. Above all, they do not

---

for Single Family Housing," *Appendix to the Report on Housing in California* (San Francisco: Governor's Advisory Commission on Housing Problems, April 1963), pp. 221–281, and my analysis in *Report on Housing in California* (San Francisco: Governor's Advisory Commission on Housing Problems, January 1963), p. 16.

[9] With the elevator, for example, nearly 1.8 million square feet of net rentable space with office room for about 20,000 tenants can be accommodated on a lot 200 by 405 feet.

reveal the competition between all these uses within rigidly circum-scribed districts. Although the theories of land shortage are as obsolete as the spinning wheel, there is still a land squeeze of a different kind. It is the shortage caused by the demand for central land in and near the cities. Though the actual land used for cities may be only 1 per cent of an industrial nation's land supply, competition for land seethes, and unless it is resolved, it may give rise to conflicts as serious as if there were an actual dearth of land.

The current land problem springs from man's need to live near his work. Despite the abundance of land, the space for all the uses de-manded by man is still limited by time, accessibility, distance, and the cost and speed of travel. He has not been able to rationalize the uses of that space, though the space is there.

The small amount of land on which man is concentrating his demands is, in the main, privately owned. As more and more people pour into the urban centers, land prices soar. Suburban lots become more expensive too. In the more developed areas, where roads and good transport facili-ties exist, the price of land is a small fraction of the combined cost of land and completed buildings—perhaps it is 10 per cent in the suburban areas, perhaps 20 or 30 per cent in the more accessible sections. In some of the poorer countries, however, land prices may reach 50 per cent of the combined cost or more, and in others, land will not be released at any price. It is in such areas that the land problem is serious and calls for corrective measures.

Land cost has soared not because there is a dearth of land or solely because of land hoarding or the increased demand for urban land per se. The reasons for rising land prices also include: (*a*) failure to provide easier access to nearby sites; (*b*) freedom from land taxation; (*c*) instal-lation of public utilities and roads that have enhanced value without equivalent assessment for benefits; (*d*) excessive concentration of owner-ship in some places and such excessive fragmentation of ownership in others that it is impossible to assemble land; and (*e*) defective policies governing land titles or lack of adequate compulsory purchase proce-dures that could bring more land into use.

High land cost may not be the only obstacle. There are other problems. In many areas income is so low that land at any price is beyond the family's means. Shortsighted transportation planning limits the land available for industry and public works. Many families who own land are frequently unable to borrow money with which to improve it. Often a squatter has preempted a key lot and made assemblage of a contiguous plot impossible. In other cases a single rent-controlled tenant may demand a fortune as a condition for his moving. In many instances, proper government policy might remove such obstacles. Governments have the power to guide the use of land, curb its misuse, prevent its abuse, regulate its nonuse or disuse, and guide its reuse. Land is the key to environment, housing, public works, and growth. But governments have failed to use the key to open the door to more rational land uses.

THE WIDENING ASPECTS OF THE LAND PROBLEM

Wherever one travels, the land problem in one form or another looms large. In India, the urban area is spreading to valuable agricultural lands; in Peshawar, Pakistan, the suburban subdivisions are engulfing soil capable of producing four crops a year. In the Philippines, the areas surrounding Manila suffer from overconcentration of landownership and excessive speculation in land. In Turkey, the land cost is sometimes 20 per cent but often 50 per cent of the total home cost. In the area of Istanbul, planless speculative subdivisions have created tiny lots, thirty feet in depth, that leave little space for living or for the most elementary utilities.

No country is without a land problem of some sort. In Accra, Ghana, land development is being frustrated by defective titles and litigation, and in the Northern Territories the same problem has brought tribal boundary disputes and violence. In Hong Kong, building land must be hacked out of the hills or created by reclamation if hundreds of thousands of small farmers are not to be deprived of their livelihoods. In Japan's Hanshin region, where subsiding land was developed with industries, the factories are sinking, with nothing but occasional smokestacks standing like headstones to mark the graves. Derelict building sites in Ireland mar the city centers. The more developed countries have their problems also. England, for example, is troubled about the pressure of housing and industry upon its greenbelts; and in California, where every week another dairy farm is lost to a subdivision, a planning commission plaintively asks, "Where now, brown cow?"

The devices for acquiring land or rationalizing land use have been changing throughout the world. The forms of land tenure are also being modified. The following are some of the tendencies:

1. A Growing Insecurity of Ownership or Possession

Security of possession has been a burning desire from the time that man first asserted his claim to exclusive ownership of a patch of ground. But insecurity is still the lot of many tenants and sharecroppers in the rural world, despite the efforts of some governments to break up large holdings and accord more sites to the rank and file.

Urbanization, which has reduced the quantity of land needed for living or working, has served only to change the problem's emphasis. Though the size of the average plot has shrunk from two acres or more to only 1600 square feet or less, the competition to acquire and hold it is no less intense. The squatter fixes his foothold on the land of another, who instead of owning a fee simple now has a fee complex. Harassed by the housing shortage, the renter waits fearfully upon the owner's decision to oust him or demand a ransom for continued occupancy. He is spared only when government decrees a blanket injunction against all evictions, after which the contest for possession becomes a continuing exercise in chicane.

With land and building costs soaring, secure fee ownership has tended to become the exceptional type of tenure. In Durban, South Africa, 99 per cent of the native Africans and 93 per cent of the colored population are renters.[10] In Ceylon, the proportion of renters after World War II was about 70 per cent; in Spain most of the people were renters; in Turkey, where 36 per cent of the housing in cities is rented, the rent paid is 37 per cent of family income.[11] The land on which houses are built in tiny Barbados is rented on a month-to-month basis; but the house is a chattel, a simple cabin set on a rockpile base and moved to another rockpile when the landowner becomes testy. Tourism, rising land prices, and requirements that owners provide roads have accelerated evictions and the shifting of houses.

Tenancy is not always a sign of poverty, particularly in the cities of the more developed areas. But in the underdeveloped countries, renting generally means low income. Nor does ownership invariably carry the same dominion and quiet possession that it once did. Even in the more developed areas where there is a functioning mortgage system, the mortgage proportion of the property's value steadily mounts, often whittling away the equity to a shell. Mortgages cover 80 to 100 per cent of cost, a blessing in inflationary periods and a bane in deflationary times. In the underdeveloped areas, mortgages are virtually unprocurable at any cost, often making tenancy or unlawful seizure of land the alternatives. Mortgage interest, when mortgages are obtainable, is rarely less than 10 per cent a year (as much as 50 per cent in Jordan). The term of the loan is usually short. To ease the problem, some governments have made mortgage loans to their citizens, but this form of accommodation is still in its infancy.

In some countries, custom and honor once exercised a restraining influence upon landlord tyranny. But the relationship is today more impersonal. The tenant and the landlord are strangers, merely part of

[10] *Durban Housing Survey* (Durban: University of Natal Press, S.A., 1952), p. 97.

[11] These figures are estimates by the Census Department in Ceylon and by officials in Spain and Turkey. See Charles Abrams, *Urban Land Problems and Policies, op. cit.*, p. 17. The figures on Turkey are from *First Five-Year Development Plan, 1963-1967* (Ankara, 1963), p. 404.

the mass seeking shelter. The relationship is no more personal between the mortgagee and the borrower. Possession in both cases is dependent upon the occupant's continued ability to pay the rent or the debt. Landlords and mortgagees are generally unmoved by unemployment, economic depression, age, illness, or death. They are not concerned about added family obligations, financial losses, shift of job location, domestic problems, or the lure of the installment salesman, who has imposed an added burden on the borrower. The homeowner's default on a single payment threatens loss of his entire investment. No system has yet been devised, even in countries like the United States, to insure individuals against such hazards, though a system of equity insurance against the risks of unemployment, illness, or death seems long overdue.[12]

Another threat to tenure has arisen in countries with minority-group problems. The expansion of government powers, while aiding the underprivileged in some countries, is being employed elsewhere to oust minorities from their footholds. Slum clearance in South Africa and in some states in the United States has become the legal device to evict the unwanted, particularly nonwhites.[13]

2. The More Intensive Use of Land

The competition for land has intensified the use of land both within the city and on its periphery. The city has become jammed with people and factories. Congestion has necessitated astronomical budgets for social services and made streets impassable. It has made the journey to work laborious and life difficult as well as dangerous, particularly for children. In some areas, the traditional one- or two-story building with easy escape to the street or yard is being replaced by vertical living quarters full of tiny compartments. Even where land has been developed under the public authority (as in Singapore's twenty-story buildings), some people prefer the one-story squatter hut with easy access to the street. As the scramble for land increases outside the central area, land that should have been reserved for recreation and other purposes is being defaced by rows of monotonous dormitories like tiers of kennels. The substantial investment made for utilities, streets, schools, and other improvements makes the sordid pattern more enduring.

[12] In a few places, mortgage payments now include a premium for life insurance. Upon the breadwinner's death, the mortgage is paid off. For a fuller discussion of equity insurance, see Charles Abrams, *The Future of Housing* (New York: Harper, 1946), p. 398, and Charles Abrams, "Equity Insurance for the Forgotten Owner," *The Housing Yearbook* (New York: National Housing Conference, 1954).

[13] Charles Abrams, *Forbidden Neighbors* (New York: Harper, 1955), Ch. 18. About 72 per cent of those evicted or scheduled for eviction from urban renewal projects in the United States were Negroes in the 1950's, and in 1963 the proportion of Negroes evicted was 65 per cent.

3. A Wider Diffusion of Holdings

Though land concentration has persisted in some places (as in parts of South America), the general trend has been toward an increase in the number of owners and parcels. This does not signify equalization of wealth but suggests instead that the soaring prices of land coming into the urban orbit have induced more owners to sell or subdivide so as to cash in on the profits. An estate of 1000 acres that is a hundred miles from the city may be valued at less than a single lot in the city's center. The diffusion of landownership has also been accelerated by division of large parcels among an increasing number of heirs and descendants, by the subdivision into building lots of former agricultural lands on the urban outskirts for subdivision, and by the voluntary sale of suburban estates whose owners have shifted their investment to industry. In some countries, laws have aimed at deconcentration, while in others large plots have been purchased by Improvement Trusts for resale. In still other cases, land parcels have been bought by government agencies for resale as housing or industrial estates, or by those who wish to build factories near the city. Where mortgage systems developed, they too have spurred subdivision of land into units suitable for building homes. Though there are still latifundia and large parcels of once-agricultural land in single ownership, the general tendency has continued toward the division of holdings. These smaller parcels will, however, often continue to be held for speculative increment rather than development.

4. Appearance of New Forms of Tenure

Partly as a consequence of rising land costs and the competition for sites, new forms of tenure have made their appearance. Some are good and some bad, but all of them are part of the contest to gain ownership or possession of a lot.

These include:

(a) EQUITY OWNERSHIP. This is the ownership of the property subject to mortgage. While a mortgage system is essential to facilitate the purchase of land and homes at ever-rising costs, it effects a virtual division of the title between the mortgagee (representing the superior interest) and the owner's claim (or equity interest). The equity continues unimpaired only as long as the owner can avoid default. When land or building costs rise, the amount of the mortgage and its proportion to value also rise. Even where the interest rates are as low as 5 per cent, the interest and amortization payments add up to more than half of the annual carrying costs of the house. In the more developed countries, the debt may run as long as forty-five years. In underdeveloped countries, where interest payments are high and the mortgage is short-term, bonus payments are exacted with each renewal. In such cases, the average family is either unable to buy or else haltered to the carrying charges of a debt that leaves little for the rest of life's essentials.

(b) CONTRACT LANDOWNERSHIP. Here the family agrees to buy the land by installment payments, hoping ultimately to pay for it out of earnings. The rising costs of land have extended the contract payments for prolonged periods. Even when payment is completed, the owner is still faced with borrowing to build a house. Buying a tract, subdividing, and retailing the land in small plots that are paid for in installments has become a frequent practice of land operators in many underdeveloped areas. Often the purchaser lacks the funds to build, so he puts up a shack from makeshift materials. Sometimes after starting his building, he runs out of money with which to pay for the roof. Ultimately the mortgagee, the weather, or the taxing authority succeeds to the property.

(c) STATUTORY OWNERSHIP OR TENANCY. In this case the government has passed laws to protect the owner against foreclosure in deflationary periods, to allow a tenant to remain in possession, to reimburse him for any improvements, or to protect him against rent increases. In these cases a statute modifies or redefines what has been a contractual relationship. Rent control is the most common example. In one form or another it exists in most underdeveloped countries. Another example is a 1958 statute in Ireland that automatically extended expiring long-term leaseholds for another ninety-nine years; where the landlord and tenant have failed to agree on the new terms, the rent is fixed at a sixth of the current rental value. While rent control and other statutory interference with the contract may be good for the tenant, it may discourage substantial investment by private capital, particularly where controls apply to new buildings. A country in which capital investment is subject to the threat of drastic government impositions must expect either stagnation of private investment or increased socialization to fill the investment gap.

(d) KEY MONEY ("SCHLÜSSEL-GELT") TENANCY. With the costs of land, homes, and rent rising, key money tenure has grown up in many underdeveloped countries—South America, Israel, and Greece among others. A premium is paid for the right to acquire possession under a tenancy. It is also often paid to tenants as the consideration for selling a rent-controlled apartment. Where mortgage money is scarce, key money is also paid to builders to help them finance new operations. The tenant is guaranteed possession for a limited period in return for a payment that is often a substantial portion of the building cost.

(e) BUILDING OWNERSHIP. Because land prices have run ahead of purchasing power, a person desiring to erect a building leases the land instead of buying it. Upon expiration of the lease, the building generally reverts to the landowner unless laws or the contract provides otherwise.

This arrangement has been common in England, where land until recently rested in only a few hands. Building ownership is common in the Soviet Union, since the government has confiscated all land titles. In the Philippines and in the British West Indies, poor people erect shacks on speculatively owned land rented to the occupant under a tenancy-at-will that is terminable summarily.

(f) SQUATTER TENURES. The growth of squatting has produced many new and unorthodox forms of tenure. As described earlier, they include squatting in which the government or the private owner tolerates possession by the squatters. A type of squatting-at-will may arise when the squatter agrees to pay periodic stipends to the owner for the right to remain. When such land is needed for other purposes, the squatter may be speedily evicted. He may resist eviction by threats or bring pressure on the government for protection against ouster.

(g) COOPERATING OR SHARING DEVICES. The inability of a single family to secure a house has given rise to mutual agreements under which several families join together to build or buy one. Cooperation for mutual aid of various kinds is not new, and its features have appeared in village economic life in China, India, and Russia and in primitive societies. It has incorporated some of the aspects of cooperation that had taken shape in Britain and France in the 1820's and some of the devices of the private enterprise system including stock ownership. Other forms include ownership of the individual apartment under an agreement to contribute to the upkeep of the building and cooperative ownership only of the common grounds. The "condominium" arrangement, under which each occupant actually owns his apartment individually, has been used extensively in Puerto Rico, Cuba, and elsewhere in Latin America and has been recently introduced into the United States. Other cooperative forms are common in Austria, Italy, France, and West Germany. In the Netherlands, Switzerland, and the Scandinavian countries, a device is employed under which the occupant never becomes the individual owner of the dwelling but participates in the administration of the cooperative and enjoys, legally or in practice, a right of extended or permanent occupancy.

(h) MOBILE OWNERSHIP. Under this form of tenure the building is not affixed to the land but remains personal property and may be moved by the building owner when the landowner demands possession or a rent that the tenant cannot afford. The number of mobile tents and houses, as well as demountable units, has increased because of migrations, hostility to minorities, landlessness, uncertainty, and social conflict. In the more developed countries, mobile living, which has its earliest roots in nomadism, is becoming a chosen way of life for many. Mobile houses may be either large self-contained units equipped with kitchen, living room, and bath or smaller caravans attached to the car or truck. In the United States, the mobile-house industry is booming, accounting for more than 10 per cent of housing starts in the 1960's. Some of the houses are deluxe models that expand into homes of 1000 square feet. They are set up on specially planned sites where as much as $60 a month may be paid as rent to the owner supplying the plot. The better camps have a common swimming pool, club room, and other amenities, but often the American mobile house is an old model bought for $1000 and set up in a stray lot. The mobile or trailer slum is an addendum to the slum catalog.

In underdeveloped countries, the mobile house is usually a small cabin erected by the owner or a carpenter and placed on rented land. Sugar workers in the British West Indies were allowed to put up such shacks on the plantations and remain as long as they worked there. These mobile shacks have now been transposed to the urban scene. A building owner may also be a squatter. Usually any moving job speeds the dilapidation of the structure, and slums of battered demountable units have become a familiar sight in poorer countries. Occupants of mobile shacks are often shunned as semi-vagrants or intruders, particularly when they require public services or have children to be schooled.

(i) HIRE PURCHASE (TENANCY WITH OPTION TO BUY). This device is employed by government to enable poorer families to rent until they have accumulated reserves or made a specified number of payments. The system gives the tenant hope of ownership and encourages him to improve his house and make repairs.

THE EFFECTS OF LAND COMPETITION

The increasing number of conflicting claims upon land in or near the city centers has become one of the most difficult by-products of industrialization and urbanization. Such land is now demanded not only for housing, industry, recreation, government, business, and trade but also for roads, bridges, parking space, railroads, water systems, airfields, electrical and gas installations, schools and universities, cemeteries, drainage schemes, and the other numerous requirements of urbanization. To these have been added the claims of agriculture, oil and mineral extraction, electric plants, military bases, harbor installations, greenbelts, and the newly emerging demands of defense, new-town building, and speculative subdivisions. The rationalization of these competing uses has been complicated by the mounting difficulty of acquiring any cheap contiguous land for essential growth and development. Where holdings are in the hands of many owners and tenants whose votes count in an election, the government may respect their views more than the single landowner's, but there is no hard and fast rule for all cases. Few underdeveloped countries are as yet prepared to assert their authority to acquire the many small parcels for more rational development or to oust those who have illegally settled. As people keep pouring into the city centers, the obstacles grow, and as taller or denser buildings go up, the cost of acquiring the land for public use or for larger private developments increases. Addition of utilities and amenities further adds to acquisition costs and freezes the pattern.

EFFORTS TO COPE WITH THE LAND PROBLEM

To cope with these problems, government power in some form has asserted itself, but too often falteringly, unmethodically, and at cross purposes. Sometimes the policy strives to prop up private investment, sometimes to restrict it, sometimes to substitute governmental for private effort. Subsidies have been granted where regulation would have done the job, or regulation has been imposed where subsidies would have been better. In some countries, pressures for action have so enlarged the definition of "public use" that almost any use will justify public acquisition. In many less developed countries, such acquisition, even for the most public of uses, is resisted.

The chosen locution is in the idiom of the day and place. In the United States, where "private enterprise" has been the national theme, mortgage insurance has been socialized in the name of encouraging private enterprise. In Europe, where "socialism" is semantically proper, subsidization of private enterprise has frequently been effected in the name of socialism. Socialization of losses is common in the developed countries, while the underdeveloped countries, looking for private investment, have employed both private enterprise and socialism in their terminology as the occasion has required.

The motivations behind government control vary. There are many different reasons that appear to have impelled government intervention. Pressures for intervention may be economic, political, or social, or a combination of all three. Breaking up larger estates in response to the pressures of tenants, squatters, or the land-hungry has become the policy of some nations whose lands are still in large-scale ownership. Beautifying landscapes and preserving the countryside have been the motivations of countries with aesthetic sensibilities. Solving the housing shortage is a third motivation. The encouragement of industrialization and defense activities is still another.

A large number of devices for regulating land use are now in operation, for better or worse. These run the gamut from outright confiscation to curtailment of rights, depending on the stage of development, the pressures, or the complexion of the particular political system. The devices include: price or rent controls; zoning; restriction on the sale price of land; subdivision controls and building regulations; purchase or regulation of development rights; public acquisition of reserve lands; tax levies to control use, to bring land into use, or to discourage its use; land, building, or rent subsidization in various forms; excess condemnation (public purchase of more land than needed for an improvement and its resale after completion); public land acquisition in advance of industrial settlement; building of new towns; joint public-private ventures of various sorts.

Policies may aim at breaking up larger landownership concentrations into smaller ones or combining smaller holdings into more practical unified ownerships. France, with diffusion of its landownership, has adopted a reparceling policy, under which small plots have been redistributed to form contiguous parcels. The segmented holdings have been turned over to a cooperative, which was dissolved after it reparceled and redistributed the land. In the United States, cities are acquiring uneconomic plots from individual owners and reselling them in blocks to private developers for "urban renewal." In Bolivia, large estates have been taken by the government for nominal compensation and distributed to civil servants or other workers for the building of homes, which they have been unable to finance.

While one form of land control may be more efficient than another, practical considerations often play an important part in shaping public policy. In Belgium, as in the United States, there is an aversion to any measures that would hamper private building. Belgium has many types of subsidies and aids to stimulate private construction. In Japan, eminent domain is often viewed as oppressive or undemocratic. Hence, the government usually builds houses only on land acquired from a willing seller. The existence of concentration or diffusion of landownership frequently determines the direction of policy.

The individual's desire to be secure on his own little strip of the earth's surface continues to be one of the great vortices around which public policy revolves. This desire is asserting itself in the pullulating cities, as it once did on the farms and in the plains. The great emerging issues are: (a) whether expansion of power can be effected without sacrificing individual rights and initiative; (b) whether an owner's duties will ultimately so overshadow his rights that he retains little more than ownership in name; (c) whether the new powers will be used to benefit the many instead of the few; (d) whether they will produce new functioning forms of community life or give rise only to new disappointments; (e) whether governmental powers will be exercised to expand opportunity and social and economic mobility or will be used to contain "undesirable groups" within segregated sections; (f) whether new laws will be respected or openly flouted; (g) whether any reform adopted will not be ultimately diverted from its original objectives or perverted to defend the interests of a more privileged class. The question is, finally, whether the cities of the new industrial world will emerge as the havens of man's freedom or as the instruments for new tyrannies and the sources of new human frustrations.

4

The Growth of Government Power and Policy

Political systems of countries may be altered through assimilation, adoption of another society's ideas, or through revolution. Revolution, however, has been violent only in a few cases, but even where the revolution was peaceful, it effected major shifts in the relationships between social classes. These shifts are still not completed, but there is nevertheless a well-defined and almost universal trend in almost all countries toward using public processes to rectify some of the social and economic inequalities of the unregulated economic process.

When social and economic inequalities first gained notoriety during European industrialization, they were cited as the inevitable results of capitalism's shortcomings. More moderate reformers in Europe and the United States thought the state could rectify some of the injustices within the existing political framework. In Russia the less moderate view was adopted. Since many developing countries are grappling with the problem of urbanization and are in the course of weighing the values of the alternate systems, the historical development of legal processes affecting shelter and urban land policy in Europe and in North America becomes relevant.

THE CONTRAST BETWEEN THE MORE AND LESS DEVELOPED COUNTRIES

The more developed and the less developed nations, though they are worlds apart in wealth and technology, are both experiencing the impacts of population inundations that have created city slums, over-crowding, and urban land problems. Both suffer from the stubborn disparity between income and shelter cost, the competition for urban land, the chaotic urban development, and the many other distortions caused by rapid urbanization, population swell, and slum living.

Yet, though the symptoms are similar, the nature of the malady and its prognosis are of a different order. The more developed nations have acquired greater political stability and can better afford to make mistakes; experiments that fail are not fatal. Their people have skills and higher incomes. They can boast of a middle class and a better opportunity for the lower class to reach a higher estate. The supply of used housing allows for a turnover of dwellings among residents as their circumstances change. Though housing cost is usually beyond the average worker's means, a construction industry functions for those who can pay the price, while the government can better afford to bridge the gap for lower-income families.

There is generally also an established legal framework in Europe and the United States within which the problems of urbanization can be tackled. Landownership is respected or restricted according to certain norms and is usually subject to compulsory purchase for the public interest. There are more likely to be well-established private mortgage mechanisms for investors and for buyers who can pay the going costs. Contracts are enforceable by courts, and if rights and duties are not always crystal-clear, they can at least be roughly approximated. Though government has intervened with sterner measures when the private mechanism has faltered, the line between governmental and private action is more or less plainly drawn; property rights are not sacrificed as the public sector is gradually enlarged. These refinements of power have taken place over a long period marked by crisis and debate, trial and error, experimentation and amelioration.

REVOLUTIONS IN THE MORE DEVELOPED NATIONS

The current pattern has evolved in Europe and the United States through what might be identified as four revolutions: political, land, industrial, and welfare. They were partly sequential, partly concurrent, producing in the end a mixed but reasonably well-articulated order which has succeeded in raising the standard of living without sacrificing individualism or its freedoms.

Out of these four revolutions has emerged a rough rule of reason defining the limitations and prerogatives of states in relation to property, as well as a reconciliation of public rights and duties with respect to the welfare of those deprived of life's essentials. The revolutions which gave rise to these reconciliations were:

1. A POLITICAL REVOLUTION, in which the individual's rights within the state were defined and protected against its arbitrary or capricious actions. The rise of merchant cities in centuries past and the traders' demands for greater freedom of action had aided the birth of individual freedoms. These freedoms have essentially survived. They include such advances as the safeguarding of property rights against unreasonable regulation, security of the home against search and seizure, and guarantee of compensation and due process in the expropriation of property.

In securing the rights of property generally, the state had been loath at first to put too great a restriction upon property of any kind, with the result that for a long period real estate (including slum property) benefited from the protection given to all property. "Police power," the fountainhead of property regulation, was an unknown term, which in fact did not receive its full christening until 1827.[1]

The imposition of building regulations as a function of police power was of course hardly novel. Such regulations had existed in Babylonia earlier than 2000 B.C., had appeared among the Chinese before 1000 B.C., and may be found in the archives of the Roman Empire. But they were always conditioned by the principal motivating forces of a particular era, and drastic restrictions on building were felt to be inconsonant with the age in which the businessman and the middle class were coming into their own.

Except for some quaint ordinances and some rare evidences of private benevolence in the nature of almsgiving, it was not until 1838 that concern for the housing of the poor began to manifest itself in England, and it was only after 1851 that the first constructive regulations against slums were adopted. But even then, and for more than a half century thereafter, many people were still holding stubbornly to the view that the slum was the fault of the slum dweller and the haven of the irresponsible, the inebriate, and the criminal. It was not until the twentieth century that a broader web of regulatory laws was spun, becoming more and more embracing as the execrations of reformers continued to chip away at the esteem of slum owners and slum builders.

Regulation required more and more of owners until hope for further reform through regulation crashed on the rock of reality. The rock was the hard fact that the more drastic the regulation, the higher the rent; the higher the rent, the fewer who could pay it. More practical devices were needed, and soon the tax power was brought to the fore as a possible alternative.

The tax power ran a course somewhat similar to the police power. Taxation was the state's special hunting ground, but at best it proved to be a limited preserve. Taxation had been viewed by Blackstone as only a supplement to other sources of revenue such as crown lands, mines,

[1] By Chief Justice Marshall in *Brown* v. *Maryland*, 25 U.S. 419.

penalties—what the great commentator termed "ordinary" revenue. Taxes he classed as "extraordinary."[2] In this hidebound context, aiding the underprivileged through taxation of the rich would be looked upon as expropriation of wealth. While the laissez-faire attitude achieved for property an unprecedented freedom from state interference, it left the alleviation of poverty to the poor and to those whose sympathy would pry open their purses. The poor in fact had long been elevated to the rank of "God's poor" and placed in the church's charge. It was unthinkable that the state would ever be allowed to become God's delegate in this respect. As recently as 1892, Charles Booth had identified the three greatest causes of poverty as old age, sickness, and drink. Manifestly good housing provided by the state would not stay old age, and while it might allay some distempers, it could not be expected to appease a poor man's thirst. The indigent, said Booth, should be taught to build their own dwellings.[3] In the United States up to the time of the New Deal, slums were thought to be the fault of the slum dweller and the product of his filthy habits.[4] That he would put coal in a bathtub, if given one, was considered gospel, at least until central heating made the tub unnecessary as a coal bin.

The compulsory purchase of property had been early recognized as a government prerogative and was in fact implicit in the government formula, though Blackstone in 1765 referred to it as "an exertion of power, which the legislature indulges with caution."[5] In the United States and England, even private parties such as railroads (and in America drainage companies as well) could use the expropriatory privilege so long as the "purpose" was public and the compensation just. But whether eminent domain was exercised privately or publicly, the scope of "public purpose" in the United States up to the 1940's continued narrow, particularly where the federal government was concerned. It was a "limited sovereignty," which meant that its power to act in such matters as war was unlimited but for "general welfare" it did not exist at all.[6] Acquiring slum property for housing as part of the war effort was lawful, but it was unauthorized for welfare. As for the states, they might use their welfare power to regulate private investment so as to prevent slums, but they could neither spend the taxpayers' money to build housing for the poor nor take land for any purpose or project that would not be "used by

[2] Sir William Blackstone, *Commentaries on the Laws of England,* American Students' Edition (Albany, New York: Banks and Bros., 1884), Book I, Ch. 8.

[3] For a discussion of the period, see *Encyclopedia of Social Reform,* edited by William D. P. Bliss (New York and London: Funk and Wagnalls, 1897), p. 1071.

[4] See, for example, *Health Department* v. *Dassori,* 21 N.Y. App. Div. 348, 47 N.Y.S. 641.

[5] Sir William Blackstone, *op. cit.,* p. 79.

[6] *United States* v. *Certain Lands in the City of Louisville,* 78 F 2nd 684.

the public." Taking land on the grounds that it would "benefit the public" was viewed as going too far.[7] Until the 1930's, in most state jurisdictions in the United States, *all* the people had to have access to a project to authorize condemnation, and the poor were not all the people.

The political revolution up to 1936 failed to solve the slum problem in the United States. But it did attack the problem in the only way that the reformers of the period had proposed and with the only tool that the era would countenance, i.e., regulation under the police power. Further, the very failure of the police power to eliminate slums served to highlight the futility of the approach and speeded the advent of more comprehensive devices.

2. THE LAND REVOLUTION had been going on fitfully for several hundred years. The revolution had been impelled by the individual's urge for a piece of ground. This generally entailed the division or sale of large estates irrespective of whether they were in the public or private domain. In the United States, denationalization of land had been the public policy almost from the beginning, so that small individualized holdings soon found their way into the hands of the many. Even the larger land grants made to railroads were segmented into smaller parcels and sold in order to speed settlement along their lines. In France and Belgium, the Napoleonic code had caused the breakup of larger holdings into smaller parcels—frequently too small for efficiency. In the United Kingdom at the turn of the century, some 600 peers held a fifth of the nation's domain, and about 7400 other individuals still owned half of its land. Tenure has been so stubborn there that some of the 999-year leases made at the time of William the Conqueror have survived and are today being negotiated for renewal. But even this stronghold of property rights has more recently been witnessing a breakup of holdings as owners have sought cash to pay death duties. Simultaneously, as England's cities expanded, suburban land was subdivided and sold to individuals for homes, further increasing the number of landowners.

Though industrialization and increased housing demands moved considerable urban and suburban land within reach of the steam shovel, it was not until after the 1940's that governments became impelled to speed the process of land deconcentration or, where oversegmentation existed, reassemblage.

Whether by economic pressures, the lure of industrial profits, taxation, contract, statute, or appropriation by the squatter on the frontier lands, the general effect of the land revolution has been not only to split up larger holdings and increase the number of owners but also to move government toward bringing land within reach of the many.

---

[7] In the opinion of the Justices, 211 Mass. 624.

3. THE INDUSTRIAL REVOLUTION (OR REVOLUTIONS) altered the uses of land from the beginning, so that many rural plots became the sites of factories, shops, public utilities, and urban houses. The whole character of the housebuilding operation was changed. The house was no longer a homemade product, whose materials were obtained and put together by the owner himself. Building entrepreneurs now took over the operation, and home building became a powerful stimulus to economic activity. With the rise of intangible personalty (in the form of stocks, bonds, patents, claims, debt, and credit), real property remained a major form of investment but lost its primacy in the new play of economic and political power.

But though industrialization brought hardship, it also expanded the individual's challenges and his opportunities; it increased the yield of the world's food-producing lands and the number of mouths to receive their product. As industrialization helped to swell the world's population, the excess was drawn to the cities, where not only man's destiny but his hopes became centered.

4. THE WELFARE REVOLUTION, the most recent of the revolutions, was marked by the assumption by governments of new functions, in an effort to remedy some of the worst deficiencies of the industrial and urbanizing processes. Greater government intervention was justified by repeated periods of depression; by the inability of private enterprise to ease the hardships of poverty, insecurity, illness, and old age; and by the failure of private enterprise to alleviate housing shortage and slums. Progress and growth, not simply continuity, became the new aim. Government took over many of the responsibilities formerly left to private charity and investment. It augmented its tax, spending, police, and compulsory-purchase powers in an effort to stimulate economic activity and remove social disparities. In addition, government entered upon new activities such as housing for the underprivileged, and it increased public works to broaden employment during depressions. Besides building dams, power plants, roads, and a wide variety of other job-making operations, it expanded public educational facilities, financed private building, and insured investment risks. It subsidized a diverse group of public and private enterprises and levied heavier taxes upon the haves to finance its operations for the have-nots. Finally government moved to control the sporadic growth of cities and improve their environments. In the process, its powers were widened so that it was in a position to manipulate the emerging scene and mold many of its prominent features.

One of the more perplexing and unsettled questions of the welfare revolution was the precise role of the private and public sectors. Hitherto, private enterprise had occupied the main field, while government operated only where "the profit could never repay the expense to any individual."[8] Schools, roads, and the post office were viewed as public operations, while housing, industry, and other profit-making ventures were considered strictly private. When the welfare function expanded, the question arose as to whether government should act directly or merely subsidize private ventures to achieve the new welfare aims. The general tendency was to do both, as the occasion demanded or the pressures forced a particular action. England subsidized the private entrepreneur at first, then built public housing itself. The United States did both, ultimately channeling the bulk of its aid by underwriting the risks of private investment. Mortgages were insured, deposits in savings and loan associations were guaranteed to encourage deposits, and aid was given to private builders who put up homes for moderate-income families and war veterans. Other aid was given to colleges and nursing homes and for building homes for the elderly. Land subsidies were given by federal and city governments for "urban renewal," and slum sites were compulsorily acquired by cities to enable private entrepreneurs to redevelop them for more profitable and more becoming uses.

The powers of police, taxation, and eminent domain have not spread without some dissent. But there is no turning back. With the accelerated trend toward greater urbanization, there is every indication that the public power plant in developed countries will never revert to its narrower limits. Neither Russia's managers nor America's entrepreneurs have come up with a magic formula for solving the trilemma of urbanism, mass migration, and housing. A modern computer might pour forth the calculus of housing need, but the solution eludes electronics. Housing programs still require identification of objectives, long periods of time, relocation of families, large capital outlays, expansion of materials production, innovation in financing mechanisms, mobilization of skills, and expert direction under cohesive, well-formulated policies.

The more developed areas in Europe and North America have taken the progressive growth of power and function in stride. The gains made 150 years ago or more in guaranteeing the individual's privacy, his protection against outright confiscation, and his rights under contract have not been drastically affected. They have simply moved into a new social context, which has been accepted as part of a new just norm. The shift to industrialization was accomplished with little or no violence. The democratic state was able to take steps—imperfect as they may be—to correct some of the inequities of industrialization. While the urban land problem continued to be stubbornly troublesome, there were few efforts by the land-needy to take law into their own hands.

Though the welfare revolution has not yet produced all the answers to the social problems of urbanization, powers for confronting them have

[8] Adam Smith, *The Wealth of Nations,* Modern Library Edition (New York: Random House, 1937), Book V, Ch. 1, Part III.

been released and the first steps taken to wield these powers more effectively. What is referred to as "social balance" now employs economic policy to stimulate private activity and generate improved purchasing power while simultaneously trying to compensate for its shortcomings through policy such as social security, public housing, and other social programs. If world tensions are eased and the enormous expenditures for defense and war can be used for more of the social exigencies, the day may not be distant when urban blight can be eliminated and when the beleaguered urban family may well be able to afford a decent home—provided, of course, that social motivation continues to have a place in political calculations.

THE POSITION OF THE LESS DEVELOPED AREAS

In contrast with the series of revolutions in the more developed countries, the underdeveloped countries are having all their revolutions simultaneously. There have been few existing patterns to build on, no firm old threads of precedent to which the new policies could be tied. Industrialization, urbanization, and the land and political revolutions have all arrived concurrently and almost precipitously.

Often a political coup by an ambitious military junta adds another complication to the problems of the developing nations. In Latin America, the military controls not only the arms but also the course of political events. Rivalries within the military establishments make for internal plotting and counterplotting, and even constitutionally elected regimes may depend on the sufferance of the generals. In the eighteen months preceding October 1963, for example, the five elected governments of Argentina, Peru, Guatemala, Ecuador, and the Dominican Republic were overthrown; in each case a military junta was the controlling element.

In Africa, new contrasts and conflicts have arisen: between barter or trade-in-kind and money; between human cooperation in meeting life's challenges and the specialization of function that accompanies industrialization; between animism and the missionary's crucifix; between the old established ethics and those imported from the more acquisitive societies; between sharing and individual savings; between the British or other prevailing system and tribal conventions; between the political demands of the rising central state and the village, the chief, the elders, the tribe, and the individual; between the representatives of the people and the determinations of the new man who heads the state. The old system of gift that once carried its own dignity confronts the interdictions against bribery in the new order. Furthermore, the task of setting up an independent civil service confronts the nepotistic inclinations which derive naturally from tribal fealty. The old reverence toward the chief is converted by some into a faith in the omniscience of a new prime minister. What would be looked upon as the loyal opposition in British politics is sometimes confused with a hostile tribe.

The shift from village to city or from tribe to family as the basic social unit has effected a mutation in ways of life that had stood fast for more than a millennium. Changes in political patterns have been sudden and revolutionary as well. Often the new state would be trestled on a constitution glowing with lofty language but with no precedents for applying it to a specific set of facts. "Freedom," "social security," dedication to the "public welfare" are all promised before there is the experience, tradition, purchasing power, or industry to bring them into bud.

Policies in the developing countries have often been inconsistent and convulsive, kind to one type of investment and harsh to another, with the prospective investor never knowing when, where, or whether the winds might shift. Raw materials lie in abundance in Bolivia's altiplano, but few entrepreneurs will gamble a dollar to dig them out. Uranium in the Congo and water power in Africa beckon for exploitation, but venturers think twice before taking the risk. Elsewhere, at the first sign of industrial activity, the human surplus disgorged by agricultural inadequacy heads for the cities, almost always in numbers far greater than the economies can absorb.

These changes are taking place in a great arena in which each of the two great ideologies is proclaiming its preeminence. Both ideologies lean on the word "democracy" as a term with strong ethical connotations and alluring overtones, but the two are worlds apart in the measure of essential freedoms granted to the individual.

One ideology is postulated on the theory that private enterprise is essential for a country's development and should be encouraged by appropriate laws, inducements, and guarantees. Where this fails to function, as in housing, government will assume the responsibility. In any event, private ownership of farms and homes is widely recognized as a paramount right.

The other ideology, based on summary revolution, at first asserted that all land belongs to the state and that neither private enterprise nor private ownership has a place in society. Private ownership, even of peasant holdings, was liquidated; farm dwellings and implements were seized; agriculture was collectivized; and urban land was confiscated. The confiscated urban land was to be publicly owned or dedicated primarily to the use of collectivized industries.

Yet it was not long before this proscription of private homeownership in the U.S.S.R. had to be modified in the face of the realities. Though all land, urban and rural, has remained in the state and private landownership was banned, the right to build one's own home has had to be conceded to some extent. The state has even granted some credits to the individual home builders.[9] Plots have been allotted for building, the right to use them has been granted "in perpetuity," and the new dwellings have been declared "the personal property of the builders." In addition to giving protection against confiscation by making adequate compensation after appraisal, the state has provided alternative land and dwelling accommodation for those displaced. Sales of residences were permitted, provided the seller did not sell more than one house within three years of purchase.

Poland, which nationalized its larger industries, passed a statute in 1947 that assisted private builders by means of land grants and priorities in obtaining building materials. It freed all new buildings from rent controls, exempted new buildings from taxation for five years, and provided that if a new building was sold at a profit during the period of tax exemption, the profit would not be taxed as income. Even more advantageous measures were granted to attract "new capital in private hands" which was being "kept under cover." A black marketeer who invested his secreted gains in building would thus be guaranteed against investigation into the source of his funds.

More recently, however, a new policy has gained ground behind the Iron Curtain. It is probably impelled partly by the seeming inability of the system to cope with the housing problem. Building of individual housing is being curtailed. Most new Soviet housing (as amplified in a later chapter) will be in multiple units. Some of the amenities (kitchens, private bookshelves, etc.) may give way to more communal facilities. Partly because of the need for female labor and partly because of the lack of individual space, there may be less opportunity for the raising and care of the children by the family. A greater emphasis is being put upon more "public upbringing."[10]

Thus while the countries with Western traditions continue their respect for ownership of homes in which family controls can operate, the bulk of U.S.S.R. families will continue to be tenants of the state, with the child shaped more in accord with the concept of the "Soviet man."

Between these two worlds, the underdeveloped countries are seeking to carve out their own values, which are by no means clear or simple. Those countries which have inherited shreds of the British system are trying to maintain them, at least in form, but are superimposing their

[9] Such building loans amounted to between 5000 and 10,000 rubles, at 2 per cent per annum with an amortization period of from five to ten years, provided that the home builder invests at least 30 per cent of the total construction costs. Maurice F. Parkins, *City Planning in Soviet Russia* (Chicago: University of Chicago Press, 1953), p. 12.

[10] "Draft Program of the Soviet Communist Party," *New York Times*, August 1, 1961, pp. 13–20.

own innovations. In others, drastic limitations on rights are not infrequent. In still others, there is respect for some types of property but not for all.

Legal processes in these less developed countries are in the incubation period, and the earliest important exercises of power are apt to occur in housing and planning. In these areas, political patterns are being set for the sensitive relationships between government and the individual, between government and property, between public and private spheres of interest, and between central and local controls.

The postwar constitutions of many of the newer governments, which proclaimed respect for the individual and for his property rights, have shown little consistency in their application. Private ownership of rural as well as urban land was usually assured. The general trend has been to break up large holdings, but sometimes, particularly in rural areas, large estates have been not only tolerated but even encouraged by freedom from tax levies. In urban and suburban areas, speculation has often been completely unrestrained. Frequently land is withheld from the market to await the inevitable upward spiral. Drastic control of real estate operations is often vexing to foreign investors in industrial enterprises, who demand guarantees from their home countries as insurance against confiscation or inflation, insist on free factory sites and minimal capital outlays as a condition for investment, or demand generous subsidies. Meanwhile, squatters extend their trespasses, and as they grow in numbers, they create their own laws and conventions.

The transition from a rural to an urban economy called for the creation of sound tenure in the cities. Homeownership programs providing a minimum of decent standards for the structures and secure tenure for the urban as well as the small-farm family might have captured the imagination of the rank and file as the concept of free land did after the American Revolution. By 1964, however, there was no evidence that the older democracies had even sensed the dangers in the leap from agricultural to urban life in the newly independent countries or the potentials for rescuing democratic norms out of the gathering chaos.

5

Obstacles to Progress in Housing

Though the contest of ideologies on the political frontiers is far from being resolved in favor of democracy, the ways and habits of democratic Europe and North America continue to influence most of the less developed world. That part of the world is buying European and American automobiles and their aspirin, duplicating their textile and cement factories, adopting their dress or religions, smoking their cigarettes, and often even importing the ethical generalizations of their constitutions. But there is nothing that Europe and North America can offer the industrializing nations as a quick specific for housing ills. The nations on those two continents are themselves still going through the paroxysms of housing disorder, and despite a hundred or more years of effort, they are still suffering from the afflictions of eighteenth- and nineteenth-century urban malformations.

Housing progress lags far behind industrial progress in every part of the world. The technical genius that broke the secrets of speed, sound, space, and light still cannot build a house cheap enough for the rank and file. While a Soviet cosmonaut can orbit the world, the state that launched him cannot establish a good housing program on the ground. A Negro laborer's family in New York and a squatter in Caracas may both have television sets, but neither can afford a decent house.

The anomaly is that the less industrialized the country, the less apt it is to have a housing problem. The moment it begins to develop industrially, its housing problem burgeons. The more it develops industrially, the more stubborn the problem becomes. In a primitive village, the housing problem is not critical. The moment the family moves from village to city, its members surrender the home that is usually their own, as well as the more ample space on which its stands, the freedom from noise, smoke, traffic, and danger, the proximity to nature, and their place in community life. What they get in the impersonal city, whatever the other compensations may be, is a crowded slum and sometimes not even that.

THE GAP BETWEEN SHELTER COST AND INCOME

It is clear that government intervention is indispensable in the new urban scheme of things, but there are still many variations in the capacities of governments to act. Low income is one of the more troublesome obstacles. Since average income per person in most of the less advanced countries is barely $100 a year, most people can buy very little, whether it is imported or produced domestically.

Though the breadwinner's earnings may go up when he leaves for the city, finding a home he can afford becomes his toughest assignment. In Africa, the average dwelling cost is about $300, though the variations are great.[1] For most cities of Asia, $1000 is the figure generally used in calculating the cost of a worker's new dwelling unit.[2] On the basis of a twenty-year amortization, 5 per cent interest, and $3.50 a month for taxes, maintenance, insurance, and utilities, the house would cost about $10 per month. If 15 to 20 per cent of a householder's income should be spent on housing, an Asian urban family would need a minimum income of $600 to $800 per year. In India, only 12 per cent of the urban population have such earnings.[3] Where is the money to come from? The outlay by the government of $1000 per house for all who need it, or even half that sum, would jeopardize other essential development.

The gap between incomes and shelter costs in the Philippines is also wide.[4] The common laborer working twenty-five days a month is apt to be earning only $50 a month and should be able to afford a house costing $1000 to $1500 if the principal and interest payments were low enough. Yet the official housing agency set up to deal with the problem, the People's Homesite and Housing Corporation, could not produce housing in 1958 costing less than $4000.

[1] United Nations, *Financing of Housing and Community Improvement Programmes* (New York, 1957), p. 13.

[2] *Ibid.*

[3] *Ibid.* See also M. Mukherjee, *The Pattern of Income and Expenditure in the Indian Union: A Tentative Study,* Bulletin of the International Statistical Institute, Vol. XXXIII, Part III (December 1951), p. 55.

[4] Charles Abrams and Otto Koenigsberger, *Report on Housing in the Philippine Islands* (New York: United Nations, 1959), p. 21.

Figures 9 and 10. Planning for the dead is often better than for the living. Figure 9 shows a graveyard in a Japanese city. Figure 10 below shows a housing project in the same city. Note the competition for land between housing, agriculture, industry, and utilities.

Figure 11. Prefabricated chattel houses in Barbados. The land is rented, and the houses are moved when the landowner requires it. (*Courtesy of the Barbados Department of Education.*) (See page 31.)

Figure 12. The author is greeted in a village in India.

Figure 13. An unpaved street in Santa Cruz, Bolivia. Only an expert can negotiate a jeep through the mud and ruts.

Figure 14. A flood scene in the Lower Volta, Ghana, 1963.

Figure 15. "The visitor to Caracas is struck by the public housing projects standing like monumental tablets proclaiming their superiority to the makeshift ranchos nearby." (See page 53.)

Figure 16. Self-help in a Venezuelan squatters' area. When tenure seems secure, the foundations are made firmer.

In Bolivia, out of 155,725 houses surveyed, 47.5 per cent were without water and 54.2 per cent without sanitation. Annual income per capita was only $65 in 1959. Yet the agency set up to build workers' homes, the Instituto Nacional de Vivienda, was building houses priced at $1600, and from 1956 to 1960 the total output was only 200 dwellings. The Instituto in fact was equipped to build no more than 100 houses a year.[5]

In oil-producing Venezuela, there is great inequality of incomes. A family in Caracas may earn upwards of $4000 a year, while a farm family may be earning less than $400. The wide gulf between incomes has driven people to the cities, with the result that already 54 per cent of the population is urban. About half of the nation's houses are dilapidated. A large proportion of the houses have thatched roofs. While thatch may be adequate elsewhere, in Venezuela it is a breeding place for the barbeiro bug, a transmitter of the parasite that causes Chagas' disease. This death-dealing disease is widespread in Venezuela. Obviously, private builders cannot replace all of these thatched slum dwellings. The visitor to Caracas is struck by the public housing projects, standing like monumental tablets proclaiming their superiority to the makeshift ranchos nearby. Actually, however, Banco Obrero, the agency set up to provide housing for low-income and middle-class families in Caracas, has in thirty years built an average of only 1300 houses a year. Most of the houses were scheduled to be sold for over $6000. Squatting is almost the only way a low-income family can get a home it can afford, though even a squatter's hut in Caracas costs $1000 and up.[6]

So far as housing is concerned, the whole world has remained underdeveloped. From Harlem to the Congo and from Peru to Pakistan, the urban worker can buy a Cadillac more easily than a good house. After the family pays for food, clothing, utilities, and other essentials, there is little money left for housing. In the United States, tenants in low-rent public housing pay about 20 per cent of their income as rent, but some slum tenants on relief actually pay higher rents than wealthy families.[7]

[5] Charles Abrams, *Report on Housing Financing in Bolivia* (New York: United Nations, 1959), pp. 15, 32, 75.

[6] Charles Abrams, memorandum to Banco Obrero, Venezuela, on *Housing Finance in Venezuela* (mim., New York, 1960).

[7] In New York City, for example, out of 14,000 welfare families housed in single furnished rooms, 86 per cent paid from $40 to $80 per room monthly in 1959. Ninety-eight families paid between $140 and $160 per room, and eighty-four families paid between $180 and $200. Rentals like these were being paid at the same time by the wealthiest families, and in many cases the rich were paying considerably less. See Anthony Panuch, *Building a Better New York,* Final Report to Mayor Robert F. Wagner by the Special Advisor on Housing and Urban Renewal (New York, 1960), p. 75. The relief families' rents were abnormally high because of the difficulty of finding dwellings for such families. Their rent is paid by the city.

The United States figure of 20 per cent is considerably above what can be paid for rent in many other countries. In Bolivia it is only 8 per cent. A civil servant in India pays his government landlord 10 per cent. Other ratios are: Australia, 8 per cent; Austria, 5 per cent; Belgium, 13 per cent; Canada, 15 per cent; and Ceylon, 3 per cent. In Turkey's cities more than a third of a family's income goes for rent. Families in the under-developed areas can allocate very little of their income for rent and often have to choose between food and a roof.

NATIONAL FINANCIAL LIMITATIONS

Although housing of the poor is a headache also for wealthy nations, they do have techniques for easing it. These techniques are used or ignored as political and economic pressures dictate. The wealthier countries also have architects, contractors, skilled labor, and available materials. While many of their families are overcrowded, virtually none are homeless and none are seizing land. Most members of their middle class are decently housed, and conditions have improved in the last few decades. Even when the European housing supply was sorely depleted by bombing, the ravaged nations were able to rebuild.

The countries in the developmental stages are operating under still greater pressure in the housing situation. Not only are the in-migrants arriving there so fast that new industry cannot provide enough jobs for them, but even the basic capital, finance, skills, and materials are lacking. Nevertheless, housing and rational urban development are the two great problems on which the prosperous nations can offer their poor relations little guidance.

The developing nations of Asia, Africa, and Latin America need a minimum of 24 million dwellings annually, or about ten dwellings annually per 1000 inhabitants. The magnitude of such requirements can be realized only when one considers that, with a few exceptions, the highly developed countries build no more than six to seven dwellings per 1000 inhabitants.[8]

It is manifest therefore that all prevailing ideas of wholesale slum clearance and building of costly housing must be abandoned, and that some fresh thinking must be brought to bear on the shelter problem. The provision of the bare essentials may have to be the world's sad but only reasonable alternative. Once we understand the enormity of the problem, however, there may be ways of dealing with it. It is only when hope is given up and eyes are closed to reality that crisis becomes inevitable.

[8] United Nations, Social Commission, 14th Session, *Report of the Ad Hoc Group of Experts on Housing and Urban Development* (New York, March 16, 1962), p. 2.

LAND COST AND LAND SPECULATION CONTROLS

In most underdeveloped countries, land for urban expansion is ample, but too little has been made accessible to urban centers. Speculation in accessible land has caused asking prices to zoom so that it now often costs as much to buy the land as to build the house. In the Lagos region of Nigeria, for example, land cost may be three or four times the house cost in the more accessible areas.

While the urban land problem varies according to the particular country and its size, topography, and public policy, one is apt to confront the following conditions, which contribute to high land cost:

1. AN EXCESSIVE CONCENTRATION OF OWNERSHIP IN SOME PLACES. In Latin America, the Philippines, and other areas once governed by Spain, concentration is partly a carry-over from the haciendas and large agricultural estates in the Spanish tradition. Some of these estates have moved into the urban orbit. But many large farms and haciendas are still run as sugar plantations, whereas their better use would be for urban development.

2. A LOW TAX ON LAND. In many countries there is no tax on farmland and in some not even on urban land.[9] Often paddy fields ripe for use as building lots are taxed nominally or not at all.

3. THE TRADITION OF LANDOWNERSHIP. In most underdeveloped countries, the tradition of landownership generally remains a powerful force on a parity with possession of precious metals. The tradition tends to make owners hold on to land and pass it on as a single parcel from one generation to another.

4. THE PAUCITY OF ALTERNATIVE INVESTMENTS. The tendency to convert landed wealth into intangibles has not yet fully manifested itself in many of the less developed countries. Government bonds, for example, are not generally a popular investment and are purchased mostly by banks and government agencies.

5. INFLATIONARY TRENDS IN THE ECONOMY. Such trends encourage landholding. The cash received in selling land, it is feared, might be

[9] In Manila, land is assessed at 30 to 50 per cent of value and sometimes even less, and the tax is about 1 per cent. Thus the effective tax rate is only ⅓ of 1 per cent to ½ of 1 per cent of value. The owner of land worth $50,000 on which the annual taxes are only $150 to $250 need not be in a hurry to develop it. A tract of 148 acres in Angeles, Pampanga, had an appraised market value of $66,000 but was assessed at only $12,700—though it was bought by the government housing agency for $463,000. Thus the tax was about $62, less than ¹⁄₁₀ of 1 per cent of value as appraised and ¹⁄₇₄ of 1 per cent of the price actually paid! The rising population makes owners feel that they can safely pay the small annual taxes and recoup many times their outlays by holding on for the inevitable price rise.

devalued, whereas the land itself will more certainly rise in value compared with the local currency.

6. ANTICIPATION OF A WINDFALL THROUGH THE BUILDING OF ROADS AND OTHER PUBLIC IMPROVEMENTS. Under most prevailing practices in the less developed countries, the government acquires only the land it actually needs for a road improvement. The increment accrues to the owners nearby, who pay no assessment. Hence, a new road could triple the sales price of abutting properties.

7. RELUCTANCE TO EMPLOY THE COMPULSORY PURCHASE POWER. Public agencies often depend largely upon voluntary sales to acquire the land they need. Official housing agencies that have the power of eminent domain either have never exercised it or have exercised it only on rare occasions. Since few owners are willing to sell, land prices are usually exorbitant.

If more land could be released for urban use, the artificially high prices would soon find their true market level. But without a mechanism for bringing land within range of the average worker's purchasing power, the central and more desirable land will continue to be the squatter's target. The choice is between legal expropriation by the government and illegal appropriation by the desperate landless. If the already critical squatting problem comes to involve many more voters, illegal acquisition of land is bound to gain political sanction in more and more countries.

In the Philippines, a country of many contradictions, the land problem is conspicuous. These islands are not land-poor like Malta, Gibraltar, or the flooded areas of East Pakistan. Some Philippine cities reach out to the wilderness, and most have open areas a stone's throw from their hubs. Even Manila has some open spaces on its outskirts, while Davao City blends into a broad rural plain. The islands, predominantly agricultural, have great fertile, well-watered stretches of land lying between their extensive mountain systems and the sea. About 60 per cent of the land is in forests, almost all government-owned.

The land problem in the Philippine cities is one not of scarcity but of refusal to sell. Much of the acreage in the urban and urbanizing districts lies frozen in the hands of owners who have no present intention of developing it. Neither the magnetism of demand nor the temptations of profit can persuade the larger landholders to make use of their holdings or sell to others who will. The situation is most acute in the environs of Manila, where land poverty exists amid land plenty.

The land concentration in the Manila area has produced economic, political, social, and physical distortions, particularly in the country's major cities.[10] It has consolidated an important area of wealth in the hands of a relatively small number of people and removed this wealth from the reach of taxation. It has also contributed markedly to the inflationary spiral by rocketing land prices, deprived people of land on which to build houses, and driven those deprived of land to seize it in violation of law. That high land costs are holding back the general development of cities is affirmed by the National Planning Commission.[11] It is one thing, however, for the official agencies to recognize the problem and another for them to resolve it.

In the outskirts of Manila, plots for homes are available to those who can afford to pay excessive prices. Speculators and subdividers are occasionally able to buy a tract, and some then retail it in small plots. Others will continue to hold the purchased land out of use or exact ransom prices. Land speculation is less often motivated by the profit to be made from immediate development than by a determination to hold on for the inevitable price rise of the undeveloped land.

There is great disparity between the cost of sizable tracts and the price of lots after subdivision. Large tracts two miles from the center of Davao could be bought at prices that would make large-scale acquisition and resale to poorer families feasible. But even in sprawling Davao, small individual plots are at a premium. A subdivider who bought a tract offered individual lots for resale at four, five, or six times the price he paid.

In the Philippines, it is land, more than building cost, that deprives the lower-income group of homeownership. In Legaspi, a small house made of bamboo, wood, and nipa would cost only $100, but a 400-square-meter lot in town would run to $3000—or thirty times the cost of the house. Because of high land cost, low-income families pay the price of slum life, overcrowding, and ransom rents—or they simply take the law into their own hands and squat on private or public land.

Land development everywhere is chaotic, with practically no controls. Manifestly, the great need is a land policy that can make properly planned land available at reasonable cost. Sound forms of tenure, regulation, use, acquisition, taxation, and financing of land should all be elements of the land policy, but rarely are such procedures used effectively.

[10] See Miguel y Garcia and Anselmo T. Quinto, "Growth of Greater Manila," United Nations Seminar on Regional Planning, July 28–August 8, 1958, Tokyo, Japan.

[11] "One of the greatest obstacles in the replanning of developed areas is the high cost of land. In many cases the cost has been found to be incompatible with the reasonable use of the land." National Planning Commission, *The Master Plan* (Manila, 1956), p. 8.

LAND TRANSFER AND REGISTRATION

Land transfer and protection of tenure by registration systems are taken for granted in the more developed countries, and they were used in Europe as far back as the Middle Ages. But they are troublesome obstacles in countries where legal systems have not matured or where stubborn customs persist. In nations where physical force guaranteed possession or where property turnover was rare, registration systems were unknown. Today, however, with the rise of individual tenancy and ownership, mortgages, squatting, multiple sales, subdivision, and inheritance laws, it is indispensable to establish property titles. The problem is particularly acute in areas where larger holdings by tribes are being subdivided into smaller parcels.

In Ghana, alienation of land had been infrequent, and unified tribal holdings had survived the early pressures for a plantation system run by foreigners. But with the demand for gold-mining concessions in the final quarter of the nineteenth century, with the growth of the cocoa industry thereafter, and with the spread of English systems of conveyancing, private forms of ownership arrived. As land development and trade increased, conflicts over titles grew with them. Builders, individuals who wanted to build houses, and government agencies that wanted to make mortgage loans all found it difficult to go ahead with their plans because of the uncertainty of titles.

Conflicts existed in Ghana over boundaries where different chiefs laid claim to the same lands and over "stool lands," which were legally transferable only for payment of debt. Purchasers also encountered trouble over defective or undecipherable conveyances, and over tracts which had been conveyed by two separate tribal chiefs, one of whom had no right to sell. Some land was held by so many individuals that it was impossible to find them all. In other cases, developers who acquired land could not find out which members of a family were entitled to the purchase price. One family bought land and made extensive improvements only to face a claim that it had bought from the wrong person. Questionable claims to large tracts were purchased by speculators solely for the gamble. Frequently, disputes between chiefs resulted in violence. A large grove of coconut trees was actually leveled by one tribe because there was no other way to settle its differences with another tribe.

Kwame Nkrumah told me that confusion over titles and land, by proving troublesome, might speed British departure. He hoped for reform thereafter, but it has been slow in arriving. There was also a prevalent feeling that acquisition by foreigners of valid titles should be made difficult as a matter of principle.

Problems of title and conveyancing are not always confined to the lack of registration systems. Where, as in Ireland, there have been few conveyances and considerable emigration, a single parcel may have as many as fifty or more heirs, each of whom must be tracked down and his consent secured for a sale. In such cases, other means must be found for facilitating conveyancing and development.

LACK OF FINANCE

In the more developed areas, the mortgage system enables most families to buy houses with a reasonable down payment and monthly payments for twenty to forty-five years. Subsidies are generally available there for lower-income families. But in the underdeveloped areas, where the average family has small savings, a house must usually be paid for outright. Even if there is a surplus from earnings, years of saving are required before a family can accumulate enough money. Where building costs are low, interest rates are prohibitive, and often high rates combine with high land costs to make homeownership impossible. In the Philippines, for example, pawnshops make mortgage loans at 2 per cent a month. Commercial banks, which rarely lend for building, charge 12 per cent a year and extend such credit only to their best customers. In Bolivia, normal bank loans to business will exact tributes of 21 per cent per annum.[12] Argentine and Peruvian interest rates of 24 per cent are common. The interest rate in a 1962 Venezuelan philanthropic project built by Eugenio Mendoza, one of its most respected citizens, is 10 per cent. This, in Venezuela, is accepted as a benefaction.

LACK OF SAVINGS

In the more developed countries, a good portion of savings is channeled through savings institutions into mortgages on homes. But in the underdeveloped areas, savings are usually in the form of jewels, cash, or tangible personalty, which is either kept on the person or concealed in the house. The average person does not trust banks. Inflation is a constant threat to savings, but it does no harm to a bag of silver trinkets. In Brazil, the worker will line up at the bank to cash his paycheck so that he can buy something with the proceeds before inflation makes prices soar by the time his next paycheck arrives.

Branch banking houses and government banks have been breaking down some of the resistance to saving, but these institutions do not usually make mortgage loans out of deposits. Absence of mortgage money has impelled some countries to make housing loans out of tax revenues, but sources of revenue are too limited to keep these loans flowing well.

[12] For an amplification, see Charles Abrams, *Report on Housing Financing in Bolivia, op. cit.,* p. 18.

ABSENCE OF A BUILDING INDUSTRY

A construction industry with the full complement of specialized trades does not often exist outside the more developed countries. The better-heeled can build a mansion by hiring a foreman to organize the labor and the operation. Some larger cities in Latin America like Mexico City, Santiago, and Buenos Aires have private contractors who build for higher-income groups. In the absence of a well-established building industry, the Bank of Chile has built apartment houses, and some semi-private banks have constructed housing for middle-income families in Bogotá, Medellín, and Cali.[13] Industrial plants and oil and mining companies have also built housing and planned communities in these cities. Some foreign-trained architects may be on hand to design a costly house or factory, and there may be a few large contracting firms concentrating on major public works or factories, financed and managed from abroad. Occasionally, some of these firms combine construction work with the import and sale of building materials. But generally the construction industry—if any—is small, disorganized, and undercapitalized.

The more developed world tends to take for granted its functioning building industries, overlooking the desultory events that preceded its present operational stage. In the less developed world, the essential crafts are at a premium. The methods and tools that built the Pyramids, the masonry achievements of the Greeks, and the use of cement and long iron beams by the Romans were never carried over from one era to another or from the old to the newly developing regions. It was only with the rise of the artisans' associations in the eleventh and twelfth centuries in Italy that craft knowledge began to trickle through to the rest of the continent, taking shape in the specialization of carpenters, joiners, masons, bricklayers, tilers, plasterers, and painters that marked the emergence of a building industry in Western Europe, notably in England. With the commercial revolution, the building entrepreneur replaced the older personal relationship between worker and owner.

In contrast with the steady development of craft and job organization in Europe, the less developed regions still tend to rely upon the single laborer who happens to have carried with him the slim knowledge he may have acquired in the building of his own rural shack. Though there are native contractors, they often are handicapped by lack of experience and capital.

While skills are advanced in some areas, the development of building crafts has been held back by government emphasis on production in other fields and by lack of knowledge of how to stimulate housing production. In-migration of skilled artisans from abroad is usually prohibited or discouraged, while the skills of many of the potential

---

[13] Frances Violich, *Cities of Latin America* (New York: Reinhold, 1944), p. 152.

craftsmen from the rural areas have not been used either because of failure to launch a housing program or because they have chosen factory work or trade. So too, the lag in construction activity has discouraged many workers from training for the building trades.

Foreign contractors have been frowned upon in nationality-conscious countries from competing with the less expert local men. In Ghana, for example, a good foreign contractor would make bids on public works through a native dummy contractor or front man. Surveyors, foremen, and architects are few or nonexistent, and where they do function (as in the Philippines), they devote their main efforts to factory or luxury construction. Building research is rarely undertaken, and where research stations have been set up, trained personnel is lacking. Costly testing machinery sometimes rusts away.

There are some exceptions. Crafts of a high order are found in Puerto Rico, where the techniques of on-site mass production are well developed. Labor in Israel, Hong Kong, and Singapore is skilled. Togoland has many good carpenters (thanks probably to original German training). There are similar exceptions in South American cities, particularly where Italian craftsmen have immigrated. Often, however, an unemployed man will say that his vocation is carpentry when he is incapable of sawing a straight line. In Singapore, where a developed contracting industry and skills make it possible to build an apartment house at as little as $3 to $4 a square foot, development is held back by lack of available sites, high taxes on rents, and rent controls.

BACKWARDNESS IN ARCHITECTURE AND USE OF MATERIALS

Some underdeveloped countries offer striking examples of public architecture and building, which the more developed countries might well respect. Much of the building is of ancient origin, some more recent. Some South American architecture exhibits both boldness and imagination, and occasionally an elaborate, extravagant venture may take form in the building of a new capital, town, or monument. Yet generally both in design and in building techniques the world seems to have embraced the dazzling age of illumination only to highlight the dark age of architecture. Considering the lack of modern equipment and materials and architectural education, the ancient Roman, Greek, Byzantine, and medieval expressions still stand as challenges to most current contributions. Some reasons for the odd contrast between past and present are that in former ages the pace was slower, the product was built for long life and with pride of workmanship, and there was greater craft skill, thanks to a system of apprenticeship.

Today there is a rush to get things built, no time for craft, and few good artisans. While the more developed nations have good modern examples of institutional architecture and have shown some technical progress, home building for the little fellow has not improved much. It has usually remained the orphan of the technical age, the waif in architectural development. Within a few hundred feet of Byzantine or Seljuk genius in the Middle East or within a stone's throw of a planned city built in Pakistan by Alexander, one is apt to see the most primitive housing and no planning at all. There is little difference between the housing of the average rural family of a thousand years ago and the rural house today, and many urban houses are probably worse. Part of the trouble is the absence of architectural education and the emphasis on speed and quick amortization of investment. Another explanation is the orientation of the architect toward engineering. But even the best architect would be hard put to design both a good multiple dwelling and one that can be rented at low cost. He is more interested in institutional or other high-cost operations. Little is known about mass construction on the site, though its beginnings may be seen in Jamaica, Trinidad, Puerto Rico, and Israel, and probably in a few other developing areas. Public building of homes and city planning in the less developed countries bear the stamp of the public works department. They are usually standardized, uniform designs that give little thought to the city's future landscape. Lack of adequate funds plays a role, but even where money is made available, it is often misspent on unprepossessing embellishments or wasted spaces. Economy, simplicity, and efficiency seem rarely to have made liaison.

In most places, housing does not get even the attention of a public works engineer, much less an architect. If, somehow, some houses do go up, they are most often neither flood- nor earthquake-proof; soil erosion undermines their foundations; primitive pit latrines abut on the living space; buildings are not oriented to the prevailing wind and rain; space is at a minimum, yet ceilings are often unnecessarily high, wasting precious materials; roof insulation is inadequate, and roof gutters are lacking; kitchens are small, and storage space for food is insufficient.

Building codes are of course essential, particularly in congested areas subject to earthquakes. Too often the codes are national regulations that do not fit some localities, or they are city codes, which do not embrace the codeless suburbs. The tendency in a number of countries is to copy the complex codes of England, Germany, or the United States as well as their zoning and planning laws, though they are irrelevant and though the talents to enforce, construe, and adapt them may be completely lacking. Zoning laws originally designed for countries with widespread automobile ownership may prescribe stores a mile away from the weary pedestrian's home.

Booming San Juan, Puerto Rico, saw large subdivisions end up in row upon row of monotonous dormitory suburbs without provision for schools, churches, community facilities, or open space. Commercial facilities were often miles from the sites. Developers who had promised to build them held back the commercial land for future speculative increment, while the harried housewives were sent on their long daily treks to the shops, or were compelled to pay tribute to itinerant peddlers who carted the provisions into the developments. A center earmarked for stores might end up as a gas station. Soon a residential area would be dotted with makeshift dress shops, groceries, barber shops, candy and pop shops, and mechanical workshops. A constellation of vending establishments of unexpected versatility would crop up through overnight conversions of residences. Playgrounds were cut off by highways or were nonexistent; open spaces were whatever empty lots might have been left behind as remnants of developments. As acre upon acre was consumed by speculative developments (financed with the aid of the U.S. Federal Housing Administration), the journey to work became more distant, to church more wearisome, to school more dangerous. In 1962, however, a dynamic chairman of the Planning Commission stopped all building until builders could revamp plans to build livable neighborhoods.[14]

Failure in other countries to develop housing programs has caused many of the relatively few materials industries to close shop or stagnate. Tile and brick factories, lumber yards, and small hardware factories struggle to stay above water. Geared to sporadic building, the industries function sporadically.

Local materials remain undeveloped. Foreign materials are imported with the notion that they are automatically better. In Ghana's Northern Territories, where adobe and thatch have survived the march of time, imported iron roofs have become epidemic, and 13 per cent of its total imports are building materials, most of which could be locally made. In Bolivia, the official explanation for not encouraging roof-tile production is that the local tile industry has failed to market its products competitively. Of course, if sufficient orders were stimulated, it could do so.

Even where raw materials are available, often there are no means of processing them. Cement is in short supply; but where lime is available, it remains unprocessed and unused, though it is one of the oldest of all materials. In Barbados, the swank tourist resorts are built with native limestone, but most families keep buying Canadian lumber for their cabins, which become termite-ridden in five to ten years.

Pakistan has building stone, sand for concrete and plaster work, excellent limestone, and a fair quantity of gypsum. Some of its areas also have brick clay, native reeds for thatching, and good timber resources.

[14] Charles Abrams, *Report to the College of Engineers, Architects and Surveyors on Resolution P-147* (mim., New York, April 5, 1962).

Though both east and west wings are short of metals, particularly iron and steel, many of Pakistan's shortages are chargeable to underdeveloped materials industries. Lime mortar can be substituted for masonry, and lime concrete for cement concrete, but they remain unused when chronic cement shortages occur.[15] Many Pakistani soils are suitable for the manufacture of stabilized earth blocks, which require only 5 per cent cement; although good blocks can be made with lime or bitumen, these opportunities also have been ignored.

For centuries, people in Cutch, Sind, and Baluchistan have used thatched roofs plastered on both sides to reduce the fire hazard. The tradition can be revitalized by using other locally made products composed of local materials.[16] But Pakistan spends millions of dollars in foreign currency to import corrugated iron sheets. The development of an indigenous material through research and construction tests could reduce the drain on currency and stimulate the country's own industries. But Pakistan is a long way from doing this.

Cement shortage is also a problem in the Philippines[17]—yet many of the islands have good, usable brick clay and coal for firing it. A few factories do make bricks, hollow clay blocks, and tiles, but production is insufficient. Encouraging brick manufacture would mean better protection against heat and would reduce the country's dependency on imported cement. Though lime is priced the same as cement and is much easier to produce, a lime industry has been slow to develop. Timber could be better utilized and many industries supported by timber by-products. This opportunity is wasted, however, for want of technical knowledge. In some countries that have built cement factories, production lags because of the lack of experienced people to operate them efficiently.

Ghana has many materials suited to local manufacture, such as baked clay products and wood and precast components of various kinds. The country could produce wood shingles, grass and reed matting for ceilings, bamboo matting for verandas and fences, and other materials. Native lime could be used as a stabilizer, and rammed-earth techniques could be pursued. Substantial economies could also be achieved by importing cement clinkers in bulk to be mixed and ground in Ghana.[18]

These recommendations were all made in Pakistan, the Philippines,

[15] Dr. Otto Koenigsberger is the authority for this. See Charles Abrams and Otto Koenigsberger, *Report on Housing in Pakistan* (New York: United Nations, 1957), pp. 100 *et seq.*

[16] *Ibid.*

[17] Abrams and Koenigsberger, *Report on Housing in the Philippine Islands, op. cit.,* p. 80.

[18] Charles Abrams, Vladimir Bodiansky, and Otto Koenigsberger, *Report on Housing in the Gold Coast* (New York: United Nations, 1956), pp. 35–37.

and Ghana by visiting experts.[19] But recommending a program is one thing, fulfilling it another. What these countries need besides advice is technical ability and administrative apparatus.

THE BY-PRODUCTS OF PLANLESSNESS

Traffic is one of the blessings and headaches of progress. The automobile and bus should provide access to and from distant villages, afford escape to recreation, and open low-cost land for building. In the more developed countries, the automobile has replaced the draft animal and won the right of way. But in cities where streets were built for foot and hoof, motor traffic must compete with wagons, cows, water buffaloes, camels, donkeys, bicycles, men, and curbside industries for use of the narrow passageways. Movement has slowed to the speed of the animal, and roads are often gullied and bridges blocked. Sidewalks are frequently lacking in old cities. When they are built in some new cities, they are soon cluttered with obstructions, holes, and traps. Meanwhile, houses have sprung up in the back alleys, and wherever space has been unused, shops and extensions mushroom, boosting land prices and making acquisition for widening and replanning too costly to be practical. Unplanned and uncontrolled, the city's hub becomes more concentrated with trade and human traffic. Workers who live only a few miles from their factories soon spend an hour or more getting to their homes. In Lagos and Apapa, Nigeria, workers spend as much as two hours for the journey to work and spend up to 15 per cent of the family budget on fares. Everything is delayed—unloading of ships, movement of goods, automobiles, and people.

Where roads have actually been widened, as in Pakistan, the widths seemed excessive to some of the home-hungry. These citizens correct the extravagance by moving onto the roadside and building makeshift settlements. Despite the increase in trucks and automobiles, streets often remain unpaved for lack of funds. After every rainfall in Santa Cruz, Bolivia, only an expert can negotiate a jeep through mountains of mud and valleys of irrigated ruts.

Foreign aid, particularly from the United States, has helped to relieve some of the traffic jams and to extend communication. Since the United States knows how to build roads better than cheap housing, roads have become popular in American aid programs. In Turkey, tens of millions of dollars have been spent on new arteries; thus cities and farms that were once isolated are now linked to Istanbul, Ankara, and other cities. But when the roads were built, no controls were instituted to hold down the rising prices of the land on the roadsides or regulate the speculative and planless subdivisions that mushroomed. In Ireland, some farseeing

[19] See United Nations reports on these countries, cited in this chapter.

officials (like the Wide Streets Commissioners in the reign of Charles II) acted ruthlessly to remove all human and structural obstructions to broaden highways. When occupants insisted on remaining, their roofs were carted away. The result of such road building is somewhat better movement of traffic, although snarls are already evident.[20] In most countries, however, the narrow streets and alleys built for the animal cannot be widened because of the interests and people that would be disturbed as well as the high cost and the backwardness of land acquisition techniques.

While the more developed countries are better poised to build throughways, parking facilities, and mass transit, the less developed areas are concerned primarily with increased productivity, hoping that someday they will get around to replanning. By that time, of course, there will be so many businesses and legal and illegal residences established that reordering will be impossible. Some countries, like Pakistan and Brazil, have shifted the seat of government to a new site, which is one way officials can escape the problems of densities and overcrowding, but the political wisdom of such decisions is still far from proved. Withdrawal from the centers of population eliminates exposure to mass pressures and problems but also makes it easier for a junta in the isolated capital to take over the government with little resistance from the masses.

The question of sanitation is always troublesome. In many of the less developed areas, rubbish is left on the streets, and dirty water is still flung from the windows without so much as a "gardyloo." Although sewers carried off surface water from Nineveh, Babylon, and Rome long before Christ, they are still unknown in many cities today. Sometimes excrement and urine pollute the wells used for drinking water.

Primitive waste disposal not only has tainted the water supply in many cities but has drawn pests and spread afflictions. Refuse left to decompose in streets and the swill from human ablutions in Karachi form iridescent pools that lose their mystery upon inhalation. Collected refuse is largely organic in the less developed areas and cannot be used for filling swamps, and because transport to distant dumps is costly, refuse wagons are often emptied near the built-up sections. Officialdom that preferred to overlook illegal colonies may be forced, through fear of epidemics, to install a common tap, but this action, while most often justified, also stabilizes the squatters' settlements by making them a little more tolerable.

Disasters such as earthquakes, hurricanes, fires, and floods compound the difficulties of building securely. Hurricanes in the West Indies often destroy thousands of houses. Earthquakes in Chile and floods in the Far East have added more hordes to the stream of the homeless. In the

[20] See Charles Abrams, *Urban Renewal Project in Ireland (Dublin)* (New York: United Nations, 1961).

Far East, millions of houses have been destroyed by catastrophes. Millions of people continually face the danger of floods in India. The Mahanadi, Orissa's largest river, marooned 300,000 people when it reached its record level in 1955.

The passions of men have added to nature's eruptions. In India and Pakistan twelve million refugees had to run for their lives across the borders following partition, leaving many of their homes flaming behind them. One million Moslems crossed into East Pakistan. They found a delta country whose water was both a blessing and a bane—a blessing for its rice crops and fish, and a bane for its constant flooding and for the land eliminated for living. The population of Dacca, East Pakistan's capital, leaped from 98,000 in 1947 to some 450,000 in 1951, and there have been an additional 100,000 people since that year. Room for expansion beyond the Dacca-Narayanganj metropolitan region is difficult, for during four months of the year the Ganges floods the region's plains, confining 60,000 villages and the few towns to islands of high ground.

PUBLIC POWER AND PUBLIC AGENCIES

Housing and public works programs require efficiency and authority to purchase land compulsorily and to regulate land operations. But in the less developed areas there has been either a lack of adequate power or an unbridled abuse of power. Compulsory purchase has been taken for granted in the United States and England, but in many of the developing countries, its use was unprecedented, and its exercise seemed tyrannical. In Turkey, however, a prime minister who had lost patience with the law boldly moved in to clear streets and tear down slum buildings without resorting to legal process at all. He was hanged a few years later by the junta that succeeded him, though his slum clearances were not listed among the charges.

In Japan, well-developed industrially but with a political system still unmatured, officials and the public, imbued with the new spirit of democracy, have felt that taking land even for public use is undemocratic. Voluntary purchase for such elementary uses as roads has resulted in astronomical compensation to owners, while compulsory acquisition has taken as much as five years. The consequence has been that Japan has located housing and some other public buildings not on the best sites but where the government happens to own some land or can buy it easily.

Financing of public improvements through local revenues is almost unknown. Most Turkish cities, for example, cannot finance housing or local improvements even if they want to. Taxes and tax sources are limited, and the inability of cities to tax the surrounding suburbs has spurred the opening of gas stations and other businesses just outside the city's boundaries where they can thumb their noses at the tax collector. The Mayor of Santa Cruz, Bolivia, levied a tax on oil to improve his streets and meet the city's other pressing requirements, but he found the levies not easily collectible. In Venezuela the local governments were reduced to impotence by the neglect and overreaching of former regimes. Some 91 per cent of the 1955–1956 revenue of the states and territories, excluding the federal district, was made up of grants from the national treasury.[21] Organized Communist insurrections and violence have checked administrative progress and private investment, and though legally elected, former President Betancourt had to depend on the army's loyalty to help him to fill out his term of office.

Occasionally the tenacity or genius of a local official evidences itself as in Manila, where the late Mayor Lacson, a dynamic official who modeled himself upon Fiorello H. La Guardia from stance to hat, made his city a more vital force in public administration. An enterprising official like the former Mayor of Kayseri, Turkey, persuaded private landowners to exchange their land so he could proceed with public improvements, which were partly financed by the city's electric plant.

POLITICS AND PUBLIC PRESSURES

To the chaos of squatting, overcrowding, filth, discontent, and social disruption has been added the chaos of politics, power, and policy. If there is an abundance of "Five-Year Plans," there is a paucity of housing objectives. There are few assessments of housing needs and few clear demarcations of functions among planning, housing, and public works agencies. The housing agency in the Philippines concentrated its main efforts on higher-cost housing. Similarly, an Improvement Trust in Lahore, Pakistan, acquired land in large parcels and built utilities, subdivided the land into lots, and sold them for the costliest housing, while the quantity of land allocated for the poor was minuscule. On the other hand, the government of Pakistan, following a United Nations mission and a United States loan, adopted a comprehensive housing law and began moving vigorously toward rehousing squatters and meeting the housing needs of its rank and file. The dictatorship has continued the program through more central orders. In India, a substantial portion of the housing program has gone to civil servants, but the masses still remain to be helped. Banco Obrero's dramatic public housing apartments in Caracas are a tiny drop in a big bucket, since the city's squatters in 1962 were coming in much faster than housing could be supplied for even a substantial fraction. Bolivia's urban land distribution program,

---

[21] Carl S. Shoup *et al.*, *The Fiscal System of Venezuela* (Baltimore: Johns Hopkins Press, 1959), p. 317.

designed to provide the sites for poorer families, became snarled in the country's deep financial and administrative problems, and the 300 houses built by the housing agency from 1946 through 1959 could hardly be called a beginning. Even in more prosperous Japan, very little housing is being built for the poor, though the better-heeled are not neglected. The reason is not willfulness or lack of humane impulses but the considerations of cost and subsidy, and the more effective pressures by the more vocal groups.

Politics and group pressures play their part in the less developed world as elsewhere. Candidates wooing popular favor and finding housing a key issue with voters, may announce programs that are more impressive in the pledge than in the performance. In other cases, political opportunists move in to embarrass housing officials trying to do their job. In Jamaica, tenants in public housing projects were urged by the opposition politicians not to pay rent. Most were happy to comply. Following my first visit to the country on a brief U.N. mission and my report recommending enforcement of rent obligations, Warren Cornwell, then the U.N. representative supervising the projects, began eviction proceedings against ten of the more flagrant defaulters, including a few civil servants. Rent collections then picked up remarkably. After Cornwell's departure, however, the government reverted to a policy of indifference, and upon my second visit to the island in March 1961, more than 70 per cent of rents were again in arrears. In 1963, a better display of official firmness increased collections somewhat. In Caracas, Venezuela, occupants of public housing were similarly exhorted not to pay rent, while other home-hungry families were told to move into new government housing free of obligation. The Betancourt government subsequently agreed to sell the apartments to the tenants, hoping that the prospect of ownership would improve payments. It has succeeded to some extent. In Barbados, with a housing program involving government advances of more than $12.7 million (B.W.I.) in 1963, 90 per cent of the renters and borrowers were in default. Though the average Barbadian is responsible, he was told during political campaigns not to pay the government's housing authority, and he happily complied. On one occasion, the staff sent a dunning letter to tenants, which doubled rent collections that month, but the staff was warned not to do this again. The new government in 1963, concerned about its ability to continue the housing program, decided to sell the houses, hoping collections would improve.

Squatters exert mass pressures upon officials before and after elections for legislation validating their tenure or giving them alternative land. In the Philippines the squatters have shown enough strength to elect their own congressman and force the government in several cases to convey land to them. In Singapore, the squatters are too numerous and too strong politically to be dealt with according to law, and a landowner will pay as much as twice the value of the cleared land for their departure.

In law-abiding Ireland, fixed rents in the older public housing are often less than the installments a family pays on its television set. They averaged in 1959 only $2.10 per week, whereas earnings were upwards of $28. Any effort to raise rent might doom the sponsor to political oblivion. Increases in income do not bring rent increases (except for the occupants who are under a differential rent system), and though the variations between differential and fixed rents are exceptionally wide, no local official would venture to narrow the gap by raising the fixed rents.[22]

✿　✿　✿

If this summary seems somber, the housing situation is not hopeless. It is bad today partly because it has been ignored, partly because the nations affected do not know how to deal with it, and partly because the countries and some of the international aid agencies which could help do not consider it one of their more vital concerns.

[22] Abrams, *Urban Renewal Project in Ireland* (*Dublin*), *op. cit.*, p. 58.

6

The Problems of Administration and Personnel

POLITICS, EDUCATION, AND ADMINISTRATION

From the Yazoo land frauds to Ivar Kreuger's financial manipulations, expanding government functions have always increased the invitations to corruption. And even when there was no corruption, excessive bureaucracy or tyranny was often the alternative.

Yet the more developed countries have generally made the transition from *laissez faire* to a mixed welfare state without excessive perfidy or loss of freedoms. Civil servants have steadily demonstrated a greater efficiency and pride of service, while the public over the years has become more exacting in its demands.

The underdeveloped countries have not been similarly blessed. Suddenly burdened with vast responsibilities, they have lacked roots in trained administration and traditions of public service. Talents to deal with even the simpler governmental tasks have been scarce. In Bolivia, where the revolution had banished many whose sons might have helped build the country, the death of a single high official was sufficient to paralyze officialdom because no adequate replacement could be found.

Politics has played a prime part in government personnel selection. Appointments have often been made on the basis of connections rather than qualifications. A good civil servant will find himself *non grata* when a new party takes office because he was too friendly with the former incumbent.

With public opinion either cynical or indifferent about its public servants, the public servant tends to become cynical or indifferent too.

Morale is often low, tenure insecure, compensation so small, and opportunity so limited that business can readily lure good talent from government service. Adequately trained clerical people are so scarce that a competent official often wastes time on details that should be handled by a subordinate or a good secretary.

The administrative difficulties are doubled in city planning and housing. Here disciplines are in their infancy even in the more developed countries. There can be no stock blueprint on how to build a functioning city or ease a housing famine. Formulas transplanted from other countries, even where valid and relevant, fail in their administration. There are few foreign investors ready to immobilize capital in a housing project as they might in oil prospecting. To complete an ordinary project, technical and professional people are needed for planning, surveying, architecture, drafting, civil engineering, contracting, and subcontracting. Skilled artisans, lawyers, and foremen are also required, but there is generally no one on hand or in training to fill these jobs.

In Singapore, where the government in 1963 managed about 50,000 public housing units, the management operation received a sudden setback when the British counterparts group left its management section with only three trained local officers to carry on. Its extensive housing program now required a large pool of trained personnel in rent collection and accounting, maintenance and relocation policy, welfare case operation, community center activities, and tenant education, but lacked both the eligible trainees and the qualified teachers to train them.

Part of the trouble in the underdeveloped areas is due to the backwardness of education. In Latin America, illiteracy is widespread, ranging as high as 90 per cent in some of the countries. There is also a lack of technical and vocational institutes, as well as of apprenticeship systems and of people qualified to enter particular fields. Ghana, for example, may have a good college at Achimota, but the primary and secondary school system does not supply it with adequate college material. One reason is the paucity of able teachers for the lower and secondary schools. Good personnel prospects for teaching, in turn, avoid the field because housing and general conditions in the school areas are often unattractive.

The problem can never be solved by attending to just one of its facets. Pakistan, India, and other former British possessions have simply copied British statutes, though their situations were quite different. Since good books on planning and housing have been unavailable, fellowships few, and teachers untrained, many of the talented students from the less developed areas have studied abroad. But they have found their courses frequently unsuited to conditions at home. Ireland, which has turned out more college graduates per capita than England, has lost many of her sons to England or Canada after graduation. In the Philippines and the

British West Indies, craftsmen have often emigrated after becoming qualified. The competition for good technicians is so keen in the more advanced nations that few can be found willing to tear up roots and settle in the less advanced areas.

Poverty often prevents promising youth from entering the universities and obtaining the better jobs in public service. Others choose academic studies for the prestige of the degree, ignoring the need for special training. On the other hand, many who do take special training lack the qualification for the policy responsibilities they are asked to assume.

The lack of training and experience is reflected in the quality of work done by the government agencies. Though one occasionally finds a government's statistical information surprisingly good, generally statistics are inadequate and dubious. Accounting systems are so primitive in some countries that the head of an agency may not know how much money his agency has spent, how much is due it, and how much is collectible. Manipulation of funds from one operation to another is frequently indiscriminate.

Conflicts between departments are common and jurisdictions hard to define. This is particularly true of housing and city planning, which cut across many official lines—finance, public works, health, industrial development, and public administration among others. To streamline operations, an Improvement Trust or a public corporation may be set up for housing, but it soon encounters the same interference as a department of government. Or the new corporation may be free of any governmental control and be part of a chain of so many other independent entities that administration becomes a freewheeling bedlam.

Sometimes, as in Pakistan, Turkey, and Latin America, administration is preempted by a military coup. Then the problems are attacked with directives—for better or worse.

CENTRALIZATION

The growing dependency on central governments is often necessary to maintain order, but it is making administration more unwieldy. Even when the central power is deconcentrated, the shift may be no more than passing authority on to regional governors, who are tied hand and foot to the central government. Although the private entrepreneur three centuries ago became the protagonist of local autonomy in Europe, he no longer exerts similar pressures upon the central authority. He takes centralization for granted. The centripetal trend has been furthered by a belief that centralization saves money, speeds decision making, makes friends, influences votes, streamlines tax collection, and strengthens regional planning. More recently, there has been concern that local governments, given their head, might build purlieus of dissent in opposition to the central power, that squatter nests might become the scene of un-controllable dissidence, or that student groups might organize and move on City Hall. Some of these fears are justified, and some simply reflect bureaucratic resistance to, or ignorance of, decentralized operations. In any event, centralization is reducing local government to a dead level of uniformity, withering the individual's role to that of an occasional ballot-caster for a prescribed central official. Variety in operational experiences and experiments is being frustrated in the process.

The answer to the debate on centralization versus decentralization cannot be categorical, but one thing is certain: giving more authority to local government and developing greater local interest is worth trying in more places. If ventured, the superior ability of central financing need not carry with it full central control. Sheer efficiency of the central agency is not the only test even if it can be shown that central operations are in fact more efficient. Housing and public works programs offer unique opportunities for the evolution of new and interesting forms of local and regional operations which, if not immediately practical, may in the longer run bring a firmer democratic vertebration to some of the growing bodies-politic.

ALIENS AND MINORITIES

A frequent deterrent to investment and to the better utilization of skills is the suppression of aliens and minority groups in economic activities. The growth of a country requires a variety of skills in contracting, building, production of building materials, development of finance mechanisms, and management. The alien may be a willing investor with the capital or the competence that a country needs. Moreover, the minority group may be a source of labor and talent. Some groups suffer the strictures of private discrimination, some of public policies. Offenses against them vary from job exclusion to persecution. One of the harshest policies is the immigration barrier that prevents an oppressed minority from escaping to a country of better opportunity or greater freedom.

To grasp the problem's full import, one has to reckon with worldwide ethnocentricism, nativism, prejudice, segregation, and the whole gamut of problems and theories concerning minority groups. As long as societies were tribal and economies agricultural, groups exhibited a greater solidarity, and conflict was mostly localized. With urbanization and the in-migration of new personalities and groups into cities, the less developed nations cannot avoid yielding to the pressures of the established majority, although a more enlightened policy might bring major benefits to their economies. James Bryce once suggested that the solidarity of modern states depends less upon the homogeneity of their populations than upon the thoroughgoing mixture of their heterogeneous elements.

But the mixture is far from being achieved, and racial, religious, or national frictions often threaten not only solidarity but also the political future of leaders advocating equalization of opportunities.

While homogeneity and fealty to the family or tribe were the basis for cooperation by the constituent members in the rural society, organization of enterprise is the key to large-scale employment in an industrializing society. The subordination or discouragement of a single organizer may make the difference between development of an industry and its stillbirth. Qualified people are the built-in "Peace Corps" of a country short of talents and training. The Italians in Venezuela advanced that country's building industry; the Chinese in Trinidad and in the Philippines have contributed much to the efficiency in trade of those areas; and the Syrians and Lebanese in Africa have often supplied the skills in building, contracting, materials production, or commerce which otherwise might have stagnated. The growth of the United States would doubtless have been stunted were it not for the liberal immigration policies that permitted people from all over the world to come in and use their energies to develop the American frontiers.

Most countries, however, tend to favor their own citizens in civil service, in extension of opportunities, in access to subsidized housing, and in other operations. They fear the competition of the foreigner and, if he succeeds, begrudge his success. Often an oppressed minority either emigrates when it can, is expelled, enters only those trades or enterprises where it is permitted to function, or remains a permanently suppressed group. Barriers that prevent minority in-migrations have produced one of the subtler forms of national oppression against the minority as well as a loss to the oppressor of the minority's aptitudes.

The problem varies widely from country to country and even within countries. At one extreme are the European minorities who with superior training or intelligence have managed to flourish in private enterprises wherever they have settled. At the other extreme are the 60 million untouchables in India whom British efforts did not elevate and who still await fulfillment of the promises of the new Indian constitution. Another extreme example is the million Palestinian Arabs who are almost completely removed from all economic life and remain one of the world's chronic headaches. In both cases, the economies suffer as much as the victims.

Many factors play a part in the integration, nonintegration, or disintegration of minority peoples. In underdeveloped countries one of the many obstacles is discrimination in education, which is employed sometimes from long-standing tradition, sometimes deliberately to stifle the emergence of a group or national consciousness. Differences in caste and national origin may be as responsible for discriminatory practices as differences in color. While India in November 1960 announced that there would be no more questions about caste in application forms for schools and universities, and Kenya made some progress in integrating its public schools, South Africa has intensified its campaign for apartheid in education. In Bolivia and elsewhere in South America, a few schools have been set up by German, Jewish, and other groups primarily for their own people, but they are open also to native Bolivians and are viewed as prime institutions. These are good examples of the help that minorities and aliens can give to a country.

Research on discrimination in employment, education, and training is scarce, particularly in the developing countries. The barriers to advancement erected against minorities in both the more and the less developed countries collectively include:

1. Deprivations in environment and home life.

2. Absence of adequate housing, which impedes mobility and free access to areas of opportunity.

3. Community attitudes restricting the hiring of workers who, it is feared, might settle in the community.

4. Resistance to hiring because of biases against a particular group by personnel managers, foremen, or employers.

5. Educational lag and defective schooling, impeding opportunities for advancement.

6. Lack of apprenticeship and on-the-job training.

7. Deficiencies in counseling services, subjecting minority youth to misdirection or bewilderment.

8. Failure of trade schools to train or encourage minority youth to enter advantageous occupations.

9. Discriminatory practices by private or public employment agencies.

10. Failure by minorities to train or apply for jobs through fear, ignorance, tradition, or unwillingness to sacrifice higher-paid jobs for longer-range opportunities.

11. Opposition by unions or co-workers because of long-standing traditions, ethnic homogeneity, or outright discriminatory practices.

12. Absence of skills acquired in the original community and inability to develop them after arrival.

13. Existence of a backlog of unemployed among the majority group who get rehiring priority in some industries.

14. Transience, which impedes the sinking of roots in the community and in its available opportunities.

15. Lack of leadership, contacts, and realistic aspirations.

16. Language difficulties, barring individuals from jobs requiring a knowledge of the native tongue.

Stubborn customs prevent many minority groups from overcoming these obstacles. Koreans in Japan find it difficult to get more than the unwholesome or menial jobs, or they may get jobs only with other Koreans. An Eta, though a native Japanese, is confined to the lowly trades, notably those dealing with hides and leather. Both Koreans and Etas live in ghettos, many of them in miserable shacks without elementary services or amenities. Urbanization and migration to the larger cities have tended, however, to free the younger Etas from the stamp of inferiority by conferring the greater anonymity of metropolitan life.

Sometimes the minority rises above the barriers and makes important contributions to the country. The role played by Jews in the shaping of modern capitalism is well known. Once among the most oppressed of religious minorities, they are now most numerous in the United States, in Israel, and in countries within the Soviet orbit. Smaller pockets of Jews, however, still live in countries where their antecedents had been permitted to settle or where they found haven from the Nazi persecutions. There are about 700,000 Jews in South America, where they have reconstructed their lives and contributed to the advance of enterprise and culture.

Before and after World War II, many minority groups were forced to leave Europe; hence, the minority problem that survived in those countries was not so prominent as after World War I. The adverse impact upon Germany's cultural enterprises is exemplified in the virtual disappearance of its art cinema production, in which Germany once ranked high. Literature and other arts have also suffered.

In Asia the minority problem remains tense, reaching its most tragic pitch after the India-Pakistan partition, which deprived both countries of skills, entrepreneurs, and capital, besides burdening each with a painful squatter and refugee problem. The continuing flight of refugees from China to Hong Kong remains one of the major human challenges as well as major housing problems, although the remarkable development of Hong Kong enterprise would not have been possible without the refugees. They supplied the labor pool, the new techniques, the commercial shrewdness of the North Chinese, and the new capital that sought investment.

The destiny of minorities in the years to come is far from certain. In the postwar period and in the wake of the Hitler outrages, many constitutions were written to guarantee equal rights to minorities. But even though the language still remains in the documents, the implied protections are not always granted.

There are signs both of betterment and of growing problems. In Trinidad, the Chinese are accepted and respected and have done much to advance development. Jamaica owes much of its building capacity to Jewish, Puerto Rican, and Middle Eastern settlers. Intermarriages in Latin America have continued as prejudice against the Negro and Indian has subsided, and the mixed offspring has tended to become an accepted part of the rank and file.

A major challenge to minority rights arises when private prejudice and discrimination are incorporated into the public ethic. Moreover, the consequences of such a policy can be tragic. Abuse of the zoning power to bar minorities from neighborhoods, use of the expanded police power to harass the minority group, and employment of the compulsory purchase power to oust such groups from their settlements are devices that have manifested themselves in the more and the less developed worlds. Legislation to bar minorities or aliens from buying land and exclusion of minorities from publicly subsidized housing are other discriminatory devices[1] that restrict a group's full usefulness in the economic structure. The worst form of discrimination, however, is the worldwide tendency to restrict immigration.

A society advances further when the labor and talents of all its people function to the fullest. The West Indian bus driver, collier, or nurse, or the Pakistani worker in England fills a need that would be unmet otherwise. The emergence of Ralph Bunche and Robert C. Weaver, as well as Albert Einstein, Jonas Salk, and the host of Jewish and other scientists, physicians, and geniuses who have added to the world's store of health knowledge and growth, is possible only in a free society and in nations whose doors are not closed to the oppressed. While the United States still has some distance to go before it can boast that its Negroes have achieved full political and economic equality, it has accepted political and economic equality in principle and is steadily moving toward achieving it. No country benefits from having to pay the economic and social

[1] For a more comprehensive statement of the problem in the United States during its developmental phase, see Charles Abrams, *Forbidden Neighbors* (New York: Harper, 1955), Chs. 1–7. The United States government has banned discrimination in employment by government contractors. A more significant step has been taken by fourteen states and many cities, which have set up commissions to pass on complaints of discrimination in employment and housing. Where discrimination is found, the employer is compelled to alter his practices as well as accept a rejected employee or rehire him if he has been unjustly discharged. Though the road to full equality still has many roadblocks and pitfalls, this is the world's most effective program to equalize rights. But few comparable protections exist elsewhere.

costs of discrimination while eschewing the dividends that might come from granting equal access to life's pursuits.

CORRUPTION

Corruption, which has not yet been eradicated in developed areas, should hardly be shocking when found in some underdeveloped areas. There are many more reasons for its higher incidence. The traditions of good public service are less matured. Too often civil servants must rely on other sources of income merely to maintain a decent living standard.[2] The few wealthy people, to whom graft would be of no real value, do not yet look upon public service as either a public obligation or a mark of distinction. On the other hand, the opportunist may see public service as a short bridge to affluence. Frequently business looks on graft as essential oil to lubricate officials when administrative delays and frustrations seem endless. Where permits are required for building or importing, there is an open black market in some countries. Those who need contraband manage to get it. Nor is the party in power always chary of accepting contributions or using public funds for promoting its reelection. The proletariat is either cynical or too preoccupied with its own pressing needs to cry out. In nations where tribal custom still plays a role, bribery is not easy to distinguish from gift. Before Ghana's independence, an African public works official who had accepted substantial sums from a foreign contractor was removed by the British governor, to the consternation of tribal people, who could see nothing venal in the gifts. When the British departed, the official was restored to respectability.

Public works and housing programs, in particular, have always provided vast opportunities for pelf and power—through construction contracts, purchase of materials, loans to the worthy, and low-rent dwellings to those who vote right. The fine line between the "contact," "connection," "contract," and "fix" tends to grow fuzzy. Some Latin-American politicians have taken enough booty from the public trough to make New York Boss Tweed's depredations look amateurish. When honesty is finally enthroned, as in Venezuela, organized troublemakers are on hand to impair confidence and stability.

Yet it would be unfair to view corruption outside the frustrating con-

---

[2] The councilmen of Kumasi, Ghana, complained to the U.N. mission about their having to work without pay. The council system was fashioned on the British model of unpaid service; the only compensation to members was a nominal stipend per meeting, of which there were eight or ten a month. Some £300 had to be spent for election campaigning alone. Thus it was not surprising that some councilmen soon made the job profitable through other devices. If, by Western standards, they were not honest in their jobs, they were forthright in confessing their predicament.

text within which most of these countries are laboring. They face new types of political organizations in which the ethics of private enterprise and government service have not yet developed, and in which political and economic stability is still precarious. Despite some less laudable examples, many officials are inherently honest and devoted to the public. Many have a sense of history, though some resort to dubious political devices to prolong their tenure.

If, to win an election, an aspiring candidate encourages defaults by tenants and borrowers in government-aided housing, one might well ask whether the incumbent would not have done likewise to assure his own reelection. If some have made empty pledges to ease the housing shortage, it is only fair to say that the fiscal limitations of the country promised nothing more. If others have yielded to the pressures of squatters or opportunists, winked at illegal imports, acquiesced in the drain on the country's currency, or given excessive concessions to those of their own political faith, ample precedents may be found in the highly developed countries during their formative periods—or sometimes even today.

The surprising fact is that many of the developing countries have actually increased their national productivity and income. That problems have not been much worse gives one hope that things may someday be better. It would, moreover, be unjust to ascribe political corruption to every country. India is one of a number of examples of a nation where standards of honesty are probably higher than those in some parts of the United States.

In general, the big problems are the lack of experienced people down the line, the fluctuations of scruple in public service, the suddenness with which the new countries have had to assume Herculean and unfamiliar duties, the phlegmatic state of public opinion and the press, the dearth of civic organizations, as well as the pressures to achieve objectives at breakneck speed. The difficulties are illustrated by the case of the Philippine Islands, which began independence under a democratic formula and with a pattern for sound administration.

THE PHILIPPINES—A CASE STUDY IN ADMINISTRATION

This new nation emerged as a beneficiary of the American partiality toward public education. In 1958 there were more than 28,000 public schools, more than 3500 private schools, and numerous institutions of higher learning. One of the educational system's dividends is a well-organized architectural profession, with houses and buildings reflecting its talents. Thus one would also expect a semblance of discipline in administration and a roster of skills to grapple with the housing dilemma.

Philippine cities suffer from a housing shortage not only because of natural population increase but because of war devastation. Bombing leveled or damaged 80 per cent of Manila's buildings, more than half of them homes. When peace came, many of the homeless Manilans were living in the wreckage, and others doubled or tripled up in what housing remained. But most other cities were spared. Fortunately for the homeless, nature had blessed the Islands with a kindly temperature, ranging from about 78 degrees in winter to 84 degrees from April to June.

The postwar housing famine in Manila and other large cities was intensified by refugees fleeing the Huks, as well as emigration from depressed areas and from farms, which in the postwar years lacked work animals, seed, equipment, and money. Manila's population swelled by 400,000 after the war. Over three fourths of metropolitan Manila's population of more than two million were crowded into one tenth of the land area. Other cities also grew. The number of Philippine cities with more than 100,000 people rose from three in 1939 to eight in 1948, while the number of cities with 25,000 grew from four to eleven in the same period.[3]

By the time the war wreckage was cleared, thousands of Philippine families had moved into the centers of the large cities. Others have kept coming. Unable to secure land, they have squatted. Manila had some 45,000 squatter families in 1958, close to a fifth of the city's population. The problems of the squatters have been described in Chapter 2.

The Philippines still have a dual frontier—the frontier of industrialization and that of the earth and forests of the hinterlands. The country's hopes should not be beyond fulfillment.

As in other countries, however, the officials have had difficulty solving the housing problem—despite the country's ample land supply, its many architects, its mild climate, and the materials at hand for simple shelters. Current policies dealing with the problem continue not only undefined but inconsistent. For example:

1. A stern policy by Manila with regard to squatters is often offset by political recognition of their "rights." Some squatters receive sympathetic indulgence or get substantial compensation, while others are summarily ousted. Most continue in limbo, hoping that massive resistance to law will bring battle fatigue to officials and ultimately convert their illegal trespass into lawful tenure.

2. A congressional mandate to the People's Homesite and Housing Corporation (PHHC) to build for low-income families (which should normally entail a maximum of economy and often public subsidy) is nullified because the agency is not given the essential funds for building. Instead, the agency is saddled by the government with unnecessary payrolls, thereby increasing operating costs, defeating the very purpose of

[3] United Nations Report of Mission of Experts, *Low Cost Housing in South and South-East Asia* (New York, March 12, 1951), pp. 166, 167.

low-cost housing operations, and turning the agency's activities toward more speculative adventures so it can balance its losses and remain in business.

3. No clear line of authority is drawn between the operations of the PHHC, the Social Welfare Administration, the Land Tenure Administration, the City of Manila, and other agencies. The results are conflict, duplication of effort, and errors in judgment.[4]

These conflicts exemplify the weakness of Philippine administration despite its high level of general education. Trained administrators are few and traditions of public service still unformed. While a civil service was introduced under American rule and continued after independence, many jobs have remained outside its scope. Professionalization of public employment and career service are not the rule. Lack of advancement opportunities (compared with private enterprise) and competition with beneficiaries of political patronage have diverted many good workers from public into private service. The morale of those remaining in public work is not high. Even when unemployment is heavy (as it was in 1958) and the government can select better people for jobs from the large pool of applicants, patronage considerations continue more important than qualifications.

Pressures of the unemployed have helped make public and civil service a receptacle for the jobless. Some 44 per cent of the government employees in 1958 were uncertified political appointees. They formed a bloc and resisted discharge when no longer needed. As a rule, administrators shrink from opposing the legislator who passes on their budgets, while harried legislators welcome the more accommodating administrator who helps satisfy painful patronage obligations.

Governors are surrounded by importunate job seekers, to each of whom they must give personal audience or deliver handwritten recommendations for jobs. The governors complain that the process takes precious time from their work, but they have no other choice. The PHHC is also invaded by scores of eager job seekers. They must all be personally interviewed and satisfied.

The effect on the PHHC has been not only spiritually demoralizing but financially damaging. In August 1958 the corporation had at least a thousand temporary employees, most of whom were useless. When the PHHC's increasing financial embarrassment left no alternative but to discharge them, the discharge was soon ordered rescinded.

Devising make-work projects for the jobless is not easy. When an

---

[4] The Fabie Estate subdivision is an example of how squatters and others were induced to buy land from the government and then afforded no services or planning of plots by government agencies. A slum formation and also a lasting suspicion of the government's good faith were the results.

agency is required to undertake such projects, they should not conflict with regular operations. The agency should also receive special funds for supervising and operating the special projects. Instead, the government pressed the PHHC to take on the unemployed without either setting up projects for them or footing the bill. The result was that the agency found itself unable to pay these extra wages from its general funds, or to pay its other debts. A housing program that served a useful purpose was thus menaced.

For example, the PHHC was operating a block-making factory with a Vibrapak machine that could turn out 6000 blocks in a single shift and 12,000 in two shifts. A house requires some 2000 blocks. The machine could produce blocks for about 900 houses a year at twenty cents a block, as against a retail price of thirty-four cents. The factory's staff, however, was soon loaded with the unemployed, making the operation uneconomical. The PHHC was thus forced to sell the factory to a private operator, who then sold blocks to the PHHC at the retail price. Next, the housing corporation was instructed to find jobs for the displaced workers in other branches of its operations.

Though the PHHC's principal function was to produce housing below cost for low-income families, it was never provided with the annual subsidies to compensate for deficits. It therefore veered toward operations that either paid their way or were more profitable. It bought more land, subdivided, improved, and sold it. Soon it was taking risks like other private companies; but, being a public agency, it was not immune from pressure, politics, and waste. It was not long before the PHHC found itself with a land inventory that it could not develop for years to come. Liquidation seemed the only way out. A public agency with a vital public purpose to perform found itself insolvent. Naturally, failure of a public corporation to pay its debts does not inspire confidence in public operations.

Coordination of the housing agencies presented another problem. Creating autonomous corporations has advantages: more freedom from bureaucratic routines, greater ease in acquiring land, and a more businesslike management in which the profit motive is subordinated to the public purpose. Autonomous corporations on the Islands, however, soon mushroomed in all directions. Then an "Office of Economic Coordination" assumed the coordinative function through a bevy of legal, research, budgeting, technical, financial, operational, and central purchasing divisions. But the coordinated corporations represented as diverse and unrelated a lot as could be assembled. The economic coordinator's functions in nine vast, complex, and dissimilar enterprises were to direct as well as coordinate and supervise the "implementation of the economic rehabilitation and development program," supervise budgeting operations, appraise accomplishments and financial operations, and "carry out the policies and measures formulated, and projects recommended by the National Economic Council" which involved the corporations.[5]

The nature of the coordination was illustrated in the annual report of the coordinator. It simply summed up the reports by the various agencies. The coordinator's budgetary supervision was exemplified by the financial anarchy into which the PHHC, one of the "coordinated" corporations, was permitted to drift. The coordination tended to build up a sort of hegemony by the coordinator over the PHHC and the other corporations, with all the incidental political pressures, but without any of the rationalization that should flow from real coordination. The coordinator became merely the political boss and patronage dispenser for the agencies.

In 1961, President Carlos P. Garcia, in his State of the Union Address, recognized the administrative difficulties and acknowledged the recommendations of the U.N. report made two years before.[6] Subsequently, a new government was voted in, and there were some indications that both public opinion and the new administration might force reform and reorganization.

LAND AND RENT CONTROL ADMINISTRATION IN BOLIVIA

Another example of a nation that lacks good administration and skills is Bolivia. Bolivia suffers from a very high incidence of bronchial diseases and infant mortality, which can be explained partly by the fact that per capita income is very low, and that most houses are teeming with people, almost half of the homes without water, and more than half without sanitation.

The country had a 1960 population of only 3,462,000 for its 424,162 square miles. More than half of its people are Indian, and about a third are mestizo (of mixed Spanish and Indian blood). Besides La Paz, with a population of 347,000, other large cities are Cochabamba, the commercial center, with 90,000 people; Oruro, a tin mine center, with 81,000; and Sucre, the legal capital, with 60,000.

Acting summarily, the state nationalized its tin mines in 1954 and broke up latifundia into smaller parcels for distribution to rural tenants. In the cities, it forced every landowner with more than 10,000 square meters of land (2.47 acres) to "sell" the excess to the government. Compensation was fixed at an official rate of 200 bolivianos per square meter,[7]

---

[5] Charles Abrams and Otto Koenigsberger, *Report on Housing in the Philippine Islands* (New York: United Nations, 1959), p. 97.

[6] *Philippine Architecture, Engineering and Construction Record*, Vol. VIII, No. 20 (January 1961), p. 20.

[7] In 1954, 12,000 bolivianos equaled $1. As of January 1963, when the currency rate was changed, 12 (peso) bolivianos equaled $1.

only a small fraction of the value. In La Paz, Bolivia's *de facto* capital, the land was then resold to workers and civil servants for a down payment of 1000 bolivianos per square meter, with the total price of each parcel to be determined later, after the city tallied up the charges for planning, roads, water, etc. The land acquisition policy was confiscatory, but Bolivia was in no mood to lucubrate on the distinctions between confiscation and due process or between token payment and just compensation.

Since 1828, Bolivia has had more than sixty revolutions, seventy presidents, and eleven constitutions, a situation hardly conducive to stable administration and administrative policy. The government of the National Revolutionary Movement, plagued by frequent strikes, rebellions, and economic crises, has nevertheless managed to maintain its popularity at least partly because of its revolutionary social program.

Under the land distribution program for cities, there was land for some three to four thousand families in La Paz as against fifteen to twenty thousand applicants. Although the government had laid down certain eligibility criteria (landlessness, war service, many children, etc.), so many applicants "qualified" that it was hard to know who was really deserving. The syndicates, each representing workers in a particular industry or operation, soon asserted their powerful influence on behalf of their members.

The main problem was not that these workers were undeserving of land but that trouble greeted those who received land—whether deserving or not. Purchasers who made down payments could not get deeds partly because of administrative inefficiency and partly because of litigation begun by former owners. Tired of waiting for bureaucracy to deliver the deeds, several hundred purchasers proceeded to build on what they did not yet own. With water as scarce in La Paz as money, the new owners could survive only by lugging cans of water from long distances. There were no plot plans for utilities and roads, and since no financing scheme accompanied the land distribution, houses remained unfinished.

About three fourths of Bolivia's urban houses are rented. There are virtually no vacancies, and an occupant's possession depends entirely on the protections of a rent control law. Because alternative shelter is at a premium, the tenant sticks to his place no matter how decrepit, crowded, or far from his work.

Rent control administration requires a sound law as well as a trained staff to enforce it. Bolivia has neither. Rent control fixes a ceiling on rents of dwellings as well as on stores and offices but permits the landlord and tenant to agree on any rent they wish. When an apartment is vacated, the landlord may charge the new tenant what he chooses. Evictions are barred even when the owner wants to occupy the house himself or erect a new building. The landlord must furnish water, light, and utilities but need not paint or repair the apartment. Theoretically, a landlord making repairs may obtain an added 10 per cent return on his new investment, but few repairs are made because few landlords will gamble on being justly compensated.

The defective rent control statute allows many rents to climb, while others remain fixed at fantastically low levels. Many renters in the large cities pay as little as eight cents a month for an apartment. Simultaneously, "frozen" rents have rocketed to many times the original maximum because the landlord can fix a new rent when his tenant dies, vacates, consents to an increase, or is bought off. Little has been done to increase unrealistically low rents or to reduce unrealistically high ones.

Despite rent control, the general rent level burst through its controls, though many still pay nominal rents. Between June 1958 and June 1959, average rents increased by 96 per cent.[8] While some tenants had no increase in rent, many others were paying two, three, or five times their ceiling rentals.

Evasions of rent ceilings by both landlord and tenant have therefore become routine. A landlord's fortunes often depend less on the value of his investment than on the sharpness of his practices or the skill of his lawyer. In newspaper advertisements, landlords offer their apartments "free"—the only condition being that the tenant deposit with the landlord a ransom that the landlord can invest for a far higher return than his property will yield.

Sometimes the landlord locks out the tenant, hoping that he won't come back. When the landlord succeeds, he rents the dwelling at many times the old rent. The death of the tenant is a stroke of luck for the landlord, a fact which generates a mortal fear of insidious owners.

In the office buildings of La Paz, elevator service has been curtailed or abandoned in an effort to force tenants out or save money. One offender is a government agency, and one victim is the agency of a foreign government set up to aid Bolivia. At an altitude of 12,000 feet, a trek up and down six flights will weary any tenant to the point of accepting terms.

Even if Bolivia had a sound rent control law, enforcement would fail. Like many underdeveloped countries, Bolivia has no facilities for enforcement, and any modification of controls would be stopped by political obstacles. The real problem is the failure to increase the housing supply by every means possible. The dearth of talent to devise the means is not the least of the obstacles.

The staff of the rent administrator's office consisted of one harried Bolivian who knew things weren't going well but could do little about

[8] Charles Abrams, *Report on Housing Financing in Bolivia* (New York: United Nations, 1959), p. 68.

it, for there are no trained people to be hired. In fact, there are few even for top-ranking jobs.

Experience in Bolivia as in other countries demonstrates the futility of relying upon rent control per se as a reform. This example also shows how—despite the stabilization of money and of prices for food, clothing, and utilities—the upward rent spiral may start an inflationary trend unless a housing program simultaneously functions. But neither a housing program nor a functioning rent control is possible without the skills to administer it.

TRAINING AND SKILLS IN NIGERIA

Nigeria still keeps her British civil servants, who work side by side with Nigerians in the administration of important public offices. This is a distinct advantage for a country that has only recently embarked upon independence and industrial development. But as in all new countries, the deficiencies are many.

Vocational training is scant and rarely related to the particular types of skills that industry needs or is expected to need. At Yaba, in the federal district, there is only one technical institute and one trade center. The trade center in 1961 could take only 180 new entrants from 1200 eligible applicants. The institute cannot accept more students because it lacks the teachers. It therefore accepts only youths who have attended Lagos schools, though national interest would be better served if expanded vocational training facilities could accommodate all eligible applicants.

Young people willing to work lack the training to qualify for jobs. Guidance counseling and a more vigorous public employment service would help, but they are missing. Data from the employment exchanges in Lagos indicate an unmet demand for skilled artisans and science and engineering technicians at the same time that there is an alarming amount of joblessness.

Nigerians are not unsympathetic, however, to educating their young. Often all the members of an extended family in the hinterlands will save their pennies to educate a child, and when a boy is grown, these pennies pay his tuition in a foreign university. When the boy goes off to a distant college, hundreds assemble at the airport to see him off on his great adventure. When he finally becomes a veterinarian, an agricultural expert, a lawyer, or physician, he in turn is expected not to forget those who helped him.

A development plan for education exists in Nigeria, but there are no targets for optimum training and employment. If a large migration is anticipated, as it well may be, both training and guidance should be available at the migration source so that frustration can be minimized when people reach the city. Often better opportunities may lie in a secondary city or one in which industry is looking for applicants. But instead everybody descends or wants to descend on the capital.

Future prospects for general education appeared more hopeful after the federal government's acceptance of the main recommendations of a British report on education. Capital expenditure on the program during the ten years 1961–1970 was estimated at £75 million and total current expenditure an equivalent amount. The United Kingdom also offered a £5 million grant in capital aid to establish teacher-training colleges and technical institutes. Simultaneously, the United Nations Educational, Scientific and Cultural Organization offered financial aid for a federal university at Lagos, while the Ford Foundation and the Peace Corps provided supplemental help for educational purposes. Although these efforts will advance general education, the gap in training for the problems of urbanization, administration, and building will still remain, and Nigeria must continue to depend on the few foreigners still stationed in its official departments for help and guidance.

7

Aid—Experts and "Inperts"

Between 1939 and the end of World War II, the Western democracies did little to improve housing for the rest of the home-hungry world. They were busily occupied with their own special problems, the unsolicited demolition of their neighborhoods by German buzz bombs and blockbusters, and the clearance by high explosives and fire storms of vast sections of the enemy's housing. But as destruction continued to sweep away homes and cities, Churchill, Stalin, and Hitler all struck upon housing as a means of bolstering hopes.

While Hitler was promising a new Berlin, and Stalin a new Moscow, plans for a new London, Manchester, Birmingham, and Liverpool consoled the harried British people. Between air raids they would trek to museums and town halls to gaze upon sketches of their dream communities. The broad highways, the playgrounds and parks conveniently situated near homes with refrigerators and central heating became a leading topic in the shelters and pubs. When the war at last ended, public demands were so persistent that there was no dissent about the prime role of housing and city planning in postwar political platforms. The surprising defeat of the Churchill government at the peak of its triumph has been ascribed largely to the public feeling that socialism could do better with the building program. The new government organized the country into planning districts, the right to develop land was virtually nationalized, and a series of new towns were scheduled to decongest the cities. The subsequent ascent of Harold Macmillan to the prime ministry is generally credited to the 300,000 houses a year he gave England during his career as Minister of Housing and Local Government between 1951 and 1954.

In the United States, prior to 1933 housing had been virtually unknown as a political issue. However, it steadily gained popularity, and in 1949 the aim of a decent home for every American family was incorporated as a preamble to the principal housing legislation.

A pledge to improve man's social and economic estate even found its way into the United Nations Charter of Human Rights. It was not surprising in a postwar atmosphere that human rights and human welfare were joined with the objective of world peace.

While the more developed areas were elevating housing and urban development to social and economic necessities at home, they gave little thought to the crucial housing problems of the less developed nations. Even when the contest between democracy and communism was revived and the support of the underdeveloped world became prized, urbanization and housing problems were still given the lowest priority in official aid programs by the more developed countries as well as by the international aid agencies and the United Nations.

When the leaders of the underdeveloped nations were finally compelled by rising internal pressures to acknowledge these problems, they could turn for help only to whatever private experts were on hand. These experts were usually either architects from the more developed areas or opportunistic entrepreneurs in quest of a fast buck through one of their pat prefabrication schemes or miracle materials. The architect could make a sound contribution to designing an industrial building or a costly house, but when called upon to advise on the problems of finance, economics, legislation, administration, development of skills, production of materials, squatting, and the many other facets of urbanization, he was at a loss. Allowing his name to be associated with a cheap shelter (which in most cases was all the country and the occupants could afford) might damage an architect's reputation—even if he knew how to design it. Building a city or a new capital was better suited to his public image and aspirations.

Since more money can be made through an architectural fee (based on the percentage of building cost) than through consultancy fees (based on short per diem assignments), an architect who was a consultant on housing problems would not be averse to recommending a costly housing job designed by him as the remedy for housing shortage. Most often the dividends of his efforts accrued to the wealthier and more vocal groups.

FOREIGN AID AND FOREIGN EXPERTS—
THE UNITED NATIONS

Toward the middle 1950's, a glimmer of recognition appeared at the United Nations. Prompted by efforts originating in the Far East, the U.N. set up a branch on Housing, Building and Planning in its Bureau of Social Affairs, which was headed by Julia Henderson. In 1951, Ernest Weissmann, a Yugoslav architect, was placed in charge of the branch. Given a staff of six professionals and three clerical people to handle the housing problems of the world, Weissmann enlisted the help of a few outside technical consultants.

Despite its lowly status and limited funds, the U.N.'s housing branch did yeoman work. It stimulated pilot projects in a few countries. It issued general studies on: urban land problems and policies; community services and facilities in large-scale projects; tropical housing and research techniques; stabilized soil construction; financing; planning of education; cooperation between Asian countries; regional planning and cooperative housing. Although some of these studies are excellent as initial points of departure, the problems of urbanization in underdeveloped areas still remain a virtually unexplored frontier.

The U.N.'s experts not only have advised governments but have aided in the preparation of master plans for cities in Asia, the Near East, and Latin America. The U.N. has dispatched some field men to Panama, Burma, Malaya, Ghana, Pakistan, Indonesia, and India, and it has co-operated in the establishment of Housing Centers in Indonesia and India. Furthermore it has collaborated with the more specialized international agencies that deal with the housing problem indirectly, such as the Economic Commissions for Europe, Africa, Asia and the Far East, and Latin America, as well as UNESCO. In more recent years the U.N. has shifted its emphasis somewhat from advice to training and education and has granted about two hundred fellowships for this purpose. It has been instrumental in setting up the Middle East Technical University in Ankara, as well as some less ambitious but more specialized training schools in Ghana and Indonesia. It has also assisted in setting up planning schools in India, Colombia, Venezuela, and Peru. More recently it has placed greater emphasis on the role of housing in national economic programs and has drawn on the limited assistance of other agencies, such as the Special United Nations Fund for Economic Development (SUNFED).

The Special United Nations Fund for Economic Development is empowered to assist in surveys, research, training, and pilot projects. It has advanced $1.5 million for the Middle East Technical University in Ankara as part of its training authorization. It has also provided $555,000 for a building materials research laboratory in Indonesia. However, it has generally not felt empowered to make housing loans, even as demonstrations, and its usefulness in housing operations is limited.

The U.N. housing branch's long subordination to a bureau evidences the low priority given to urbanization problems. (Housing and urbanization up to 1962 were not elevated to commission, committee, or special agency status in the same way as health, education, economic reconstruction, etc.) The attitude stems from the survival of the idea that housing is a "social problem" that can wait. Up to 1962 the U.S. State Department had made no move to raise the U.N.'s housing branch to a more vital place in technical assistance. At the urgent request of Philip M. Klutznick, erstwhile U.S. representative at the U.N., elevation of the branch to a committee reporting to the Economic and Social Council was finally recommended. But in February 1962, after a two-week meeting of delegates from twenty-one nations, all of whom agreed on the vital need for more U.N. housing aid, it appeared that not more than one or two in personnel would be added to the existing U.N. housing staff.

Nevertheless, the United Nations had moved into a vacuum. Interest was aroused and the way opened for other agencies to fill some of the gaps. An underdeveloped nation could get advice from an impartial expert or group of experts not out to make a killing. That the U.N.'s housing branch has accomplished as much as it has with so little is a tribute to Ernest Weissmann and his staff.

An evaluation of the U.N.'s contributions can be made only in the light of its limitations and the inherent complexities of the problems. The money for the U.N.'s whole technical assistance program has come from the voluntary contributions of members and has averaged only about $25 million annually for technical projects of all kinds. The total expenditures for housing staff, technical assistance, and regional economic work in housing have been about $1 million a year. Such a budget for the whole world automatically restricts technical assistance, excludes financing aid, and must go mainly to pay the salaries of the small staff, the fees of the experts, and the costs of the missions, conferences, publications, and other expenses.

One of the U.N.'s greatest problems has been in recruiting experts for missions. There were architects, engineers, and other specialists agreeable to making a short visit to a country during the appropriate season. Sometimes a specialist discovered upon arrival that he lacked the particular knowledge required for the area. A qualified architect might know little of finance, while a financial expert would know little about materials or building codes—and neither would know anything about the urban land problem or the preparation of legislation. A team of experts might be better equipped, but they could generally stay only for sixty or ninety days and draft a report. The recommendations would then fall on the shoulders of an untrained and beleaguered national who could not translate the recommendations into mortar. When I asked a Turkish official why he had urged his government to apply for a United Nations mission, he replied frankly: "It's the prestige of having a foreign expert. . . . If the report agrees with what my department wants I consent to its release. If not, I shelve it."

American experts were especially hard to enlist partly because of the small fees (a maximum of $50 a day for a thirty- to ninety-day mission) and partly because every candidate was subjected to a rigorous search by the Federal Bureau of Investigation into his personal life, loyalty, and security. Since the 1950's were hardly marked by calm impartiality, and since Anglo-Saxon rules of evidence have never won a place in the investigatory encounter, loyal Americans often shunned U.N. service when they learned that investigators would visit their former landladies, employers, and disgruntled employees, scour their pasts, and compile all the hearsay into a file[1]—all for a two- or three-month visit entailing a fee of $50 a day or less. Even in the more reasonable atmosphere of the 1960's when the procedures have been speeded, few qualified experts are willing to have a dossier compiled on them by a government sleuth. Thus nationals of other countries or private experts have preempted most of the jobs, and the prestige of the United States has hardly been advanced by the absence of its qualified nationals.

Preparation of essential studies on various aspects of world problems was no easier. Since the U.N.'s housing staff was small and occupied with administrative tasks, outside experts had to be solicited. The budgetary allocation allowed for studies provided only for payment of honorariums, and often not even that. Some of the U.N. reports on specific countries might compose an initial literature on housing and urbanization problems. But few have been published. Most remain in the secret archives of the U.N.'s basement. For example, my 1954 report recommending the establishment of the Middle East Technical University in Ankara was still restricted in New York nine years later—though it had long been public in Ankara and the university had graduated its fourth roster of students. A similar U.N. report on Pakistan recommending housing legis-

---

[1] Even where there were no charges or suspicions, these investigations would take months. On one of the early U.N. seminar missions to India, a team that included a top-ranking Puerto Rican official, a nationally known planner who headed the planning department of one of America's best universities, a respected federal official, and the author was held up for more than four months while the mission members were being investigated. When the seminar began in Delhi, the team was still in the United States being checked. After this delay was reported by the Indian and American press, the search was speeded, and the members were finally dispatched to make their belated appearance at the seminar.

lation remains secreted at the U.N. six years after the law was enacted in Karachi. The writer's report on the Philippines has been published in a Philippine technical journal, but remains restricted at the U.N. The varied reports in the U.N.'s files that are withheld from analysis probably number in the hundreds, but there is no way of knowing what they contain, or of evaluating them. That these reports have not been exhumed is not entirely the fault of the United Nations but also of the countries themselves, which somehow find it easier not to approve what they are not required to approve. A U.N. rule calling for an itemization of specific objections and a policy declaring that reports must become public unless the particular government objects within a prescribed period might resolve the difficulty. This procedure, however, has never been favorably considered.

Of course, every nation is afflicted with bureaucratic routines, and an organization that must respect the foibles of one hundred nations is sadly handicapped. An extravagant reference to the desirability of private enterprise may stir up Russian criticism, while any recommendations for socialization may alarm the capitalist nations. Reports must therefore be neutral on political issues and not too critical of people, policies, or programs. The result is that reports are too often written in guarded language or fail to grapple with all the realities. If the expert wants his report made public, the price is compromise and often approval or omission of what should be criticized.

In recent years, countries have become more concerned about housing problems and have pressed for broader U.N. action. After the Secretary-General in 1960 circulated a request for comments on a "long-range program of concerted international action" some twenty-one governments generally endorsed the need for programs of one sort or another. Some called for pooling research results and organizing more international seminars for specialists. Others emphasized the need for increasing the productive capacity of the building industries. Education and training were singled out as important gaps, with the Federation of Malaya commenting that lack of technical personnel was one of its primary obstacles. Better financing devices and long-range programs were cited as vital by other countries.

But all of these suggestions added up to no more than general advocacy of a wider role for housing, with no specific steps to implement it. Such generalizations are the main spawn of such conferences, and they rarely mature into specific forms of aid. However, the annual meeting of national representatives, recommended in 1962 by the delegates of the twenty-one nations, promises to keep the housing issue before the U.N.'s Economic and Social Council, and some more positive recommendations may eventuate in the years to come.

THE WORLD BANK AND ITS SUBSIDIARIES

Among the more important agencies that have either done something in housing and city development or are empowered to do so are the International Bank for Reconstruction and Development (the World Bank) and its affiliates.

The World Bank makes loans or guarantees to its member countries primarily to facilitate investment of capital for productive purposes and to promote private foreign investment. A large part of the World Bank's portfolio is made up of loans for utilities, transportational development and communications, pipelines, highways, and roads; it makes loans to development banks and for the expansion of agricultural production, irrigation, flood control, land clearance and improvement. As a service to its member countries, the World Bank provides technical assistance and survey missions. The Bank has extended its technical assistance activities into an Economic Development Institute, which trains officials. The International Finance Corporation was organized by the Bank to assist the financing of private enterprise, but housing has been ignored.

In 1960 the World Bank organized another subsidiary, the International Development Association (IDA), to make more flexible loans. Seventeen of the more prosperous countries have contributed in gold or convertible currencies, and fifty-one others pay 10 per cent on this basis and the balance in their own currencies. The IDA can make housing loans, but by the end of 1963, not a single housing loan was made. Moreover, it is doubtful that this organization will do anything significant in this field, since eligible projects must have "high economic priority."

Although housing aid has not been favored by the World Bank or its subsidiaries, a representative told the meeting of twenty-one U.N. experts in February 1962 that a pilot project might be considered, but he feared that giving housing aid to one nation might spur other nations to ask for similar aid. With one exception a housing expert has never been assigned to the Bank's various missions, and the official told the meeting it did not need a housing expert on its staff. As for the pilot projects, there were no applications, since most countries expected a cold reception. In recent missions, however, housing has figured indirectly in the recommendations—an occasional loan to a materials industry or to a city for water might be acceptable.

The World Bank's position was summarized by its representative at the Eighth Session of the Social Commission. The basic test was "productivity." Housing aid may be considered where it is "an integral part of a directly productive project" like workers' housing for an industrial plant. "However, the staff of the Bank is inclined to believe that in most cases the Bank's aid to housing will take the form, as it has done in the past, of investment in basic utilities and industries, thus helping to build economies, in which housing industries can become progressively more active."[2] In other words, housing production will occur as a spontaneous result of aid given for everything except housing.

A probable reason for the World Bank's record has been a feeling that housing is a bottomless pit. In an address to the United Nations Economic and Social Council on April 24, 1961, Eugene Black, then the Bank's president, said:

> I find myself increasingly doubtful whether domestic savings and foreign aid together will be sufficient to allow real progress, if present rates of population growth continue for long. . . .
>
> Some calculations have been made about the cost of providing houses in India during the next generation, if the population continues to grow at its present rate of about 2% a year. If you disregard the cost of rural housing, on the somewhat optimistic assumption that it can be carried out entirely with local materials and labor, then you still have to pay for the homes of nearly 200 million extra people who, it is expected, will be living in India's cities 25 years hence. . . . A sober estimate of the cost suggests that in the 30 years between 1956 and 1986 a total investment in housing of the order of 118 billion rupees, or roughly $25 billion, will be needed. If you find a figure like that difficult to grasp, I may say that it is well over four times the total lent by the World Bank in all countries since it started business 15 years ago. Put another way, it is more than 30 times the initial resources of the International Development Association—and those resources are supposed to cover IDA's first five years of operations.[3]

This argument may highlight the magnitude of the problem and the financial limitations of multilateral agencies. But it also recalls the arguments made in the United States against federal aid to housing in the 1930's when it became the fashion to use the adding machine as the field-piece against all social programs. It is neither good accounting nor good sense, however, to confuse loans with subsidies, then to bundle them together and multiply them by thirty. Loans for housing come out of a revolving fund composed of initial advances and of repayments with interest, and the total of loans made may be only a fraction of the initial funds. Most of the capital, moreover, should be raised internally through the development of savings, though some external aid is useful as a primer. Also, the amount of external aid will depend on the type of housing and on whether the aid given will have multiplier effects, and will develop local skills and materials and the use of local currencies. So

---

[2] See United Nations Meeting of Experts on Housing and Urban Development, February 7–21, 1962, Working Paper 6, *Mobilizing National and External Resources for the Extension of Housing and Urban Development* (New York, 1962), p. 29.

[3] Eugene R. Black, *Address to the Economic and Social Council of the United Nations, New York, April 24, 1961* (mim., Washington, 1961), p. 13.

long as indifference to housing influences the policy, little hope can be held for housing development through World Bank assistance.

The order of thinking that would relegate housing problems to Providence and prayer stems partly from the exhortations of some of the architectural philosophers who urged that the underdeveloped countries avoid the errors of the developed nations and not build slums. The theory was that anything built lasts and that no expense should therefore be spared in providing the best from the beginning.

The fact is that in the more developed countries, cheap houses and even slums were built in the first stages of growth. Many of these houses were owner-built. Thereafter, as productivity improved, the countries began to rehabilitate or clear the slums and build better neighborhoods.

What are called slums may have to be built at first, but they ought to be the kind of slums that can be improved when the families can afford it. A sensible program may have to tolerate some crowding at first, some help at the beginning with a roof, and some subletting. But with proper planning of the land and utilities, and with proper siting of the houses, later improvement is possible. Meanwhile, a planned building program could encourage the development of internal financing devices, skills, and a building and materials industry that can ultimately meet the fundamental and inescapable need for shelter as well as for jobs and greater social and economic stability.

OTHER INTERNATIONAL AGENCIES AND AID

Though there is no single agency, national or international, set up to deal exclusively and directly with world housing and with urban land and planning problems, there are many that are indirectly concerned or that give it honorable mention. A listing of official, semiofficial, or unofficial international agencies that are indirectly concerned would cover several pages, for they involve the whole gamut of human activity, though each agency functions only at the fringe. A man from the U.S. Department of Commerce, for example, may be interested in the export prospects of American materials industries, or a department of an international agency may want to know the number of housing starts in a country, or the impact of slums on juvenile delinquency. There are also international housing organizations like the International Federation for Housing and Town Planning, and various architectural associations, but their concerns are mainly informational. The wide involvement with housing makes it almost a common denominator in the calculations of development. It is a weathercock of economic activity and social conditions and plays a part in cost-of-living indices, political stability, employment and unemployment, etc. But this essential of life gets more mention than it does attention.

The Organization for Economic Cooperation and Development and the U.N.-sponsored economic commissions for Europe, Asia, Africa, and Latin America make studies and advise and confer on collateral or incidental aspects of housing or urbanization. Studies dealing with materials, urban renewal, and other subjects have been made available. These organizations also cooperate with the United Nations in its work, but they render no financial aid.

The Caribbean Commission, set up to improve social and economic conditions by nations with territorial or economic interests in the area, does some research and collects statistics in specialized aspects of housing, and there are similar organizations, such as the South Pacific Commission.

The Colombo Plan concentrates its technical assistance on British Commonwealth countries, but housing plays a minor part. The British Colonial Office advises on housing and has issued some interesting reports by G. Anthony Atkinson on building techniques. Great Britain has also made some money available to its colonies for housing, while the Commonwealth Development Corporation (CDC) has made investments in savings and loan associations in some of the Commonwealth countries and financed housing in Jamaica and Trinidad insured by these governments. The CDC is the British counterpart of the Agency for International Development of the United States but makes its loans on a business basis and charges market interest rates. It often takes in private business partners to share the risk and occasionally has sold part of its holdings to the public.

Other international agencies include the Agency for International Development (formerly the International Cooperation Administration), the Organization of American States, and the Inter-American Development Bank. These are discussed later in this chapter.

A few governments and even some religious groups have also supported housing. Denmark is providing technical assistance for the planning of a project in Indonesia for 5000 people. A fund of $140,000 has been established to which the American Society of Friends has contributed $50,000 and the U.N. $20,000 (plus two experts) for a self-help project in Somalia. The U.S.S.R. is building houses in Ghana, the Swedish government in Ethiopia, and the governments of Israel, Poland, and Yugoslavia are helping in Guinea. These projects, however, are limited, isolated efforts when viewed against world needs.

AID TO LATIN AMERICA

The only area in which housing aid of any magnitude has been forthcoming is Latin America. Up to 1960, the mention of housing or urbanization problems to an ICA (International Cooperation Administration) man evoked only an icy glance, and almost nothing from the $1.4 billion authorized for aid between 1957 and 1959 ever found its way into buildings. It was not that urban housing was politically inconsequential. To the unsteady dictatorships in that troubled area, housing was in fact an important prop. Meetings of inter-American public agencies stressed continually the importance of the urban housing problem. But the prevalent Washington ideas on the distribution of aid were those of the economists to whom housing had no place—political, social, or otherwise. A lonely housing man stationed in the Washington office was rarely consulted, and his memoranda to higher officials were pigeonholed.

The situation changed abruptly with the challenge of Fidel Castro and his promise of social reform to Cuba's proletariat. Now statesmanship suddenly overshadowed economics, and social reform gained headway as a device for achieving hemispheric amity and stability.

In September 1960, after a pledge of $500 million by President Eisenhower, the United States and Latin America outlined in the Act of Bogotá a broad program for cooperation in social improvement. After President Kennedy took office, he requested that $394 million of the sum be assigned to the Inter-American Development Bank (IDB), a multilateral loan agency of the Organization of American States. Simultaneously the Agency for International Development (AID) absorbed ICA and continued to administer bilateral assistance through the Development Loan Fund (DLF).

From 1957, when it was set up, until mid-1960, the DLF advanced no money for housing. Thereafter, an amendment to the Mutual Security Act (Sec. 202) authorized housing loans and guarantees. Instead of providing for the squatters and low-income families, however, DLF poured its moneys into savings and loan institutions, which in turn re-lent the moneys at profitable interest rates to the more vocal in the higher-income categories.

After the clarification of Castro's long-term Communist aims and the organization of the Alliance for Progress in August 1961, housing money began to be dispensed in earnest. The DLF was absorbed and became part of AID's more comprehensive effort. With a pledge of $20 billion of aid over a ten-year period under the Alliance, money began to flow into housing faster than ever before. A Senate subcommittee now recognized the relationship between housing and "the stability of the underdeveloped free nations of the world," since "social and political unrest and communism are natural consequences of such conditions. The actions of these large masses of underprivileged and ill-housed people can wipe out all the gains from economic assistance in these countries."[4]

[4] *Report on International Housing Programs,* Subcommittee on Housing, Committee on Banking and Currency, U.S. Senate, 87th Congress, 2nd Session (Washington, 1962), p. 1.

OPERATIONS OF AID AND IDB

As of December 31, 1962, eighteen loans totaling $152,650,000 were made by IDB alone. Simultaneously AID as of that date had also paid out about $100 million for various housing projects independent of those of IDB, so that about one quarter of a billion dollars of housing aid had gone into South America by the end of 1962. This amount does not include another $60 million authorized as a guarantee of private investment in housing. By the close of 1963, AID advances amounted to $150 million, while federal guarantees represented another $150 million.

After years of ignoring housing, this sudden rush of funds into the field was like a dam burst. About 44 per cent of the loans granted by IDB were for housing, as of mid-1962.

Since $300 million of United States aid dispensed in so short a time is a major commitment and may represent only a beginning, it becomes important to find out who is benefiting and whether the expenditures are serving the best interests of the United States and the receiving nations.

Until 1963, AID was an acknowledged administrative jungle. Though housing aid had become a vital part of American political policy, at least in Latin America, there were only two people in the central organization of AID who knew anything about housing at all. One was a kind of roving advisor, and the second was given the administrative tasks and the supervision over some thirty field experts scattered all over the world. A third staff member was added later. Before AID had given any financial assistance to Latin America, there had been a staff of twenty-six people in the field. In 1963, when $300 million in aid was being given, the number was only sixteen. There was not a single housing expert in Asia or the Far East.

The incoming Kennedy administration had recognized what had long been generally known about AID and its predecessor ICA, i.e., the "fall in the morale and the efficiency of those employees in the field who are repeatedly frustrated by the delays and the confusions caused by overlapping agency jurisdictions and unclear objectives" as well as the lack of a "highly professional skilled service."[5] These defects, however, were not cured after the Kennedy administration took over, and for two years thereafter organizational chaos continued and in some respects grew worse.

The Regional Housing Advisor in charge of AID's housing in Latin America was isolated from the stream of policy making and was often unable to obtain information about housing loans until after they had been made by somebody else somewhere above the vague line of authority. Policy depended on who knew whom among the personnel instead of who was responsible for what. On paper, nevertheless, the

[5] *New York Times,* March 23, 1961, p. 14.

Regional Housing Advisor had the responsibility but not the authority to decide on hundreds of millions of dollars in housing loans and investment guarantees. He had to assume this task without a staff to process or supervise the advances, at the same time working out a tenuous liaison with some thirty desk officers and fourteen general loan officers. Simultaneously, he also had to maintain contact with six or seven other federal agencies, and take care of the usual rounds of meetings, memoranda, and other matters that compose the workload. Some clerical assistants could have relieved him of the detail work, but for unknown reasons he failed to get them.

There was no identifiable policy concerning the relations between AID and IDB. Both were operating in the same areas and in the same countries. In the absence of an effective liaison between the responsible personnel of AID and IDB, applications for loans were made to both, and neither knew much about what the other was doing. Both were in competition, though the same United States government had retained the veto power over applications. Finally, on August 7, 1962, an effort was made to clarify the line of policy demarcation. From that day on, AID's resources were to be considered as "supplementary" to those of IDB.

This decision brought still more confusion and even the discontinuance of some missions. A better solution might have been to define the categories of assistance for AID and IDB. At first, IDB had provided loans to governments for direct government construction of housing, while AID had made loans to savings and loan institutions and housing cooperatives. But it was not long before IDB became interested in savings and loan associations and cooperatives as well, while AID departed from an earlier expressed policy of not making loans for projects, and made advances both for slum clearance and direct construction as well as loans to the savings societies. There was now no clear division of authority whatever, and both agencies made separate deals with the same Latin-American officials and in the same countries—a kind of interagency *laissez faire*.

Though policies roved, crisscrossed, and intermingled, neither agency was very much concerned with housing the low-income group in Latin-American countries. Most of the loans continued going to savings and loan associations, which in turn re-lent the money at extravagant interest charges to higher-income families. Frequently the money was lent at rates of between 0.75 to 2 per cent, but by the time the money reached the consumer, there had been so many markups along the line that the rate to the ultimate borrower was 12 per cent. In Peru, the disclosure of the interest spiral became a national scandal and the leading issue in Peru's election campaign. One of the unspoken reasons for ignoring the low-income families was that they were not as politically influential as the higher-income groups. The latter, it was thought, were therefore the more deserving beneficiaries.

While there were one or two self-help projects by AID and a strong desire even among squatters for homeownership, the aided projects were more in the nature of isolated pilot operations that proved little even after they were built.

Holding the purse strings is no guarantee of popularity, and sometimes the holder gets the blame for what is a government's own default. In Argentina, blame for the failures and delays of the government in helping to launch a major cooperative housing undertaking was laid at the door of the Alliance for Progress and the United States. No effort was made by American officials to put the blame where it belonged.[6]

While AID and IDB funds were being poured into Latin America, housing aid to the Far East and Africa was all but ignored. The regional director in Africa (at least up to 1964) was affirmatively opposed to housing aid of any kind. In Pakistan, where military considerations dictated cottoning to the country's demands, a $50 million housing program (financed through "480" counterpart funds) was being administered without supervision of expenditures by a housing expert, and approvals were being given almost *pro forma* by an engineer. The explanation was that "no housing advisers from the United States have been requested. . . ."[7] The official record of accomplishment in other parts of the world outside of Latin America was composed largely of brief visits or junkets by American housing officials, "advice," and inactivated programs.

The conflict between agencies and the contrast in the volume of housing aid between Latin America and the rest of the world was due primarily to the lack of a policy at the top levels. Although President Kennedy had seen aid programs all as part of the one world effort, the transmission belt of aid outside Latin America had somehow never gotten moving.

Yet if the same spurt of liberalism had characterized aid outside of Latin America, it would have been equally ineffective. For even had there been any constructive objectives written for the AID program, there were no trained people to carry them out, and there was little data on which judgments could be made. The operating efficiency of existing agencies or programs was virtually taken for granted. The over-all land problem and the tax situation were accepted as they existed. The weaknesses in mechanisms for developing skills and materials were tolerated. Basic questions that might have had impact on equipping the countries

[6] Abner D. Silverman, *Report on Housing Visit to Argentina,* memorandum to Harold Robinson, AID (mim., Washington, August 14, 1962), p. 6.

[7] *Report on International Housing Programs,* Subcommittee on Housing, *op. cit.,* p. 28.

for a broad-scale approach remained unanswered, i.e., the nature of the over-all housing and urban situations in each country that was aided; the economic, technical, and human resources available for the tasks; the types of facilities and programs that would best serve the lower-income group; the resources that could be mobilized without prejudicing national development; the external assistance—material, financial, and technical—that would be required for a real program. Instead, the feeling was that there were pat remedies—housing cooperatives, savings and loan associations, self-help, and federal guarantees of private investment —which were uniformly applicable to all the nations in the South American continent, and substantial advances and guarantees were made in line with that theory.

Progress in housing is made when the facts are known, the aims and priorities are spelled out, the legislation is drafted to fulfill them, an agency is set up with the powers to carry out a program, the skills and materials are mobilized for building, and a competent administrator is put in charge. Each country and most often each city has a special problem that has to be diagnosed by qualified people as a separate case to be tackled by an individualized program. Nor, despite AID's leaning toward quick and general remedies, can the problem be solved in a month, or even in years. Selecting and implementing a few special aspects like materials production, training, financing, and legislation might start the circulation going more effectively than a federal guarantee of an American builder's investment in a local housing project. But such a program needs people who can identify the areas that will respond to specific advice or help. In the long run, housing aid makes sense when the dollars advanced have helped provide the mechanisms essential to build a country's housing apparatus so that it can go ahead on its own after the impetus of the initial aid dollars has had its effect.

THE NEED FOR INTERNATIONAL EXPERIENCE

A by-product of the worldwide indifference to urban problems is the absence of an international pool of experts. This also explains the prevalent ineptitude in dealing with housing and urbanization. They are both part of a single problem. Furthermore, housing does not mean houses alone but is part of the whole framework of utilities, transportation, schools, recreation, finance, materials production, training, and all of the other essentials of urban life and urban formation. Seventeen years after World War II there was not a single comprehensive university course in the problems of international urbanization, housing, or international urban land economics.[8] Such training was needed to develop a

[8] Some courses in the planning problems of underdeveloped areas have, however, been started. In London, Otto Koenigsberger gave occasional briefings on tropical

pool not only of visiting experts but of "inperts," i.e., qualified nationals within the countries themselves.

The field requires people who have a grasp not only of economics but of the related disciplines—housing policy, urban land problems, administration, sociology, city planning, finance, law and legislation, transportation, architecture, building and building materials, and public relations—plus a large gift of common sense. They must be able to identify the more pressing aspects of a problem while visualizing them in the broader perspective. They should be adroit enough to generate progress with the limited tools available in a given country. But the experts from the more developed countries are largely specialists trained only in a single phase of the problem, or they are civil servants trained only in routine administration. Too often they see the solution only within the context of their own limited fields.

As the situation stood in 1963, economics still ruled the aid program and restricted housing programs in most regions of the developing world. Housing, city planning, urban land, and similar aspects of the urbanization process continued to be accorded a low priority except in Latin America. Though the United States was beginning to give such matters some recognition where its more immediate political interest lay, a sound approach at the international or the American level still needed to be formulated. Even if the logic of such an approach were at last to be recognized, the lack of knowledge, the failure to formulate goals, the absence of research programs, and the paucity of experts foreshadow years of delay before a realistic start can be made.[9]

---

housing; recently Jacobus Thysse at The Hague and Constantine Doxiadis in Athens have been giving courses. The U.N. has helped establish a small School of Town and Regional Planning in the University of Indonesia to attract students from Indonesia and other parts of Southeast Asia. In Ghana, following the U.N. mission, planning and development assistants were receiving training. The U.N.-sponsored Middle East Technical University has scheduled a planning course in Ankara. The Inter-American Housing and Planning Center in Bogotá (Colombia) trains people for special tasks in Latin America. Some single courses have been started at Harvard and the Massachusetts Institute of Technology. All of these courses are helpful, but none is sufficiently comprehensive to produce the general expert needed in the field.

[9] With the designation in 1963 of David E. Bell as AID Administrator and his appointment of a committee to reexamine housing policy, such a start seemed at long last to be in the offing.

8

Economics and Housing

The initial flow of housing money into Latin America may have brought no major improvement to its masses, but it was at least an official acknowledgment that housing was no longer an orphan. In other parts of the world, there was neither enough money for housing nor any serious effort to devise the essential means of production. Some governments among the less developed countries tried to weather the popular pressures for shelter by making promises they could not fulfill or by providing a few sporadic projects to buoy up hope. In the absence of a policy, unnecessary imports of building materials for higher-income groups were draining precious foreign exchange. In still other cases, unemployment that could have been substantially absorbed by a sound building program grew worse with the increase in urban migration. Meanwhile, squatters took over, adding to the general demoralization and hopelessness.

Although the less developed countries were now allocating from 12 to 30 per cent of their gross fixed investment to residential construction, it was not benefiting the people whose needs were the most pressing. Not only were housing conditions deteriorating, but in some instances they were twice as bad as a decade before.[1]

As for international aid, these poorer nations had to be satisfied with advice or a pilot project here and there. Of the billions spent on aid

---

[1] United Nations, Social Commission, 14th Session, *Report of the Ad Hoc Group of Experts on Housing and Urban Development* (New York, March 16, 1962), p. 10.

since the end of World War II, little went into housing or urbanization programs except for Castro-challenged Latin America.

An important reason for the neglect of housing was that it was viewed as a subordinate requirement in the estimates of international aid economists and among the economists within the countries themselves. Both groups had read the same texts, attended the same colleges, or learned the same theories. The old texts survived to influence teaching and policy even after some of the authors had modified their views. The cold calculations of "input-output ratios" had dominated postwar economic thinking in development economics. Housing, it was felt, called for a large input and yielded little output.

THE THEORY OF LOW-PRIORITY HOUSING

From the beginning of international aid programs, there were two schools of economists, both opposed to housing expenditure. The first advocated what may be termed "the devil take housing" theory, which asserts that housing is a durable form of investment requiring a substantial outlay to create it but paying off little per year. It generates no foreign exchange, competes with industry and agriculture for capital, draws off needed labor and materials, and may even be inflationary. A poor country, it is said, cannot spend much on assets for future consumption. It should focus on more food production and on assets that advance productivity, such as factories, machines, better seed and livestock, railroads, highways, and power plants. Use of a country's limited resources for housing consumes the funds needed for productive development and for better nutrition, health, and medical care. For these reasons, according to the theory, housing deserves a low priority in both internal spending and in international aid. This, in the main, had been the view of most American and international policy makers since postwar foreign aid began.

The theory was succinctly stated in 1953 by Sir Percy Spender, Australian Ambassador to the United States:

> There are too many urgent things to attend to . . . the problem of house building in this part of the world is one about which we don't want to be too urgent. The more important thing is to help people to obtain the facilities to increase production and progressively they will thereby solve the problem of housing in their own way.[2]

Other economists, whose line may be called "the modified devil take housing" theory, think that there may be a case for some, but not much,

[2] Burnham Kelly, ed., *Housing and Economic Development*, the Report of a Conference Sponsored at the Massachusetts Institute of Technology by the Albert Farwell Bemis Foundation on April 30 and May 1 and 2, 1953 (Cambridge, January 1955), Sir Percy C. Spender, "The Colombo Plan," p. 18.

housing. Housing in the United States was cited as an example. There it took $7.00 of investment to produce a $1.00 increase in the value of additional housing services per year. By contrast, only $1.80 of added investment was required in a steel plant to yield a $1.00 increase in the value of steel produced per year. "If our objective is to obtain the fastest possible rate of growth of output, and if these United States ratios are at all representative, investment in housing should be kept down close to the lower limits of requirements."[3] Some housing, however, is justified but only where "the objective is to encourage relatively small scale enterprise in the essentially rural areas in India, rather than to put a heavier load on the large cities," or as in Indonesia "for reducing the over-concentration of population on Java by moving people *en masse* to some of the lesser populated islands such as Sumatra."[4]

If housing is built, this theory holds, it must be confined to the "musts": that is, where plants are put up in remote locations, where an excessive journey to work produces labor problems, and where houses can constitute "concrete demonstrations of the rewards that may be obtained from greater, disciplined productive effort."[5]

It is difficult to argue with the contention that a poor country should not spend "too much" on housing. Indeed it should not spend "too much" on anything. But the trouble with both the extreme and the modified theories is that they assume, as Catherine Bauer Wurster said when the issue was first joined in 1953, that there is a "sharp academic distinction between 'economic' and 'social' change, and between 'production' and 'consumption' standards." They assume also that it is possible to concentrate on increased productivity

. . . while postponing any general changes in the social environment until such time as adequate resources may be available for this purpose. . . . Economic development invariably *forces* population redistribution, which in turn means radical changes in the basic pattern and structure of man-made environment. Economic and social change are integral parts of *one* process, the process of development. . . . The remote mine or power plant, where new housing is obviously necessary, is only a small if dramatic example of what is going on at a much larger scale in the cities.[6]

[3] *Ibid.*, Max F. Millikan, "The Economist's View of the Role of Housing," p. 26.
[4] *Ibid.*, Max F. Millikan, "The Economist's View of the Role of Housing," pp. 24, 25. More recently, however, Professor Millikan has said, "the problem is not a choice between housing and other investment; the problem is how much housing you must have in order to make some other investment pay off."
[5] *Ibid.*, Leo Grebler, "Possibilities of International Financing of Housing," p. 32.
[6] *Ibid.*, Catherine Bauer (Wurster), "The Case for Regional Planning and Urban Dispersal," pp. 40, 41. Most good economists now seem to have veered toward the position that Mrs. Wurster and a few others at the conference espoused, although it was then a minority view in economic circles.

It is probable that the "no housing before factories" proposition may have been influenced by two kinds of programs, popularized in the more developed nations in the postwar era. One was new towns, which, it was thought, should be close to the human dream, with a slum-proof guarantee against megalopolis. Another was the costly slum clearance and public housing programs. Economists took these programs as criteria, and they concluded that the cost of new cities or housing would be so great that it would leave nothing for factories. They failed to see that the problem of easing the shelter problem in the less developed areas was not solved by building a host of costly public housing projects or a cluster of Welwyn Gardens; that what Lewis Mumford wanted for England was inapplicable in Calcutta; and that Le Corbusier's Chandigarh was a special situation, which hardly provided the prototype for the cities of the underdeveloped world.

Despite earlier reticence on the issue, a number of respectable economists have rejected the theory that social change can be ignored as a factor in economic change. The General Assembly, the Economic and Social Council, and the Social Commission of the United Nations have moved toward the position that balanced social and economic development is essential, and have adopted resolutions to that effect.[7] But few theorists have attempted to set forth any ideal conception of balance or order of priorities.[8] The truth is that social change may often come before economic change or be concurrent. There are so-called social overhead projects like education and health, which are comparable to economic overhead projects in that they provide little or no dividend in foreign exchange; they also yield low returns and take time before their real benefits can be counted. Nevertheless, they are indispensable to the

[7] See Draft Resolution I, United Nations, *Report of the Economic and Social Council, 16th Session* (New York, December 14, 1961), p. 37, and Resolution 830H, United Nations, Economic and Social Council, 32nd Session, *Resolutions, Supplement No. 1*, (New York, July 4–August 4, 1961). See also Gunnar Myrdal: "There is no doubt that very generally the poor countries in their understandable eagerness to raise production levels in agriculture and industry rapidly are putting too little emphasis on the need for productive investments in human beings and directing too little attention to the need for raising labour efficiency." "The Theoretical Assumptions of Social Planning," in *Transactions of the Fourth World Congress of Sociology*, Vol. II (London: International Sociological Association, 1959), p. 162. See also Simon Kuznets: "For studying economic growth . . . the key is not in the physical stock of plant and equipment; it is in large part in the capital invested in human beings and in the whole economic and social structure that conditions the use of plant and equipment." "Population, Income and Capital," in "Factors of Economic Progress," *International Social Science Bulletin*, Vol. VI, No. 2 (Paris, 1954), p. 170. See also T. W. Schultz, "The Role of Government in Promoting Economic Growth," in *The State of the Social Services*, Leonard D. White, ed. (Chicago: University of Chicago Press, 1956), p. 379.

[8] United Nations Economic and Social Council, *Report on the World Social Situation* (New York, April 1961).

proper balance of development and to the economic activities that require them.[9]

In the long run, the economists' "exceptions" for permissible housing tend to multiply and render their main argument suspect. The resources and capital that these economists wanted to devote to more vital uses are somehow consumed for housing anyway. The pressures and needs for housing are too often so great that more of the scarce resources are consumed than would have been if there were a sensible policy of resource allocation. The employer is often forced to build for his executives or skilled personnel as part of his industrial investment. Each special group —privileged workers, executives, government employees, teachers—demands housing and often gets it, while the rank and file suffer. The wealthier citizens build costly houses of imported materials without regard to the shortage of exchange. The more desperate cannot wait for economists to settle the fine points of their disputes and are taking over land illegally, preempting whatever materials they can buy or forage.

THE EFFECTS OF HOUSING ON ECONOMIC DEVELOPMENT

General economic principles on productivity do not apply equally in all areas, all cases, and all times. They may be valid in the United States and not in Ethiopia; they may apply to one type of housing program and not another. In Israel, where the population doubled between 1949 and 1957, an enormous housing program did not halt economic progress generally but probably aided it. Despite the extensiveness of the country's commitment to housing, the excess of imported over exported building materials was only 4.2 per cent of the total deficit on the balance of payments in 1957. To set up a rule with a long list of exceptions is less realistic than conceding that a housing program is essential, allotting a practical portion of the budget to it, and picking sites where houses will do the economy and the society the most good with the least expense and the minimum of imports.

While there are no accurate yardsticks to measure its impact, housing should be acknowledged as a necessity of life. To exclude its production under any general rule makes little more sense than to ban production of clothing or milk. The building of homes is "economic" in that houses in the less developed areas are often the small production centers for the tailor, dressmaker, or storekeeper. Housing also plays a major role in stimulating employment, direct and indirect; it activates other industries and adds to local purchasing power. Whether "social" or "economic," it may be a wise expenditure simply in terms of balanced growth.[10]

[9] United Nations, *Financing of Housing and Community Improvement Programmes* (New York, 1957).

[10] *Ibid.*, p. 5.

One of the main needs of underdeveloped countries has been to absorb unemployment, particularly in cities where there has been an influx of migrants.[11] When rural migrants come to the city, they are apt to look to the construction industry as one of their primary sources of livelihood. Because of the prevalence of extensive unemployment during the formative period, a housing program properly organized that uses a maximum of domestic materials could be the principal means of employing people productively. If excessive home construction might be inflationary, almost any other make-work program would also be inflationary. But housing production at least contributes an essential good while simultaneously mitigating a possible rent inflation. For the many countries that are experiencing depression and growth at the same time, a housing program can employ funds constructively that might be otherwise wasted on improvised projects or relief payments. In 1963, about half the unemployment in some of Ghana's cities was among construction workers. Yet these cities were experiencing a severe housing shortage. In Ireland, housing proved a mainstay of economic activity when the unemployed had no other opportunities, and it trained men for jobs. The war-torn countries of Europe planned not only for housing but for new towns as a part of their over-all programs for recovery. The devotion of vast amounts of capital to rebuilding did not impede their remarkable industrial growth thereafter. Housing and recovery proceeded hand in hand.

Elsewhere the production of considerable housing (particularly in rural areas and small towns) may be homespun without affecting the labor market or other productive apparatus. In other cases or places, what may be needed to get housing started is a community block-building machine, some tips on rammed-earth techniques, or loans only for roofs or doors. If a proper program is instituted, it will emphasize the low-income worker's needs, drawing on a minimum of imports and foreign exchange, expanding local materials production, and increasing local purchasing power.

A housing program can also play an important part in developing savings and in releasing unproductive capital into the economy. People will save for housing even when they might not save for anything else.

Housing fosters the development of other industries, such as production of building materials, not only for dwellings but for all types of construction. The construction and building industries produce not just dwellings but the related services and utilities, shops, and communal facilities. They also build factories, transport, and power plants and play

---

[11] In the more developed countries, total employment in construction usually equals about 20 to 30 per cent of employment in all manufacturing industry. Housing probably accounts for about half of direct and indirect construction employment.

a dominant part in the capital formation process. Since a fourth to a third of labor engaged in all manufacturing industries are employed in building industries, they influence many levels of economic activity.[12] A housing program may indeed be essential to keep materials factories functioning which produce for all types of construction and productive enterprises. Without an adequate demand for such products, factories would cease functioning and the country might be forced to increase its imports.

If the general business cycle declines while building activity is high, a depression is usually mild, but if both building and other activities decline simultaneously, the depression is severe. Moreover, for every worker employed on a site, at least one other job is provided collaterally, and one out of every ten jobs in the United States is directly or indirectly provided by the construction industry as a whole. In Israel, the proportion is about one in eight. Residential construction is the largest sector of the construction industry and is therefore accepted as an important device for stimulating employment during periods of depression. It serves a similar purpose during the early periods of a nation's development when there is considerable unemployment, particularly of migrants.[13] The importance of the home-building industry to the health of the general economy was realized during the worst American depression, when the government worked to stimulate construction and repair, to free mortgage money, and to encourage materials production. If the drop in American residential construction could have been halted in 1925, the downswing in industrial production that began in 1929 might have been checked.[14] Today, the *Wall Street Journal* regularly features the increase or decrease of housing starts as a main index to boom, recession, and bust.

Housing is also "economic" in that industrial production will be hampered or stopped unless workers are sheltered. During World War II, the United States temporarily curtailed housing programs; but despite the stringency of labor and materials, it soon had to resume them on a major scale. Labor turnover among poorly housed workers was so great that general productivity bogged down. Americans will die for their country, but they balk at doubling up with their in-laws.

[12] United Nations, *Report of the Ad Hoc Group of Experts on Housing and Urban Development, op. cit.,* pp. 13, 38.

[13] "The unstable situation in the field of employment compels the State to engage in active intervention and, among other measures, to take steps in order to secure a suitable amount of building and public works in general." H. Drabkin-Darin, *Housing in Israel* (Tel Aviv: Gadish Books, 1957), p. 174.

[14] See statement of John Blandford, *Hearings before the Subcommittee on Housing and Urban Redevelopment of the Senate Special Committee on Post-War Economic Policy and Planning,* 79th Congress, 1st Session, Part 6, January 9, 1945, pp. 1233 *et seq.*

While doubling up with in-laws is less objectionable in the low-income areas, a failure to provide housing in a mining or oil-producing area is apt to cause not only labor turnover and squatting but inordinately high wages and fringe benefits to compensate for the lack of housing or the long journey to work. Thus the general manager of Ciudad Guayana's steel mill in Venezuela estimated that the difference in cost per ton of steel between workers living four to six kilometers from the plant and workers living fifteen kilometers away represented 1 per cent of the average selling price per ton and 7 to 10 per cent of the expected net profit on the average ton sold.[15]

The location of housing influences the site of industry as often as the placement of industry influences housing location. The existence of an adequate housing supply often ties workers to their existing environments irrespective of the pains and hopes of governments and economists to lure them to a particular industrial site. The sharp differentials in earnings between one section of a country and another reflect to some extent the availability of better housing and community life in one place compared to another.

Where housing is built—whether by private builders, self-help, or squatting—it fixes the public investment in the vast network of public utilities and facilities. Environment cannot be easily altered, and, in the long or short run, enormous public investments are required to reorder and rationalize an established pattern. Thus the descent of masses of people upon a city and their makeshift construction of dwellings may raise the cost of installing utilities thereafter to excessive levels. Providing the housing and utilities from the start may therefore prove a wise economy in the long run, particularly when the transportation routes are planned simultaneously. Nor can slums or squatter huts once built be easily torn down. With sixty million people being added to the world's population each year, and with large-scale urbanization inevitable, there is no longer any alternative to finding a tolerable place for housing investment. Putting it out of mind is closing one's eyes to the facts of world life.

[15] Under the Labor Law of Venezuela the company must provide transportation as well as pay wages from portal to portal. The steel mill figured that the mill would have to pay half the estimated time for travel, which would represent 1.50 bolivars per man per day for those living in Puerto Ordaz, 15 kilometers away, and double that figure for those living in San Felix, 25 kilometers away. It also estimated the average cost of transportation at 1.50 to 3 bolivars per man per day. The steel mill pleaded that the government build the housing closer to the plant. While the mill's cost calculations for the travel of its workers may be questioned, there is little doubt that housing location would measurably affect the cost of steel produced. For the calculations of the steel mill, see memorandum of Charles Abrams to Joint Center for Urban Studies of the Massachusetts Institute of Technology and Harvard University, *Report on the Development of Ciudad Guayana in Venezuela* (mim., New York, January 25, 1962).

Thus there are few countries today that have not been forced into housing programs because of the political if not the social or economic realities. These events have almost made the debate academic. In postwar England, Sweden, Denmark, and other countries of Europe where housing has played a significant role in national programs, a political party could hardly expect to win approval by an electorate without pledging itself to a housing program. What is true of developed areas is true in poor countries as well. Squatting in underdeveloped countries exerts its own forms of political pressures and creates its own economic forces in the process. When Jamaica elected to earmark 60 per cent of a United States grant to rehouse squatters and made housing its top priority, it was not because there was no need for more factories. The reason was that the whole economic program would bog down, foreign investment and tourism might begin to sense danger, and political stability would be threatened unless the housing problems were solved. In Colombia, squatters caused so many social problems, political discontents, and disorders that industry in one of its cities began to move and the country had to initiate a crash housing program to induce the rest of industry to remain.

Once housing is accepted as an integral part of any development program, a nation is then better poised to plan its most effective and most economically practical production. It can earmark the amount of money it can afford for housing. A developing country may need to encourage programs that will use the smallest amount of materials, labor, or imports, and to sponsor self-help and core-house construction. It can also restrict the production of luxury housing. The government may promote the growth of factories that produce materials from local raw materials. It can specify the local materials for its housing programs and keep factories functioning that might otherwise close up. Moreover, it can attract savings by promising homes to savers and foster mortgage lending out of sources that do not compete with loans for industrial development. The country can prepare a land distribution program that will confine squatting to the proper areas instead of allowing the squatters to create their own settlement patterns. It can program housing where it is most needed and dovetail housing with industrial settlement policy. Production can be stepped up in areas of depression and curtailed where it is less essential. Often the inflationary threat of a rent spiral can be held down. Finally, a nation can demonstrate to its people that it is interested in their needs and thereby bolster the political and social stability required to make economic investment safe and viable.

9

Background of Public Policies

THE INFLUENCE OF BRITAIN

With the postwar liquidation of empires, the underdeveloped countries that had won independence were forced into industrialization as the only way to employ and feed their surging populations. The more they industrialized, the more serious became their urban housing problems. For solutions, they often turned to the devices employed by their former colonial rulers, who were believed to have all the answers both to industrial maturation and to its growing pains.

The main arena of nineteenth-century housing reform had been the greatest colonial power of all—England. England's civil servants had already carried some of their planning ideas to her possessions during the colonial period. Her more prolific writers had spawned stacks of books on housing and new towns, while her officials and reformers had preached the gospel of better cities at meetings and seminars around the globe. As a consequence, some of England's planning laws and land acquisition procedures had become models for her departing colonies, and even after their independence her example and influence carried on.

England was not without a background of experience to be drawn upon. During the nineteenth century, she had seen the small country towns of Birmingham, Liverpool, Manchester, and Sheffield expand five to ten times. People in the swelling cities had huddled together on earth floors, sharing outside toilets and pumps that often failed. With cholera epidemics erupting and a death rate among the poor three times that of their "betters," England in 1875 had imposed minimum standards of building, drainage, and ventilation upon her private slum builders and owners. Such regulations were by no means novel, for ever since restrictions on builders had first been hand-delivered to Hammurabi by Shamash, the sun god, they have intermittently appeared as the inevitable "thou shalt nots" in the relationships between urban man, his fellows, and his government.[1]

By the beginning of the twentieth century, when slum life and social reform had attained prominence, Britain had not only expanded her inventory of restrictive laws at home but had already begun to export similar legislation to her colonies. The colony of Aden, for example, provided a whole series of "thou shalt nots"[2] to control or limit: (*a*) the location of buildings, the space around them, and the types of housing that could be built; (*b*) the conditions of sanitation or health; (*c*) the subdivision of land and the size, spacing, design, materials, or external appearance of buildings; (*d*) the use of land or buildings and the height or position of walls, fences, or road bends; (*e*) the accommodations for parking, loading, and unloading; (*f*) the objects affixed to buildings and the exhibition of advertisements; (*g*) the neglect of buildings or land.

Similar restrictions are now widely employed throughout the developed world. Recently they have been extended to preserve beauty and nature, limit population densities, and protect the vested interests of residents. Zoning is one of the accepted devices for specifying residential, commercial, and manufacturing uses.[3] Building regulation, originally designed for fire protection, structural safety, and sanitation, now controls the strength of materials, the condition of plumbing and electricity, elevators, heating, ventilation, and other aspects of buildings. Still another restrictive device is subdivision control, which governs the shape and sizes of lots and influences land use, street patterns, play spaces, and utilities.

Though restrictive devices are accepted almost everywhere, they have their limitations when applied to housing. Every restriction increases the cost of the dwelling. If too stringent, restrictions may curtail or stop building altogether. They also tend to perpetuate the older buildings which, if rebuilt, would violate the newer codes. They cannot prevent slums, overcrowding, or squatting in the face of a mass migration. There is no question that restrictions upgrade quality for those who can afford the higher standards and they preserve both the quality and the appearance of new neighborhoods. But inevitably such regulations, by raising

[1] Restrictions governing the burial of the dead and prohibition of party walls were early regulations among the ancients. N. D. Fustel de Coulanges, *The Ancient City* (New York: Doubleday, Anchor Books, 1956), pp. 63–65.

[2] *Aden Colony Gazette*, December 30, 1948, Legal Supplement No. 1, Sec. 17.

[3] These are usually broken down into further subclassifications such as single-family, two-family, and multiple-dwelling districts for the residential zones, and retail and light and heavy industry for the commercial or manufacturing zones.

building costs, remove a considerable sector of the population from the
benefit of the private building product. Restrictive legislation that may
work in a developed country with an adequate public housing program
will bog down elsewhere unless land and housing are provided for those
who need it and at costs they can afford.

GOVERNMENT-ASSISTED HOUSING IN BRITAIN

When the limitations of restrictive laws were acknowledged in England and when housebuilding had still failed to keep pace with the demands of her urban-drawn population, direct government aid to housing
was considered. The movement for subsidized housing started haltingly
at first, breaking into a full gallop following World War I. But since
industrialization was not one of Britain's colonial policies, subsidized
housing remained a policy for home consumption only.

At first the subsidies in England were dispensed to private entrepreneurs on the theory that helping the private sector would accrue to
the general good. The entrepreneur could be regulated and taxed, but
it was thought wrong to displace him save in those very limited fields in
which it was not profitable for him to venture. And it was felt that even
in these fields, if subsidies were channeled through him, he would rise to
the occasion. To depart from this general principle and make government the owner and operator of an enterprise would represent a sharp
break with tradition and a move toward "socialism." England in 1919
therefore authorized payment to private builders of lump sum grants per
house, but when the cost of building soared, the programs had to be
modified to fix annual subsidies per house. Under Britain's legislation of
1924, houses were no longer to be sold but rented, while later acts
stepped up subsidies to meet both the increasing costs and the growing
housing needs.

Subventions to private builders ultimately proved a disappointment,
and direct public building was finally adopted for Britain's cities. This
worked better, and by 1956, three million dwellings had been produced
for rental by local authorities. Private building, however, was not
abandoned altogether. The growth of building and loan societies provided new sources of mortgage funds for private homeowners, and at
the end of 1955 these associations had accumulated assets of close to
$6 billion.

Thus in a very general way a political dichotomy had been achieved
in England. Private enterprise was to build for those who could pay its
costs, while public enterprise would build for the rest, mostly for rental.
In some countries, a third force, i.e., nonprofit enterprise, would function
as a sort of middleman free of the blandishments of the profit motive and
therefore eligible for special government dispensations.

The introduction of publicly built and owned housing did not meet the political resistance anticipated. Popular pressures were on the rise, and private enterprise could not effectively answer the claim that it was ignoring the lower-income classes. In any event, it was argued that the housebuilder was not being supplanted even in public housing, which, by buying private materials and employing private contractors, was actually stimulating the private building process. Nor, it was felt, should industry object, since government was assuming the burden of housing its workers, thereby increasing the stability of the work force and quieting the thunder from the left.

DEVELOPMENT OF HOUSING POLICY IN THE UNITED STATES

The policies of the United States have also had influence in the less developed world. Not only did such influence permeate through AID programs, but the United States was looked upon as the most technically advanced country on earth, which therefore had all the right answers.

In the United States, housing programs were not formulated until the depression of the 1930's, and they took a somewhat mixed course. The federal Home Loan Bank System helped give the savings and loan associations access to liquid funds and freed the associations from dependency on the commercial banks for loans. Deposits in savings and loan societies were insured, thus increasing depositor confidence and making the societies the principal sources of home mortgage credit. When the depression deepened, a number of experimental programs were launched to aid private housing operations. Private lending institutions whose portfolios bulged with frozen mortgages were rescued and the mortgages extended for the homeowners.

At the same time, the Federal Housing Administration guaranteed private mortgage loans on homes to the extent of 90 per cent or more of "value" (often equal to 100 per cent or more of cost), which spurred additional private mortgage lending and accelerated home building and ownership mostly by middle-class families. Construction of multiple dwellings was encouraged by a similar formula. Simultaneously a public housing program was initiated through municipal housing authorities that built subsidized rental housing for low-income families. The program was fought by private building interests, was successfully hamstrung in a number of cities, and thereafter was blunted by Congress.[4]

Housing aid oscillated in its motivations from economic recovery in

[4] For a fuller discussion of this program, see Charles Abrams, *The Future of Housing* (New York: Harper, 1946), and Charles Abrams, *Forbidden Neighbors* (New York: Harper, 1955).

the 1930's to slum clearance in 1937, to housing for the defense and war workers during the prewar and war periods, to providing for war veterans in 1946, and in 1949 to helping the ailing central cities. More recently, aid was also extended to include direct loans to colleges for student dormitories, housing for displaced families and elderly people, for nursing homes, rehabilitation of old buildings, and loans to cooperatives, most of which were privately sponsored.

Under an urban renewal program authorized by the 1949 legislation, cities could buy slum sites, relocate the occupants, and sell the cleared land to private developers, who would build private dwellings and commercial buildings that would elevate the character of the old slum neighborhoods. The land would be sold at discount prices with the federal government meeting two thirds to three fourths of the loss and the cities the balance. The cities would more than recoup their outlays through the increased revenues accruing from the new improvements.

Thus in the United States the private mechanism was recognized as the principal sponsor and was given priority. Direct public operations were held to a minimum with no more than about 550,000 low-income families housed in municipally owned, federally subsidized projects up to 1964. Some of the tenants were evacuees not only from the publicly subsidized but from the privately redeveloped urban renewal areas. Recently direct 100 per cent loans at $3\frac{1}{8}$ per cent interest to nonprofit corporations have been authorized, and though a few genuine nonprofit operations have emerged, private builders in the main have been the beneficiaries of the liberal credits and the building fees permissible under the program. The entrepreneur has done what the municipalities have not—he has built in volume, and he has operated in the burgeoning suburbs, which are beyond the control of the central cities. The role of these central cities was to build some housing for deprived families, but most of the recent efforts have been centered on acquiring and clearing slum sites for private builders under the urban renewal formula.

SLUM CLEARANCE IN BRITAIN AND AMERICA

A main motivating force for housing reform in both Britain and the United States has been the slum. No word in the language has called up more horrible images of the poor man's lot or is more capable of marshaling the forces of protest. Although reports and investigations of slums in Victorian England had shocked the British conscience, a "slum" was not easily defined or definable. British social planners had at first applied the term to any squalid neighborhood inhabited by the lower and criminal classes. Later this definition was qualified to refer only to houses rather than to both houses and people. Slums came into disrepute everywhere, and officials generally agreed that future slums should be prevented and existing slums razed as soon as possible.

During England's industrialization period, Karl Marx had charged that demolition drove the poor "into even worse and more crowded hiding places. . . . The labourer, with his wife and child and chattels, is thrown into the street and if he crowds in too large numbers towards quarters of the town where the vestries insist on decency, he is prosecuted in the name of sanitation!"[5] The charge was not without merit, but gradually the recriminations were shifted onto the slum landlords, more subsidized housing was built, and the demands of conscience were appeased. In the United States, the plight of displaced families (particularly minority families in slum quarters) continues, but a growing resistance to wholesale displacement in the name of social reform has finally asserted itself.

SLUM CLEARANCE IN THE UNDERDEVELOPED AREAS

With industrialization, the less developed countries are currently experiencing inundations of people similar to those which brought slum life to Europe and the United States during their industrializing periods. Yet even in the most advanced of nations, house production has not succeeded in keeping pace with mass in-migration—and slums persist. It is even harder for building to keep pace in the less advanced countries, where the population inflow is like a deluge and the resources to cope with it are minuscule.

Slum clearance, however, which had gained headway both in England and the United States, began to influence the developing countries as well. It was seen as the final answer to the slum's social by-products, to squatting, and even to overcrowding. The way to get rid of slums and all their distortions was to level them.

In 1954, pressures in Accra, Ghana, by British-trained planners and their local disciples were for clearing such areas as Ushertown, Bentsir Asafo, and Jamestown, despite an intense housing shortage. That year, at a Cambridge University meeting of British and other foreign officials concerned with African problems, there seemed to be almost complete agreement on the need for tearing down slums without regard to housing need or shortage. The evictees would include West African and South African Negroes, but there was also a sincere feeling among most that the way to clear slums was to tear them down. By the definition of the "slum" agreed upon at the meeting (age, obsolescence, and lack of amenities), ancient King's College—where the delegates were housed—

[5] Karl Marx, *Capital*, Modern Library Edition (New York: Random House, 1906), pp. 722, 725.

would have qualified, though of course this was not thought of and was in fact unthinkable.

In 1955, at about the time the pressure to clear the slums of Accra had reached its high point, a United Nations mission on housing arrived and, after surveying the housing shortage and the effect slum clearance would have in aggravating it, recommended that slum clearance be stayed until there was a more adequate supply of housing. Instead, a program to increase the housing supply was recommended. It shocked the British intelligentsia in Accra, but the recommendations of the U.N. mission were adopted.

THE LAGOS SLUM CLEARANCE SCHEME

In neighboring Nigeria, which at the time was also about to achieve its independence from Britain, the pressure for slum clearance met no such opposition. British officials and Nigerians were persuaded that slum clearance was the only right way to attack slums. Lagos, said the Minister of Lagos Affairs, is "the mirror through which foreigners make their initial appraisal of Nigeria."

Lagos, the federal island capital of the Nigerian Federation, is about 27 square miles in area. It is the Federation's chief seaport as well as a bustling trading center, with a population of about 300,000 in 1952, which grew to 450,000 by 1962. Metropolitan Lagos embraces both the federal territory and the periphery, which is part of the Western Nigerian region, and in 1962 had a population of 726,600.

A slum clearance scheme, prepared in 1951, became operative in 1955. The first target for clearance was a 70-acre section in a densely populated trading, industrial, residential, and market area containing more than 30,000 poor people. The agency designated to carry out the task was the Lagos Executive Development Board (LEDB), which, after acquiring the plots by compulsory purchase, was instructed to replan the area with roads, open spaces, and new plot layouts. The new plots were thereafter to be resold and rebuilt for what the LEDB would consider more sanitary and more appropriate development.

Lagos is a city that has skyscrapers but no sewer system. The Western regional government put up the first skyscraper, and the central government, not to be overshadowed, went up higher with a rival skyscraper. Installation of a sewer system, however, which a World Bank mission had described in 1954 as "the most important single contribution which could be made towards improving the health of the inhabitants of Lagos," could gather no official support. It had to give way to more alluring schemes like dams, state buildings, bridges—and, of course, slum clearance.

In the absence of sewers, human excrement in the capital of Africa's largest nation is deposited daily in some 13,000 night-soil buckets, which are gathered up by 400 collectors and then tipped into the lagoon at an annual cost of about $600,000. The collectors know the city's health depends on them, so they are not averse to making unreasonable demands or threatening walkouts. Since the city makes a charge for collections, a small black market enterprise is functioning that offers to do the job more economically, and it is not always the lagoon into which the black marketeer deposits his contraband.

Night soil, sewage, kitchen wastes, and drainage are disposed of by every means available. Waste water pours through ruts that run beside the houses. Rain cuts off access to houses, and mud remains for days, always to be replenished by the waste water. The hotels, office buildings, and industrial estates use septic tanks, which discharge their effluents into soakage pits. Often the larger office buildings must emit their waste into the nearest storm drain, but a good part of it flows into the ground, which is laden with sewage and could conceivably contaminate the water supply, one of Lagos's main defenses against epidemics. An indication of the seriousness of the problem is that all but 15 per cent of the schoolchildren have either hookworm or roundworm; more than 10 per cent of all deaths in Lagos are attributed to dysentery or diarrhea.

The 70-acre site chosen for extinction was a slum by any definition in the international city-planning glossaries. Though not all the houses were physically bad, they were crowded and lacked amenities. After the area was condemned, moreover, repairs virtually ceased, and deterioration was speeded, making the slum designation less questionable than ever.

Bad as it was, the slum was not without some redeeming features— the central location of the area, the proximity to work and friends, and the fact that a number of slum buildings had been occupied by the same families in common for generations. They were in the nature of family compounds that housed the elders as well as the younger members. Within some of the cramped dark houses, craftsmen plied their trades and depended upon the central location for their livelihoods, as did hundreds of female traders, who displayed wares from their homes while caring for their children. Older members of the families benefited from the presence of the working members. There were also many other tenants who helped meet part of the family's living expenses.

One of the attractions of slum clearance schemes is that a rented steam shovel can do the trick at little cost and in a few days. If the land is valuable and can be sold for private redevelopment, the transaction may even prove profitable. Slum clearance and urban renewal expenses therefore contrast favorably with those of a sewer installation, which in 1954 was estimated to cost £5 million.

Slum clearance and summary sale of houses to outsiders, however, is apt to meet the resistance of the established dwellers, particularly in land-conscious countries where alternative investments for cash are few. The intervention of 200 helmeted policemen was in fact required to disperse a mob in Lagos when the LEDB proceeded to take over one of the houses. Lagos officials, however, thought they could both clear the slum and appease the displaced owners. All land acquired after the replanning of streets and facilities would be reoffered to the original owners at 120 per cent of the public acquisition cost. Thus it was thought that much of the £2.95 million outlay earmarked for the operation would be recovered through the resales, and the old owners could have their plots back.

One problem remained, i.e., where to put the families while the site was being rebuilt. This was solved by planning a housing development on vacant land in Suru-Lere on the outskirts of Lagos to be simultaneously undertaken. Terraced cottages containing one to four rooms would be provided at a subsidized rent of twenty-five shillings a month per room for the temporary accommodation of the displaced residents. After eighteen months, it was thought, the new development would be ready, and they could return to their former neighborhood, now spruced up and no longer a slum.

By 1962, however, Suru-Lere had expanded into a major venture of 1513 costly housing units for displaced families and another 1300 units for others. It was no longer solely a temporary rehousing scheme and indeed was beginning to run into real money.

Slum clearance in Lagos soon met a series of snags. Seven years had passed, and the LEDB had succeeded in demolishing only 25 of the 70 acres. About 11,000 persons were displaced, and hundreds of small shops and stands that had been the source of livelihoods were uprooted. By this time, the £2.95 million that had been allotted to the project had grown to an estimated outlay of £3.5 million (exclusive of Suru-Lere). But this is still far from the final outlay. Suru-Lere has become a heavy drag on Nigeria's budget.

Eventually, the LEDB ran into financial difficulties even with the continuing government advances. The former owners who had been expected to lose no time in buying back their land in the slum were not appearing with their cash. All the government had received from them was £728,000, and a substantial number of those who had put up this money were hardly prepared to rebuild and resettle according to the original plan. As some of the plans began to materialize, somewhere in the background lurked a new crop of entrepreneurs who had bought up many of the claims from the impecunious old owners for a pittance.

The redemptions by the original owners did not materialize for several reasons. The net area that would be available with the full 70 original acres replanned and rebuilt would be only 42 acres. Half of the reduced area was zoned for commercial and half for residential use, so that the space available would be inadequate to satisfy all or even a good part of the demands for rehousing the old owners on the site or providing them with the old opportunities to trade. A substantial fraction of the redemption rights of some owners, therefore, had to be foregone.

Yet even if there had been enough land to go around after road building and replanning, most of the owners were financially unable to buy their land back. Even if they could have scraped together the money, they could not finance the new buildings as they were required to do. Most were small traders or workers unschooled in the strategies of finance, negotiation, and rebuilding. In many cases, ownership of the land had been vested in a large kinship family comprising several households thereby making the achievement of a consensus difficult. The compensation upon receipt was divided into so many portions that, once distributed or spent, it could no longer be reassembled for the repurchase. Borrowing for rebuilding was difficult and only possible at ransom interest rates—often as high as 100 per cent. Some therefore put down deposits for the land and could never pay the balance. Many who should have helped with the financing now lived in Suru-Lere, and they were generally the younger members of the family who were no longer interested in returning to the city center to resume the interdependent family patterns of the former common household.

The end product of all these laws, policies, and compromises has been frustration. Despite a displacement of thousands and the breakup of family relationships as well as a burdensome outlay for the 25 acres acquired, only a fraction even of that acreage has been resold and redeveloped. Those who have redeemed and redeveloped, moreover, are generally not the former owners but more affluent purchasers who have bought the owners' rights or leased from them at very advantageous terms. The few new developments on the site, moreover, while better than the old slum buildings, are not the munificent ones that were anticipated. Most of the old slum persists, and further improvement is stalled.

The most ironic by-product of the clearance scheme is that a good portion of the already cleared 25 acres has been reoccupied mostly by those originally displaced. They have not built new buildings but have rented makeshift shops on the cleared land, some of which are now occupied as sleeping quarters by the evicted. The presence of the unused land and the pressures of the displaced shopkeepers to eke out a livelihood had succeeded in forcing the LEDB to allow them to go back. Thus, as of mid-1962, over 400 stalls had been put back, and 57 more were in the process of being set up in 1963.

It would take at least another £5 million (the estimated cost in 1954 of a Lagos sewer system), and probably much more, to complete acquisition. The recovery of the government's investment is by no means sure.

Further slum clearance would entail fresh displacements, if not fresh resistance from the petty traders and owners on the 45 uncleared acres as well as on the vacant sites on which the displaced occupants have now won repossession. Above all, the new development and the rest of Lagos would still be without a sewer system. Even if the whole site were cleared, it is unlikely that the end product without a sewer system would be a worthy symbol of "the progress and prosperity of Nigeria" as officials had hoped.

If there are to be any more displacements, Suru-Lere will have to be expanded considerably and at a far greater expenditure than the government is prepared to make for rehousing the evictees. Suru-Lere, moreover, does not appear to be the unchallengeable alternative to slum life that the sponsors of the scheme had envisioned. It may provide housing but not the livelihoods the old slum afforded. Even if the whole slum had been cleared, it would have made only a small dent in Lagos's total slum inventory; many of the evicted slum dwellers had simply crowded into the adjoining slums, intensifying overcrowding and making their future clearance more remote. According to a study by Peter Marris,[6] despite the heavy subsidization of rents, the cost of living is considerably higher in Suru-Lere and takes a larger bite out of income, the cost of food and transport is higher, the journey to work longer and more tedious, and the distance of the petty trader from his work greater. Worst of all is the attenuation of family life, which has disrupted group relationships. This is particularly hard on the old people who had lived on the family property and been cared for by relatives. The isolation of Suru-Lere has impoverished social life and broken up strong familial attachments.

The benefits of slum clearance should mean more than exchanging a shoddy home in a convenient neighborhood for a convenient home with a tiresome journey to work. The combination of isolation, higher expenses, and lower incomes has threatened an established way of life and livelihood for many. Not only do the Suru-Lere occupants see less of their relatives, but the quality of the relationships has changed. In central Lagos, even though the communal family houses were gradually being broken up, the unity of the extended family had survived in day-to-day visits, in regular meetings, and in the mutual-help characteristic of these people. But the families in Suru-Lere have been finding it less and less easy to maintain these visits or to discharge their obligations. Forced into a self-sufficiency alien to their traditions and harassed by the demands on their overstretched resources, once-unified households have been shattered. Time will tell whether Suru-Lere has won more benefits

[6] P. Marris, *Family and Social Change in an African City* (London: Routledge & Kegan Paul, 1961).

in the long run than it has lost, but one thing appeared certain in 1962 —the slum clearance scheme was inextricably snarled.

In view of the government's financial embarrassment, the U.N. mission to Nigeria advocated a new plan for the development of the land already acquired, a conservation and improvement plan for the remaining 45 acres in place of the old slum clearance operation, and a loan program to help owners improve their existing properties. It advocated that further rerenting of the cleared land to traders be stopped so that the rebuilding of the 25 acres could proceed. The mission also suggested a cash settlement for the redemption rights of the owners who had not yet reclaimed their property. Some low-cost units to accommodate those displaced from the site were also recommended, though it appeared that not more than about 10 per cent of the displaced families could in the long run be accommodated on the remainder of the 25 acres. What was already begun would thus be completed, and the reslumming of the area that appeared inevitable would be avoided by assuring the remaining families on the 45 acres of their possession. By replanning the site for rehabilitation and conservation, the site would be improved, and further displacement and extensive government outlays would become unnecessary. In fact, the government in 1962 was not prepared to pay the cost of further clearance operations anyway, so that the issue had become academic. At some future time, perhaps, when a sewer system is installed and when the housing shortage in Lagos has been eased, slum clearance may be resumed. While the cost of slum clearance may be greater at that time, the rebuilding of the area, when coupled with the installation of a sewer system, would at least make better sense.

SLUMS AND GROWTH

It may have to be conceded that in the formative years of industrialization, the slum will be the inevitable by-product of urban development, like the abdominal distortion that precedes birth and growth. The trouble has been that reformers have always called the swelling a cancer to be excised wherever it appears.

Any effort by a poor country with a fast-growing population to counter slum formations by building high-quality housing generally produces few houses and keeps slums forming elsewhere. The population pressures are simply too strong to be met by building a few costly projects while ignoring the slum problem as a whole. India tried costly houses and then had to cut her cloth to her meager measure. There has been a similar lack of results in Manila and other parts of Asia.

Manifestly, if housing needs are to be met on the scale and character required in the swelling urban areas, the program must weigh all the social effects of disruption by clearance against the social benefits of rehousing in an environment that retains or restores as many of the institutions as are lost in the clearance. This is not accomplished by building a development too far from the work centers and without the other advantages and opportunities of central city life. Furthermore, public operations must provide a maximum number of houses at minimum cost, widening the area of choice for the slum dweller and meeting as much of the housing need as possible.

In a housing famine there is nothing that slum clearance can accomplish that cannot be done more efficiently by an earthquake. The worst aspects of slum life are overcrowding and excessive shelter cost. Demolition without replacement intensifies overcrowding and increases shelter cost. It may also increase squatting and thereby quickly create slums that are more stubbornly enduring than those removed. Continued residence in slums may be a necessity for some time to come.

As for overcrowding, it is less serious when there is easy access to the outdoors. Sharing of apartments by several families may be necessary at the beginning of a program, and despite its disadvantages it helps pay the shelter cost and mitigates the evils of homelessness.

Slum clearance, as the following chapter indicates, may be inevitable in some cases. But on a wholesale basis it is generally justified only when a country can afford it financially, and then only after sufficient vacancies have been created. Clearance should be the second, not the first, phase of a housing program, though both clearance and housing may in proper cases be undertaken as part of a single program.

In Singapore, the Improvement Trust had long been clearing slums as well as building some housing, but it soon came face to face with the consequences of its slum clearance policy, when those who were displaced proceeded to squat.[7]

A final lesson is that when slum formation is inevitable, it should be planned rather than denounced. Laid out properly and on carefully selected sites, the cheap structures, particularly when they are one-story buildings, can be improved or replaced when the time is ripe. If slums are unplanned, however, they may defy government correction forever. Planning housing of minimum standard may be contemptuously called slum building. The term "planned slums" may raise the reformer's eyebrows, but enable him better to see. If slum building shatters Utopian dreams, it may soften the rudeness of the awakening.

[7] "In the face of this problem it may well be that central area clearance schemes will have to be postponed and all efforts concentrated on new housing." *Annual Report,* Singapore Improvement Trust (Singapore, 1957), p. 4.

10

Proposals for Solving the Problem

PUBLIC HOUSING

One of the reasons for Nigeria's difficulties was that in the more developed nations, slum clearance and public housing had been made inseparable parts of a single program. The slum had gained prominence as a bane, and its elimination was declared a blessing. The theory was that no housing program could be valid without simultaneously leveling the slums. As slums were razed, new units subsidized by the government would be built at the same time to rehouse the displaced families on the rebuilt slum sites or elsewhere, and all would be satisfied and happy.

Actually, the provision of public housing is an independent undertaking that need not be part of the clearance operation. Though slums cannot be cleared without providing alternative housing, public housing can be built on vacant land without clearing slums at the same time. Nor has public housing proved itself the only satisfactory program for slum dwellers. Not all who are evicted want to become government tenants. Others may not be qualified because their incomes are too high or their families too large or too small. The site may be inconvenient to their work place, or the slum dwellers may prefer living in houses they own or in older dwellings among their own friends and institutions.

Nor does slum clearance inevitably mean slum demolition. Slums may be cleared by constructing enough housing in advance so that the range of housing choices is enlarged and the move to another dwelling is free of duress. Worse than slums is a slum shortage that provides no shelter, good or bad. Wholesale demolition produces such a slum shortage and compounds the slum's evils by forcing the poor and the evicted to crowd into what remains.

There is a wrong way and a right way of accomplishing slum clearance. The wrong way is exemplified in countries like the United States, where slum clearance is occurring under the urban renewal, public housing, and public works programs without adequate alternatives being made available to the displaced families. Ireland did it the right way by building enough housing for slum dwellers first. After undertaking one of the largest public housing programs per capita in the world, Ireland in 1963 was moving to acquire slum sites in the central areas for more practical uses. This could now be done less painfully.

Ireland's housing program dates back to 1866, when its Commissioner of Public Works first advanced money for working-class dwellings, but it was not until 1948 that the public housing program was stepped up. Since then, this program has been the principal influence on its urban patterns. Between 1948 and March 1956, the Dublin Corporation alone had built almost 16,000 dwelling units for its low-income families. The Dublin Corporation felt that "thinning out" the central city was desirable, and acquired large tracts of land on the city's periphery. It also encouraged private builders to build on the peripheral land through easy public credits, and it simultaneously built most of its public housing there.

Once-vacant land outside the Dublin center was soon covered with long rows of homes, most of them two stories high. What was formerly farm or pasture land became the sites of the new neighborhoods of Finglas, Ballyfermot, Coolock, and Wilkinstown. Industries are moving where the housing is, and the housing is not too far from work opportunities in the city proper. Dublin still has 600 acres available for future building in such outlying areas. Holding reserve land for future use is a sound policy.

Altogether Dublin now owns about 42,000 houses. Overcrowding and the pressure for housing have eased. There was, in fact, a vacancy turnover during 1962 of some 1500 units in its publicly built houses. Unless population and in-migration to Dublin increase beyond expectations, the housing situation now seems under control. The same policy and the same situation apply to Ireland's other large cities.

By 1963, Ireland was ready for clearing the older areas in the central city that were ripe for use as offices, high-cost residences, and commercial properties. By assembling the small, privately owned parcels and replanning them for private and public redevelopment, Dublin's traffic and parking problems can be eased, worn-out sections of the city redeveloped, business offices accommodated in the central sections, open spaces provided, and private investment spurred in the proper places.

There are other phases of public housing programs in the more developed nations that are either questionable or inapplicable to the less developed areas. Britain, from which many public housing principles were derived, is a country in which the less privileged classes are usually renters. The United States adopted Britain's policy and built all its subsidized housing for rental. But by subsidizing interest instead of rent, the less privileged families can buy their houses. Except where there is land shortage, both ownership and rental should be available forms of tenure in the developing areas. Where, as in Ireland, individual houses can be built on vacant land, it is easier to sell the houses to the occupants, and my U.N. report recommended this procedure.

Income limits are set on public housing in the United States, and if a family improves its income, it becomes ineligible for further occupancy. Not only does this rule encourage misrepresentations, surreptitious informing by hostile neighbors, and uncertainty of tenure, but it penalizes ambition. Again, Ireland's policy in this respect is more sensible. It fixes an economic or unsubsidized rent for each unit, and the tenant has the option either to divulge his income and pay rent commensurate with his ability or to refuse, and pay the higher economic rent. Greater certainty of tenure makes for more personal freedom, better tenant relations, and better care of the dwellings, and avoids economic segregation. It also cuts down official arithmetic. In most of the developing areas, continued occupancy can be permitted without any requirement for disclosing incomes.

In most of the highly developed nations, subletting is prohibited in public housing, and here this policy is doubtless justified. But in the less developed nations, subletting, like the sharing of apartments, may be the logical, if not the only, way of helping to pay housing costs and providing a roof for many whom public programs cannot accommodate. As income and housing supply increase, crowding will diminish. In Lagos, Nigeria, where interest rates on mortgages by the Nigerian Building Society are at least 8 per cent, a poorer family that builds a house actually depends on subletting a room to be able to buy the house and maintain it. If a room is sublet at $6 a month, the purchase price would come within reach of a family earning as little as $30 a month. The majority of houses, according to the U.N. mission, could be built for about $2500 apiece, and each would shelter one and a half families. With a secondary loan made by the government and a first mortgage loan by the building society, 5000 homes could be financed and housing provided for about 7500 low-income families.

These examples suggest the caution with which foreign public housing policy should be recommended for the less developed countries. The wide variations in conditions, costs, and customs require a study of each country's housing problem in its own light.

URBAN RENEWAL

With the growth of the world's cities, the urban renewal concept which had been launched in the United States in 1949 gained headway in Europe, and more recently it has also drawn the attention of less developed nations. Urban renewal entails the acquisition of large tracts by the public authority, replanning the area, and then reselling or leasing the land not required for public uses to private developers for rebuilding or rehabilitation. Although the clearance of slums had been the main motivation behind the program's origins in the United States, the rebuilding of declining central areas of cities has been recently receiving the primary emphasis. The need for wider roads, parking, apartment houses, offices, shops, and industries has intensified the competition for the centrally located land. By developing such land as a unit, better sections would be created.

Urban renewal is by no means a new concept. Baron Georges Eugène Haussmann transformed the face of Paris during the reign of Napoleon III, and despite vigorous opposition and his ultimate dismissal, he gave Paris the broad boulevards, its water supply, the sewer system, bridges, the Opéra, and other public buildings that make Paris the envy of the world. Glasgow and Birmingham a century ago also bought substantial slum acreage in the cities' slum centers and, after replanning the areas with new roads, disposed of the excess land for private redevelopment.

Yet evicting people from their footholds—even when those footholds have been secured illegally—is meeting far greater difficulty than it did in the days when the city's slum dwellers were looked upon as so much human surplus. Today the public obligation is not only to evict but to rehouse. Without an ample public housing program, even those countries with a liberal compulsory purchase power must soon face resistance. To satisfy the opposition, the Netherlands not only rehouses its displaced occupants but gives them subsidies on a declining basis for five years to compensate them for the higher rents they must pay in their new dwellings. In Europe, flatted factories are also being built for displaced businesses, and in some cases payments are made not only for moving expenses but for goodwill. Although in the United States occupants must be assured of alternative accommodations in public housing or elsewhere, they are not always being rehoused adequately, and opposition to urban renewal has grown.

The problems facing the developing areas are more serious because of the hordes of people descending upon their cities, the limitations of their building industries, the lack of private investors in building financing and transport, and the numerous other impediments to growth. There are nevertheless some developing countries with housing programs—among them, Singapore and Israel—that are looking to urban renewal for a more rational development of their city centers. Israel has not yet finally formulated its urban renewal plans, but Singapore, which is producing more than 12,000 public housing units annually, called upon the United Nations in 1963 to help it set up such a program. Because it is one of the first to do so, its situation has special significance for other developing countries.

More than a million of Singapore's 1,730,000 people (mainly Chinese) are concentrated in the Singapore City area, where entrepôt trade supplies the main form of activity and livelihood. Despite its extensive housing program, Singapore's squatter problem and its housing shortage have caused people to jam into tiny rooms and cubicles in the central areas. One such crowded area is Chinatown, which adjoins the city's constricted business center.[1]

The island's population has doubled every twenty years since 1921. The shortage of office space and housing led the government to impose rent and eviction controls in 1947, and in 1961 repossession by owners was barred even for demolition and new buildings.

Rent control has compounded Singapore's problems. One tenant of a small downtown office, for example, demanded $100,000 for his possession. But settling with him would only mean having to face even higher demands by the remaining tenants. Another by-product of rent control has been the growing decay of buildings. A landlord whose gross rent is limited to $15 monthly is hardly likely to keep his building in repair when he sees his main tenant garnering $100 or more from the subtenants. Nor does an administrative device exist for compensating the landlord for repairs—he must repair first and depend on the court to grant him a slight increase thereafter. In 80 per cent of the cases in which tenants sought to compel the owner to repair, owners have asked the court to declare the building uninhabitable and to order it demolished. (An empty lot is worth more than three times the value of a rent-controlled house.) In one case, tenants who repaired their own dwelling units in an effort to avoid their eviction after they complained lost both their $2000 and their possession. Few tenants now dare to complain to the authorities about the condition of their dwellings.

With no repairs being made to houses, they will soon be ripe for the wrecking crew. Because possession of valuable commercial buildings cannot be secured, Singapore's central business section is facing stagnation. Urban renewal appeared as a way out of both these problems.

Under an urban renewal program, Singapore's Housing and Development Board could acquire contiguous parcels, improve the traffic and

---

[1] Charles Abrams, Susumu Kobe, and Otto Koenigsberger, *Report for the Government of Singapore*, prepared by an Expert Mission appointed under the United Nations Technical Assistance Programme (mim., Singapore, August 1963).

parking patterns, and sell the remaining land for badly needed office, commercial, and residential buildings constructed according to plan. Commercial tenants would be compensated for the fair value of their possession. Since rent controls have reduced the values of shophouses to a pittance, the Board could acquire the land cheaply and resell the cleared land for more appropriate uses, often at a profit. Singapore's extensive housing program could provide quarters for the displaced occupants and stores for some of the evicted shopkeepers. The new buildings would yield the government many times the revenues it presently receives. With an urban renewal program, the government would also be accomplishing a much needed public service. This plan looked good on paper until all the stumbling blocks were identified.

Though the 12,000 public housing units that Singapore built annually made it possible to provide a tenant with a new dwelling unit on a week's notice, most of the slum dwellers preferred staying where they were. Most of the housing projects are too far from work. If there is to be a major displacement of occupants by urban renewal, more housing projects would have to be built closer to the centers or in new self-contained neighborhoods with industry and shopping of their own.

Another problem is finding private builders who would be willing to buy and redevelop the sites, particularly for moderate-income families for whom no rental housing is presently provided. The main stumbling block is that Singapore's tax laws take 36 per cent of a builder's gross rent, leaving him with only a 6 per cent return. Worse still, he is obliged to pay another 40 per cent as income tax on the small profit he receives. The U.N. mission recommended a reduction of the gross rent tax to 20 per cent on urban renewal investments. This would give the investor a return before income tax of about 9 to 10 per cent, which would make rental housing attractive to the private redevelopers.

Still another problem involved the Chinatown area, which adjoins the business section. No houses in all of slumdom compare with them in the human crowding and dinginess, airlessness, and lack of privacy. But once outside the house, the Chinatown section offers other compensations in its restaurants, shops, and temples, its street scenes and its bustle, its central location and its jobs. No replacement, however ingenious the architect, could recapture the section's magnetism and its interest for tourists and residents. But the buildings need preservation against the elements, and the population has to be thinned out to alleviate the overcrowding. A sensible renewal scheme would identify and reinforce Chinatown's existing values rather than destroy them. The U.N. mission recommended careful selection of unsafe or dispensable structures and the erection of "vest-pocket" buildings in Chinatown that would blend with the environment. Additional public housing would be built on nearby government-owned land. Simultaneously, a more workable code enforcement and rehabilitation program would be undertaken to make the remaining buildings safer and more habitable.

The lessons to be drawn from Europe and the United States as well as from the fragmentary evidence in the less developed areas are that urban renewal can be an important tool in the planning process—not only or even mainly for the clearance of slums but for making central city sections serve their most useful functions in national development. In addition to opening up traffic arteries, providing parking spaces, public improvements, housing, and the industrial and commercial buildings required by the growing economies, an urban renewal program would make it possible to assemble fragmentary parcels, remove the clouds on titles that frustrate improvements, and provide a politically acceptable device for selective releases of property from the strictures of rent controls.

Urban renewal, however, entails a drastic use of the public power and must be scrupulously exercised. It should be one tool but not the only one in the planning process. It should not be employed mainly as a device for increasing tax revenues, making profits on land operations, or for ousting "undesirable" people from their shelters. In most cases, it should be launched only when housing shortage has eased or when, as in the case of Singapore, it is coupled with a vast rehousing program. Adequate compensation for moving and other expenses as well as for losses and goodwill should be provided as part of the program's cost. Above all, it should be undertaken only after its benefits to the community as a whole justify the impositions it enforces, and it should be launched only after it has received wide public acceptance.

NEW TOWNS

Another concept that has impressed the less developed nations is New Towns. It gained prominence in the more developed nations as a way of achieving the better life and was being offered as a remedy for the problems of the swelling cities of the developing world. The question was whether industries and people should be left to accommodate themselves in existing cities, be siphoned off into satellite formations around these cities, or be distributed in new self-contained cities elsewhere.

In Asia and the Far East there seemed at first no alternative to enlarging already existing industrial plants in preference to creating new units. As the existing plants in the big and more established cities expanded and took on more workers, the cities grew, the housing shortage intensified, and community facilities such as water, schools, and traffic arteries became overloaded. When it looked as if the limits of space, efficiency, and human endurance were being reached, some means had to be found for decentralizing industry and population. Again the echoes of England

and the continent were heard, and the influence of the former empire was felt.

One of the ascendant influences in nineteenth-century urban reformism was the New Towns movement, launched by Ebenezer Howard.

> These crowded cities have done their work [wrote Howard]. They were the best which a society largely based on selfishness and rapacity could construct; but they are in the nature of things entirely unadapted for a society in which the social side of our nature is demanding a larger share of recognition. . . . The simple issue to be faced, and faced resolutely, is can better results be obtained by starting on a bold plan on comparatively virgin soil than by attempting to adapt our old cities to our newer and higher needs?[2]

To Howard, the solution was to build new garden cities that were self-contained social and economic units of about 30,000 people. Each town would be built on about 6000 acres and would be held in single ownership. The towns would contain homes, industries, and community buildings with reservations of permanent farmland and parks as greenbelts.

There was nothing novel in the idea of building new towns, but Howard had the distinction of propagandizing the idea when it was needed, and not only shaping the concepts but advancing them into actual demonstrations. The concept of functional balance between industry and people, the ownership of the land by a common authority to whom increment in value would accrue, the deliberate limitation on increased population density, and the use of the greenbelt to guarantee it distinguished Howard's from most other New Towns ideas. At a time when every effort to clear slums and reduce overcrowding faced frustration in the more developed areas, Howard's proposal came like a fresh breeze into a stuffy council chamber. "Town and country," said Howard, "must be married, and out of this union will spring a new hope, a new life, a new civilization."

A new hope did spring up, though a new life can hardly be ascribed to it, and a new civilization is a long way off. Yet out of Howard's inspiration sprang the Garden City movement. Five years after Howard's death the first garden city was built in Letchworth, and another was built some years later in Welwyn. Sir Frederick J. Osborn and Lewis Mumford assumed the role of disciples, reechoing the idea and arguing its case with passion in Europe and America.

There were other forces in Britain's crusade for better environment—among them the Fabians, who saw housing legislation as the beginning of socialism within the capitalist framework. By their attacks on concentration of ownership and by Henry George's single-tax crusade, impetus

[2] Ebenezer Howard, *Tomorrow: A Peaceful Path to Real Reform*, reissued as *Garden Cities of Tomorrow* (London: Faber and Faber, 1945), p. 146.

was given to the feeling that the incremental value of land should accrue to the people. Sir Raymond Unwin popularized the thesis that "nothing is to be gained by overcrowding." With reform in the air, the only question was how to get its product on the ground. Utopian communities and Marxism shared common inspiration, but in England Marxism would have meant throwing out the capitalist baby prodigy with the slum bath water. New towns and better housing seemed like alternatives worth trying.

As the breezes of Utopia swept through the world, the New Towns idea sailed along with them. As one Englishman put it, "In the world of practicable ideas, new towns were one of our most substantial exports."[3] Hilversum in Holland and the new satellite communities in Frankfort on the Main are said to have embodied some of Howard's ideas. In India, new towns for steel and railroad building have sprung up. A self-help community for refugees was built in Faridabad, about fifteen miles from Delhi and planned for 30,000 people. (The same number set by Howard was, according to Mumford, "a shot in the dark.") With the end of World War II, the planning of new towns received impetus in Greece, France, the Philippines, and South America. Today they are being planned or have been developed as national policy in Israel, Singapore and Malaya, Ceylon, Venezuela, Norway, Puerto Rico, the Netherlands, Ireland, the Soviet Union, Poland, Hungary, and Yugoslavia.

Though the new towns built varied from Howard's conceptions, the building of new towns was inevitable. Population pressures were forcing it, and improved communications were making it more possible than ever. The decision of an industry to locate a plant on a vacant site would gradually attract another factory nearby. Though the population influx might at first be mainly workers, traders, and those involved in secondary services, the settlements would soon begin to spread at or around the core. An unplanned new town would result.

Planning new towns should be part of the growth process, but the motivations and principles that applied to Britain and Europe were too often irrelevant for other parts of the world. As Otto Koenigsberger noted in the report of the mission to Singapore, the planning of British and European new towns presupposed a steady rate of social and economic change. These nations laid primary stress on individual enterprise and confined government action largely to preserving the prevailing economic substructure and relieving distress. The European society was fundamentally conservative in outlook and concerned with preserving the achievements and institutions built up in the past.

In contrast, the less developed nations are experiencing sudden population inflows (even England's own assumption of gradual population

[3] Preston Benson, "Czechoslovakia," in *Town and Country Planning*, Vol. XXIX, No. 9 (London, September 1961), p. 351.

increase proved unrealistically conservative). These countries are acting more directly to spur production and investment. Finally, preserving the past and its institutions is less important to the developing nations than shaping the immediate future. Even in England, moreover, the earlier dream of self-containment (espoused in the case of much publicized Welwyn) gave way to a growing dependence upon the metropolis.

While many of the theories in European town creation were inapplicable elsewhere, the British New Towns movement nevertheless provided both an impetus for planning industrial development and a laboratory for probing city-planning processes, rationalizing land uses, and learning about industrial location, urban finance, comprehensive site planning, and improved environment. The towns built after World War II afforded new outlets for some of the overspill from Britain's crowded cities, and the movement filled a similar need in some other countries.

If it served some of Britain's purposes, however, the New Towns movement did not always meet the high level of the hopes and prospects of those who planned them. Tel Aviv, originally a small Jewish suburb of Jaffa, was planned by Sir Patrick Geddes in 1925 as a garden-city dormitory for this commercial city. He had envisaged a population of only 40,000 in an area of about a thousand acres. When Tel Aviv became Israel's metropolis, its streets were far too narrow, land was lacking for public buildings and parks, the residential plots were too small, and what remained of the original town plan was a few pleasant streets and gardens.[4] Similarly, Ankara and Manila received very little respect from the squatters and migrants who poured into them. While stately Chandigarh rose troublesomely and expensively in the cool foothills of the Himalayas, Calcutta kept teeming, with little hope that new towns would ever filter off its surging homeless people.

It soon became clear that while the idea of building new towns was as sound as when God ordered his first six built, the old crowded city could not be counted out. The limited-population new towns were localized in their aesthetic effects and represented only one of many devices rather than a universal solvent. They were too costly for many developing countries[5] and failed to offer the varied opportunities and attractions of the larger cities.

No planned city in a world where freedom of movement exists can

[4] Arieh Sharon, "Urban Land Policies: Israel," *Urban Land Problems and Policies, Housing and Town and Country Planning, Bulletin #7* (New York: United Nations, 1953), p. 84. See also pp. 46, 47.

[5] One of the costliest items in the private development of new towns has been the financing of utilities and services. Mohone, a town built by the National Rayon Corporation near Bombay, exemplifies the exceedingly high cost of such services and utilities.

sustain its assigned population quota or its plan in the face of a mass inundation of people. Unless the housing famine and the economic problem are eased, the aesthetic and numerical integrity of cities (planned or unplanned) will not be respected by the irrepressible masses. If new towns are to accommodate the surging populations of the less developed areas, they may have to be built for ten or twenty times the number Howard projected. Existing towns will have to be extended, and metropolises will have to look to their borders for further expansion.

An existing city, nevertheless, can reach the limits of its utility. The tyranny of topography, the strangulation of traffic arteries, or the uneconomic cost of moving goods may leave a country no alternative but to build new towns. Caracas, Venezuela, for example, is so crowded with squatters, traffic, and people that unless other cities are built or at least expanded, the continued inflow of people and automobiles will throttle it. Jobs must be found for expanding populations, and often new industrial magnets outside the existing ones can accomplish the purpose. In a world pressed by home-hungry squatters, planning makeshift shelter may be the best that can be hoped for at present, and a new town may have to be a slum town in whole or in part.[6] Whether they are lasting failures in the long run will depend not alone on whether they are slums when built but also upon how they are laid out initially and on their capacity for rebuilding when the opportunity is ripe.

Lagos, Nigeria, illustrates the need for new towns as well as for regional plans. The population of the Western sector just outside the federal jurisdiction grew from 36,000 people in 1952 to 277,000 in 1962. The people of this island capital have pushed out into the Western region of the new Federation partly because of the island's topography as well as the number of swamps that limit the usable land area within the capital. Not only do thousands of workers in Lagos spend as much as two hours traveling to their jobs, but as much as 10 to 15 per cent of their family budgets goes to pay for commutation. The evident alternative is to acquire tracts of land large enough to compose satellites of Lagos close to mass transportation that can bring people to their work at low cost and without overburdening existing transport services. The U.N. mission to Nigeria therefore recommended a satellite town in Agege to accommodate about 250,000 people, some of whom would be employed in the town, while others would commute to Lagos and to the adjoining port city of Apapa. Considerable commutation would thus be drawn in the opposite direction from Lagos and lighten its traffic load. A

[6] In Ciudad Guayana, Venezuela, plans call for designation of sites on which the squatters will be permitted to settle. Land will be laid out into plots and aid given for building. See recommendations in Charles Abrams, *Report on the Development of Ciudad Guayana in Venezuela* (mim., New York, January 25, 1963).

number of other settlements on vacant land would also be planned. Altogether the proposed satellites would accommodate about 500,000 Lagotians.

Singapore island, which is diamond-shaped and about 26 by 14 miles, is planning a new town in Jurong which will accommodate 200,000 people in ten years and will have a variety of industries. The location and regional relationship of Jurong and other new towns on the island will have a lasting effect on the location of industry and people and on the nature of their environment. The United Nations mission in 1963 recommended that Jurong and other new towns projected for the future be located as "ring cities," accessible to the sea, but with an open "lung area" between them and Singapore City. This open area would serve a combination of purposes: the greenbelt for the new cities that surround it, a catchment for drinking water, the site for the island's airfield and for cultivation. It would also contain the roads across the island for communication between Singapore City and the new coastal cities.[7] Without new towns, the central city would spread into the interior, and all the advantages of location and easy movement would be sacrificed.

The successful development of new towns is related to the ability to earn a livelihood. In the most home-hungry of countries, a new self-contained town will not hold workers if there is no prospect of jobs, trade, or progress. Israel, one of the world's laboratories of new-town building, has experienced trouble with at least four of the twenty-one new towns it completed by 1963 because the few factories that employed the population experienced slumps. The industries and social life also lacked variety. Even in the case of some other towns, people drifted toward the bigger cities, where the job choices and chances for advancement were better.

The concept of self-containment in planning will too often have to give way to the satellite alternative, for it is the core city that provides the greater variety of choices and the interest which the satellite often lacks. The availability of cheap land and the preference of the entrepreneur for one-story plants is nevertheless likely to induce a fanning-out of job opportunities into the satellite. The satellite entrepreneur thereby has the advantages of less crowding and freer movement while being near the city with its skills and other perquisites. A satellite location also affords the worker a wider choice of jobs both in the main city and in the satellite. In time, the workers in the city may tend to locate in the city, while those who work in the satellite will settle in the satellite. The shorter journey to work is ultimately the inducement for the worker's locating his home within convenient distance to his job.[8]

[7] For details of the plan, see Abrams, Kobe, and Koenigsberger, *Report for the Government of Singapore, op. cit.,* Ch. 3.

[8] This finding was made in the United States. See *Report on Housing in California*

If a new town is set up on land that is distant from a large city, it should be sufficiently varied in its industries, opportunities, and interests to have its own polar influences. This is illustrated by the success of the new town of Beersheba in Israel.

If industries in a new town are of a major order like a substantial steel plant, then secondary industries like cement (made from steel slag), fertilizer (using coke oven and refinery gas for ammonia synthesis), and rolling mills as well as trade may contribute to making the new industrial town a diverse organism with a wider choice of jobs and a better opportunity to shift from one job to another. Government policy in the form of inducements and regulation can often spell the difference between the success and failure of such new formations.

DISPERSAL OF INDUSTRY

Britain's early planners also thought that the congested cities made dispersal of industry mandatory and that dispersal could best be achieved by building new towns on the one hand and by controlling industrial settlement on the other. The same principles were soon carried over into the less developed areas. If industry could be placed near where people farmed, it was thought, it might stem their descent upon the metropolises and help maintain them in their established rural communities. It would reduce the burden of unemployment and cut down the cost of new transport and public facilities. Catherine Bauer Wurster in 1953 urged that "if limited resources are to produce maximum social-economic progress in underdeveloped countries, concentrated metropolitan growth is to be discouraged in favor of a network of smaller cities and towns related to the rural hinterland."[9]

Few could disagree with the need for a policy of industrial decentralization, and industry should certainly be encouraged where the smallest number of houses need to be built. But, as in the case of new towns, desired effects do not always issue from policies. A nation's desire that industry settle where it is good for the nation is not always what the industrialist thinks is good for his business. In the less developed areas,

---

(San Francisco: Governor's Advisory Commission on Housing Problems, January 1963). It would probably be true wherever human movement and housing availability made it possible. On the other hand, in Ciudad Guayana, workers preferred to live not near the new steel mill but in an adjoining community. But they could easily move by car to the mill within a fifteen- to twenty-minute ride from their homes.

[9] Burnham Kelly, ed., *Housing and Economic Development*, the Report of a Conference Sponsored at the Massachusetts Institute of Technology by the Albert Farwell Bemis Foundation on April 30 and May 1 and 2, 1953 (Cambridge, January 1955), Catherine Bauer (Wurster), "The Case for Regional Planning and Urban Dispersal," p. 47.

where capital investment is at a premium, the inclinations of the investor are apt to have more weight than those of the planning officials.

The metropolis has a host of intangibles and incalculables that work like a magnet on the businessman and induce him to settle either in the big city or near it. They include:

1. THE INELUCTABLE LOGIC OF THE BIG CITY FROM THE STANDPOINT OF BUSINESS CONTACTS. The big city has the banks, the universities, and the better newspapers. It is where executives meet face to face; where the distributors and buyers are located; where foreign businessmen are most likely to visit; where the best professional and skilled workers are available; where the stock exchange functions; where there are secondary service industries; where air and rail service is best. The big city also supplies a ready-made consumer market for goods.

Tokyo, the world's largest city, is also among the most overcrowded. Japan has sought desperately to hold down her population by controlling births as a national policy. Yet Tokyo continues to grow. It would seem logical for Japan to foster the building of new free-standing cities elsewhere, or at least to encourage the growth of secondary areas such as sparsely settled Hokkaido, or Hanshin, which has a good port and other facilities. The obstacle is that too many Japanese industrialists find that the advantages of Tokyo outweigh the disadvantages. An Osaka industrialist with a fine home, major investments, and many friends in the Hanshin region told one of the members of the U.N. mission to Japan that despite the advantages of Hanshin, he had decided to take an apartment in Tokyo. In a bank-note world, it is better to be as near as possible to the bank notes.

2. THE LOGIC OF THE METROPOLITAN AREA FROM THE STANDPOINT OF CONTACT WITH GOVERNMENT. Government today regulates business, makes loans or subsidies, and grants export and import licenses. It manipulates the national economy through currency, tariff, and other controls that can make the difference between profit and loss. The big city is where approaches can be made to consuls, embassies, tax officials, and men of influence. The delays of beadledom in the modern world can frustrate any business activity. But personal contact keeps the businessman *au courant* on government policy and facilitates the cutting of red tape.

3. THE LOGIC OF THE BIG CITY AS A RESIDENCE FOR THE EXECUTIVE'S FAMILY. The business executive's wife has become a potent factor in his choice of a residence. Despite its inconveniences, the big city offers good schools, department stores, doctors, dentists, psychoanalysts, safer water, theaters, restaurants, bridge clubs, and first-rate beauty parlors. One has more privacy and more social opportunity. After an altercation with Mrs.

Grundy, the executive's wife can turn to other fish in the big city's social stream. As for the inconvenience of the big city, she can deal with it, usually by living in the suburb, but the city must not be too far away.

* * *

If the big city must inevitably grow bigger, what will happen when a city like Calcutta reaches twelve to sixteen million in 1970 or a conceivable fifty million by 2000? While not every city is Calcutta, there were in India in 1963 some 106 cities with populations of 100,000 or more that might form the basis for extension and industrial development in the ensuing decades. In fact, enlarging existing cities and suburban areas offers less risk than building isolated new towns.

The task is great and the way full of hazards as well as productive frontiers. The burning ideal must always be damped down by the realities of enterprise and investment. Yet one thing is clear—there is no spatial shortage for industrial man. Nor is there a world shortage of materials for shelter. The principal shortage is one of ideas, policies, and the ability and will to face the problem and to help those who do not yet know how to help themselves.

11

The Problem of Finance

Absence of a mortgage-financing mechanism is one of the most telling indexes of underdevelopment. The nineteenth-century caricature of the mustachioed villain threatening to foreclose unless the defaulting home-owner gives him his daughter's hand in marriage is now only a tintype in the archives of American development. A mortgage system is accepted as essential almost everywhere. Polonius's advice, "Neither a borrower nor a lender be," would, if followed, make it impossible for most people to own their homes.

In countries with the highest per capita incomes, a middle-class bread-winner must still have twice his annual gross income to buy a modest house, but by the time he can accumulate it, he may be dead. Since urbanization has been universally accompanied by rising costs of homes, a shortage of capital for the purchase, and a gap between income and shelter cost, the only way of acquiring a home is by going into debt.

Yet, although the mortgagee in Europe and America is no longer a villain but a respectable businessman, the vilification heaped upon him elsewhere is not without a basis. Lending by private usurers in low-income countries carries interest rates ranging from 20 per cent to 100 per cent, and much of what a worker earns often goes to the lender. Considering that even in developed countries, interest and amortization payments on a 6 per cent mortgage constitute over 50 per cent of monthly carrying charges, the rates exacted in underdeveloped areas make home buying for the average worker little more than a fantasy.

A good house should last at least a lifetime. In the more developed nations where a mortgage system exists, the house is built first and paid for in installments out of earnings. If there is no financing mechanism, families have no alternative but to rent (if they can), build a cheap makeshift, crowd into small spaces, squat, or sleep on the streets. Absence of a mortgage system can lead to stagnation of the building and materials industries, increased unemployment, social discontent, and in some instances even political upheaval.

Underdeveloped nations have sought to set up various mechanisms to finance home building. Most of the devices are crude and ineffectual. When a credit pool is created out of tax revenues, the resources are so small that only a handful of houses can be built. Some governments have considered floating bonds on the capital markets, but the unfortunate experiences with Latin-American mortgage bank flotations in the past have not improved their prospects. The uncertainty of the security, the lack of purchasing power among the rank and file, the fear of inflation, and the higher yields available on other investments are other factors that have impeded the growth of home financing.

DEVELOPING CAPITAL FOR HOUSING

There is no uniformity in the financing needs of developing nations. Most lack capital for projects, but a few can raise funds privately in the international market, others can get private loans if payment is government-guaranteed, and some can raise capital internally by stimulating savings or borrowing from such private sources as insurance companies. In exceptional cases, like Puerto Rico, bonds are floated in the United States. Many developing nations can pay the periodic housing subsidies out of taxes, but getting the initial capital for development is their primary problem.

The diversion of excessive capital for housing handicaps industrial growth, which also needs capital for new structures and equipment. To minimize the capital required for housing, the dwellings may have to be low in initial cost and should be built with local materials. Sometimes they may be erected by unemployed or partly employed workers building their own dwellings.

How can capital be accumulated for a housing program without jeopardizing other aspects of development? The following are good general answers:

1. Capital outlays for housing or new towns and subsidies for lower-income families should be viewed as two distinct items and budgeted separately. Subsidies should be paid out of annual revenues. Capital lent for housing should be repayable with interest so it can form a re-

volving fund for the production of more housing. Subsidies and rents (or interest receivable) should be the collective pool used to service and repay the capital loans.

2. Capital accumulations for housing should come as much as possible from sources that are noncompetitive with capital needed for other enterprises. This is already the case in most developed countries, where loans to industry and loans for housing draw differential rates and are made by different kinds of lenders. Commercial banks lend most of their funds to their industrial and commercial depositors, while institutions such as savings and loan societies lend on mortgages but do not make business loans. Other sources of capital accumulation such as pension and social security funds frequently earmark some money for housing loans that pay higher-than-market interest rates for fixed terms. In these cases, loans for housing are often made to those who contribute to the pension fund formations.

3. There are untapped savings, only a small part of which can be drawn into commercial banks or business investment. They can, however, with proper incentives, be drawn into housing loans not only because interest rates can be more attractive but also because the ability to borrow for a home can be made the incentive for deposits in mortgage-lending institutions.

4. There are in a number of underdeveloped countries counterpart funds due the United States in local currencies for purchase of farm products. These funds are not fully used by the debtor country for developmental purposes and in some cases the debtor country is unaware that they may be used for housing. A part of these funds should be earmarked for low-cost projects, mortgage institutions, materials production, or other stimuli to housing activity.

5. Some countries that can borrow foreign private capital for housing by guaranteeing payment are not taking full advantage of the potential. Countries within the British zone of influence should be able to borrow from British and Canadian life insurance companies and other institutions looking for investment outlets, and from Commonwealth investment funds. Germany and Japan are other possible sources of aid that should be solicited.

6. Investment by industries in housing for workers can be induced by government guarantees, aid in land acquisition, or other assistance. Many industries whose workers need housing would prefer making loans directly or through the proper agencies that they can carry on their books as defined assets. They would prefer this to carrying illiquid real estate at undefined or nominal values and having to manage the property

to boot. In several instances, employers have offered to invest the capital for the formation of savings and loan associations, if the funds would help house their workers. Proper government policy can often influence a company's decision to invest.

7. Government guarantees should be given to savings deposits in institutions with mortgage investments. Liquidity would thereby be assured and deposits encouraged. The existence of the guarantee and the availability of government funds to meet large withdrawals would also spur more savings institutions. Rarely would actual government advances be necessary.

8. Life and other insurance companies can become a more important source of capital for housing, particularly in cases where governments require companies entering their markets to invest part of their revenues within the country. A substantial portion can be invested in mortgages and prove profitable for the companies.

9. The development of international sources of capital for housing has hardly been considered. Some of this money flows into housing anyway (particularly in Latin America) and disappears into a few costly projects. Loans are often made without analyzing how they can do double and triple duty, how they can help build up savings, or how they can best serve underprivileged families. As discussed later, the development of an international device for loans secured by mortgages or rents repayable in local currency is still unexplored and also deserves attention.

THE FINANCING OF COMPANY HOUSING

The financing and building of housing have often been undertaken by employers, particularly in areas distant from established cities. Company housing has a long history; its less respectable roots run back to the era of agricultural feudalism, in which master provided shelter for serf. With industrialization, the motivations have included the need to attract workers and to minimize labor turnover. Sometimes benevolent motives have prompted company investment. Other employers have felt that being landlord gave them a double grip on the labor force.

In the more developed areas, company housing and company towns have gradually receded. Architecturally, they were rarely the best exhibits of employer magnanimity. Though rents were low, so were wages. In the United States, agricultural camps for migratory workers are still a national blemish. Often entire families are crowded into a single small room. Facilities for washing and cooking are primitive or missing altogether.[1]

[1] *Report on Housing in California* (San Francisco: Governor's Advisory Commission on Housing Problems, January 1963).

The main reason for the decline of employer interest in the United States has been the unpopularity of company towns and company dwellings and the rise of governmental concern with housing. Properly devised housing and homeownership programs that are publicly assisted enable the worker to live with greater comfort and privacy (and often at lower cost) than in company housing.

In the less developed areas, the building of company housing is not uncommon. Such housing has been built in the Far East, the Middle East, South America, Canada, and other areas. In Japan, home-hungry workers eagerly await the opportunity to move into employer houses. About 700,000 dwellings were financed by Japanese employers between 1945 and 1951. In Argentina, Industrias Kaiser Argentina has offered to build several thousand houses for sale to its workers if it can be helped with the financing. Its survey shows that the houses can be sold with a 20 per cent down payment and fifteen years to pay the balance.[2]

In India, major industries like the Bata Shoe Company build housing for their workers. India requires oil companies to provide housing as part of the oil concession agreement, and there are similar requirements in Venezuela. The building of industrial housing in India is frequently based partly on grants and loans made to the employers.[3]

The Standard Oil Company's concern with housing goes back to a Peruvian venture at the time of World War I. At first, Standard provided rent-free camps, supplying free or cheap food as well, compensated for by lower wages. The free perquisites were withdrawn when the workers pressed to get other things free. Wages were then adjusted and charges for the perquisites resumed.

Camp life, however, left many aspirations unsatisfied. A Standard Oil official says the average worker wants: (1) his own home, and one he can keep after retirement; (2) a house that suits his tastes and is in a location of his choice; (3) neighbors of his own choosing, whether or not they are company employees; (4) roots in a community with a built-in economic stake for the future; (5) a measure of economic freedom without dependence on his company; (6) the dignity associated with the rights and responsibilities of citizenship. To fulfill these aspirations, the official says, the company's policy has now veered toward building houses and selling them to workers.[4]

[2] Abner D. Silverman, *Report on Housing Visit to Argentina,* memorandum to Harold Robinson, AID (mim., Washington, August 14, 1962), p. 6.

[3] United Nations Economic and Social Council, *Financing of Housing and Community Improvement Programmes* (New York: United Nations, 1957), p. 22.

[4] Burnham Kelly, ed., *Housing and Economic Development,* the Report of a Conference Sponsored at the Massachusetts Institute of Technology by the Albert Farwell Bemis Foundation on April 30 and May 1 and 2, 1953 (Cambridge, January 1955), K. H. Quick, "Housing Experience of the Standard Oil Company," pp. 99, 100.

The practices of companies vary. Some prefer to pay a fixed housing allowance to the worker, who then proceeds to find his own housing. Ninety per cent of the workers in Venezuela's new steel town of Ciudad Guayana take the portal-to-portal pay rather than live in company houses. At first, the steel company provided rental housing close to the mill, but the tenants, viewing upkeep as the company's obligation, neglected the grounds, and a drab cluster of houses lacking the qualities of a neighborhood was the product.

In Aruba in the Netherlands West Indies, a foundation was organized to help finance construction of homes that were then sold to workers with a small down payment and a mortgage with interest at about 4½ per cent; the loans were made by private banks and were guaranteed by the foundation. In western Canada, a company that viewed its workers' shacktowns as "incompatible with operating efficiency and with the company's employee relations and public relations position"[5] bought land, provided streets and utilities, and then sold the improved land to the workers, who built their own housing. A company in South Sumatra, Indonesia, provided the materials as well as the land and utilities. A town for 50,000 people was built by the Aluminium Company of Canada in Kittymat. After sale of the homes, the town was incorporated; a town council now operates the public facilities and services. In Pakistan, where employers have made substantial contributions toward housing their workers, some workers beleaguer their employers by running up rent arrears in the firm belief that an accumulating debt is a continuing guarantee against dismissal.

Most of the objections to company housing can be eliminated if the dwellings are sold to the workers. When the house is their own, they tend to maintain and improve it, and they no longer feel that the employer holds a whip hand over their shelter as well as their job. Financing of workers' dwellings can be handled in a number of ways, such as:

1. A fixed tax on each employer based upon the number of workers.

2. A prescribed loan per worker housed either in a company-built or a publicly built project, with the loan repayable in monthly installments by the workers.

3. Provision of government-owned land, schools, and roads by the government, with the employer contributing the entire housebuilding capital.

4. Organization of a worker's self-help building cooperative, with a joint loan per member-cooperator for land development and building cost.

[5] *Ibid.*, K. H. Quick, "Housing Experience of the Standard Oil Company," p. 101.

5. Provision of loan funds by a building and loan association, with the equity capital provided by the employer and/or the government.

6. Provision of loan funds by the employer, with the loan guaranteed by the government.

In some Latin-American and Caribbean countries, the government has generated employer construction through a special tax on incomes (in Colombia, 2.5 per cent of incomes above a specified level) or by granting tax deductions for part or all of the employer's outlays.[6]

Under any formula, the bargaining powers of the industry and the nation must be weighed. Excessive requirements will discourage investments. In other cases, new investment by an industry can only be induced by government housing aid. Sensible negotiations and reasonable contributions by the employer may produce communities of satisfied workers with a dividend worth the employer's investment. There is no one formula that works everywhere and at all times. Sometimes the housing needs of many workers might be met by giving the employer property tax exemptions, liberal tax deductions for depreciation, or help in the financing.

GOVERNMENT GUARANTEES

Guarantees of mortgage investment by government agencies, such as the Federal Housing Administration in the United States, have facilitated financing in a number of countries. Under FHA, mortgages on homes and larger structures are government-insured with ½ of 1 per cent of the mortgage paid by the owner annually as a premium. A somewhat similar—but cheaper—formula operates in Canada, financed by a single premium of 2½ per cent paid at the closing.

On the whole, the FHA formula has helped owners buy homes with small down payments and has spurred ownership. The wisdom of the insurance formula, however, has not gone unquestioned. Many mortgages in the United States are made without benefit of the insurance scheme by builders who dislike its restrictions or shun its red tape. Some loans actually cost less than those with the FHA guarantee. A fair test of the actuarial risks has not been made, because building costs and home values have risen ever since the formula was initiated.

---

[6] In Chile, employers may subscribe to 3 per cent bonds of the public housing fund to the extent of about a third of the employer's tax liability. United Nations Economic and Social Council, *Financing of Housing and Community Improvement Programmes* (New York: United Nations, February 1957), p. 38. Under another law, 5 per cent of the employer's profits is earmarked for housing, but the employer is given the option to deposit the equivalent in savings and loan associations.

The government guarantee has been responsible for the flow of substantial mortgage funds from Britain to Jamaica (B.W.I.); a similar formula is functioning in Trinidad. In both areas, British capital had been slow to finance housing investment, and its interest in lending was accelerated only by the government guarantee.[7] Barbados authorized government guarantees of mortgages in 1963, hoping similarly to attract British capital. But government guarantees or FHA formulas are not workable universally. Where interest rates are very high or there is a threat of inflation, a government guarantee will not suffice to induce investment. However, pension funds can sometimes be tapped by government guarantees. Guarantees can also stimulate the investment of institutional reserves, such as those of foreign or domestic insurance companies, and idle funds of public and quasi-public corporations. Should a device for international lending be formulated, the guarantee may also be necessary.

SOCIAL SECURITY FUNDS

Social security and pension funds are a form of forced savings employed in a number of underdeveloped countries to finance housing. Although housing can be a sound investment for pension funds, one danger is the temptation to use the funds for those social or governmental purposes which should normally be a charge on the general taxpayer. In these cases the pension funds may be lent under pressure at nominal rates or on dubious security. It is important, therefore, that the administration of the funds be independent and the administrator free to make sound investments. When such funds are invested at the market rate, however, the lowest-income groups are not apt to benefit substantially. But there are sound ways to make these funds more socially useful. One is by making lower-interest mortgage loans guaranteed by the government. This was done in the Philippines when Gonzalo Gonzalez, head of the social security system, lent a portion of the social security funds for mortgage purposes. The mortgage loans are guaranteed by the Home Financing Commission, the Philippine equivalent of FHA in the United States. Pension and social security funds can also be employed to house lower-income groups if the loans are made at market rates and if the government not only insures the loans but agrees to subsidize the interest payments so that housing charges will be within the borrower's means.

Another possibility is placing a fraction of the pension funds as an in-

[7] Charles Abrams, James G. Banks, J. Robert Dodge, Marvin S. Gilman, and Dr. Kalervo Oberg, *Report of Housing Team of the International Cooperation Administration to the United States Operations Mission* (Jamaica, April 1961).

vestment (preferably government-guaranteed) in a savings institution which can stimulate further deposits from more people and relend the deposits on mortgage.

THE DEVELOPMENT OF SAVINGS

The only real way to break the log jam in mortgage financing is by attracting savings or other idle money into the home-financing market. But systems of savings as a spur to mortgage investment are still in their infancy. The low income level in poorer countries naturally limits savings, but at least some people have enough earnings or profits for comfortable living, with a little left for savings.[8] Little effort is made to tap them, however.

When income increases, the average family is apt to embrace the spending patterns of Western nations instead of copying their habits of saving. The television aerial, for example, may not be simply a means of tuning in a love song, but a symbol of status.[9] Likewise, the announcer's eulogy of the newest mechanical kitchen utensil too often incites the housewife to trade the nest egg for the eggbeater. Those with free money in the less developed nations often lend it on short-term high-interest loans to installment houses which relend to farmers, consumers, or traders. In Jamaica a fierce competition has set in for investment funds, with both long- and short-term investment opportunities competing for savings in a narrow market. Mortgage financing is under a handicap in the face of the loan charges made to installment purchasers by the "hire-purchase" companies. These charges run between 17 and 30 per cent, which enables the companies to entice savings by offering 6½ per cent on time deposits.

Other families with savings buy and hoard goods against inflation. A commercial banker in La Paz complained that he had long sought the magic formula for disgorging the cash hidden away by some wealthier Indians in Bolivia's altiplano but had achieved no success.

In many developing areas, savings and loan societies are nonexistent, and whatever savings go into commercial banks are lent to business rather than on mortgages. Even these loans often command fantastic rates. In Bolivia, for example, normal bank loans may cost 21 per cent. When such profits can be made on commercial loans, there is little incentive to lend money for housing. Commercial banks in some countries

---

[8] J. J. Polak, *The National Income of the Netherlands Indies, 1921–39* (New York, n.d.), pp. 64–66. See also W. W. Lockwood, *The Economic Development of Japan* (Princeton, N.J.: Princeton University Press, 1954), pp. 278–280.

[9] This is not peculiar to underdeveloped areas. Sir William Holford of London told me that when television was first introduced, not all the aerials of the poorer classes in England were actually connected to a television set.

occasionally issue mortgages to a few of their good customers, but these are generally short-term accommodation loans secured by additional collateral.

Such savings as can be harnessed for housing loans are often brought in from pension funds (as in Turkey and the Philippines) or through lottery systems. Nevertheless an opportunity exists for attracting savings from the rank and file into a mortgage system, but a main obstacle to be overcome is one of changing the habits and traditions of the past.

THE GROWTH OF SAVINGS AND LOAN SOCIETIES

One of the largest sources for mortgage funds in developed areas has been the savings and loan association or the building and loan society. The association began in eighteenth-century England, but the modern fruit is far different from the original seed. Some of the early associations actually built their quota of houses and then dissolved. Membership called for systematized thrift; the members were required to make regular payments for prescribed periods and were obligated to share losses. Today the shareholder is more like a depositor, while the borrower looks upon the association as his impersonal mortgagee. Almost all of the associations accept funds at interest and lend them out to home buyers or builders at higher rates, retaining the differential for overhead, reserves, and dividends. Those who deposit the funds may be either depositors or shareholders free to withdraw their money unless the demand for cash is concerted, which is rare. In that case, they will get their money as mortgages are liquidated. In the United States, associations are chartered by the states or the central government. They usually receive federal loans and insurance of deposits. In England, the societies are supervised by the Chief Registrar of Friendly Societies and are an important source of mortgage credit.

Similar associations are found in New Zealand, Ireland, New South Wales, Canada, South Africa, and Central and South America, as well as Western Europe. In 1962, there were twelve in Jamaica and not one in Barbados.

Bookkeeping and administrative practices of savings and loan associations in developing countries are too often old-fashioned, and servicing costs are heavy. In the Philippines, there were seven associations in 1957, but their resources totaled only $5.8 million, which was 3 per cent of the total resources of all banking institutions. The Manila Building and Loan Association, the largest, was paying 6 per cent to shareholders, with interest increasing by another 2 to 4 per cent upon maturity. The Association quoted 8 per cent for mortgages, but not many loans could be made from its meager resources. For the average man, getting a mortgage was like hunting big game in Mindanao with a slingshot. A family might save money to buy land on the installment plan, but never have enough to complete the payments or build the house.

A number of obstacles check the flowering of building and loan associations in the underprivileged areas. One is lack of practical knowledge. A second (common to associations everywhere) is the provision for postponing payment should cash demands exceed cash resources. A government-sponsored formula for assuring greater liquidity during periods when cash dries up would help.

Another problem is the attitude of government officials themselves. In the Philippines, the Government Central Bank has viewed mortgage loans as inflationary, thus strengthening the reluctance of commercial banks to help the associations with credit. When these commercial banks do make a mortgage loan to a customer, they charge him 7 to 10 per cent in interest (as against 3 to 3½ per cent paid on his deposits); this is a better deal than lending the money to an association at 5 or 6 per cent, which is all the association can afford to pay.

The experience has not been much happier in Venezuela, where wealthy citizens could have launched savings associations. But opposition by commercial banks coupled with a lack of initiative and expertness militated against them. In 1961, however, Eugenio Mendoza, an influential Venezuelan industrialist, became interested in the housing problem and proposed to help solve it by putting his own money and that of some fellow industrialists into a nonprofit home-building company. The $2.5 million he corralled was hardly enough to start a major demonstration building project. While on an assignment for the Venezuelan government, I induced him to convert his building foundation into a building and loan society that could receive savings and thereby expand operations as well as garner cash that was then pouring out of the country.[10] The foundation in 1961 negotiated a $5 million loan from the Development Loan Fund for the launching of the operation. By 1964 there were fifteen such associations.

While American dollar loans for such associations are helpful, what many countries mainly need is the agreement of their own government to make cash available against mortgages pledged by the associations in the event of heavy withdrawals. This aspect has not been fully worked out in most countries and continues to be a principal deterrent to expansion of the associations.

After 1960, the partiality of American aid and of the Inter-American Development Bank toward savings and loan associations spurred their expansion in Latin America. A Federal Home Loan Bank Board and a system of savings and mortgage insurance were set up in Chile, and as of July 1962 there were eighteen private savings and loan associations

[10] See Charles Abrams, *Housing Finance in Venezuela,* memorandum to Banco Obrero, Venezuela (mim., New York, 1960).

with 19,000 savers and about $10 million in savings. National housing banks have been set up in Ecuador and the Dominican Republic providing for savings and mortgage insurance. Peru passed similar legislation in 1956, and in 1962 it had nine associations with 9500 accounts. In December 1961, a $10 million AID loan went to Venezuela to speed establishment of a savings and loan commission. A $5 million loan to encourage an association was also made to Colombia. This financial assistance to Latin America was in addition to substantial loans for housing construction of various forms.

A greater emphasis in American policy on expanding savings and loan associations would doubtless help to attract savings and advance mortgage lending as well as construction activity. As noted earlier, however, the benefits of American aid at nominal interest went largely to the upper-income groups in these countries, while the loan associations were allowed to charge the people as much as six times the cost of the borrowed money. The price ranges of homes on which loans could be made in Chile ran up to $9500, up to $7500 in Colombia, and up to $7000 in Peru. Though the encouragement of savings and loan associations was important, and though some loans to higher-income families might often be justified on economic grounds, the question was whether this form of subsidized American aid was justified, since the lower-income group received little or no benefit.

In contrast to the American program of aid at nominal rates to savings and loan associations is the British businesslike approach under which the Commonwealth Development Corporation buys stock in the associations or makes loans to them at commercial rates—$7\frac{1}{4}$ to $7\frac{1}{2}$ per cent in 1962. The associations charge their borrowers rates that permit repayment of the British loans plus their own profit. When the association is a going concern, CDC sells some of its stock to the public. In 1963, when it offered some of its stock in the Malayan society to the public, it was oversubscribed thirty times.

One of the policy determinations in the less developed areas is whether the enabling law under which associations function should allow only for mutual (or nonprofit) associations or for stock corporations operating for profit. In a number of countries, the statutes permit only the former. The best policy is to permit both and pass on each application on its merits. Nonprofit corporations, while sound when operated by reputable citizens, can prove to be fiascos because of insufficient capital, absence of incentive, the indifference of the directors, *sub rosa* profits on land, lawyers' fees, and other perquisites garnered by the "nonprofit" managers. Stock corporations in which adequate capital is invested and in which profits are the reward of the investors are not immune from similar chicane but may also be better operated and safer for the depositors. The greater the stake of the stockholder-investors, the more apt they will be to make careful loans, plow back profits, and hold management costs to the minimum. An inflexible statute that permits only mutual companies limits the number of such associations and tends to discourage the very investment of fixed capital and financial know-how that the country desperately needs.

SAVINGS AND LOAN ASSOCIATIONS IN AFRICA

Savings and loan associations exist in Africa, but operations have not always been ideal. Ghana was spurred into organizing a society in 1954, but its loans are made only to the higher-income groups. It was thought that people might be induced with proper stimulus to put their money into savings deposits instead of into building blocks.[11] The government had announced a plan for making mortgage loans through a government-sponsored organization to the extent of some $2.5 million, reserving another $3 million if and when required. Although the government called its plan a building and loan society, it was actually a government-sponsored mortgage bank. In a country where impartial relations between government officials and government beneficiaries was not yet a fact, the U.N. mission felt that loans would soon go to the government's favorite sons.

What was needed desperately in Ghana was a handful of enlightened businessmen to organize and direct a savings and loan association and to show more interest in the country's development than was manifested by selling the Africans canned goods from England. But despite the U.N. mission's efforts, the businessmen at the time showed not a glimmer of interest. The mission was able after a spirited meeting with Prime Minister Nkrumah and his cabinet to induce the government to divert some of its investment into a "roof-loan scheme" for the less privileged and to use the balance of the authorization for a society.[12]

In Nigeria, the need for developing personal savings was acknowledged in the National Development Plan for 1961–1962, which stated that savings "must be increased by at least one quarter over the present level to sustain the contemplated growth rate of Gross Domestic Product at a little over 4 per cent compounded per annum."[13] Personal savings were not unknown in Nigeria, where a Postal Savings System and the facilities of commercial banks had been set up to accept deposits. But the

[11] See Charles Abrams, Vladimir Bodiansky, and Otto Koenigsberger, *Report on Housing in the Gold Coast* (New York: United Nations, 1956), p. 25.

[12] For a fuller exposition, see *ibid.*, pp. 71–81.

[13] Otto Koenigsberger, Charles Abrams, Susumu Kobe, Moshe Shapiro, and Michael Wheeler, *Metropolitan Lagos*, a report submitted to the Ministry of Lagos Affairs (New York: United Nations, 1962), p. 151.

channeling of such savings into a mortgage system was still relatively new.

The Nigeria Housing Development Society had been set up in 1956 with an advance of share capital of £1,625,000, of which Britain's Commonwealth Development Corporation invested £975,000, while the federal government invested £500,000 and the Eastern regional government £150,000. Additional funds were made available by CDC through long-term credits at 7½ per cent interest.

Operational prospects up to 1962 seemed good, and dividends on share capital (at first 2½ per cent) rose to 5 per cent in 1962. The investment was not a bad one for the Nigerian government, for while it held only 32.5 per cent of the stock investment, it received about 40 per cent of the profit in the form of income tax from the Society in addition to 20 per cent of the profits for its share capital. This was made possible by the charges on mortgage loans made at 8½ per cent and in some cases 9½ per cent.

One of the troubles with the operation, however, was that its total savings in 1962 were only £60,000 and the total number of savers was only 200. This was not due to the absence of available savings, for licensed banks held more than £21 million in such savings in 1962, Nigeria's Postal Savings System had 287,000 depositors, and the Chase National Bank had acquired about 2200 thrift accounts in a single year, though it paid only 3 per cent in interest. The reason for the Society's small amount of savings was that it had made little effort to attract savings, and such efforts as it had made were far from effective. Its offices were located on the second floor on a side-street building that was hardly conducive to inspiring confidence or making its presence known. It also required that initial deposits be not less than £50 (later reduced to £10). At the Society's discretion, funds could be withdrawn only after a ninety-day period, which should have been shortened. No deposits were required of borrowers, who might have contributed captive accounts of at least £50,000 to £75,000. Advertising and additional inducements to attract savers were negligible.

One reason for the Society's indifference to savings was the fear of the British directors that deposits might be suddenly withdrawn, a fear which the commercial banks did not share and which they took care of by a system of "activity charges." These were levied on accounts with more than a specified number of withdrawals.[14]

In sum, the Society was less a savings society than a mortgage company making loans almost exclusively from its capital funds and bor-

[14] The Bank of America in Lagos imposed such charges when there were more than six withdrawals in a given month, besides a charge of seven shillings when the account was closed within three months.

rowings. In its role as a mortgage company, it had filled a gap in the economy, brought British funds into the country, and operated independently of the government and its pressures (CDC held the controlling voting shares). But failure to draw savings limited its effectiveness as an instrument for retarding inflationary movements as well as for encouraging more home building through mortgage lending. If most of its funds were derived from deposits drawing 4 per cent interest instead of from CDC's loans bearing 7½ per cent interest, it could also afford to lower its rates on borrowings below 8½ per cent.

A government guarantee of deposits would allay the fear of withdrawals, and this was recommended by the U.N. mission.[15] The mission also suggested a reduction by the government of income taxes, removal of the office to a more accessible location, and a better public relations program. Because of the fifteen-year mortgage term and the 8½ per cent interest rate charged by the Society, the carrying charges of homes were too costly for most low-income families. The U.N. mission therefore recommended that the Society make only a 50 per cent loan to some of these families and that the government take back a second mortgage at 3 per cent for twenty-five years. With the lower average interest rate and the longer mortgage period, families earning as little as £20 per month would be able to acquire homes.

ATTRACTING SAVINGS

To attract savings, something more than wishful thinking is needed. Safekeeping at interest is one of the classical inducements, but it is not enough to buck more enduring traditions.

Inducing people to save will entail more than hanging out a bank shingle. In addition to paying interest, the association must search for other devices that will challenge the established habits and stubborn folkways. A proved device is the lottery, which is used to raise general revenues, funds for hospitals, etc. If with every deposit the depositor received a chance to win a home, this might supply the incentive needed.

The lottery is a more respectable device than is generally believed. The distribution of the Promised Land among the Twelve Tribes of Israel involved a decision by drawn lot. As a source of national revenue, the lottery was introduced in England as far back as 1569 and continued in use until the 1920's. A lottery helped pay for the Virginia Company's colonial expedition, and lotteries were partly responsible for financing the establishment of Harvard, Columbia, Dartmouth, and Williams colleges in the United States. The abolition of lotteries in England and the

---

[15] Abrams, Kobe, Koenigsberger, Shapiro, and Wheeler, *Metropolitan Lagos, op. cit.*, pp. 156, 157.

United States was later inspired by corruption and counterfeiting of tickets.

Yet some governments employ or permit lotteries today (with ample justification) for hospitals, as in Ireland and Australia, and some conservative churches are not above using it to raise funds. In Colombia, the beneficiaries are not only hospitals but old people who are given housing. Lotteries have a long and uninterrupted history in Central and South America and in several European countries, while even England has adopted the lottery idea for recent public bond flotations. Banks have offered houses as prizes in Turkey, and the cost of the prize is recouped through a proportionate reduction in the interest rate on deposits.

While objections to lotteries exist (e.g., they may induce people to rely on luck more than labor), the argument against use of the lottery to draw savings is without much force. The benefits of savings are retained, and thrift rather than speculation is encouraged when the gamble is the inducement to thrift. In this context, it is less a lottery than the accepted and respected prize for participation.

Fear of inflation has frequently intimidated savers, but there are ways of reinspiring confidence by linking the value of savings to the cost-of-living index or to particular commodities such as cement. Such devices have been employed in Chile and Scandinavia. In Israel, a "Saving for Housing" project, initiated in 1955, encourages people to save for an apartment. To offset fear of a rise in building costs, the value of the depositor's funds is linked to the cost of an apartment in the year the deposit is made. If, upon being awarded an apartment, the cost of acquisition is higher than in the year the account is opened, a premium is paid, based upon the amount of the deposit. Interest (exempt from taxation) ranging from 4 per cent on deposits of three-year duration to 6 per cent for five-year deposits is paid meanwhile. Savers of IL3000 (about $1000) become eligible for an apartment and are chosen by lottery. A candidate who has failed to win in four consecutive draws is automatically entitled to an apartment in the fifth year. The apartment owner gets an IL5000 ten-year mortgage bearing an interest rate at 8 per cent which fluctuates with the cost-of-living index. Up to January 4, 1962, the project had attracted 55,503 savers with deposits of IL152,787,000, and some 20,000 apartments have been supplied. Parallel "Hemed" and "Shevah" schemes operate on somewhat modified terms and provide for mortgage loans up to IL6000, with the saver entitled to a new home after saving IL3000 within three years.

Other reasons for resistance to savings include the fear that the government may find out that a person with a bank account has dodged his taxes. This is an exaggerated fear for smaller savers, but it has nevertheless discouraged savings.

Still another deterrent to savings is the unnecessary impediments placed upon withdrawals. The Nigerian Postal Savings System, for example, allowed withdrawals of no more than £5 at a time, and getting one's money back may take as much as a week because of the need for identification and other complicated regulations.

Public relations devices should be part of the savings association's tool kit. Associations in the United States not only advertise in the press and on radio and television but also give casserole sets, clocks, and prizes of various sorts to initial depositors and employ many other techniques to lure savings. Barclay's Bank in Singapore gives every saver an accident policy carrying insurance equal to the amount of the deposit. There is no good reason for leaving the field exclusively to the installment salesmen, whose ingenious techniques for attracting idle money have proved magnetic.

MORTGAGE SOURCES IN UNDERDEVELOPED AREAS

The sources for mortgage funds in underdeveloped areas are wide in variety, but they are ineffectually used. The housing cooperative that has flourished in Europe and the cooperative that also accepts savings, like HSB (Hyresgästernas Sparkasse-och Byggnadsförening) in Sweden, have played a minor role in Asia, Africa, and South America. In England, Ireland, and elsewhere, government savings banks have done reasonably well in garnering savings, but postal savings in the United States fell below $600 million in 1962 because of the nominal interest rate and the competition of other savings institutions. Rarely are government savings funds anywhere put into mortgages.

The fact that a government mortgage fund exists does not always mean that it functions. In Pakistan the government-financed Home Building Finance Corporation in 1957 made loans up to 80 per cent of estimated house value at 5 per cent for individuals and at 4 per cent to cooperative housebuilding societies. Loans were for a maximum of fifteen years, and the ceiling was $8400. An applicant was required to show proof of adequate income, an approved plan of the house, an architect's estimate of cost, and proof of title. The intentions were good, but fewer than a thousand loans were made from 1952 to 1957. There were no loans at all to cooperative building societies and few to lower-income families, the average loan being about $4400 (21,000 rupees). One reason for the dearth of applications was red tape and delay. Another was the requirement for proof of valid title over a twenty-year period, which in Pakistan was difficult. Still another was that the repayment period was too short and payments were too heavy for many families.

In Ghana, at the time of the U.N. mission in 1954, mortgage lending under a Housing Loans Ordinance was experiencing similar difficulties.

Among the factors responsible were: the requirements of residence in the house by the applicant and a provision that no one was eligible who had had a previous loan (these restrictions virtually denied loans to contractors who built in volume); a requirement that an applicant must have title to the land or a lease for at least sixty years (the unmarketable titles in many parts of Ghana limited the number of qualifying applicants); a requirement that there had to be a contractor for every house (this limited lending to the very costly houses and all but eliminated homeowners who built their houses with their own hands or with the help of hired laborers). Added to these problems was the lack of experienced personnel, who in bewilderment exercised so much caution that few loans were approved.

The statement in the U.N. report is as relevant today for many countries as it was in 1954:

. . . the mere passage of a law does not mean it will work; a loan program must be so drawn as to reach the greatest pool of possible borrowers; experienced personnel is indispensable; restrictions might express the desire for safety but simultaneously be too unpractical to allow the program to function; the whole business of mortgage lending is a highly technical operation which calls for the best skills available in the business; the experience of one country in financing cannot be blindly copied by another and made to work.[16]

In the Philippines, mortgage programs were limited in volume and in the number of lower-income families they served. The Home Financing Commission, modeled on the FHA, was established in 1957 and undertook to insure loans up to 95 per cent of appraised value, charging a premium of 1 per cent for the insurance. Mortgage loans were for periods up to twenty-five years, and interest in 1957 was fixed at 5 to 6 per cent. To attract capital, interest received on the loans was exempted from taxation. Though a few institutions did take loans as an accommodation, most could see no advantage in making illiquid mortgages at 5 or 6 per cent when interest rates on commercial loans were 8 per cent or better.[17]

The Philippines had a number of other mortgage agencies of lesser importance,[18] but there was still a shortage of mortgage money, and as

[16] Abrams, Bodiansky, and Koenigsberger, *Report on Housing in the Gold Coast, op. cit.,* p. 28.

[17] Charles Abrams and Otto Koenigsberger, *Report on Housing in the Philippine Islands* (New York: United Nations, 1959), p. 51.

[18] These (in addition to the building and loan associations, commercial banks, and the pawnshops) included the Agricultural Credit and Cooperative Financing Administration, which made loans to small farmers and tenants. The Philippine National Bank (a government-financed agency authorized to make loans up to 60 per cent of appraised value at 6 to 8 per cent interest and usually for five-year periods)

elsewhere it was hard for the average worker to borrow the money with which to build his house. Interest rates were from 8 to 13 per cent and frequently twice that. Steady workers with good credit often bought land on the installment plan but never could borrow the money to build.[19]

Colombia has grappled with its problem more tenaciously.[20] Its Land Credit Institute, set up in 1939 with a capital of $518,000 (3.5 million pesos) to promote creation of territorial banks for rural housing aid, enlarged its activities in 1942 to include urban loans to cities and cooperatives. In 1961, the programs were directed mainly to financing self-help projects for those with monthly incomes of $52 (plus $12 for each dependent), mutual-aid projects for groups of twenty members with incomes of $52 to $104 monthly, and core housing. A 6 per cent tax on the net income of stock companies was levied in 1959, and the proceeds were earmarked for the Institute's purposes.

Another financing agency is Colombia's Banco Central Hipotecario, a mortgage bank financed by the government and by compulsory subscriptions of private banks. Loans are 65 per cent of cost; most loans have been made to contractors. Interest rates go up to 11 per cent for houses costing over $7400 and 10 per cent for others.

Because Colombia's mortgage system has solved only a small fraction of the housing problem, the city of Bogotá launched its own program in 1959 to help low-income groups. The city assigns 5 per cent of its annual income to the municipal housing agency (Caja de la Vivienda Popular), while the rest comes from borrowed funds.[21]

Almost everywhere, however, mortgage systems are underdeveloped. Funds are too small and down payments too large (up to 50 per cent of cost); mortgages are of short duration (less than fifteen and frequently five to ten years) and interest rates too high. Fear of inflation has also discouraged loans, particularly those for long terms.[22]

---

made a few loans. The insurance companies made some loans at rates up to 12 per cent interest, and one, the Philippine Life Insurance Company, built a housing project which it sold to higher-income policy holders on credit.

[19] As of March 1961, the collecting capacity of the Social Security System had reached 5 million pesos. (Address by Rudolfo P. Andal, Commissioner, Social Security System, March 11, 1961.)

[20] Pan American Union, *Housing Institutions in Bogotá* (Colombia, 1961).

[21] All municipalities with an annual budget of more than $148,000 must invest 5 per cent of their budget in housing—either in their own housing or in the Instituto de Crédito Territorial.

[22] "Mixed economy" companies such as the Crédit de l'Afrique Equitoriale Française, Crédit de Madagascar, and similar agencies have been created in French territories. They borrow from the Caisse Centrale and relend to individuals for home purchase. In the Belgian Congo, advances have been made to provinces for building loans to Africans. Japan's loan funds have been extensive, but little money has trickled down to the underprivileged worker.

THE FINANCING OF HOUSING FOR PUERTO RICO

An interesting example among the developing areas is Puerto Rico. Under the administration of Luis Muñoz Marin, the Commonwealth has made startling advances, with its net income rising from $225 million in 1940 to over $1465 million in 1961. While the island was making remarkable strides in industry, it put no damper on building. Thus the construction industry, while building a good deal of housing of poor standard, has also developed ingenious large-scale building programs with on-site fabrication, which have helped expand the value of new private dwellings from $29 million in 1951 to $82 million just ten years later. Puerto Rico is cited as a foremost example of progress in housing, but its case is special owing to its link with the United States, the benefits of tax exemption, mainland financing schemes, mainland builders, and unrestricted emigration to the United States, which helps to ease its population pressures.

Puerto Rico has had a serious housing problem, which has manifested itself in squatting, overcrowding, slums, and a scarcity of housing for lower- and moderate-income families. Industrial expansion pushed family income from $660 annually in 1940 to $2300 in 1956, intensifying the housing need of the new middle class. The United States housing program had proposed or provided more than 30,000 public housing units, which, though helpful, were not enough, nor were they the type of housing that most of the people wanted. Another objection was that the public housing projects provide no opportunity for ownership and impose income limits for eligibility.

Financing of homes was undertaken partly through savings and loan associations, whose assets had swelled with the rise in incomes, but mostly through FHA-insured mortgages made by island or mainland lending institutions. The beneficiaries under both were only those who could afford houses costing in 1963 over $9000.

Puerto Rico enjoys a number of advantages over other developing countries: (1) the large pool of skills, (2) the marketability on the mainland of tax-exempt bonds, (3) the mainland FHA mortgage insurance system, and (4) a tax exemption on houses worth less than $15,000.[23] If a program could be designed for ownership and if a good core-housing scheme were devised for lower-income families, many could enjoy the advantages of homeownership at prices they could afford.

The main problem is to finance such a program for those with incomes between $2000 and $4000. Puerto Rican tax-exempt bonds (as well as

[23] This was introduced under the pressure of the election campaign. For the good and bad aspects of such a measure as well as for a critique of current private building operations, see Charles Abrams, *Report to the College of Engineers, Architects and Surveyors on Resolution P-147* (mim., New York, April 5, 1962).

those of Puerto Rican cities) have sold on the New York market at rates comparable to those of mainland cities, i.e., approximately 3½ per cent. This is clearly an untapped source for low-cost mortgage credit.

Written assurance has been given by a large investment firm that it would lend up to $90 million for the program—provided that either a limited amount of tax proceeds be earmarked to guarantee payment of the interest or the Commonwealth of Puerto Rico guarantee the bonds or payments as they accrued. But there were legal problems due to archaic debt-limitation provisions in Puerto Rico's constitution. The Puerto Rican government revised the document, and by 1962 the legal obstacles no longer existed.

Tax-exempt housing bonds in the United States have won high rating in banking circles, and they have been issued under a variety of schemes. New York State in 1961 floated a $56 million issue under which the proceeds were re-lent at low interest to limited-dividend corporations or cooperatives that had been set up mostly by private builders. The bonds to finance the builders provide for a one-year reserve to cover interest and sinking-fund requirements on the bonds. While the state does not guarantee the bonds (they are issued on the credit of a special financing agency), it does guarantee that the annual reserve will remain intact and that it will make good any deficit in the reserve fund.

A similar formula could be used for Puerto Rico's new housing program. Mortgages taken back by Puerto Rico's housing agency would provide an interest and amortization rate sufficient to pay the charges on the bonds. A core-housing scheme (already begun) could reach some families earning even less than $2000. Thus a new way of further easing Puerto Rico's housing problem moved into focus.

Puerto Rican financing is, of course, a special case. But it demonstrates how a country with a good credit rating can raise housing capital in world markets. Sources of credit at low interest could be tapped for those countries that have demonstrated their competence, their solvency, and their political stability, particularly if there were proper international mechanisms to help guarantee or supply some of the capital.

✿   ✿   ✿

The intricacies of housing financing do not make easy bedtime reading. In the underdeveloped world, even the most elementary principles are not yet understood. Their refinement will take years, and the continued help of seasoned experts is a necessity. While international aid is essential as a pump primer and private foreign funds can be drawn upon, it is within the borders of each country that the bulk of the credits must be found. Savings, which must be the source of internal loans, can be expanded if, coupled with the inducements of interest and safekeeping, there is the prospect of getting a mortgage loan. The development of such savings is a task to which the World Bank and other international agencies have given little attention.

The development of savings for housing need not interfere with the development of savings for industrial expansion. A savings system (whether it is in the form of a savings and loan association or a government fund) can often be used to finance low-cost as well as other housing, if governments guarantee mortgage investments and if interest subsidies are developed under intelligent formulas. While some general theories are relevant in financing, they must be adapted in each country to its own circumstances, to the indigenous traditions, and to overcoming the obstacles that such traditions impose. Not only is technical advice needed in the underdeveloped areas, but there is also room for ingenuity in the development of international devices that can help break the housing blockade in the underdeveloped world.

12

Self-Help, Core Housing, and Installment Construction

THE TECHNOLOGICAL LAG

For most of the world's people, there have been no major changes in housebuilding since Neolithic man produced his first flint ax. His lake dwelling, 750 square feet in area, with a fireplace, porch, pitched roof, and walls plastered with clay, was owner-built, and was in many ways superior to most houses of contemporary urban man.[1] In fact, occupied caves near Rawalpindi, Pakistan, the handiwork of nature, are better shelters than most squatters' makeshifts in Manila, Algeria, Venezuela, or Hong Kong; their roofs, though massive, are weatherproof, while their egress to the open fields is a happy contrast to many a dungeonlike tenement. In cities of Latin America or Africa and in the rural backlands elsewhere, man still makes bricks in the same way from mud, compresses them by foot in the same kind of wooden molds, dries them in the same sun, and puts them together by hand to form the same type of shelter as in the Stone Age.

In southwestern Anatolia, near Burdur, recent excavations disclosed a Sumerian settlement harking back to 5600–5400 B.C. At the Stone Age level, the occupants had built houses of mud brick with floors laid on a pebble base, covered with lime plaster, and painted in various shades of burnished red. The courtyards were paved with green and yellow painted plaster; the ovens and hearths were not unlike those used today. In the later layers of the Neolithic period, houses had windows, large wall cup-

[1] For photographs of a Neolithic house and a comparison with a present-day house in Pakistan, see Figures 25A and 25B.

Figure 17. Housing is more than houses. Homes are often the small production centers for the tailor, dressmaker, or shopkeeper. The picture shows a house and shop in San Salvador. (See page 109.)

Figure 18. Reoccupied shops on the Lagos slum site. The shops are also used as sleeping quarters. (See page 120.)

Figure 19. A new housing project in Morocco with a squatter settlement the background. (*Courtesy of Photographie Aérienne Verbelke.*)

Figure 20. Four-family houses built for low-income families by the Barbad Government. Each apartment consists of a living room, two bedrooms, and kitchen, with running water and sanitary facilities. With a 37 per cent subsid an apartment rents for $2.00 a week. The problem in these houses was m defaults. (See page 69.)

Figure 21. A typical scene in Africa, the common water tap.

Figure 22. A street in Accra, Ghana, showing the contrast between old and new.

Figure 23. Rent-controlled shop houses in Singapore. (See page 131.)

Figure 24. A new town in Upper Nazareth, Israel, with water tank and n● buildings in the foreground. (See page 138.)

Figure 25A. A model of a lake dwelling in the Neolithic period, 700-900 square feet, with a plastered porch and clay walls. (*Courtesy of the American Museum of Natural History.*) (See page 164.)

Figure 25B. A comparable house in Pakistan today. How much have we advanced?

Figure 26A. Native housing in Kano, Nigeria.

Figure 26B. A typical house in the Ashanti region, Ghana, built without bene-fit of an architect.

Figures 27A and 27B. Building wattle and daub houses in Morocco. (Courtesy of Laboratoire Photographique du Service de l'Urbanisme du Maroc.)

Figure 28.   A squatter settlement on a tidal swamp in Puerto Rico.   (*Courte͏* *of the Government of Puerto Rico*.)

Figure 29.   Unloading goods in Ghana.   Prefabricated panels were unload͏ similarly before the building of the pier.   (See page 166.)

boards or niches, plastered bins and platforms used for grinding cereals or grains, and refuse pits. The Neolithic houses were similar to those presently occupied in the nearby village of Hakilar.[2]

That housebuilding and shelter standards have not changed substantially since the dawn of civilization is not proof of man's stagnation. Left to his own devices, he can learn to build his shelter, as indeed he still does in the world's rural areas. Nor are his minimum housing needs much different from what they were a thousand years ago.

The industrializing city has complicated man's efforts to obtain the shelter that he was once able to build with his own hands. Disposal of wastes becomes an almost insuperable health problem for the poorer countries. The long trek to and from the job and the dependence on the market for land and materials and on community organization for vital services have altered the simple patterns of life in village and field. A new form of social organization is needed if man is to survive and function. The requirements of health and sanitation and the menaces of overcrowding and squatting are demanding not only the strong intervention of political processes but the knowledge, which has not even been formulated, of specially trained people.

PREFABRICATION

When government proved unable to meet the problem of building the millions of new houses needed, it was not surprising that officials looked at once to technology in the more advanced nations for the answer. The gilded age of mass production that had produced the TV set and the airplane would, it seemed, certainly have the answer to the shelter problem. It was considered impossible that housing would be the perverse exception.

One of the more alluring devices of the immediate postwar period was therefore the prefabricated house. The war had given the prefab a fillip when the United States government poured tens of millions of dollars into subsidizing the industry. The venture ended as a fiasco. One company experimenting with a single prototype, the "Lustron House," had been able to draw more than $40 million from the national treasury, with not a row of Lustrons ever rising to adorn an American suburb. Prefabs of another variety produced in the United States during the war and shipped to England tarnished the luster of American industry's escutcheon almost as much as the B-29's brightened it. But no real evaluation of prefabrication trickled across the seas to alert the officials of the underdeveloped areas.

Indeed, India, Ghana, and even more advanced Israel acquired a faith in prefabrication that was beyond argument. Wood, aluminum, and pre-

[2] *New York Times,* February 12, 1961, p. 25.

cast concrete prefabs began to crop up near city centers. Most often they looked out of place and were expensively priced, but disillusionment could not dispel the official confidence in technology.

In Ghana, a firm of consultants, who charged $210,000 for their guidance, told the government in 1952 that their own prefabricated product would help resolve Ghana's housing enigma. Soon precast concrete walls poured in Europe were hauled across the seas to Accra's promontory, lowered to rocking canoes, and paddled precariously by intrepid natives past pitching breakers to the distant shore; then they were laboriously transported and set up, miles away, to compose a few lonely exhibits. The company contracted to build 168 model houses at Accra, Kumasi, and Takoradi, and set up three factories in Ghana to manufacture its product. But when the cost of sixty-four completed houses ran up to $448,000 and had been translated into the number of cocoa beans needed for payment, the government, on the advice of a United Nations mission, quietly gave up the venture. As the U.N. report put it,

> The Company thus acquired a double role: as authors of the . . . report they were consultants and trusted advisors to the Government, and as producers of the sample houses they became suppliers of the very commodity on the suitability of which they were to advise.[3]

In more advanced Israel a gigantic Le Tourneau-layer crane appeared in Beersheba on the hot sands of the Negev desert. After quaffing and crunching tons of cement and stone and water and pouring the compost from a huge iron maw into a floor-shaped mold, the crane carried the hardened slab to the site of the cement house. The quiet little Bedouin trading post where Elijah once sought refuge from Jezebel's vengeance continued to resound with its clatter until the imperfections of its product and the cost of its performance brought a sober reversion to slower but surer handicraft.

In Karachi, Pakistan, small aluminum prefabs were soon added to with adobe, discarded wood, or other makeshifts, composing the first prefabricated slums. Private companies supplying prefabs to their workers fared little better than government. When the Standard Oil Company procured some European-style prefabs for its distant oil centers, local workers refused to occupy them. The workers wanted houses built according to local design, though they were of lower quality than the prefabs.[4]

[3] For the full U.N. report, see Charles Abrams, Vladimir Bodiansky, and Otto Koenigsberger, *Report on Housing in the Gold Coast* (New York: United Nations, 1956), Appendix M.

[4] Burnham Kelly, ed., *Housing and Economic Development,* the Report of a Conference Sponsored at the Massachusetts Institute of Technology by the Albert

It is only fair to say that officials who yielded to the magnetic qualities of prefabrication were not entirely to blame. Aluminum manufacturers in the United States and Canada, looking for new outlets for their merchandise, were hawking the virtues of aluminum prefabs as the solution to the world's housing shortage in the underdeveloped as well as the developed countries.[5] They were peddling a final answer long before they had perfected the product or established low or competitive costs. Home magazines were displaying the examples of twentieth-century genius in multicolored photographs; Madison Avenue in New York and its equivalent in Scandinavia were ballyhooing the universal validity of the prefab.[6] Packaged houses were also appearing in oil fields, where, because speed counted more than cost, they sometimes made sense. But there was little disposition by government officials to check comparative costs—what was good for oil seemed good for all.

It must be remembered too that in the developed countries, prefabrication was being viewed even by experts as an infant prodigy with a big future—which indeed it should ultimately enjoy. But it was not broadcast that in the postwar period the infant had proved to be a troublesome, delinquent dwarf, lacking the extraordinary qualities of the precocious child. Though the prefab industry has recently made marked gains in quantity and quality, prefabs are still not cheaper than traditional houses even in mechanized America.

"Prefabrication" is a term with many connotations, and products have been precast ever since brick was baked for the tower of Babel. A house is only a composite of numerous items prepared on the site or elsewhere, none of which exceeds 30 per cent of total cost.[7] In some areas, timber, precast concrete, or asbestos cement walls have long been locally prefabricated, as distinct from a wholly manufactured package delivered to the site.

Farwell Bemis Foundation on April 30 and May 1 and 2, 1953 (Cambridge, January 1955), K. H. Quick, "Housing Experience of the Standard Oil Company," p. 102.

[5] See Dwight Macdonald, *The Ford Foundation* (New York: Reynal, 1956), pp. 91–93, for an interesting experience of the writer regarding the techniques of prefabrication and modern public relations.

[6] The postwar difficulties included one or more of the following: inability to finance mass orders, absence of distribution outlets, high production and sales costs, inadequacy of research, public squeamishness about prefabricated products, obstructive building codes, labor troubles, peculiarities of individual terrains, and high freight rates. Furthermore, the price of the prefab does not include site, site improvement, and other charges that cannot be prefabricated but represent a large proportion of total house cost.

[7] The percentages, of course, will vary with countries, standards, climates, shipping costs, etc. See for example, Charles Abrams and Otto Koenigsberger, *Report on Housing in Pakistan* (New York: United Nations, 1957), p. 94.

There is a future for on-site prefabrication and quantity on-site production as well as for prefabricated parts. Efficient mass-produced walls, roofs, pipelines, doors, and windows will help reduce the cost, and economic prefabrication of a cheap shell will save money, too. In the more developed countries, apartment houses are made of precast sections. In Jamaica, a combine of Jamaican entrepreneurs and a Puerto Rican building firm in 1961 put up a thousand houses of concrete precast on the site, claiming a saving of 15 per cent in labor cost per house. A two-bedroom house of 760 square feet sold for $5530 and a three-bedroom house of 860 square feet for $6400.

Though experimentation should go on, especially in on-site prefabrication and in the prefabrication of parts and of core houses, most areas[8] will have to rely on handicraft for some time to come, and use of local labor and materials is still more economical for most developing countries. The campaign to sell the exported prefab as the proved product of the industrial age has been stayed for the present, but its energetic salesmen are far from discouraged. In fact, one can still see these agents of industrial enterprise in Nigeria, Latin America, and elsewhere, waiting for home-hungry buyers to nibble.

REVERSION TO SELF-HELP

After disillusionment with technology had set in, it was not unnatural that officials would try the other extreme—to encourage the homeless to provide for themselves as they had done when man first moved out of the cave. If man's skills were employed and some materials were supplied to him, he might be induced to build as he once did (and indeed as he was still doing wherever industrial progress had not encumbered him). The formula seemed logical. By shifting the onus from technology back to the individual, there would be hope for a cheap solution.

As in the case of prefabrication, however, a good deal of wishful thinking accompanied the self-help formula. Soon it was viewed as a panacea for the housing problem of the industrializing nations. By the mid-1950's, movies were recording its miracles. In a number of programs, Neolithic techniques were "updated" to include tutorial instruction, and the most modern cost-accounting methods kept track of hours spent and materials used. Speed of block production was increased in pilot areas by more modern hand tools to achieve self-help mass production. Sometimes the program was marked by a missionary element (i.e., "God

---

[8] "Most areas" is used advisedly. It is entirely possible, for example, that a prefabricated aluminum house may be made in Jamaica and sold at low cost. The company, by operating its main plant in Kingston, could sell the houses cheaply there while using Kingston as a base for export to South America.

helps all those who help themselves"), which became partly responsible for the faith and zeal associated with the expensive programs.

THE NATURE OF SELF-HELP AND AIDED SELF-HELP

Despite the advance of technology, owner-built housing—the earliest form of construction—is still the most common in the world today. Mutual aid in building is not novel either. In the older communities friends, tribesmen, clansmen, and neighbors have long cooperated in the placing of walls or beams.[9]

The official self-help programs simply tried to incorporate as policy what already existed, but the aim was to adapt the formula to urban environments. In the cities, however, a money economy exists; a specialized laborer can be hired for the work and can do it better. The factory worker lacks the time and energy to build, and there is no seasonal interim when he can accelerate his efforts. Nor is the cooperation of neighbors and family, of clan or tribe, available for mutual aid. In short, while self-help and mutual aid still function in most parts of the world, carrying it over into an industrialized environment and speeding its processes by organization is a different and more difficult task.

The nature of the public assistance and the degree of self-help effort vary with each area. In villages or small towns where the self-help tradition is strong, the government may supplement the independent self-help building of the farmer with projects for the self-help improvement of roads, sanitation, water, markets, schools, or squares. In some places, self-help spurs erosion control or rearrangement of houses when a service road is cut through.[10] Government may also supply the worker with the particular parts of the house that are difficult for him to obtain.

In the cities, loans have been made for materials and purchase of sites, workers have been supervised and trained, and block-making machines have been provided.[11] In still other cases forms for walls or preassembled

[9] In Japan, "self-help construction of dwellings in the farm areas is decreasing as a result of the increased use of money in the farm economy. Today with more and more houses being built under contract, the need for labor furnished by the farmer and his family is rapidly disappearing, while mutual aid labor is being dispensed with because of the high cost of entertainment." Ryoichi Ura and Chihoko Shimokobe in *General Report on Self-Help and Mutual Aid Housing*, World Planning and Housing Congress, May 28–June 3, 1960 (San Juan, 1960), p. 2.

[10] What the public authority thinks is a better arrangement is not always what the villagers think. In a Turkish village, when a road was cut through and the villagers were made to push back their houses from the roads in the interests of safety, it was not long before the villagers moved their houses right back to the roadside.

[11] In Bogotá, block making by the much vaunted Cinva-ram machine was found too tedious. The machine is now used mainly in the rural areas.

roofs have been supplied. Sometimes self-help has been limited to a few simple tasks, with the plumbing, wiring, and masonry assigned to paid skilled workers.

ORGANIZED SELF-HELP OR MUTUAL-AID PROJECTS

In urban housing projects, the more self-help required of the occupant, the greater must be the inducements, supervision, and administrative costs. The more trained craftsmen placed on the job, the more efficient the operation. When construction standards are simple, fewer skilled craftsmen are required.

In organized mutual-aid projects, the workers are taught certain jobs, and they move from house to house. The workers are usually not told which house they will own so they will not skimp or loaf on other houses and take special care with their own.

The United States has had a few organized urban self-help projects. From 1955 to 1960, Flanner House, a settlement house in Indianapolis, sponsored an undertaking by Negroes, who built 237 very good houses under inspired leadership. With the aid of grants, cheap land, a workshop for precutting, and intensive training under seven experienced craftsmen and four organizers, savings were about $2000 on each $10,000 house built. Construction of the first house took some 5600 hours of the prospective owner's time. After backbreaking experiences and frustrations, the contributed time per owner was reduced to twenty hours a week for sixty weeks. Even with expert supervision, the sponsor found it necessary to let out a number of the contracts. Although there was no long line of candidates for the self-help housing in 1961, it cannot be denied that there were values derived for those who participated —the nourishment of a cooperative spirit, the training of men[12] (a few of whom might enter the building trades or repair their own houses), and the emotional satisfaction of having worked on one's own house.

Complete reliance on self-help in cities is apt to bring disillusionment, and failure has occurred even where outside aid was given. An experiment in Pakistan in which an American religious group tried to demonstrate how to build ended up with the teachers doing virtually all the work. In a pilot project in San Juan, prospective occupants were required to spend weekends and one extra day each week in building their houses. A bartender-builder told me he would just as soon have paid a laborer for the day's work, since he had lost a day's pay.[13]

[12] Self-help projects have been responsible for augmenting the number of carpenters and masons in British Honduras. See H. C. Fairweather in *General Report on Self-Help and Mutual Aid Housing, op. cit.*, p. 11.

[13] After a review of Puerto Rico's urban self-help housing efforts, I concluded that like other pilot schemes, self-help is a valuable demonstration, but one must consider

Often the added task leads to the practice of moonlighting, in which the worker doing two jobs does neither job well. He comes in tired when his regular job begins, worries about whether the rains are enfeebling his foundations, and makes frantic telephone calls to his wife when he should be cleaning the empty glasses at the bar.[14]

Because Puerto Rico's demonstration programs are widely publicized and sometimes adopted by other countries before they have been proved, the Puerto Rican Planning Board's recital of problems in its organized self-help programs is informative:

1. Too long a time is required to build self-help houses. (An average of six months to construct about twenty houses.)

2. To construct the dwellings under a cooperative arrangement with small groups that consist of fifteen or twenty families is difficult owing to the delicate job of orientation.

3. An organization of engineers, inspectors, and administrative personnel is required in the agency to administer the program.

4. The cost of these dwellings, especially in the rural areas ($350), does not reflect the true costs, since this figure ignores the cost of the parcel in the rural community, the salaries of the technical and administrative personnel, and the cost of future improvements to be made in the rural communities to fulfill the government philosophy of providing essential services.

5. The need of acquiring and operating costly construction equipment is another obstacle.

6. Construction by the families is imperfect because of the lack of experience.

---

the difficulties of securing the day off, the over-all costs of the undertaking if administrative costs are added, and the feasibility of the device for expansion into a definitive program. I recommended the development of a core-housing scheme, planned and designed so that the owners can improve core houses to their own taste or preference. Carlos Alvarado, director of Puerto Rico's Housing and Redevelopment Agency, told me in April 1962 that 1000 houses had been built or were under way and that the scheme was working well.

[14] Grenfell Ruddeck of Australia confirms this. "If . . . the self-helper works night and day on his dream house, he ends up by helping himself from the boss's time. He is distracted for months, tired on Mondays, in a hurry to leave on Friday, and all the week making liberal use of the office phone to check on his suppliers. His employer is not likely, during this period, to see him in the best light for a raise." Grenfell Ruddeck in *General Report on Self-Help and Mutual Aid Housing, op. cit.,* p. 7.

7. No great economies or efficiency in construction is obtained since the modern techniques of mass production are not used.[15]

Houses built with substantial or partial self-help have nevertheless proved practical in some of Puerto Rico's rural areas. It is claimed that an average of 3000 houses are built annually. Small houses, 18 by 18 feet, are built of reinforced concrete with one large room designed to be divided into a living-dining room and two bedrooms. Communities of thirty families join in the work, and a trained foreman supervises it.

Self-help and mutual-aid operations have experienced both success and failure. They have succeeded among those with a common aim or drive and when some in the group possess skill and ability. Although self-help may fail for want of inspiring leadership, it has often succeeded with it. In a town in Ghana, a young former post office clerk, newly elected to a chieftaincy, was able to inspire his people to build a community center that, if done under contract, would have cost a small fortune. Self-help operations have a better chance where the financing inducements or subsidies are compelling and where self-helpers have the time and can reap rewards commensurate with their efforts.

Ownership is almost always a precondition to successful self-help operations anywhere. Unsightly slums have frequently resulted from schemes in which the occupant was to be only a tenant. The degree of cooperation will rise with ownership and decline with tenancy—the occupant will put in more work on his own home.

Success is claimed for self-help operations in Trinidad and in Chile and Guatemala, where the Agency for International Development has sponsored several extensively supervised projects. Prospective owners precast blocks, walls, or roofs, but they hired skilled labor for the electrical, plumbing, and masonry work. Self-help projects have failed in Barbados and Costa Rica.

In Bogotá, Colombia, where Cinva (the Pan-American Housing Center) makes the city the center for Latin-American expertise in housing, various experiments have been tested. They include partial self-help projects and mutual-aid undertakings. In mutual aid, workers are carefully selected on the basis of a point system. A class of fifty is indoctrinated by an architect and a social worker at four weekly meetings. At each meeting a film prepared by the United States Information Agency is shown. During the training period, the social worker interviews each family head so that his qualifications can be assessed before a lot is deeded. In selecting applicants, the agency chooses a skilled worker in each building trade. Since the terms are attractive, the agency has little

---

[15] Puerto Rico Planning Board, *A Proposal for a Low Cost Housing Program* (Commonwealth of Puerto Rico, Santurce, Puerto Rico, undated but probably 1958), p. 9.

difficulty in finding applicants. Unlike experiments in other countries, each worker knows the plot and house he will own.

Simultaneously, so-called self-help projects in Bogotá have been undertaken for families with monthly incomes up to $44 (plus $10 for each allowable dependent). In one type, the Instituto de Crédito Territorial buys the land and improves it with private sanitary facilities and water supply for each lot; in another type, there are communal washrooms and baths, but private toilets are provided. In either case, the family buys the lot, agreeing to complete the house within a specified time. The Institute not only supervises the operation but makes loans for building materials up to $437. The land, sold to the prospective occupant for $175 to $187, is paid for in installments concurrently with those on the materials loan. The house is designed by the owner himself, though the Institute provides six optional plans.

General inquiries in Bogotá yield several conclusions. The mutual-aid program has proved costly and cumbersome and will probably be abandoned. The self-help projects, however, are working, though usually they are land and utility undertakings in which the worker is sold a plot with utilities and then left to his own devices. With the financial aid, he finds it attractive to get a piece of land, and with the loan for materials he is able to hire skills to complete the house. It may, in short, not be self-help at all. My investigation disclosed skilled hired workers laying floors, building exteriors, and doing other work for the occupant on contract. Where the worker was specially skilled himself, he contributed his own labor. In general, however, the worker finds it better to earn his pay at his job and hire the necessary craftsmen for most or all of the work.

POTENTIALS AND LIMITATIONS OF SELF-HELP AND MUTUAL-AID PROJECTS

Because of the excessive claims made for self-help and mutual aid, an impartial assessment of the programs seems essential. My conclusions, based on the projects I have seen in the more and the less developed countries, are as follows:

1. The success or failure of self-help and mutual-aid projects depends largely upon conditions in each area. The more rural the environment, the more likely it is that self-help is already functioning and will continue, since it is part of the contest for survival. Aid in materials and land buying will speed the process of building.

2. In areas favorable to self-help, it should also be possible to stimulate the building of roads and schools, the digging of wells, and the provision of communal facilities if the government helps with equipment, facilities, guidance, and money.

3. While organized and aided self-help can be undertaken in urban sections of the underdeveloped areas, it can play only a limited role in the rehousing of populations. Self-help works best in small communities because such building traditions still prevail, life is less turbulent, relations are more intimate, land for the house is not scarce, and urban problems are minimal.

4. Since craftsmen can build all or a substantial part of their own houses, there will always be room for such craftsman-built houses in cities as elsewhere. Some form of financial aid will help stimulate building.

5. Reliance on industrial workers to learn building crafts and to find time and energy for building generally will prove disappointing. The forty-hour week is still a long way off in many places. Selection of those with common objectives and free time is essential, but this tends to make each project a special case, and such benefits fail to accrue to the bulk of the working population.

6. Despite their limitations in industrialized areas, partial self-help and mutual-aid projects are not devoid of values. Self-help trains men to build, and some indeed enter the construction trades as a result of learning. Where idleness exists, it is a good device for consuming free time (on sugar plantations, for example, where employment may be only four or five months of the year). Self-help and mutual-aid techniques might show more promise with greater prefabrication of essential parts.

7. Reliance on self-help is misplaced when it is offered as the solution for the housing problem of cities. It may consume time and money that could have been spent more usefully elsewhere. Though claims of savings have ranged from 20 to 25 per cent, the offsets (losses of time and efficiency from the main job, loss of supplemental earnings, initial cost of plant, supervisory and administrative costs, deficiency in the product, etc.) are not always fully calculated.

8. Where the aim is not primarily the training of workers, it is preferable for the government to lay out and provide plots and utilities and let each owner decide whether to use his own skills or hire others for all, most, or part of the work.

INSTALLMENT CONSTRUCTION

When mortgage financing is unavailable and housebuilding is dependent wholly or partly on a money economy, many in the less developed areas build their houses serially. After the family has bought a piece of land, it waits until it can afford to buy some building blocks. At that time the family may either put up the wall with the help of its members or hire a professional worker or a handyman. The family then may wait until it accumulates enough money for the roof, doors, and windows or can borrow it from friends or moneylenders. The interval between the building stages is usually long, and sometimes years pass before the family is in a position to pay for the land and for enough building blocks to go ahead.

The roof is usually the costly item that keeps the family from completing the structure. In the villages of Araromi and Ajegunle in Nigeria, 514 of a total of 3070 houses counted by the U.N. mission were roofless. The situation is similar in Bolivia, Ghana, and other countries.

Installment building is not a new concept. In the United States, frontier families often dug cellars which they roofed over temporarily and inhabited until they could build above ground. (Occasionally, small church congregations still do the same thing.) Simple shelters have been built in all parts of the world and then expanded room by room or floor by floor until the house met the family's ultimate needs. Squatters have also put up rude shells and later extended them.

Installment building is the only way many families without savings can get their houses built. It may seem more practical to deposit the savings until there is enough to pay for the house, but savings systems are not always developed or convenient. In any event, it may seem more reassuring to see one's savings in the form of bricks. Brick saving is nevertheless a tedious process, tying up family capital and often ending in frustration.

The installment builder needs financing to help him complete his building, and often a small loan will be sufficient. But not enough attention has been paid to this aspect of the housing problem.

STANDARDS FOR CORE HOUSING

Core housing is a major variant of the self-help technique. Introduced into the underdeveloped areas by United Nations missions,[16] it has now become part of the housing vocabulary. It aims to provide an organized, cheap, and practical scheme for the urban and urbanizing areas of poorer countries. Since the U.N. missions, the idea has spread and is on its way to becoming an important building device in the less developed areas.

One of the shortcomings of the self-help operation is that the worker

---

[16] See Abrams, Bodiansky, and Koenigsberger, *Report on Housing in the Gold Coast, op. cit.;* Abrams and Koenigsberger, *Report on Housing in Pakistan, op. cit.;* Abrams and Koenigsberger, *Report on Housing in the Philippine Islands* (New York: United Nations, 1959); and Abrams, *Report to the College of Engineers, Architects and Surveyors on Resolution P-147* (mim., New York, April 5, 1962).

has no place to live while he builds his house. Frequently he has already spent his funds and efforts on a squatter's hut, or he lives miles from the site of the house he is building. The core-house scheme rests on the premise that a family, with little additional work, can move into the core right away and thereafter expand the house as time and funds allow. In this respect, it is a variant of installment building and an important accessory for the installment builder.

One advantage of core housing is that it can be mass-produced on the site at a considerable saving. It entails no extensive supervision. It requires a tract of land and the essential utilities, after which the cores can be erected in one mass operation.

The core house should conform to the following principles:

1. The house should be a livable minimum unit which provides a good pattern for later extensions. Where larger families are the rule, the core house should, if possible, have not less than two rooms at the start.

2. Construction should not depend on self-help exclusively or even mainly. Some workers skilled in building should be selected as occupants in the area where the cores are built. They can be hired by other owners, and their own improvements will often provide the inspiration and prototype for the extensions.

3. Homeownership or hire purchase should be a prerequisite in any project, since ownership will stimulate investment of funds and labor toward expanding the core. Loans should be advanced in installments to finance both the core and its additions. The loans may be made to individuals or preferably to villages, clans, tribes, or cooperative units for relending to their people. The loan to a group ensures more responsibility and supervision and a better chance of repayment.[17]

4. Training in housebuilding should be concentrated on those who can devote their new skills to continued building. The core-house principle need not depend on training the owner for building. He can do the work himself or hire another.

5. The lot should be sufficient to permit expansion according to one of a series of alternative plans. One or several houses with completed extensions should be built as models. The core house need not be freestanding but may be attached if land or utilities are costly. In these cases, the houses should allow for additions at the front, rear, side, or top.

6. Local industries should be developed to provide materials for completing the cores. These may include clay, tile, lime, or other industries. If such industries already exist locally, they should be encouraged and

[17] This was the scheme adopted in Ghana. See Chapter 13.

aided to extend their operations. Reliance on imports should be minimal; when imports are required, mass purchases should be made to save money.

7. Materials used for the core should also lend themselves to house expansion. The interiors should be planned so that improved facilities can be supplied without breakage or difficulty. Aluminum or concrete cores would be inadvisable if expansion in wood is likely, nor would a wood core serve if a cement-block extension is contemplated.[18]

8. In tropical climates, the rooms in the house should have openings on two sides for through ventilation; the windowsills should be low and openings large enough for a good breeze; the roofs should be built to exclude heat. Common walls should be fire-retardant. Although electricity is not always immediately necessary, the core houses must have access to good water and sanitary facilities at the outset.

VARIETIES OF THE CORE

No single type of core can be uniformly applied to all countries and all climates. Each country, and in fact each region, may call for a particular design. These include: the one-room core for small families in very poor countries; the two-room core to be expanded horizontally for the growing family; the core that can be added to vertically; the row-house core, the front and rear of which is expandable; and the core built as part of a compound. There are also the core composed of a room that can be subdivided and the core in warm climates composed of a roof, supports, and a floor to be walled in by the occupant.

Ghana has used the core house to facilitate resettlement. George Nez, Chief of the U.N. Regional Planning Mission there, wrote me on December 6, 1962, as follows:

Remembering your success with the roof loan scheme [see Chapter 13], we probed the problem of rapid and cheap resettlement housing for the Volta Lake relocation (two years, 70,000 people) and designed a "nuclear house" with concrete strip foundation, stout framing, roof and one room walled in, which can be fast-produced with unskilled labor at a cost the Volta River Authority can afford, leaving the finishing to self-help labor of occupants. Out of desperation, this scheme is beginning to work all-right.

[18] A virtually indigenous core has developed in Barbados, where the timber house is placed on rented land and must be mobile in case the landlord makes harsh demands. Local industry has developed a small two-room worker's house to which the owner may add a prefabricated shed. Hence the house is both a core and a demountable. See Charles Abrams, *Report to the Barbados Government and the Barbados Housing Authority* (mim., New York, May 5, 1963).

Row and attached houses cut down on utility costs. On the other hand, where bore-hole latrines are provided, land space should be liberal enough to prevent pollution of the water supply.

A core can be prefabricated, but the material should be locally available for extensions. Core prefabrication and core design are frontiers for research, but by 1964, research had hardly begun.[19]

Local building techniques, including those displayed in squatter colonies, will suggest the type of core most suitable. The squatting colony in fact can be an important source of information on the available local skills and techniques. Houses built as complete units are often improved by an extra bedroom, kitchen, workroom, or a place for the livestock. In Japan, where wooden buildings are traditional, owners remove the wooden roofs of one-story buildings to add a second story. Vertical expansions have been proposed for the Delhi area in India. In Puerto Rico, where building block is commonly used, horizontal expansion or both horizontal and vertical expansion would work. Cores being built in various areas include not only the roof, roof supports, and floor but the large one-room subdividable core.

APPLYING THE CORE-HOUSING SCHEME

No single scheme or device works everywhere or the same way everywhere, and this includes core housing. The core house is no substitute for high-rise buildings in dense areas. Its greater use is linked to the development of transportation and the opening-up of land areas on the outskirts of cities. It faces obstacles where land costs are inordinately high. In the Philippine barrios, for example, where the cost of shelter has a wide range, a small house made of local materials and put together with the help of friends may cost $150, while a house in Manila built privately would run to $4000 or more. In other parts of the country, where land is not dear, core housing is practical. The Department of Household Statistics reports that the urban family in the Philippines spent 17.9 per cent of its income on shelter and utilities in 1958. A low-income family anxious to own a house could, by restricting other expenditures, spend 20 per cent of its earnings on housing. For the family earning the legal minimum wage, this would mean $10 a month. Since a finished house at $10 a month would be too small for most Filipino families, the erection of a core shelter is the practical alternative. Development of transportational access to work is, of course, imperative. Experience in the Philippines and in many other countries shows that even families in the lowest-

[19] In the United States, the mobile housing industry has made marked technical advances in the design of movable structures and might offer a laboratory for core prefabrication.

income group manage to improve and enlarge their homes as the years go by, if they have a stake in doing so.[20]

It is significant that Colombia, which prior to 1959 built complete houses, has modified its program in favor of core housing. Up to 1961 the country had built 1254 houses in Sosiego, La Fragua, and El Tejar. The land is purchased at thirty to fifty-five cents a square yard, and the contract for building the cores is assigned to a private contractor. The buyer makes a down payment of 20 per cent and pays the balance in monthly installments scaled to his income.

Unless a house is planned as a core from the beginning, a core-housing project may deteriorate into a slum. Hence the layouts and placement of the houses must be planned for expansion and provision made for common grounds, tree planting, and play spaces. Loan funds must be available for interior improvement and extension, and competent officials should be on hand to give encouragement.

It is important to measure the cost of the core and of the house as ultimately completed. There is no point in building cores where only a small further outlay would have built the addition as well. This may be the case in the more developed areas where plumbing and kitchens account for a high proportion of cost. Furthermore, the core should be simple, with no extravagant interior trappings. They can be added later by the owner.

When sound principles of core construction are violated, the results will be painful if not ludicrous. In Quezon City, the Agency for International Development financed a core composed of four toilets back to back. The Agency promised only rental of the core and expected each tenant to build a house around his toilet. The unique core with no ownership as an inducement was not enough to inspire Manila's squatter families to invest their time and effort to add to the land and toilets offered them. The project, which came to be known as "Flushing Heights," extinguished AID's interest in Philippine housing.

The relationship between the quality of the completed house and the type of tenure is significant. In Puerto Rico, complete houses built to FHA specifications were after six months improved by the owners and augmented by costly extensions that made the original house pattern no longer recognizable.[21] Some of the work was done by the owners, some by

[20] Abrams and Koenigsberger, *Report on Housing in the Philippine Islands, op. cit.*, p. 67.

[21] In a discussion with Puerto Rican officials on the construction of core housing for self-help and public housing programs, estimates in 1957 for such a core came to about $2500, which in Puerto Rico was cheap compared with public housing costs, which ran to $9000 a unit. Many Puerto Rican families are adept at putting up their own walls, and FHA houses built for them have been measurably improved either through their own or hired labor even though houses with FHA standards are not planned for expandability.

hired workers. In Pakistan, those who were living on land left by evacuees and who were more certain of being given its ownership built good houses, while squatters on government land, expecting displacement, erected makeshifts. On land rented for short terms in other parts of the world, houses are most often primitive huts which the occupants make no move to improve or expand.

Care must be exercised in selecting applicants. Temporary residents and transients are not likely to invest in additions. Where the house is too far from work, the occupant will hesitate to make improvements. Jobs and security of job status are factors in all housing undertakings, and core housing is no exception. Since people with common interests are more apt to cohere into a community and help one another, the aim of a sound community interest should be kept always in mind.

Since individual ownership of the land encourages improvements, ownership arrangements must be carefully weighed. Should the owner, for example, be permitted to sell only to an approved person? Where there is danger of speculative resales of the aided housing, sales should be subject to a public agency's consent or should require that the agency have first refusal. If it buys the land, the owner should be compensated for any improvements. If the formula provides for an interest subsidy (e.g., a mortgage loan at less than the market rate), the interest may rise to the market rate in the event of an unapproved sale. Or if a capital subsidy is given, the sale may be authorized only upon repayment of the subsidy. If the government aid is nominal, however, the restrictions on the owner should be minimal.

A country must choose between building for the few and demonstrating little, building for the many and exhausting its resources, or providing for the many with a minimum outlay. Core housing provides for the many.

While housing can be built as a rigid final product that resists improvement even when the national income has improved, it can also be built with a potential for improvement paralleling the national progress. A core-housing program makes this possible.

The demands of an expanding industrial population assert themselves irrespective of the best-laid plans. No nation has yet proved able to avoid slum formation in the face of a mass migration. Whether the formula can be altered depends primarily on the layout of the site and of the utilities. If the layout is good and the utilities are provided, the houses can be improved without the built-in blight of a bad plan. The core house can be adaptable to increases in family size. It can more easily be sold to those who may wish to alter it. It is dispensable at less cost, should mass clearance be necessitated by a major urban expansion.

A slum clearance enthusiast may call a core-housing project a slum, but if under that ubiquitous definition it *is* a slum, it is at least a more

Figure 30. Women workers transporting concrete for core-house settlement in Ajena, Ghana.

Figure 31. Filling in the walls of a core house in the new town of Ajena.

Figure 32. Foundation frames and roofs of core housing in Nkwakubio, Ghana.

Figure 33. Completing a core in Nkwakubio.

Figure 34. A typical northern savanna village in the Upper Region, Ghana.

Figure 35. A common fishing scene as nets are hauled in by tribal members in Ghana.

Figure 36. An outdoor kitchen in the midst of a new town under construction in Nkwakubio, Ghana.

Figure 37. The roof-loan scheme's dividend. Villagers building a bridge through self-help in Ghana. Some traditional houses are in the background. (See page 190.)

Figure 38. A typical house in Tanganyika with coral stones used to strengthen walls, supports, and plastering.

Figure 39. A hut in the Philippines landscaped by a squatter.

alterable and improvable slum. Planned as minimum housing, it will lend itself to adjustment and improvement more than the compromises that obsolesce quickly and leave their sad remains for a century or more.

Though core housing is no more a universal recipe for housing shortages than is self-help, it should be considered in almost every underdeveloped country as one part of the program. It requires no crusading spirit. It is no substitute for the traditional self-help or mutual-aid techniques in the rural areas, though it should be employed as a supplement there when possible. Often it is more efficient than the organized self-help operations now being laboriously launched in cities. Where land is available at reasonable cost, core housing is more likely to produce shelter than is organized self-help. In the long run, if programs are planned properly, it will produce better housing as well.

13

The Roof-Loan Scheme

When the poor man expresses his yearning for "a roof over his head," he highlights one of the principal housing needs in the less developed areas of the world. The roof is the part of the house most exposed to the elements. The most important part of the structure, it is also the costliest and the most difficult to acquire.

Building a roof was one of man's earliest engineering accomplishments. When the dweller in the cave discovered that he could enlarge his home by piling rocks in front of the cave wall and roofing them over with logs or skins, he had taken his first step toward civilization. Yet today he is still striving hard for his roof. As he moves away from the places where wood, thatch, or bamboo can be obtained easily or where tile can be baked from local clays, he becomes more and more dependent on buying a ready-made cover, fabricated in some distant rolling mill or shipped thousands of miles across the seas.

In many areas where self-help or mutual aid still functions, the average family, if helped with a roof, will manage to make or buy the earthen bricks or blocks with which to put up some sort of shelter. For this reason, if national and international agencies could assume the responsibility for making roofs available to families at reasonable costs and terms, a solution of the housing problem would be closer in many areas. Yet this approach has been completely ignored in aid calculations.

Although providing houses for the masses is becoming an increasingly complex process, a case study will illustrate how help with roofs can stimulate relatively unsophisticated people to grapple with their own shelter problem and to master some of its perplexities. The first use of the scheme was in Ghana, where the operation incidentally also helped solve some other problems. Thus a brief description of the country as it appeared to the U.N. mission and an outline of the circumstances that gave rise to the plan are relevant to the discussion.

GHANA—CONTRASTS AND CONFLICTS

To the United Nations mission[1] in 1954, Ghana (then the Gold Coast) was a country with many types of people, tribes, languages, religions—and problems. Between the capital city of Accra and the savanna villages of the Northern Territories lay the extremes of old and new: the automobile and the tom-tom; the proficient mammy trader emulating the ways of the West and the tribal woman with only a leaf to clothe her.

Tribal life itself may seem as strange to a visitor as polygamy or the animism that is Ghana's dominant belief. Yet Ghana's ancient tribal structure is a proved social and political organization with its own culture, traditions, rituals, and loyalties. Its cooperative features would win the admiration of the most committed Utopians. Whether the work is setting the sprawling fishnets and pulling them in laden with herring or gathering food and fuel from the soil, an orderly life has been built around communal effort and communal ownership. In a precarious environment that few white men could endure, the primordial tribe has held its members together for centuries in simple dignity.

Ghana had a population in 1954 of 4,333,000, which was rising annually by about 225,000 people. Many of them were moving into the cities, and these cities soon revealed afflictions in common with the rest of the world. Accra became a bustling capital with a major airport, department stores, and modern buildings only a stone's throw from tribal communities. In the cities, rental property replaced tribal tenure, and a disparity manifested itself between rent scales and wage scales. A housing shortage and overcrowding appeared. The old communal lands within the urban environs began to be fragmented into individual parcels measured by metes and bounds. Increasingly, there were conflicts over titles, competition for land, and some squatting. As urban problems grew, the government began to regulate property and to seek methods for relieving the housing shortage.

Whereas changes had occurred gradually and successively in Western nations, the transitions in Ghana were arriving almost simultaneously.

[1] The U.N. mission was composed of Charles Abrams (Chairman), Otto Koenigsberger, and Vladimir Bodiansky. The report, *Housing in the Gold Coast* (New York: United Nations, 1956), is now an official document and is available at the United Nations.

Emerging from a virtually pedestrian mobility, Ghana made way for the automobile by cutting roads through the old elephant runs of the savanna.[2] The harbor installations at Sekondi-Takoradi bristled with cranes, and warehouses became packed with seaborne goods. Plans to diversify productivity sought to free the country from dependency on cocoa. An important project was the harnessing of the Volta River for hydroelectric production of aluminum from the abundant stores of bauxite. A new port was built at Tema Harbor near Accra, where goods had previously been carried in by canoes from freighters anchored three miles out. As labor moved out of the tribal environment, it confronted the opportunities and novelties as well as the conflicts and bewilderments of city life.

Sharp social transitions accompanied urbanization. The small family was replacing the tribe as the social unit, and the individual was withdrawing from the communal group and the tribal organization. In the villages, too, the ways of the West were influencing the hinterlander, whose thatched roof lacked the magnificence of the galvanized iron that kept the envied British civil servants dry.[3]

Pressures to abandon older values, older styles, and older modes of life began to alter housing needs and desires. A curious tribesman would move down to the Bibiani gold mines and work for years (perhaps contracting silicosis in the process). Then he would return to his tribe, only to find that his savings lacked the luster for him as a tribesman that they had held for him as a miner. He might dissipate the money for the pleasure of the tribe in one extravagant adventure, or he might move down into the city's ferment, spending his days and earnings in an orgy with strangers.

GHANA'S HOUSING

Despite its mounting urbanization, the Gold Coast in 1954, like many other developing countries, was still predominantly a country of fields, tribal villages, and compounds. Most of the people lived in hamlets with a population of less than 1500, which were governed by chiefs. Houses in the north were made of sunbaked swish (laterite), while the urban and near-urban folk lived mostly in houses of cement block, swish, swish-concrete, or wattle and daub.

In the towns there was a composite of modern houses, slums, shantytowns, and office buildings. Cooperation was no longer tribal but more

[2] When the U.N. team tried to land on an airstrip in the Northern Territories in 1954, thousands of natives stormed the strip to greet our huge "bird." After three attempted landings, the police forced back the people, and we were able to land.

[3] In some countries, after thatch had been replaced by more modern material, the thatched roof regained its respect as an antique with an honorific value.

often practiced only among members of the same family. Dwellings were larger, took longer to build, and called for more skill. From Takoradi to Accra the road was punctuated with mud houses in villages enlivened by occasional marketplaces.[4]

Virtually all building in the rural areas (80 per cent) was accomplished by self-help. Though there was room for improvement in village layouts, in drainage and water supply, in foundations, cattle pounds, and grain-storage facilities, almost everyone in the rural sections was a builder of a sort. Labor was divided between the men and the women: the men put up the walls and roofs, and the women rendered (plastered) the walls and finished the floors.

Roofs were made of various materials: thatch was most common in the rural north, while in the towns corrugated iron sheets, asbestos clay tile, and aluminum began to appear more often. (Occasionally one might see signs of primitive genius, as in a distant isolated village near Lawra where the villagers built their houses half underground. They connected a road that served as a ramp to a walk of flat roofs forming a parapeted plaza for the villagers and children.)

Though the housing problem has been intensified by industrialization, Ghana has advantages not shared by other developing areas. At the time of the U.N. mission in 1954, Ghana had 92,000 square miles of land for its 4.3 million people. But even with its sharp population increase since then, it is still not crowded.[5] Its climate is tropical, and its terrain is relatively level. While the urban land problem had become complex, most people in the rural and village areas could still get land for housing without paying a ransom price. Considerable acreage, formerly Crown land, is in public ownership.

The cooperative spirit, which some of the more developed countries are trying hard to recapture, still exists in many aspects of tribal living. In fact, one of the indicated frontiers in housing production seems to be the salvaging and strengthening of these cooperative practices of tribal and village life.

THE SEARCH FOR A HOUSING SOLUTION

When the U.N. mission arrived in Ghana, the government was recovering from the costly prefabrication hangover resulting from the advice of its enterprising European consultants. (See Chapter 12.) Since housing

[4] These were run by enterprising "mammy traders," who peddled domestic and imported goods, gave limited credit, and often served as their own bill collectors or petty moneylenders.

[5] Ghana's population of 4,118,450 in 1948 grew to 6,690,730 by 1960, an increase of 62 per cent.

had become a more pressing political problem in both the cities and the hinterlands, another scheme had to be produced quickly.

The main factors weighed by the U.N. mission in its search for a workable financing scheme were: (1) the keen desire for homeownership; (2) an apparent willingness to save, though the forms of saving were primitive; (3) the ability of many people to build; (4) the availability of some good indigenous materials; (5) the inability of most people to pay for a satisfactory house; and (6) the absence of a financing mechanism.[6]

The desire for homeownership was evidencing itself in the painstaking accumulation of building blocks. Savings that might have been channeled into long-term investments lay immobilized in blocks that might never feel the mason's trowel. Often the blocks were actually set up on a lot, but the house remained unfinished until the day when the owner could buy the roof and perhaps the doors and windows as well.

In many areas, good indigenous materials were available for building walls. The termite, whose tall mounds interrupted the plains, had helped compose a material from Ghanaian soil that held together fairly well, and with a little cement added it could be made into a lasting mural material. In the backlands, the natives used no cement, but covered their walls with a colored preservative taken from local trees. However, except in the Northern Territories and in areas where bamboo or thatch was still used, no indigenous roofing material was available.

By helping to finance the roof, doors, and windows, the government could help lower-income families and encourage self-help. Such a plan would utilize local materials in the walls and spur the building of many houses. It would also hold loans on new houses to a minimum, develop a program of mass purchase, minimize the need for public subsidies, and help stabilize and improve some of the areas outside the large city centers.

Among all existing programs, there was none for the predominant portion of Ghana's population, i.e., the low-income family, the subsistence family, and the family in self-built housing. These people could still build homes with their own hands. Theirs was the strongest moral case for government loans or subventions.

But when the U.N. mission arrived, the government had already earmarked $2,492,000 as an initial investment for what it called a "building and loan society" (actually a government mortgage bank) and had reserved another $3,080,000 for additional capital. This was the plan that the government had proffered as a substitute for the prefabrication scheme of its former consultants.

[6] Though some of Britain's banks had established branches in the colonies, their operations were commercial. They accepted savings, but did not funnel them into mortgage loans. Savings accounts were not common.

When the roof-loan scheme was presented at a cabinet meeting, the government, after a lively debate, agreed to allot $2,100,000 for roofs as a revolving fund out of the moneys earmarked for the mortgage bank. As for the bank, efforts would be made to interest entrepreneurs in a genuine building and loan society to dispense with direct management by the government.

THE ROOF-LOAN SCHEME

The U.N. mission's plan was simple. Loans would be made for roofs, doors, and windows, repayable over a fixed period. For a two-room cottage of about 260 square feet in plinth area, the roof cost was estimated in 1954 at about $196, doors and windows at about $22, and lime wash at about $6—a total of $224. This amount would be about one fourth to one third of the value of a completed building. No loans would be necessary for the wall structure. In the Northern Territories, loans would be made as often on foundations, doors, windows, and finishes as on roofs, because the mission felt that the use of thatch should not be discouraged.

Simultaneously, separate loans would be made available to communities or councils for concrete mixers, block-making machines, vibrating tables, woodworking machines, etc. Loans for equipment would include advances for forms for making rammed-earth walls, a technique that had had an important demonstration in the Northern Territories and seemed worth encouraging.[7]

The mission recommended that loans be made by a central agency to the local or municipal societies or councils, which would be responsible for repayment. The local and municipal societies formed out of the tribes would, in turn, make smaller loans available to individual borrowers at interest rates sufficient to cover expenses and to provide reserves for losses. Loans would also be made to local cooperating or common-interest groups that looked like good risks.

Since the purchase or production of prefabricated roofing materials would be made in bulk by a public agency, it might be possible, the mission thought, to program total national requirements and spur wholesale purchases of the roofing materials, windows, and doors. Sizes and specifications could be standardized and arrangements made with foreign

[7] In this respect, the mission was impressed with the pioneering work of Lloyd Shirer, who worked with the natives and taught them how to use rammed-earth techniques in housing, building dams, and other essential work. The report emphasized the importance of on-the-ground experts working with the people. Shirer had come to the Northern Territories as a missionary and was later employed by the government. He was made a chief by one of the larger tribes for the valuable services he rendered, but later he left Ghana with his wife because, following independence, he was not encouraged to stay.

firms for manufacturing roofing material of prescribed size and quality. All or most of a foreign factory's output could be contracted for at an attractive price.

THE SCHEME IN OPERATION

By the time the scheme was put into operation in Ghana, roof costs had risen. The government offered a roof loan (including doors and windows) up to $560 for anyone who would put up the walls. To qualify, borrowers had to be members of a village housing society that would agree to guarantee the loan, and the house had to be finished except for materials financed by the government.

Each village society (usually thirty to forty members) requires the approval of the regional Rural Housing Assistant, who works with the Department of Social Welfare and Community Development. This assistant tells the applicants where they can get materials, and after approving the quantity needed and the prices, he issues a warrant authorizing pickup at the store. He collects repayments and proceeds against defaulters. The Department of Social Welfare and Community Development advises the government on the villages in which societies are to be formed, and on the preparation of plans and site layouts for small estate developments.

A village society is set up in a prescribed way. First, a name is decided upon and registered. Then the objects of the society are stated, i.e., to erect houses according to the specifications of the Ministry of Housing, so owners may qualify for loans.

Membership in a society is open to families who intend to build a standard house or have one built. In all negotiations, one person speaks for the family. The society at its first meeting elects a chairman, vice-chairman, and secretary. The meetings are held at least once every two months.

Roof loans are granted to members who have built their houses to wall plate level, according to specifications. Applications for the loans are made on a form countersigned by the chairman of the society, who underwrites the loan on the society's behalf. In requesting a roof loan, members enter into a solemn obligation to repay, at stated intervals, the installments due. No further loans will be made to a society that has a member in arrears.

Membership in the societies totaled about 25,000 in 1960, and loans aggregated nearly $1,850,000. A staff of only eight Rural Housing Assistants (in addition to instructors in the Department of Social Welfare and Community Development) has been responsible for the operation. At first the societies met without women, but many "mammies" soon became members and sometimes have become vice-chairmen.

By May 1959, repayments amounting to just under $420,000 were due, and $378,000 had been collected. Most of the temporary arrears appeared collectible.

The mission had recommended the loan scheme with the ominous feeling that repayment might suffer the same experience as the unrepaid loans under an agricultural program. Hence the mission cautioned:

> In dispensing the loans, the most serious consideration must be given by the lender to the reputation and credit of the individual borrower. With the credit system in its infancy, the crucial period is the beginning, when borrowers of government assess their benefactor. They may look at their government as a father to whom debts are never in fact repayable rather than as a creditor whose goodwill it is important to maintain for future indulgences. Enforcement of debts should adhere to the bond and prompt payment [should be] insisted upon. If loan practices follow the practice in cocoa lending by the Ministry of Agriculture, there will be little investigation, loans will be made almost pro-forma and a sound credit system will hardly be expected to mature.[8]

The mission had expressed its feeling that, even if the loans were not repaid, they would at least become unintentional subsidies for the lowest-income group. That there has been so little arrearage is a tribute to the scheme and to the people who participated in its operation.

COLLATERAL DIVIDENDS FROM THE SCHEME

The roof-loan scheme has had wider implications. Walls that were formerly built amateurishly were now more substantial because of the rigid loan requirements and the public supervision. Most important, the societies have generated many other activities and interests. Members get together to discuss local problems, build better roads, improve sanitation, and even to advance their educational status. This has happened because the Department of Social Welfare and Community Development keeps in touch with each society and tries to develop leadership and to encourage cleanliness and cooperation among the people. Furthermore, the government supplies bulldozers and tools where necessary and gives instruction in their use.

Before the societies were organized, a loudspeaker device had been employed to convene tribesmen and exhort them to make physical and social improvements in their villages. All too often the loudspeaker reached deaf ears. Now a government representative borrows a chief's "gon-gon" (a rod and a bottle-shaped iron sounding instrument) to summon the people to a meeting. The representative tells the assemblage, "You have to sign a paper for a roof loan, and you can now put only

[8] Abrams, Bodiansky, and Koenigsberger, *Report on Housing in the Gold Coast, op. cit.*, p. 23.

your thumbprint on the paper. It's time you were able to sign your full name. You should attend classes in school." A person in the region who knows how to read and write in one of the many vernaculars is designated as the leader to teach the others to read.

Moses Awoonor-Williams, a Ghanaian who helped direct roof-loan operations, says:

> Since people work during the day, a lamp is important, and societies are induced to buy lamps—one big lamp for the literacy club and others for individuals. The roof-loan scheme has therefore become a device for literacy as well as for general community development. The same people who teach are used to organize road-building. The members of the roof-loan society, when they don't fish or work on farms, work on the roads. Schools are roofed over, too. The chief signs the note for the roof, which is paid back by voluntary subscriptions or through a levy on each man's cocoa crop.[9]

The roof-loan scheme has won another appropriation similar to the first, and Ghana is planning roof loans in some of the cities.[10] The example of the scheme has sparked the organization of benevolent societies fashioned on the roof-loan society formula. There were said to be about a thousand societies in 1960. As in the case of the roof-loan arrangement, the society is responsible for the loan, which is repayable in four years.

On November 25, 1960, the Chief Town Planning Officer of the Ministry of Works and Housing wrote to a U.N. representative, giving this assessment of the roof-loan scheme:

> Generally speaking, the Roof Loan Scheme has intensified building activities in those villages where it is operated. . . . The very fact that the scheme is operated through societies (and therefore the latter have had to be formed) has in itself had a beneficial effect in bringing people together for a practical purpose and has, I believe in any case, re-orientated their interests toward their villages. . . . [It] has led to a demand by the people for planning schemes and amenities of all kinds, including water and roads. Because the societies are operating a financial scheme it makes people aware that generally speaking you cannot get something for nothing. This is to my mind a tremendous step forward. . . . The people do realize that improvements to their villages and to their living conditions rest very largely on themselves and their own efforts with guidance from government.[11]

[9] These details of how the roof-loan scheme was operating were obtained in November 1960 from Awoonor-Williams, formerly director of the Department of Social Welfare and Community Development, while he was in the United States. Much of the organizational work that helped make the scheme a success was undertaken by R. K. A. Gardiner, former director of the Department of Social Welfare and Community Development.

[10] In a 1962 *New York Times* supplement on Ghana, the government pointed to its roof-loan scheme as one of its outstanding accomplishments.

[11] From a memorandum by B. A. W. Trevallion, Chief Town Planning Officer, Ministry of Works and Housing, Ghana.

The roof-loan scheme is far from a complete answer to the housing problem in the large cities. Nor is there ever any guarantee that even the best plans will retain their original form and integrity in countries in institutional flux and where politics intervenes to discourage repayments. But the experience has demonstrated that out of the ancient cooperative aspects of the tribal and village system can be forged a new device not only for producing homes but also for making public improvements, achieving greater cooperative effort, advancing education, consolidating community life, and developing social and communal responsibility.

ROOF LOANS FOR BOLIVIA

Though it is the poorest South American nation, Bolivia is endowed with an abundance of raw materials for building. In La Paz, Cochabamba, and elsewhere, adobe may be taken out of the ground, mixed with a little straw and water, and placed in a wooden form, and in less than a week's time it is dried into bricks suitable for building. Elsewhere wood abounds. Local industries can provide roofs of clay, tile, or cement, though transportation problems may impede delivery to the landlocked cities.

A second advantage that Bolivia enjoys is the availability of land around the city cores. Bolivia's population density is low—about three persons per square kilometer as compared with seven for Argentina, Brazil, and Peru.[12] Its city populations are relatively small.

A third advantage is that Bolivia's climatic conditions make cheap housing feasible. Seventy per cent of the population live on the high plains at 11,000 to 14,000 feet. Here the climate is dry, favoring the use of adobe and simple construction. In the valleys, the climate is usually subtropical, varying with the altitude. Cochabamba, Sucre, Tarija, and Potosí are in this area. The eastern lowlands, comprising about 70 per cent of Bolivia's area, are sparsely populated, and the climate is subtropical or tropical.

A fourth advantage is the people's aptitude for building and the use of self-help. The population is overwhelmingly rural. The men of the altiplano have had to build houses that can keep out cold and rain. Rural and city life converge or adjoin, and the average Bolivian still retains and passes on to his sons the knowledge of how to put up a simple structure of clay or wood.

Unlike many other underdeveloped nations, Bolivia is not yet suffering from a serious squatter problem. This advantage stems partly from the slow pace of industrialization and the relatively small movement of population and partly from the breaking up of the latifundia and the redistribution of land to workers already in the cities.

[12] *U.N. Demographic Yearbook* (New York, 1954), Table I, p. 102.

In sum, Bolivia, while a poor and underindustrialized country, is not poor in the land, labor, or materials with which to undertake a minimum but feasible housing program. But Bolivia nevertheless has a serious housing problem, which manifests itself in the cities in overcrowding, rising rents, and illegal building.

Lack of water and sanitary facilities is common. Out of 155,725 houses surveyed in 1950, 47.5 per cent were without water and 54.2 per cent without sanitation. This is not because the country lacks water, but because supply systems are inadequate. Wells for common use are sunk in the streets of tropical Santa Cruz, but even these crude facilities are lacking in other cities—including the poorer sections of La Paz.

Most of the dwellings in cities are rented, but there are few vacancies and therefore few opportunities to change homes when family needs expand. Owing to the dubious protection of Bolivia's rent control law, tenants are glued to their shelters no matter how decrepit, crowded, or unsuitable.

Bolivia's main problem is how to build houses in quantity with the limited funds available. Since the houses must be cheap enough for the average worker, they must be provided either by self-help housing or by core housing that the workers could expand.[13]

My U.N. report in 1959 recommended the creation of an initial revolving fund of a million dollars for loans to help workers develop their land and build. The loans would bear interest at 9 per cent (not exorbitant in Bolivia) and would mature in fifteen years. A program might have been devised under which owners would receive a loan for the cost of a roof, doors, and windows, provided they first erected four walls on land approved by the government for development. Demonstration houses would be erected and technical assistance given.

On the basis of cost estimates that I obtained for roofs, doors, and windows in La Paz, Cochabamba, and Santa Cruz, some 3000 houses could be built through a million-dollar fund, and more could be built as repayments came in or as the fund was augmented. With such a program a further distribution of land could be made. The government would prepare simple roads and make land available where water existed or could be provided. Such a program could reduce the trend toward a continuing inflation in rents and create jobs in the production of materials.[14] It would reduce the tendency toward illegal building,

---

[13] To allay political pressures, the country had embarked upon a housing program under which houses were being built at costs upward of $1600 per unit, financed by social security funds. Bolivia's financial condition being what it is, only a few hundred houses could be built.

[14] Many small materials companies were operating precariously because of the paucity of orders.

provide an important source for municipal revenue through its levies, and give people homes and incentives.

I laid the plan before His Excellency Dr. Hernan Siles Zuazo, then President of Bolivia, and his cabinet in 1959, but the country simply did not have a million dollars. Bolivia in 1959 was an anomaly. It had a stable currency and an unstable social, economic, and political structure. The international agencies had been liberal to a point—but they had not faced the popular need for hope, security, stability, and decent family life.

My plan was approved by the cabinet, with an understanding that an effort would be made to raise the money. The country could scrape together less than a fifth of it. When the proposal was released to the press, it was greeted with enthusiasm and made front-page headlines for days thereafter.

When the plan was put before the International Cooperation Administration (now the Agency for International Development) in Bolivia, it was flatly rejected. The official attitude was: "If the Bolivian knows the money comes from the United States, he won't repay it. We therefore have no interest in helping him with housing." The AID officials rejected proposals under which the powerful labor syndicates might sponsor the program or assume some responsibilities for repayment. They were simply not interested in anything that had to do with housing.

Cities like La Paz are nerve centers, and their slums are the festering places of revolt. Even if housing is not a prime factor in promoting productivity, a million dollars lent for housing in La Paz could have prevented incalculable losses over the longer run. Though more aid money has been poured into Bolivia since Castro's challenge to Latin America, the only housing assistance has been a small loan by the Inter-American Development Bank to spur a savings and loan association. Even this had not gotten off the ground by 1964, and if it should, it would be of little benefit to low-income families.

ROOF LOANS FOR NIGERIA

A U.N. mission in 1962 proposed a roof-loan scheme for Nigeria.[15] Here too it was recommended that societies be formed that would be responsible for the debts incurred by members. The society would be composed of twenty heads of the leading families of a neighborhood. Each society would propose five of its members annually for a roof loan. Specially trained government inspectors would check the loans and sup-

[15] See Otto Koenigsberger, Charles Abrams, Susumu Kobe, Moshe Shapiro, and Michael Wheeler, *Metropolitan Lagos*, a report submitted to the Ministry of Lagos Affairs (New York: United Nations, 1962).

ply the owners with vouchers, against which they could obtain the necessary materials from a local merchant. Maximum loans were to be $560, but most would be for less. They would be repayable in installments over a five-year period. The amount of each loan would be adjusted to the quality of the materials.

Since loans are made only for the last sections of buildings, the quality of the foundations and walls can be inspected (as in Ghana) before loan approval, and corrective suggestions made where required. The government would be enabled to encourage the use of local materials and influence better construction and planning.

In 1862, Governor Oliver had suggested that the houses of the poor in Lagos be covered with corrugated iron sheets at the expense of the government and that the owners be made to repay the cost by easy installments. The proposal had been made as a precaution against fire. It is a coincidence that precisely a century later, the U.N. mission, knowing nothing of Oliver's proposal, recommended a similar scheme as a partial solution for Nigeria's housing problem.

Like core housing, roof-loan schemes are not applicable everywhere, nor are they the last word in home construction, but they offer a cheap solution in many areas. Properly implemented, they can also provide a demonstration of how existing values, even if primitive, can be built upon to meet a new problem in a changing societal pattern.

14

Education and Research: A University Is Born in the Middle East

THE NEED FOR TRAINING

Progress in a country depends not only on a few people who are talented, resourceful, and wise but also on a larger pool of people who are instructed, experienced, and willing. Education and training are essential to bring out the abilities and usefulness of both groups.

Too often, however, the development of training facilities is viewed as too long-term and remote. The temptation is to proceed at once without planning simultaneously for the wide variety of skills essential for development and operation. Some think that the needs of a developing area can be satisfied by financing a dam, a series of broad road belts, or a steel mill built by foreign contractors. Others feel that housing pressures can be relieved by instituting a crash housing scheme employing whatever skills are on hand and without developing more skills and more materials factories. Both approaches may do some good in a few countries, but in the absence of a simultaneous longer-term development of the major skills and professions that an urbanized economy demands, they will prove inadequate.

The main task in most countries is to define and provide for both long- and short-term requirements as part of a development plan. Education for the varied skills and professions needed in the production of housing as well as in the operation of industry is indispensable. The most constructive device is the presence of a technical university whose disciplines are closely related to those required by the urban industrial society. The importance of such facilities for training and education was dramatically demonstrated in Turkey in 1954.[1]

THE TURKISH SCENE

Turkey is a country of striking contrasts in terrain, customs, occupations, backgrounds, and social and economic conditions. Few countries possess such a variety of scenes and surprises. The tourist finds Istanbul very different from Ankara; a visitor to Bursa, Yalova, and Izmir cannot picture Tarsus, Amasya, Sivas, or Konya. Much of the country, particularly the smaller towns and provinces of the interior, was long cut off from communication with European Istanbul and with the world in general.

Barely a generation before my visit to Turkey on a United Nations mission, the government had sought a new concept of cultural life through major social and political reforms. Dress was transformed, and old customs were challenged. A new constitution was introduced together with a legal system patterned upon the Swiss model. Industrialization was speeded, improvement in agricultural methods fostered, and the need for education emphasized. Though the masses still knelt toward Mecca, Turkey's leaders turned to the West.

By 1956, the chemistry of progress had not yet fully dissolved the sediment of old routines. Turkey remained predominantly agricultural, with wide social and cultural distances between its regions and persistent conflicts between old and new ways.

Yet the same manifestations of industrialization and urbanization that were occurring elsewhere in the world had already begun to assert themselves in Turkey's cities. The change was accelerated by an American-aided road program that had shortened the distances between cities and hinterland.

The pace of the urbanward migrations allowed little time for planning to accommodate the new populations. Since housing was very scarce, the migrants preempted whatever land they could. The planned city of Ankara, with squatters forming almost half of the population, no longer looked planned, particularly on the hills and outskirts overlooking its broad, well-ordered center. Istanbul and Izmir teemed with makeshift hovels. Action was needed to control further blight and to prevent continuing trespasses on government and private lands.

---

[1] See Charles Abrams, *The Need for Training and Education for Housing and Planning,* prepared for the Government of Turkey (New York: United Nations, 1955).

THE SHORTAGE OF TECHNICAL MANPOWER

In Turkey as elsewhere, urban life calls for a versatile group of artisans and technicians. The required skills are interdependent, particularly in building. If skills are available, policy and program can be formulated; if they are not, or if one important skill is lacking, even the best policy will fail.

Among the many elements that shape the urban environment are the architect and town planner. They influence the design of the house and neighborhood as well as the subdivision layout; they help draft building laws and affect other aspects of physical development.

Turkey had too few of either profession, and in some cities there were none at all. There were fewer than six city planners in all of Turkey. The only two architectural schools in the nation, both in Istanbul, accepted fewer than 200 applicants a year out of almost 2000 seeking admission. Most of the architects received their training through a discipline that combined architecture and engineering. After graduation, some left to work abroad; others practiced engineering or another profession. But very few hung out their shingles in the cities beyond the Istanbul-Izmir-Bursa region.

There was no effort to teach or discover an indigenous Turkish architecture. The tendency was rather to import foreign concepts and impose them on the Turkish scene. Planning concepts, though drawing on British policy, were predominantly German in execution, with monumental structures overwhelming the narrow streets. A pension housing plan, which allowed for housing loans to civil servants, had borrowed its "90 per cent of cost" mortgage-insurance formula from the Federal Housing Administration in the United States, though the circumstances were different.[2] French design influences could be noted here and there, too, making the physical product an odd hybrid, a mixture of elements extracted more often from the worst examples than from the best.

Because of the dearth of architects and of men with technical training generally, cities were unable to hire civil servants who could interpret plans. In Adana, for example, I noticed a new building that violated the existing building code by omitting the prescribed lateral areaway and by covering 100 per cent of the lot area. Were the adjoining buildings to follow its example, as indeed they were bound to do, there would be no light, no yard space, and no ventilation for any of the buildings except on the street side. When I questioned the contractor, he exhibited the city's approval stamped on the plan. Approvals of illegal plans by city officials were perfunctory, owing partly to inability to read plans and partly to a building code so general and confusing that it

---

[2] For a critique of the pension housing plan, see *ibid.*

supplied no clear directions. Cities violated the code themselves when they put up public buildings, hardly setting a good example for the citizens.

To complicate matters, the surviving provisions of an ancient code had to be read in connection with the more recent regulations. Every point in the regulations seemed arguable. For example, a setback from the road is required. One owner found that if he observed this rule, his building would be too narrow to be economical. So he built with no setback whatever. Once an illegal house is erected and occupied, it is unlikely, because of the housing shortage, that it will be ordered torn down. In fact, in its effort to ease the shortage, Turkey granted a ten-year tax exemption on new buildings. The nation was not only permitting the erection of illegal structures but subsidizing them as well. Everyone seemed to acquiesce in the illegalities, to the despair of a few higher officials. However, nothing could be done in the absence of trained people, acting under comprehensible, publicly supported, and enforceable laws.

The product was a bizarre pattern in which new buildings obscured ancient monuments. Frequently the number of stories in buildings exceeded the legal limit. Materials used were often illegal and buildings sometimes unsafe. Knowledge of building specifications was scant—a perilous void in a country subject to floods and earthquakes. In Amasya one could still see flood markings on buildings along the main street, but neither zoning to regulate the use of such land nor adequate flood control measures were in evidence.

Without facilities for specifying and testing materials, the country had drawn on foreign precedent for its specifications. The acceptable brick in Turkey, for example, met the needs and standards of Germany in 1930. When this specification was approved by Turkey in 1938, it had already been modified in Germany. The obsolete German standard for brick, however, still was applicable in Turkey, and all locally made brick had to conform. In the effort to be "practical," violations of materials standards became as common as violations of the building code.

OTHER BY-PRODUCTS OF LACK OF TRAINING

The cities of Turkey are rich in architectural heritage. The genius of Byzantium has survived, a partly ruined monument but still a splendid contrast to the tawdry results of private and public effort a millennium later. Few places in the world, in fact, offer such an interesting record of Hittite, Roman, Byzantine, and Seljuk monuments. Despite the ravages of time and the unregulated speculator, they still dominate the scene in Konya, Bursa, Kayseri, and many smaller towns.

The incongruous architecture of foreign countries was imposed upon an ancient scene without respite. A cheap, characterless cinema blocked out an ancient mosque in Sivas. A natural blend of hills and plains that formed one of nature's miracles in Bursa was marred by a series of speculative makeshifts. Turkey seemed to cry out for a renaissance that would see the birth of an architecture of its own, but there was no one to spawn it.

Lack of training and craftsmanship was manifested on the Turkish scene in other ways:

1. SPECULATION AND BLIGHT. Much of the "planning" of Turkey's new environment is that of private speculators. These men buy large aggregations of land from farmers or from the state or city, run a line through each plot horizontally as many times as possible, then as many times vertically as possible, leaving as little room as they can for streets. The tiny parallelograms are then disposed of as building plots to as many buyers as possible. A full-page advertisement in the government's official publication announced a new subdivision to house at least 10,000 people on lots that were to be all of 900 square feet (equivalent to 25 feet by 36 feet); the corner lots were even smaller. This is not enough space for a house of the humblest standard. It leaves no place for play, recreation, or laundry; no yard or garden space; no room for expansion of the house and no relief from the drab monotony of house upon house upon house.

Since the development was in a rural area (though within easy commuting distance of Istanbul), the subdivision was completely free of any regulation in design, materials, and specifications. If precedents are a guide, however, the demands of the new population for water and other public services would soon compel the city to include the tract within its jurisdiction. Thus, on one side of Istanbul stood the miles of squatters' mushroomlike houses, on another the crude, unhappy subdivision.

A similar situation confronted Ankara, the core of which is the planned city built by Atatürk. Outside the planned city was the vast army of peripheral squatters, their holdings often sanctioned and legalized, their minuscule byways and alleys tolerated. Inside the planned and once orderly center, however, shanty extensions were protruding from the recently built houses, while, for the lack of zoning enforcement, petty shops were beginning to sprawl over the residential centers. Zoning, subdivision controls, and extension of planning regulation over peripheral areas were either unknown in Turkey or could not be properly administered.

2. FRUSTRATION OF CITY PLANS. Inspired by British example and by the postwar European city-planning renaissance, the government had required each city to file a plan of improvements, showing new squares, streets, public buildings, etc. But the plans never saw fulfillment for one reason or another—lack of finance, the prospect of fantastic awards in

compulsory purchase proceedings, the visionary nature of proposals when weighed against the ability to fulfill them, and above all the absence of know-how at the local level. A blueprint left at a local city hall was likely to end up on some shelf, never to be unrolled or translated, but the private building would go up anyway.

Yalova boasted one of the finest resort areas in Turkey. It had been improved by Atatürk and had been one of his favorite retreats. More recently plans were made for a square near the present pier in the city center, and this proposed square was expected to adjoin the existing public park. Soon after its blueprinting, however, an entrepreneur built a costly apartment house and garage almost in the center of the projected square. Since the cost of public purchase would have taken half of the city's annual budget, the plan for Yalova was no longer practicable.

3. ADVERSE EFFECT ON PUBLIC AND COOPERATIVE HOUSING. There were numerous settlements built for Bulgarian refugees under a specially administered housing program. No matter what the area or the nature of the terrain, the houses and design were part of a stock plan of brick houses, placed in monotonous rows. Orientation to sun and winds was often disregarded. In one case it might have made more sense to use the rolling portion of a plot for building and leave the flat portion for farming. In another case the houses might have faced the sea, but the stock plan prepared hundreds of miles away could take no account of terrain or topography.

A large portion of Turkey's housing was built by or for cooperatives. Cooperative housing was in no sense as advanced as Sweden's or Denmark's, and cooperators were often merely a small group of individuals working for a state-operated or private enterprise; sometimes they were a disparate dozen families banding together to negotiate a loan from Emlak Bank (a public institution) or for the purpose of dealing with a contractor as a unit. Here, too, as in the housing of refugees, selection of house type was from a dull stock plan that paid little attention to topography or landscape.

4. LIMITATION IN USE OF PENSION FUNDS. This scheme in 1954 represented the largest single effort to build housing for workers. But owing to the absence of financing knowledge and experience, the fund of $3 million produced only one tenth of the housing possible if the money had been handled properly. By using the fund as a capital reserve for a cooperative savings institution, a major mechanism could have been devised for channeling such savings into long-term mortgage financing. But this approach would have called for housing and financing experts as well as good housing administrators, which were not available. Absence of technical knowledge of cooperative undertakings was also

reflected in the enabling legislation and in the administrative formula, both of which were monuments to administrative confusion.

5. IMPAIRMENT OF INDIVIDUAL RESOURCEFULNESS AND INITIATIVE IN CITIES. Some of the better squatter houses in Ankara and Istanbul suggested the existence of a pool of workers with a natural aptitude for building. Since many of the houses were built of mud brick, or rocks gathered nearby, or scrap wood and tin, and had been put up in as little as twenty-four hours to avoid public interference, one could not help acquiring a healthy respect for these people. Some of the better houses cost only a few hundred dollars. Only a few passed city standards, and some were precariously located near landslide areas. Yet a good development might have emerged, given some initial planning of streets and utilities at the site, somewhat better materials, more time to build, some intelligent supervision, and some assurances of security of tenure. Instead, the squatters built what they could, and what they built will haunt the landscapes of Ankara and Istanbul for generations. They help to reinforce the theory that no planned city like Ankara can remain unimpaired when challenged by a mass influx. The housing problem must be solved before a planned city can retain its prescribed contours, or squatting locations must at least be simultaneously planned for as part of the development of the city.

6. ADVERSE EFFECTS IN THE VILLAGES. In the villages, the problem was not shortage of materials, for Turkey is rich in local materials that can be used for village housing—sun-dried and baked brick, clay roof tiles (locally made and purchasable at low prices), stone, and lumber. Nor was the problem land shortage. What was needed was better planning and land policy, good design of villages and housing, better shelters for livestock, improvement of roads, better information on agriculture, improved school and community facilities so that life could be more productive and more interesting.

Much of the life in the villages entailed cooperation in the sharing of grazing lands, helping a kinsman to build his house, or working together in supplying a common village need. This type of cooperation could have been used to greater advantage. The villages, however, were too often cut off from the life of the rest of the country. Though a village improvement program was begun in 1954, and a few pilot operations showed promise, the trained personnel was inadequate to launch or supervise a meaningful effort.

The deficiencies in personnel and training, of course, were not only in architecture and planning. Turkey also was short of engineers, surveyors, lawyers, builders, legal draftsmen, people trained in finance, economics, and sociology, and the host of other professions and talents a developing country needs. She had relied to some extent on foreign aid to fill these gaps, but the visiting experts usually stayed a month or a year and left. Their reports were filed away, often because there were no people to implement or even interpret them.[3] It was apparent that what Turkey needed was not only foreign experts but trained people who remain in the country and who can only be trained through an internal educational program.

CONCEIVING A UNIVERSITY

When I went to Turkey on a U.N. mission, I had not the slightest notion that a university would be the outcome.[4] Certainly the odds were against the success of any mission, for an expert carrying no funds in his portfolio was just another expert. In 1954, he would rarely get to see anyone with the rank of a cabinet minister and was more often assigned to a minor functionary who would spend an occasional hour with him lamenting the predicaments of officialdom. A U.N. economics mission with three prominent experts, after struggling to make an impact on the government, had packed its belongings and left in despair.

There was, nevertheless, one important factor favoring the prospects for a university in Turkey, i.e., the sheer need for it. A university could do more than train people, more than simply develop an indigenous competence in architecture.[5] The need for architects and planners was

[3] This was the fate of a report on housing made by the architectural firm of Skidmore, Owings and Merrill, which, though printed and bound, lay inviolate under a stack of forgotten papers in a petty official's file.

[4] In my first letter to Ernest Weissmann urging the United Nations to take up my recommendation for the establishment of the university, I wrote:
. . . After 5 weeks in Turkey, it became apparent to me that any technical recommendations I might make would make no more dent than a mosquito's bill on the hull of a battleship. The Turks, however willing, simply have not the administrative or the technical equipment with which to implement any technical recommendations I might make. Any laws I might prepare would not be enforced and a detailed report with elaborate recommendations would be relegated to the dust-bin.
Ankara itself, which hums with civil servants engaged in the nation's development, has no technical university in either engineering or architecture so that the city in which policy is made for the whole country and which is the seat of almost all technical work and equipment is an intellectual desert as far as architectural and planning talent is concerned. The country with a people who solved the problem of the true pendentive centuries ago and contributed originality in art and structure to a dark world is now, architecturally speaking, in the darkest ages itself and shows little hope of emerging unless the base of a revolution in design and structure is indigenously developed under a long-range scheme.

[5] It was not the first time that absence of good architects and of a good architectural school impeded Turkey's progress. Edward Gibbon records that in the building of Turkey's capital, "Constantine soon discovered that, in the decline of the

the wedge, but engineering and training in other disciplines were also essential to build the country. A university could be the focus of much-needed research. If located in Ankara, it would be oriented toward Asiatic Turkey, as well as Istanbul. It could draw upon the pool of experienced personnel in the nation's capital to help with training. An interchange of ideas between teachers and government officials would benefit both, and the country as a whole. If opened to students throughout the Middle East, the institution could help expand training in other countries as well.

Official experts from the United States had considerable influence in Turkey thanks to the millions of dollars behind their advice, but U.N. missions got no cooperation from them either in money or in sympathetic interest. There was in fact a hostility among ICA officials to the idea of a U.N.-sponsored project that either emanated from or was carried over into the State Department in Washington. In any event, a competitive feeling was manifest and persisted for years after the university had begun to function. The fact that the proponent was American, the teaching was to be in English, and an American university was to be later involved as advisor never altered the American attitude.

It was not until I met an American-trained Turkish engineer named Vecdi Diker that I found a sympathetic response to the idea of a new university. He introduced me to Fatin Zorlu, then Acting Prime Minister. After a conference, I prepared a memorandum, dated October 1, 1954, setting forth the following justifications for the institution:

1. There was a shortage of architects and planners (city, village, and regional) qualified to help in properly developing the country.

2. With the country in the process of growth, building was proceeding rapidly, and physical patterns were being created that would have a lasting influence upon the future formation of the country.

3. The proper development of the country could not be assured through the aid of foreign experts alone, although they were needed to advise on the creation of an institution, to help staff it with competent teachers during the early years, and to train Turkish architects and planners both in teaching and in the practice of the professions over the long term.

4. Though there were more trained engineers than architects in the country, there was a shortage of engineers as well—thus after the school

---

arts, the skill as well as numbers of his architects bore a very unequal proportion to the greatness of his designs." He directed his magistrates to institute schools and appoint professors and spur "ingenious youths who had received a liberal education" to become architects. Edward Gibbon, *The Decline and Fall of the Roman Empire* (New York: Washington Square Press, 1962), Vol. I, p. 309.

of architecture and community planning was organized and in operation, the scope of the school should be expanded so as to embrace engineering. However, the teaching of architecture should be directed toward a specialized profession, not coupled with engineering as a unit either in training or in the conferring of degrees; the same principle should apply to the engineering profession.

5. The necessity for such an institution in Ankara was emphasized by several facts: Ankara had no such institution, either within its boundaries or within the immediate region; architecture, engineering, and planning policies vitally affecting Turkish development were being made in Ankara; there were many students as well as civil servants who could benefit from study or association with competent experts and teachers from abroad, and who would apply for entry; their training and association with a university and with such experts would improve the quality of design and the physical development of national undertakings as well as the quality of private developments.

At Zorlu's request, I prepared a tentative budget for a university showing, among other things, how much would be required in foreign funds and how much in Turkish lira. I also appended a brief memorandum on the details of fulfillment dealing with the following:

1. Temporary quarters for the institution could be made available by the government during its initial stages at one of the schools in Ankara or in some other suitable place.

2. The project could best be implemented by having an established university abroad assume the primary task of advising on the budgeting of the program, programming the courses, aiding in the staffing of the professional and administrative personnel, and prescribing the requirements for entry and for degrees. I suggested that the School of Architecture and City Planning of the University of Pennsylvania (where I was then teaching) be requested to advise on these phases of the program.

3. The further aid of the United Nations toward implementing the program was to be solicited.

4. A committee, to be designated by the Turkish government, would further the proposal. The committee would study financing requirements, confer with those concerned with the proposal's development, and make the proper recommendations. As soon as possible the committee's composition would be broadened to include foreign experts, particularly from the United States, who could establish desirable liaisons with foundations, the University of Pennsylvania, the United Nations, or other groups whose technical or financial aid might be helpful. Steps would be taken to have the committee designated and have it con-

fer with the Minister of Education, the Minister of Public Works, and others involved with the program.

5. At the appropriate time the government would announce the appointment of the committee, the purpose of its formation, and the preliminary plans to be taken toward initiating the undertaking.

On October 6, 1954, Olle Sturen, the officer then heading the U.N. office in Turkey, sent a memorandum to the Turkish Minister of Education, setting forth the objectives of the university. Simultaneously, Sturen wrote a letter to the United Nations in which he said:

> The reason why this project to me seems so important is that as far as I understand, it is the first time since we started our technical assistance programme in Turkey, that our recommendations have been so rapidly accepted and not only that but have been discussed, considered and accepted on the absolutely highest governmental level. I am certain you agree with me that if we achieve success in this project, it will reflect on the future of the whole U.N. technical assistance here in Turkey.

After receiving approval of the plan in principle from both the United Nations and the University of Pennsylvania, I asked the government to release the plan to the press. Though all the details were still to be worked out, I felt that a public announcement while I was still in Turkey would make the commitment firm. The announcement met with an enthusiastic public response.

Early in 1956, Turkey's Ministry of Education officially opened the Middle East Technical University. After preliminary assurances of interest by the United Nations Technical Assistance Administration, the United Nations Special Fund appropriated $1.5 million for the venture, and Thomas B. A. Godfrey was selected to represent the U.N. and help get the university started. Under a second team, headed by Dean Holmes Perkins of the University of Pennsylvania, a faculty of architecture and community planning was assembled, and classes were started in October 1956 in temporary quarters. During the next two years, M.E.T.U. added three more schools, one in engineering, one in the administrative disciplines, and another in the arts and sciences.

THE UNIVERSITY IS CHARTERED

Though functioning since 1956, the university was formally chartered by the government in 1959 as a government-owned but quasi-autonomous institution similar to state universities in the United States. While the Minister of Education has a voice in financial matters, the university's president and Board of Trustees make the policy. In 1960, Turkey was paying the largest share of the school's annual budget ($2.4 million); international sources contributed approximately $600,000. The United States up to 1960 was still not among the contributors. In 1960 the first 30 students were graduated out of a total of 515 matriculants.

Since the teaching staff would be drawn from all over the world (Great Britain, Norway, Japan, Italy, Canada, the Netherlands, Sweden, Finland, and the United States), it was obviously necessary to choose a single language for studies. Because of Turkey's close ties with the countries that use English as their language for the teaching of the sciences, and because of the abundance and availability of English literature in technology and other important fields, English was selected.

The original plan was to grant a master's degree after four full years of study, the students spending two semesters a year in study and the summer season in supervised employment in the field. Most of the departments now, however, have redesigned their curricula so that a bachelor's degree is given upon completion of all courses at the end of four years, and a master's degree is conferred upon those found competent after a fifth year of study. The development of a city-planning course was one of the original objectives, but it did not get under way until 1961.

The university has a unique staff pattern, which might well be studied by institutions of higher learning in other developing countries. From the president on down to the academic level of deans, directors, and department chairmen, there would be both a Turkish and a foreign counterpart, until time and experience had given the Turkish administrators a solid basis in Western techniques of higher education. For example, while the charter requires that the permanent president be a citizen of Turkey, his consultant president in the early period was to be a scientist or engineer of international reputation from another country. Two American educators, Dean W. R. Woolrich and later Dr. Edwin S. Burdell, were the first consultant presidents. After Dr. Burdell resigned, Kemal Kurdaş, a dynamic Turkish educator, was officially named to head the university.

In November 1959 the Board of Trustees established an architectural competition for design of the university and University City.[6] In 1963, M.E.T.U. was in the process of completing a university that will ultimately be teaching 12,000 engineers, scientists, and other technicians on an 11,000-acre University City located five miles from Ankara. The Turkish government expects to spend the equivalent of $12.5 million on the grounds and buildings. In addition to the $1.5 million contributed initially by the United Nations Special Fund, the Ford Foundation has given $250,000 for graduate studies and research projects, and after a

_____
[6] See *Time*, Vol. LXXVI, No. 2 (July 11, 1960), p. 81, and the Middle East Technical University release dated February 1960 and signed by W. R. Woolrich, consultant and interim president of M.E.T.U. at that time.

long delay, AID gave $350,000 in equipment and the services of four Cornell University professors for the university's Faculty of Administrative Sciences.

In November 1963, M.E.T.U. began its sixth year with an enrollment of 2100 young men and women. The student body in 1963 was twice that of 1962. It was described in 1963 as "the fastest growing university in the world."[7] About 10 per cent of the student body came from other Middle Eastern countries, and some from Africa.[8] There were 300 on the teaching staff, 65 of whom were non-Turkish nationals. All around them, contractors and construction men were busy building additional laboratories, dormitories, and facilities.

On November 5, 1963, President Kurdaş wrote me that the university was then

. . . engaged in completing the first phase of this program which will be sufficient to meet the needs of 6000 students. This first part of the construction program, which I am determined to have finished before October 1964, includes fifteen buildings with the utility services of water, electricity, roads, telephone, sewage system, gas and heating. As of the end of October 1963 we have already completed a substantial part of this building program and all the utility services.

On October 1, 1963, the students were enrolled as follows: engineering, 952; architecture, 228; administrative sciences, 441; arts and sciences, 439. The engineering department included chemical, civil, electrical, mechanical, and mining engineering. The architecture department embraced city and regional planning as well as architecture. The administrative sciences covered economics, statistics, management, and public administration. Under the department of arts and sciences were the departments of chemistry, education, humanities, mathematics, physics, theoretical physics, and the social sciences.

Turkey has been a troubled country. When the Menderes government was succeeded by a military group, the university naturally experienced some difficulties, but so far it seems to have survived the transition period. UNESCO has taken over the United Nations' representation and has helped in staffing and other aspects.

Institutions of learning cannot avoid the problems of flux and of rapid and sometimes even violent change in developing nations. The Middle East Technical University is no exception. But already the university has made an important contribution. That it has continued and

[7] *New York Times,* October 21, 1963, p. 2.

[8] In the letter to the author dated November 5, 1963, the university's president, Kemal Kurdaş, wrote: "We have had serious difficulties in recruiting foreign students. In general, they do not qualify in the competitive entrance examinations which take place every July. In order to overcome this difficulty we have established a special quota for foreign students."

grown under the new government, though a creature of the old, is a tribute to Turkish officials and an indication that the struggle for improved education has been placed above the battle.[9]

Training is a long and tedious process, but there are no shortcuts. Ventures like M.E.T.U. are indispensable and, it is hoped, will continue to find a prime place among Turkey's interests, in international aid programs, and in the aid programs of the United States.[10]

As the years pass and the thousands of trained young men and women take their places throughout Turkey's cities and farms, M.E.T.U.— though it was unsupported until recently by United States aid programs —will have a greater and more lasting impact on Turkey and perhaps on the Middle East than most other aid programs to which the United States gave its money and support.[11] A university teaches many lessons to many people—and here is at least one lesson for the United States as well.

THE NEED FOR RESEARCH

Education and research go together. Both are imperatives in the struggle for development. "Billions of dollars of investment have been lost," says Paul G. Hoffman, "because millions were not spent in adequate preparatory activities. Many sound projects have been passed by because of inadequate investigation. Investment opportunities are not usually found. They must be created."[12] In the 1950's wholly inadequate attention was given to "surveys of resources, technical training and industrial research."[13]

The main criticism of research into the problems of underdeveloped areas is not its inadequacy as a tool but the inadequacy of hypotheses to

[9] Vecdi Diker is no longer a trustee, but without his untiring efforts on behalf of the university, it could not have emerged. In the bitterness that followed the downfall of the Menderes government, Fatin Zorlu in 1961 was among those executed. I have no way of knowing the merits of the charges or the justification for the punishment. I know only that this highly cultured man was unselfish in his firm support of the university in its formative years.

[10] Credit for launching a university rates far less than credit for seeing it through. In that perspective, the trustees during its first hard years, the teaching and administrative staff, the American and Turkish presidents, and the United Nations and UNESCO deserve the accolades. Had U.N. officials, particularly Julia Henderson, Ernest Weissmann, Arthur Goldschmidt, and Tagi Nasr, not relied on my representations by letters from Turkey, the university would never have been born.

[11] At long last in 1963, Cornell University, with AID sponsorship, undertook to give its course in public administration.

[12] At the National Conference on International Economic and Social Development, Shoreham Hotel, Washington, D.C., June 15, 1961.

[13] Paul G. Hoffman, *One Hundred Countries, One and One Quarter Billion People* (Washington, D.C.: Albert D. and Mary Lasker Foundation, 1960), p. 31.

follow up. If research is the "diligent and systematic inquiry or investigation into a subject in order to discover facts or principles,"[14] the quest can take on meaning only when one has decided what it is that one wants to ascertain. A formula that is simple and practical in England may bog down administratively in Ghana. Corruption, ignorance, lack of skills, politics and opportunism, centralization, the stubbornness of custom or disrespect for prevailing traditions, and other intangibles may doom the best findings—while the genius of a few leaders or the lucky disclosures of nature may validate a recommendation ordinarily destined for failure.

Other deficiencies include the low priority given to program and policy research. Though the evils of a particular situation may be shown, the means for eliminating them are often ignored. A study may emphasize the economic aspect of a problem and neglect the legal and political factors. So too, remedies that originate abroad are too often adopted irrespective of their applicability.

Research into urbanization embraces not one problem but a score or more of related problems, and it is impossible to isolate one from the others. The problems include, among others, economics and the land problem, the relationships of the urban to the rural economies, population problems and demography, tax, finance, and subsidy policies, manpower problems, public works and transportation, sanitation, administration, politics, community and social organization, regional policy, housing policy, architecture and city planning, materials production, code enforcement, and industrial location.

For example, take the single item of urban land. Although considerable data exist on rural land and on a few phases of the housing question, the urban land problem has hardly been recognized even in the more developed countries. When urban land theories do receive notice anywhere, it is by the realtor, tax collector, or subdivider who is concerned with the problem only in a very specialized way. With even the developed countries confronted by urban land problems for the first time, preliminary data are required on urban land tenure, land regulation, land use and planning, land acquisition, land cost, land financing and subsidies, and land taxation.[15]

Research into design and materials is of a different order and is a virtually uncharted field, particularly in tropical building. Good building research institutes are needed to study climatic problems, make economic analyses of the building industry, and collaborate with design centers in

[14] Clarence L. Barnhart, ed., *The American College Dictionary* (New York: Random House, 1949).

[15] See, for example, my checklist in Charles Abrams, *Urban Land Problems and Policies, Housing and Town and Country Planning, Bulletin #7* (New York: United Nations, 1953), pp. 137–139.

the study of materials costs, productivity, and the best means for increasing labor efficiency and reducing house cost. Local building methods as well as the use of indigenous materials should be studied also.

Where building research stations and centers of design already exist, improvement of training and facilities is generally essential. One of the most important aspects of building research is to identify the particular priorities for study.[16] Sometimes a building research station will waste time exploring items of minor importance or will spend money on studying something already determined in the School of Tropical Architecture in London or some other institution.

The lack of research tends to give the few available studies the character of gospel. The AID man charged with responsibility for housing in the field will find little information of value to him except perhaps a few papers on self-help housing in Latin America or some of the studies of the United Nations experts. The emphasis of American aid programs on building and loan societies in Latin America is due at least partly to the inadequacy of data on other aspects of housing and cities.

Implementation of research also requires a new look at the existing studies not only by the low-income countries themselves but by the United States, the international agencies, foundations, and private industries. For almost a decade, the Housing and Home Finance Agency and AID in the United States were unfamiliar with the reports on housing and urban land problems made by experts at the United Nations, while the United Nations has never published more than the few national studies officially released. Nor has any foundation or independent expert ever evaluated the reports of U.N. experts to determine whether their recommendations worked or failed.

Few foundations have been interested in the urbanization problems of the less developed areas. However, in 1961 the Joint Center for Urban Studies of the Massachusetts Institute of Technology and Harvard University accepted a contract for the planning of Ciudad Guayana, the new industrial city in Venezuela, and the Ford Foundation thereafter

[16] In the Philippines, for example, the subjects for building research recommended by Dr. Otto Koenigsberger included, among others, the following: (a) replacement of imported asbestos in cement-asbestos sheets by local fibers such as abaca, copra, or ramie; (b) prevention of fungus growth on cement asbestos sheets that causes discoloring and loss of reflectivity; (c) development of surface treatments and paints for galvanized iron sheets to increase durability and reflection of radiated heat; (d) treatment of nipa and cane matting with fireproofing agents to make them usable in urban areas; (e) development of fiber-and-chip boards (building boards) from bamboo or the discards and by-products of the lumber industry (a beginning has been recently made with the manufacture of "lawanit" boards); (f) insect-proofing of bamboo and bamboo matting; (g) use of plywood shingles as roofing material; (h) discovery of new roofing materials that can be processed from indigenous sources; (i) design of earthquake-proof masonry buildings with minimum steel consumption.

undertook the planning of the Calcutta region. These pioneer efforts should help develop experts and information, though they deal with only a tiny fraction of the problems of more than one hundred countries.

The proper development of research programs will depend substantially on the availability of statistics. But the availability and accuracy of the statistics depend on the skill of the statisticians as well as on the willingness of the governments to release them. Sometimes statistics are part of a country's propaganda process and are shaped to fit the requirements of public relations and politics. Nor are data always current; with the rapid changes in cities, information is soon outdated. Frequently a real expert's small sampling in a country is likely to be more valid than a handsomely bound departmental report processed from the latest-model IBM machine. Often the hunt for data will be as rewarding as seeking a bear in the desert. In Barbados, for example, there is no lack of historical material and general tourist information; but there is no income study, no information on family budgets, no essential data on what people earn and how they live.

Private industry could help considerably, if it were interested. But only a rare entrepreneur will explore techniques and indigenous products uniquely suited to the developing countries. The typical American manufacturer is interested primarily in selling an American-made wallboard, just as the Briton is seeking customers for his plumbing and the Swede for his latest prefab. Research in the use of local materials may result in a competitive product which would not be welcomed by the home office.

A primary need is for the development of a comparative science of urbanization that can make strides like those made in comparative jurisprudence, comparative psychology, and comparative religions. This discipline should aim to identify and inventory the successions of social, political, legal, and economic phenomena that determine the evolution of urban institutions. It should explore the nature of the rhythms and the cross-fertilizing influences that affect institutions in the process of growth. It should encourage the much-needed interpretive works of specialized scholars familiar with the materials and methods of the various relevant sciences and critically relate them to the organic whole within each society. With a more scientific approach, the practice of applying loose generalizations and standardized remedies to situations that are vastly different might then be challenged.[17]

---

[17] It was this lack of integration of the sciences that prompted the "Delos Conference," called by Constantine Doxiades. [See my article in *International Science and Technology* (New York: Conover-Mast, November 1963), p. 90.] The conference was significant in that for the first time it called together a cross-section of people in the sciences and professions to discuss the problem. Besides the author, the conferees, among others, included: Lady Jackson (Barbara Ward), the economist and author;

If research into the varied problems of urbanization is to be launched, at least the following are essential: (1) the skillful assemblage of all relevant material into a few central places; (2) the selection of a few competent and experienced people for chairs at key universities throughout the world; (3) the encouragement of studies by qualified people in universities in the developed and underdeveloped areas; (4) the encouragement of more meetings and seminars, dealing with specific problems of experts working in the field; (5) the identification of experts and scholars who have been working in related fields and the enlistment of their interest for United Nations, World Bank, AID, and other missions.

Because the problem is many-sided, the people best qualified for research will fall into two categories: (1) those whose professional attainments qualify them for specialized research (experts in materials, tropical architecture and design, town planning, administration, and similar subjects); and (2) those who have broad experience in a variety of fields, enabling them to identify the interrelationships among city-planning and housing principles and sociology, public administration, land and general economics, law and legislation, politics, etc. Out of their over-all knowledge might come hypotheses that could serve as a foundation for broader as well as specific research.

In undertaking research, the emphasis should be on policy investigation and on field studies rather than research of the chair, though the latter should not be excluded. Studies should be of two kinds: "tourniquet research," for obtaining answers needed immediately, and "leisure research," for problems that are more theoretical and not so urgent. Yet even the first small step—assembling the relevant materials—has still to be taken.

Professor C. H. Waddington, the geneticist, of Edinburgh University; Sir Robert Watson-Watt, the physicist; Sir Robert Matthew of Edinburgh University; Siegfried Giedion, professor at Zurich and Harvard universities; Edward S. Mason, professor of public administration at Harvard; Lyle C. Fitch, president of the Institute of Public Administration; Clifford Furnas, president of the State University of New York at Buffalo; R. Buckminster Fuller, professor at Southern Illinois University; Charles H. Page, professor at Princeton University; David Owen of the United Nations; Margaret Mead; Edmund N. Bacon, Philadelphia city planner; and leaders from the underdeveloped nations in Asia and Africa.

Figure 40. A public housing project Singapore.

Figure 41. Old housing and the new homes started under a United Nations Technical Assistance program in Esmeraldes, Ecuador.

Figure 42. An occupied core house in Nkwakubio, Ghana.

Figure 43. A group of core houses in Nkwakubio.

Figure 44. The U.S.S.R. has achieved much in prefabricated housing production. It has also achieved monotony. Its housing problem remains one of its serious headaches. A prefabricated room is shown en route to a housing project.

Figure 45. One of the U.S.S.R.'s urban projects.

Figure 46. A self-contained project in Bredalspark, Denmark, for low-income families.

15

Development Planning
and Housing

Under nineteenth-century capitalism, the individual pursuing his own best interests was thought to further the interests of all. Businessmen claimed that government meddling would jar natural harmony and diminish the total wealth produced.

That era, however, has passed into history as governments everywhere have been forced to reassert the right, indeed the necessity, to intervene in the economic process. They are initiating, influencing, and regulating economic activities as they once did under mercantilism but with other motivations.

With the unremitting pressure to feed, house, and clothe their growing populations, the less developed nations have had to plan their intervention far more carefully than the developed ones. They must build up inventories of capital, equipment, and raw materials, develop demands for their products in world markets, balance their payments, stimulate and diversify their industries. They have had to plan investments of all sorts, budget their expenditures, educate and train their people, program their public operations, and stimulate their private ventures. Moreover, they have had to do this with meager revenues and tools, and do it all at once. Almost overnight the number of their departments and civil servants has soared, their cities spilling over with people demanding jobs, food, and housing.

More government intervention has meant more taxes. The need for more sources of revenue has called for greater production. Hence, the new governments have had to create a favorable climate of investment, mellowed by subsidy and other encouragements. The road to industrial development is particularly treacherous, for the developing nations cannot afford the luxury of error. Error may spell famine, bankruptcy, or revolt.

To cope with their developmental problems, a new discipline of "country programming" or "development planning" has been born. A new school of experts claiming to know the answers seeks to mark out the guide lines for public and private activities.

These answers are by no means simple. The experience of the more advanced countries is only partly relevant for nations that are being compelled to capsule into a decade or two what has evolved elsewhere over the course of centuries. While trying to respect the established economic principles of the foreign experts, the leaders of developing nations are obliged to maneuver through political chasms, satisfy prospective investors that their money will be safe against inflation, rebellion, confiscation, and corruption, and simultaneously resist the allurements and provocations of communism.

If anything has been demonstrated in the brief period since World War II, it is that not all development follows accepted economic rules. Stabilizing a currency in Bolivia or elsewhere, while important, is no panacea for unemployment or political instability. The leadership of one man or a few men at the top may make the difference between progress and defeat, particularly when politics and economics must go together.

DEFINING THE TERMS

The new vocabulary of development planning needs to be more carefully defined than it has been in the past. The planners begin with the identification of objectives. Though some theorists have sought to break down country planning into *objectives, goals,* and *targets,*[1] the categories are inadequate. Objectives should include those which must be immediately attained and those which are ultimately attainable. Flood control may be the *immediate* objective of a project, while the *ultimate* aim would be conservation of water power, increased production, and better living standards. The term "goals," which is used by economists as synonymous with "objectives," implies, in a strict sense, cessation of effort upon attainment.[2] It is used also in the sense of "paramount goals" which "bring to fruition the dreams of the men who laid the foundation of this

[1] Gerhard Colm and Theodore Geiger, "Country Programming as a Guide to Development," April 12, 1961, a paper prepared for the Brookings Institution Conference on Research for the Improvement of Development Assistance Programs and Operations, May 25–27, 1961, Washington, D.C.

[2] Webster's *Dictionary of Synonyms* (Springfield, Mass.: G. & C. Merriam, 1942).

country."[3] Though a city may plan its goals for maximum population and development, a nation is engaged in an unending effort to make living standards better and better. "Aims" and "objectives" are therefore more accurate words than "goals" to describe the national ends sought.

"Target," which has been drawn out of archery and ballistics into economic jargon, denotes something less than long-range aims or objectives. The five-year plans containing targets imply an effort to reach a specific increase in food, road mileage, construction, etc. Targets are important because they imply commitments and therefore call for firm direction of efforts and allocation of revenues. An adroit politician might explain that he has met an objective, but he would have a harder time demonstrating that he has met a target.

Other terms used in planning include the means for fulfilling programs in terms of *schedules, projects,* or *schemes.* The words "program" and "plan" have the widest meanings, implying proposed methods of action or procedure—the "five-year plan" was the name given to the industrialization program of the Soviet Union, but "program" also implies a design for the orderly achievement of certain ends that may be part of a general plan. "Schedule" emphasizes the importance of the time element and also implies a commitment. "Project" is much like "scheme," and the two words are often used interchangeably. But "scheme" (suggesting more imaginative scope) implies the careful choice or ordering of details (e.g., a housing scheme in England), and "project," which originally was broader than "scheme," is now used for specific undertakings as well (e.g., an urban renewal project).

DEVELOPMENT THEORIES

Defining the terms is easier than spelling them out in practice. The two dominant theories among economic writers seem to have become (1) quantitative economic theories identifying capital saving and investment as the vortex around which development moves and (2) qualitative theories accenting the procreative or productive aspects of economic operations. A third theory (currently viewed as lowborn) is that no one factor can fully account for the intricacies of the development process—it is a social process with a measurable economic aspect. In developing areas, however, the "non-economic factors do not express themselves in the kind of economic behavior which conforms to the conventional assumptions of Western economic theory."[4] Thus housing is not only shelter but a device in Kingston, Jamaica, for breaking up social trouble spots in squatter areas that threaten major political eruptions. Housing

---

[3] *Goals for Americans,* the Report of the President's Commission on National Goals (Englewood Cliffs, N.J.: Prentice-Hall, 1960), p. 1.

[4] Colm and Geiger, "Country Programming as a Guide to Development," *op. cit.*

consumes a large part of Ireland's national budget because the emotional background of absentee landlordism and the influence of Britain's housing programs moved it ahead of industrial development.

The tendency to develop categories in the urbanization process leads to a kind of Sisyphean embarrassment. Housing has a capital and a savings aspect, a generative aspect, and a social or attitudinal aspect that should normally endow it with political and social as well as economic respectability. When it is ignored by the economic planner, it will move into focus through the politician.

Before housing and urbanization are placed in the context of plans, programs, objectives, and goals, ten ways in which governments are acting today in relation to economic activities should be identified. They are:

1. Abstention

This emphasizes *laissez faire* as the best means of encouraging development. Examples are allowing a builder to put up what he chooses, and giving industry free rein to settle where it wishes and determine the hours and pay of its labor.

2. Persuasion

This implies an appeal to industries or developers to do something they will ordinarily not do. In India, for example, large concerns have been persuaded to make social contributions that most industries concerned solely with self-interest will normally refuse. In the United States and England, capitalists may be persuaded to go into nonprofit or limited-profit enterprises or even to subordinate the profit motive in an emergency.

3. Regulation

This refers to restrictions by government in the interests of health, welfare, or safety. It is the most tempting power in the government power plant since it entails no budgetary outlays, but it can cripple incentive and investment if used to excess. The regulative power may also be relaxed to stimulate private operations.

4. Inducement

This implies giving considerations in one form or another to lead to certain desired action. Such considerations include subsidies, guarantees, concessions, loans, favorable tax policies, tariffs, and other aids to stimulate investment or venturing. Government mortgage insurance and free factory sites are examples.

5. Direct Operations

These include the building of roads, schools, and the like, but they may also embrace a wide variety of operations in one country that are left to private investment in another. When direct operations are very extensive, they identify the system as socialist, state-capitalist, or other authoritarian form.

6. Desocialization

This may occur in the sale or disposition of a socialized or government-owned asset, property, or enterprise. Sale of government lands to encourage settlement is an example.

7. Public-Private Joint Ventures

Here the government may join by investment or credit in an undertaking with a private enterprise. The Voluntary Home Mortgage Credit Program in the United States and mixed investment mortgage banks are examples.

8. Regulated Monopoly

In this case, the government grants or tolerates exclusive control of a service but supervises it as a condition of the franchise. A franchise to a telephone company in Latin America or to a cement manufacturer in Jamaica is an example. Monopoly can be consistent with free enterprise if the monopolized activities are carefully selected and regulated in the public interest.

9. Planned Inevitability

Here the government plans the installation of roads, power, or other works so that the site becomes the logical and even inevitable locus of development for industry, private housing, or other operations. This can be a useful device for planning industrial estates or for influencing settlement in a new town.[5]

10. Cooperative or Nonprofit Enterprise

Here government may stimulate or create types of ventures with a philanthropic or public aim or one in which the profit motive is subordinate to the general or the cooperative good. There are many types of cooperatives, of which credit associations, housing cooperatives, self-help, agricultural, and consumers cooperatives are a few. The forms of nonprofit ventures are also varied. The most recent example in housing is the

[5] Charles Abrams and Otto Koenigsberger, *Report on Housing in Pakistan* (New York: United Nations, 1957).

nonprofit housing enterprise sponsored by religious, social, and even private venturers in the United States [under Section 221(d)(3) of the 1961 Housing Act]. Inducements of various kinds may spur the formation of cooperative or nonprofit associations.

The way in which these policies are employed and the extent of their use help explain the complexion of a particular political system. The problem in the so-called "mixed economies" is to manipulate these policies adroitly without allowing any one sector to become so top-heavy as to distort the mixture.

IMPLEMENTING HOUSING DEVELOPMENT

Planning policy calls for implementation through the wise use of a government's inherent powers of police, eminent domain, and tax (and spending, including credit facilities).[6]

A plan for an entire nation is incomplete unless each item of the plan has objectives. In fact, the objectives of the subordinate programs should be part and parcel of the over-all plan or program. Housing and transportation programs with their own defined objectives, for example, should also support the main objectives.

Though government powers are used more in urban development than in any other activity, most of the existing programs are still in the demonstration stages. In some countries, programs are in search of powers; in others, powers are in search of programs. In few cases are powers and programs linked to well-defined objectives.

Housing, city planning, and city replanning are only some of the many elements in developmental planning. But they are root programs, out of which other activities spring. They can no more be allowed to operate in isolation than can any other major activity. So too, the amelioration of agricultural distress will reduce migration and hold down the urban housing demand. Stimulation of industrial activity will expand housing demand, and a policy that disperses industry will distribute the housing demand. An over-all policy favoring production of materials will encourage housing production. A policy that increases incomes will stimulate savings, raise housing demand, and perhaps funnel savings into home production and help spur economic improvement.

Although a nation may embark upon a housing program simply to provide homes, its economy will benefit in many other ways, such as the absorption of unemployment and the increase of local purchasing power stimulated by building. A housing program will encourage local materials industries as well as many secondary industries. These new industries in turn will lessen a country's dependence on imports that may

---

[6] The tax and spending powers have usually been construed as part of the one tax power.

unnecessarily drain cash resources. Other advantages include the encouragement of industrial production and efficiency by convenient housing sites and the development of crafts and skills in an economy devoid of them. A good housing program will contribute to the proper development or preservation of a nation's physical environment and to the rationalization of the vast pool of public works, roads, schools, and other public improvements. It will stimulate savings and the organization of a mortgage system offering reasonable interest rates. Moreover, new and important sources of tax revenues will be created. Finally, such a program helps to stabilize home and community life.

Few countries have effectively stated the objectives that should influence the urban patterns being formed today. Generally we find a number of housing or planning agencies operating at cross-purposes or in areas alien to their stated aims. In the Philippines, the squatter family is virtually ignored in publicly aided programs. In the United States, where housing and urban development objectives are stated in broad generalizations in the law, federal aid is extended to middle-income families, colleges, cities engaged in slum demolition, and lending institutions whose mortgages or deposits are insured. But there is only a small rental program to aid the low-income families, whose need is greatest. Although the vastly increased powers of government now give it the ability to create and manipulate environment, not all nations give housing an important role in shaping urban patterns.

THE AIMS OF A NATIONAL HOUSING POLICY

Although housing objectives in underdeveloped countries will vary with political and social pressures, financial conditions, existing housing supply, and a host of other factors, certain objectives are probably appropriate for most countries. These are as follows:

1. Priority in Housing Production for Lower-Income Families

When there is a dearth of building materials or funds, the least privileged must not be pushed out of the program. These people can obtain decent shelter only by public initiative or assistance. Yet aid to them need not exclude other objectives. When a government guarantee might stimulate building, help support local building and materials industries, and assist other groups, the two programs may be undertaken jointly.

The vast numbers of deprived families make it impossible, however, to meet the demands of all in a short time. The dilemma is that if a substantial and costly program is undertaken for the masses, the country's resources may be sapped; but a limited program simply helps a favored few and creates troubles that are thereafter hard to tackle. The dilemma is not easily resolved, but some headway can be made with a program that produces the maximum number of houses with the minimum outlay, employs the maximum practicable amount of domestic materials, and leaves to the occupant as much of the work as he can handle. This can be accomplished either by planning houses that the occupant can build himself with some technical aid or help in purchasing land or materials, or by building a core house, to which the occupant can add as his circumstances permit. Furthermore, an effective program lays out the houses and land so that a practical minimum of utilities is supplied which can be added to or improved at a later time. It plans transport routes and facilities so that more cheap and accessible land is brought within the work orbit. Finally, the program must provide a system of loan financing that requires repayment of principal so the funds can revolve for the benefit of others.

Building new houses for a higher-income group does not release many secondhand dwellings for lower-income families. A few houses may enter the lower-rent market, but the demand is so great that this does little to enlarge the low-cost housing supply. The period when vacancies occur in the higher-rental housing is apt to be the time when it becomes unprofitable to continue building. When further building ceases, so does the filtration process.

One of the greatest threats to public housing programs is the irresponsible attitude of opportunistic politicians who try to pick up a few votes by toadying to the government's housing beneficiaries. It is easy, of course, to tell housing tenants not to pay rents or to advise borrowers of government funds not to pay their debts. In a close contest, it might even win an election. But the consequences for the country's well-being can be disastrous. The continuity of housing programs depends upon repayments as well as subsidies. The failure to make repayments means that only the favored first get the benefits, while the rest, including those who may need housing most, will be ignored. But there are more serious implications. Default fosters a growing dependency on government in place of honest effort, a breakdown in morale, and the growth of a cynicism in the relationship between government and its beneficiaries. It tends to make the rest of the people look to government for the big handout and to spur their resentment when they do not get it. By providing an unwholesome precedent for a widespread evasion of obligations, it threatens other vital programs. Default by some people encourages others who are honorable to misrepresent their needs and turns them into willful defaulters. Finally, the failure to pay debts justifies the refusal of international aid agencies to support housing and even threatens other aid programs where such a practice might be repeated.

As previously noted, I have encountered three countries—Jamaica, Venezuela, and Barbados—where wholesale defaults have been encouraged or sanctioned, but there are doubtless others. In Jamaica, as of

January 24, 1963, more than 15,000 tenants owed the government a total of a million dollars.

The Barbados housing authority in 1955 built housing for sale and for rental to families earning up to $30 (B.W.I.) weekly (one B.W.I. dollar equals fifty-eight cents in U.S. money). By 1963, it had received housing funds from the government of more than $12 million (B.W.I.), a substantial sum for an island of only 240,000 people.

Yet almost from its birth in 1955, the authority made no effort to establish a responsible relationship with its tenants and borrowers. About 90 per cent of the money due the authority in 1963 was in arrears. No request was made to pay rents or loans, though every now and then a statement of the amount due would be mailed. On one occasion the staff decided to send a new type of statement on a blue paper demanding payment, and collections doubled. But when the authority (doubtless reflecting the attitude of the government at that time) instructed the staff not to do the same thing again, collections returned to their previous low level. Needless to say, the morale of the staff was hardly advanced.

By 1962, the incoming government was faced with a painful dilemma. It had no funds with which to continue the housing program, but failure to do so would have political repercussions. In its embarrassment, the new government decided to offer the homes to the renters, hoping that freehold tenure would inspire more responsibility. Under this plan, only a 5 per cent down payment will be required, and arrears will be funded into a mortgage at 2 per cent interest. Sale of homes will help, as it has helped in Venezuela, but much will continue to depend on whether the government and the authority are prepared to enforce payment on the new mortgages.

Barbados is a fortunate island in many respects—in its climate, its people, and its literacy. But Barbados also exemplifies dramatically how a land with one of the lowest rates of illiteracy in the world can also be one of the least enlightened as to the citizen's responsibility to his government.

2. Opportunity for Homeownership by Low-Income Families at Low Costs

To the poorer family, homeownership is a prime hope, representing not only shelter but lifelong security. The emotions underlying the homeownership structure may or may not be based on reality,[7] but they are powerful enough to win respect.

[7] There has been much literature emphasizing the dangers of homeownership, but most of it, including my own book *Revolution in Land* (New York: Harper, 1939), is in the context of pre-1934 uncontrolled depressions, when poor people were induced to buy homes at costs they could not afford. Much of the risk has been and can be removed by sound policy.

Opportunity to own homes may be accorded by permitting purchase with a small down payment, by a rental agreement with an option to buy, by a rental agreement providing for conveyance after a prescribed number of rental payments, or by selling land to the family and helping to finance construction. Whatever the method, it is vital that the terms be tailored to the family's means.

3. A Housing Program Offering Reasonable Choice of Environment

Since not all families want to own homes, other forms of tenure must be provided. There is an almost universal tendency to plan for the "typical family," but the typical family today may be atypical tomorrow as it moves to the city, as its children mature, as it doubles up with another family, as it ages, or as the family unit breaks up for one cause or another.

Some families prefer the flexibility of tenancy to homeownership; some choose a short journey to work from a city apartment in preference to a suburban dwelling. Certain people function well in cooperative housing, while others view it as a burden. There are single persons and elderly folk for whom special types of housing may be desirable, yet their desires are not uniform; some prefer life in the urban hub, while others hunger for a garden. Some, like the Chinese, have a capacity to endure privation and overcrowding that is perhaps unequaled by any other people on earth.

For those undergoing the paroxysms of the urban transition, variety as well as variability in design, use, and tenure may be indispensable. A government in particular cases will have no choice but to build rental housing or multiple-story units, as in Hong Kong or Singapore, where there is a dearth of good land. Occasionally, houses should be designed for multiple uses—in Bolivia, for example, many families want to have some room for selling comestibles and soda pop to supplement their meager earnings. House and shop can well be combined. Room may often be provided for sewing or tailoring or for a rent-paying lodger. In other cases (in parts of Pakistan, for example), making room for the joint or extended family will be prudent.[8]

4. A Sound Financing Policy Enabling Low- and Moderate-Income Families to Buy Homes

Some underdeveloped countries have no financing programs whatever;

[8] "The tradition of the joint or extended family system . . . will persist as long as it helps assure a cohesive existence and a greater economic security. The joint family (which tends more often to grow than to shrink) presses constantly for additional room. But as it grows, it also acquires more contributors to the shelter cost." Rigidity of the dwelling unit, whether of vertical or horizontal design, prevents expansion and additions as required by the growing family unit. Abrams and Koenigsberger, *Report on Housing in Pakistan, op. cit.*, p. 22.

in most, they are defective. In Ecuador, housing has been financed with the proceeds of a tax on bananas; in the West Indies, export crops (mostly sugar) have been taxed; and in Chile, Colombia, and Peru, funds have been raised from coffee. Since taxes are only collectible annually while the cost of a house should be amortized over its life, only a few houses are built before the tax resources for housing are consumed. If taxes for housing are levied at all, they should generally be earmarked for annual subsidies, whereas loans made on the housing should be financed by borrowing. Concrete formulas should be devised for setting up mortgage systems affording reasonable interest rates over long terms. Without proper financing, a nation's housing program will be small or nonexistent.

5. *Encouragement of Savings*

Just as the key to housing production is finance, so the key to housing finance is savings. If people can be induced to save, the savings can be channeled into mortgages. Savings are voluntary and do not discourage investment as taxes do.

Constructive programs for stimulating savings are scarce. Savings and loan societies either do not exist in the new countries or receive little encouragement. Deposits in postal savings banks are rarely used for housing development. If saving is to be stimulated, not only must incomes be improved but more imaginative schemes must be devised to draw savings into constructive channels. Since a house is the most impelling motivation for saving, a housing program should be part of any scheme to promote deposits.

6. *A Sound System of Subsidies*

Subsidies in the first stages of national development are neither new nor socialistic. For example, a subsidy was extended to the salted-codfish industry just after American independence. One myth about subsidies is that they always mean losses. Subsidies for housing low-income families need not cause extensive losses if the housing is simple and sensible. In Singapore, for example, public housing entails virtually no subsidy at all. Nor should a loss be sustained in writing down the cost of slum land to induce its purchase for private redevelopment. Such a reduction should be more than compensated for by the annual increased revenues the government would get from the new improvement. Subsidies may entail losses in the short run and stimulate profits over the long term.

Any one of a variety of subsidies may be used. The list includes capital subsidies, deficit subsidies, cash subsidies, interest rebates, and write-downs of land or building costs. Subsidies are given to industry to induce choice of sites in particular areas or, as in Sweden, to families according to the number of children. Other forms include leasing or sale of projects at advantageous terms, rent subsidies to help families pay for housing they themselves select, government guarantees of investment, and cancellation of part of an indebtedness. Government may subsidize transportation that opens up cheap land to housing or give special subsidies or inducements to cooperatives. Tax exemption is also given on houses or on bonds issued for project building.

Because subsidies are natural targets for pressure groups, and because underdeveloped economies are peculiarly vulnerable to pressure, their dispensation should be guided by clear principles. Four basic principles are discussed below.

(a) A SUBSIDY SHOULD SERVE A PUBLIC PURPOSE AND BE PART OF DEFINED LONG-TERM OBJECTIVES. A theoretical public benefit can of course be ascribed to almost every subsidized operation. The principle therefore becomes meaningful only when subsidies are geared to a comprehensive policy. The granting of tax rebates for a fixed number of years and a free site to a new factory in an underdeveloped country may serve a public purpose by stimulating employment and productivity and thereby raise the general standard of living. Whatever loss may be suffered during the exemption period may be recouped through tax revenues in later years.

Subsidies for programs to improve health and safety should have a high priority. Low-cost housing is an almost universally acknowledged purpose for which private land may be acquired and public moneys spent. One check against diversion of subsidies is a specific legislative authorization that clearly defines the purpose. The legislation should also prescribe the standards and require an annual account and report from the agency administering the subsidy. By making the appropriation periodically instead of giving the agency a blank check, the government can better scrutinize the agency's operations. The government's commitment to a subsidy, however, should be unalterable where it is a contractual obligation servicing private loans or investments.

(b) THOSE SUBSIDIES WHICH SERVE A MULTIPLE PURPOSE SHOULD BE PREFERRED. Stimulation of a developing economy is a public purpose when it absorbs unemployment and fosters the country's growth. Housebuilding has been acknowledged as an important economic pump primer. It also helps remove social tensions induced by housing shortage and squatting. A subsidy to low-cost housing therefore qualifies as having a variety of social and economic benefits.

(c) THE SUBSIDY SHOULD BE DEFINED AND CERTAIN. Generally, subsidies for the underprivileged should be budgeted in the same way as are subsidies for schools and other recognized public uses. In this way, the legislature and the public may measure the costs and benefits of the program, and reduce or expand the expenditure as merited. Though some hidden or devious subsidies may be necessary, they frequently cost the taxpayers more than open and direct subsidies. They often conceal the true cost and divert public funds to those least deserving help. Examples of hidden subsidies are loans to businesses or banks at nominal rates, tax advantages for special purposes, tax exemption on government bonds, insurance of risks without adequate premium, and loans to civil servants for housing at below-market interest rates.[9]

One of the reasons for large-scale defaults on housing projects and housing loans is that the housing agency has had to provide both for the families who cannot pay rent and for those who can. A housing agency should require everyone to pay rents. If a subsidy is needed to enable the authority to meet its obligations, the amount should be carefully estimated and periodically paid to the authority to balance its accounts. Those who can pay no rent should be subsidized by a public-assistance agency that pays the rent for them until they can do so themselves. The public-assistance agency should be set up to make investigations of a family's situation, help it get employment, and assess precisely how much it needs to live. The authority should not assume these functions. When it does so, an epidemic in defaults is likely to be the consequence.

The same principle can be applied to the sale of housing. In this case, the mortgage taken back by the government can bear a market rate, but an interest subsidy would bring monthly charges down to what lower-income families could afford. In such cases, the family's situation can be examined every three years and the subsidy readjusted. This recommendation was made by the ICA mission to Jamaica.[10]

(d) SUBSIDIES SHOULD BE DISPENSED IMPARTIALLY TO THE CLASS SERVED. A frequent objection to subsidies is the unjust priorities they tend to foster. There may be a temptation to grant subsidies to the administration's friends while denying them to its opponents. Fair treatment can be assured by a sound civil service, independent boards, well-defined criteria for qualification, boards of review, and selection by lot from housing applicants. Individual negotiations with new industries are

---

[9] See Charles Abrams, *Report to the Barbados Government and the Barbados Housing Authority* (mim.; New York, 1963), for a discussion of the consequences of hidden subsidies and their consequences.

[10] Charles Abrams, James G. Banks, J. Robert Dodge, Marvin S. Gilman, and Dr. Kalervo Oberg, *Report of Housing Team of the International Cooperation Administration to the United States Operations Mission* (Jamaica, April 1961).

of course unavoidable, but dispensation of subsidies should follow general rules, which as far as practicable will be the same for all. Of course, no device is either foolproof or safe against political irresponsibility, particularly in countries where the ethics of the public-private relationship are still in the process of evolution.

7. A More Effective Building Industry

The primary needs of a housing program in an urban economy are personnel and materials. Development of skills will depend on the availability of opportunities and on the type of construction scheduled. When the approximate number of building units needed and the types of structures are determined and scheduled, a rough estimate can be made of how many people should be trained.

There is need for technical training centers and trade schools as well as secondary technical schools and apprentice-training opportunities. Two types of skilled personnel are required: (1) the highly talented manpower, such as architects, engineers, city planners, administrators, and (2) mechanics and craftsmen. In too many developing countries, the training of architects has emphasized engineering, sometimes with only occasional attention to architecture. Although building skills are found among many of the rural migrants, failure to schedule building sends many of these people into factory and other work where their skills are lost. Considerable skills, however, can be acquired by on-the-job training in self-help projects supervised by trained foremen.

8. Reduction of Home Construction Costs

Another key to the housing problem is low building cost. Costly housing meets the needs of only a few, cheaper housing the many. The best way of saving on cost is for the housing agency to take responsibility for land planning and utilities and to leave as much to the occupant as possible thereafter. Where the government builds, however, there may be many ways of saving on house costs, such as by economizing in design, standardizing parts, prefabricating shells in volume operations at the site, organizing labor and materials more efficiently, reducing the cost of materials in the factories, developing and using cheaper local materials, employing the labor of the occupant or his neighbors, providing core housing, economizing on utilities, and reducing administration costs and overhead.

No single economy will, by itself, achieve substantial reduction of house cost, and savings are often consumed in the rising costs of land. To effect the necessary savings all along the line will take on-the-site efficiency plus much ingenuity.

Houses in a warm climate can be simpler and cheaper. There the outdoors (front and rear) is really an appurtenance of the house.[11] The simpler the house, the greater the proportion of local materials used. Native building traditions have been too blandly dismissed as outmoded, but sometimes one sees strong flat roofs made of local soil, and in the most primitive tribal villages, one sometimes finds houses that are better examples of indigenous building craftsmanship than those found in some of the more developed countries.[12]

The opportunities for reducing costs are suggested in this sampling:

(*a*) Ceiling heights are frequently excessive. Whether a ceiling is cool depends on its construction and on the roof material. A galvanized iron roof without a ceiling radiates heat requiring at least a ten-foot height.[13] Thatch is often the coolest type of roof and, in areas where it does not nest dangerous vermin, is serviceable as well as cheap.

(*b*) The wider the plot, the higher the cost of roads, mains, sewers, drains, etc. Low-cost houses should be designed with the narrowest road frontages practicable. They can have through-ventilation and a private yard while avoiding the narrow spaces between houses that sometimes become the harbor for refuse and illegal shacks. Houses can also be ranged around an open courtyard or patio, as in North Africa, and in other hot, dry climates, such as Tunisia. Semidetached houses also bring economies in public services.

(*c*) Lime mortar might be used in place of cement for masonry and rendering, while lime concrete might replace cement concrete for reinforcement and foundations.

(*d*) Many local soils can be used to manufacture stabilized earth blocks, and by careful selection of soils, only 5 per cent of cement may be adequate instead of 10 or 15 per cent. Good stabilized blocks using earth lime or bitumen as a stabilizer might obviate the need for cement altogether.

(*e*) Where climate impedes storing cement, a grinding plant for clinkers can sometimes ensure a better synchronization of supply and demand.[14]

[11] Tropical climates differ, as do the uses of materials. The three basic climates are: hot and dry, hot and humid, and cooler upland. Cold generally affects tropical people more than those in the more temperate zones. See G. Anthony Atkinson, "Design and Construction in the Tropics," *Housing in the Tropics, Housing and Town and Country Planning, Bulletin #6* (New York: United Nations, 1952), pp. 7, 8.

[12] See Charles Abrams and Otto Koenigsberger, *Report on Housing in the Philippine Islands* (New York: United Nations, 1959), p. 69.

[13] In two-story buildings, ceiling height can generally be lower for the ground floor.

[14] See Charles Abrams, Vladimir Bodiansky, and Otto Koenigsberger, *Report on Housing in the Gold Coast* (New York: United Nations, 1956), Appendixes I to L.

(*f*) Although reinforced concrete-slab roofs are the most popular in Karachi, the housing authority could use other types of roofing. In Cutch, Sind, and Baluchistan, thatched roofs plastered on both sides to reduce the risk of fire have been used for centuries, and "Jax Boards" manufactured from local reeds in the Indus Valley may help revitalize the tradition.[15] Alternatives like these should be explored at least until more durable materials are found.

(*g*) Timber costs can be reduced by more careful utilization of existing resources. The high cost of timber is due partly to high transport costs and partly to the fact that only a fraction of the tree is used for boards. Wood shavings and sawdust can often be used in laminated boards, which are durable and less subject to warping.

(*h*) Simple earthenware sanitary fittings, as well as hinges, locks, and bolts, can often be locally manufactured.

(*i*) Small local kilns (as in Turkey), publicly aided where necessary, could rationalize brick and tile production.

Since each country has its own special materials, standards, climates, skills, and traditions, techniques and experiments must be related to each particular area. Above all is the need for painstaking research in design and building materials.[16]

9. *The Placement of Industry Where a Minimum of Housing Has to Be Built*

Much has been said about the desirability of locating industry where people already live. The new-town dweller in India often undertakes an arduous and costly journey to his native village on a weekend to abate his yearning for friends, family, and familiar scenes. Many Indian villages, deserted by their younger men, have a surplus of younger women destined for spinsterhood unless the father raises a small ransom for a dowry.[17] Of Calcutta's 1960 population, exceeding six million people,

[15] While the Jax Board roof requires more maintenance than concrete slabs, proper maintenance is more likely in owner-occupied houses. Such roofs are repaired once a year, according to the custom in rural areas and small towns.

[16] See, for example, the various proposals made for materials research in Abrams, Bodiansky, and Koenigsberger, *Report on Housing in the Gold Coast, op. cit.*

[17] In 1953, I examined the vital statistics being collected on several hundred villages in India. The statistics uniformly revealed a surprising surplus of male infants over female. The sex distribution was equalized at the age group over fourteen. Upon returning to Delhi, I suggested to an official that a possible reason for the discrepancy was deliberate neglect of female infants. Equalization after fourteen might be due to the male migration at that age. The inference was not denied. The situation dramatizes the privations of village India and the pitiful efforts to control life in areas that are not yet able to control births. These villages were the sites of small

65 per cent are male and only 35 per cent female, while in Bombay there are 663 females for every 1000 males.

A sound industrial-location policy can alleviate many of these distortions. It can minimize the vast expenditures for new housing and improvements, alleviate the crowding and irregularities of city living, and help preserve the social and economic solvency of the hinterland. The automobile has lessened the importance of distinctive locations, machinery is no longer the exclusive possession of a few nations, while the rigors of a tropical climate have been mitigated by the use of refrigeration and air-conditioning processes. Suburbanization, satellite towns, sister towns, and new independent units are among the forms decentralization can take. The devices for achieving decentralization include resource-development projects, subsidies, industrial-zoning laws, transportational development, and various forms of inducements and compulsions. But there is a vast gulf between what a developed country can do to *influence* industrial settlement and what an underdeveloped country desperately bidding for industry is *compelled* to do. Industry's main concern is profit, not a country's social or economic needs. It finds the drawing power of the larger city strong, its advantages many.

But industrial managers can often be influenced by government. Some of the ways worth trying are suggested below.

(*a*) Frequently an industry's decision to settle in a particular place is not strategic at all. Had its executives been approached, they might have made their decisions fit the country's needs.[18]

(*b*) There are many industries in underdeveloped areas that are owned or controlled by government agencies, but often these agencies are as difficult to deal with as the most contentious competitor. The trick —a difficult one—is to get them back into the family and make them share its responsibilities.

(*c*) Government agencies are often set up to make substantial loans to industries or to acquire some of their shares to help finance them. But they are frequently out of contact with the other agencies concerned with providing roads, power, planning, or housing—factors that ought to influence the industry's decision to settle on a particular site. In still other cases, the government itself may plan a large manufacturing

---

two-acre farms barely yielding enough food to support the existing population, much less any additions to the family. The statistics were only samples, but more substantial and more recent studies might confirm what I can only call a surmise.

[18] In Pakistan, for example, one industry chose a particular site far from housing and transportation solely because one of the owners had bought the land at a bargain price. An exchange for other land could have placed the industry more advantageously.

operation yet make no plans for housing the workers or building a cohesive community.

(d) There are numerous industries that need not be situated in a large city and can use local labor advantageously because of lower wage levels and less turnover. There may also be better access to local materials (grain, cotton, hops, lumber, lime, etc.) in a nonurban area, plus accessibility to water power, coal, or the by-products of a nearby industry. Officials should be masters of these facts, and such facts might often persuade an industry to choose a government-favored site.

(e) Many industries make decisions after only brief inspections of a few potential sites. They consider a study of all possible sites an arduous process. But an official agency could present comprehensive data for an entire region.

(f) With modern transportation, areas on the fringe of a city may combine all the advantages of the city without its traffic or other inconveniences. A relatively cheap expenditure for a road link may be enough to induce settlement of an industrial plant.

(g) Efficiency, fair dealing, proper public relations, and the elimination of beadledom by official agencies can often speed an advantageous site selection.[19]

(h) In a number of underdeveloped countries, the feeling still persists that industrialists will arrive with purse in hand and bow to local regulations, official red tape, nuisance taxes, and directions to build housing for workers. Some investors indeed may submit, but many will not. For all of the valuable metals in Bolivia's tin mines and rich mountains, the fear of communism, political instability, expropriation, excessive regulation, and labor troubles are still sufficient to discourage American companies. In Shannon, Ireland, on the other hand, a twenty-five-year exemption from income tax is attracting industries prepared to build and produce for the European market.[20]

[19] An American textile manufacturer recently went to Venezuela seeking a site for a factory that would have employed a thousand hands. Unaware that he could have obtained central information on site location in Caracas and the help he needed, he spent a month in fruitless negotiations with lawyers and "contacts" representing officials of various cities. Ultimately he departed in despair. The widespread and often unwarranted feeling that bribery is part of the business inventory in underdeveloped areas dissuades some entrepreneurs from moving in, while many pay for influence unnecessarily.

[20] The long respect and protection of large British holdings in Dublin's hub shows a laudable regard for property rights, particularly when one considers Ireland's longstanding opposition to British absentee landlordism. At the same time, laws compelling rent reduction on expiring building leases tend to confuse the picture. Instead

(*i*) Countries that are aiding the underdeveloped areas can and should do more to persuade their home industries to choose sites that will help the country being aided. The right choice of a location for an industry could sometimes do more good than a $5 million grant for a new road.

(*j*) A developed city with fixed investments is sometimes threatened with loss of an important industry, which would leave a large number jobless. Many of the unemployed will join the swarm of migrants descending upon other cities, thus adding to the cost of housing programs and social outlays. It is just as important to keep industry where it is as to attract new industries. A government can reduce the danger of an industrial flight by acting in time. It can make public improvements, ease traffic conditions, or add public offices to help business deal with officialdom locally.

(*k*) All too often an intense competition rages between cities hungry for industry. By offering extravagant inducements, one city may gain an enterprise at the cost of wreaking havoc in another. The winner is then compelled to make enormous new investments in public services, utilities, and homes already available in the losing city. Since the location and migrations of industry are national concerns, unfair inducements should be subject to national scrutiny.

(*l*) Physical improvements by official agencies—such as power lines, water mains, and highways—are vital factors in attracting industry. A developing country should project and chart its industrial growth and settlement, use persuasion and inducement as often as possible, and employ regulation as carefully as is practical. When persuasion fails, national inducements can be offered in the form of free or cheaper sites, lease of sites, aid in building the factory, tax exemptions in whole or in part, and provision of some housing, utilities, or public services for workers. Differential regional inducements should be extended to stimulate proper settlement. Industrial zoning should never be so rigid as to dissuade industry from coming at all.

(*m*) Proximity of schools and universities is one of the most important factors affecting executive decisions to move to a particular location. Settlement of a number of industries in an area makes the school problem easier (besides attracting other trades and professions). The existence of a good university improves the social magnetism of the area while simultaneously facilitating research for the benefit of business.

---

of allowing the property to revert to the owners upon the lease's expiration, the law preserved the tenant's possession and fixed the rent at a sixth of current market value.

(n) Feasibility studies followed up by skilled negotiation can often make the difference between the settlement or expansion of an auxiliary industry in an area or its settlement elsewhere. A steel mill, for example, may spur the building of a refractory brick factory or a cement plant.

(o) The conditions of the labor market are among the most important determinants for industrial settlement. Bolivia's social, labor, and tax laws, which put heavy burdens on any operation employing more than five workers, were enough to discourage large-scale operations. Vague laws requiring employers to furnish travel accommodations or portal-to-portal pay in a projected city like Ciudad Guayana tempt entrepreneurs to settle in established cities where the transportation problem is the worker's own problem. Labor strife and unreasonable demands by unions and labor syndicates are hardly conducive to industrial settlement. Settlement of the labor problem and clarification of laws and rights of the employer and the worker would do much to encourage investment.

(p) The general interest, attractiveness, and safety of a community have much to do with an industry's settling or staying in it. Drab, isolated towns will not tend to draw either the investor or the executives and skilled workers upon whom the success of ventures depend. Governments should aim to plan cities and provide amenities that attract the executives and their wives and are convenient for children and family life.

10. A Reasonable Program for Rehousing Squatters

When a country's policy is to ignore squatting, illegal settlement will usually mushroom. Acquiescence in a trespass ripens it into a perquisite, and once a sufficient number of squatters have established their stakes, their political power may be enough to defeat any corrective program.

Policy for dealing with squatters cannot be uniform, for in many places the colonies are so large as to call for special concessions. Where squatters are few or arrivals are recent, they may be satisfied with a grace period in which to move or with payment of moving costs. In more established settlements, the government may have to grant tenancy for a fixed period, with the distinct understanding that possession by the original owners will be recovered. A rent should be charged in the interim. In other cases, it is best to leave the squatters where they are and help them improve their conditions. Policy must never be self-formulating or uncertain, but must be clearly defined.

In cases where the government undertakes the clearing of squatter areas, a policy (with variations to fit particular conditions) may encompass the following: First, a commitment should be agreed to by city, provincial, and central governments denouncing squatting. Cottoning to squatters for votes or implied approvals are invitations to invasions. Second, a proper legislative and operational program must be prepared for the housing as well as the relocation of squatters. Mass eviction without housing invites trouble and achieves nothing constructive in the long run. Third, the required funds should be appropriated for a rehousing program. Finally, public support must be obtained for the efforts of the authorities and the orders of the courts. The aid of business and civic leadership should be enlisted and approval of the other political parties obtained if possible.

As part of the program, the following steps are suggested:

(*a*) A squatter census should be undertaken to get information on family structure and accommodations, type and location of employment, earnings, age, training, and experience. One of the aims of the census should be to find out which squatters are casualties of the land and housing problems, which are problem families, and which are trouble-makers and professionals trying to cash in on the nation's predicament.

(*b*) Registration cards should be distributed to families covered by the survey to enable the resettlement agency to check on squatter migrations, on influx of new squatters, and on the progress of resettlement and rehabilitation efforts. Aerial photographs can help identify new incursions.

(*c*) Where the program provides for resettlement, payment of moving expenses, or other benefits, a cutoff date should be set and announced, following which no benefits or payments would accrue to anyone without a registration card. Squatters arriving in a locality after the fixed date would not be entitled to registration cards and would be subject to prosecution for trespass. Every effort should be made to remove squatters before they have completed their huts. Public acquiescence after completion makes the task harder and the compensation for moving greater. Private owners should be adequately protected against the threats of opportunists, and summary proceedings should be available with quick hearings and determinations. Simultaneously, an educational campaign explaining the aims of the program should be launched. Properly undertaken, it should help prevent the spread or resumption of squatting and could win the cooperation of the squatters themselves against further invasions.

(*d*) Funds for clearance and resettlement should be allowed to those qualifying. Small long-term loans might be available for self-liquidating projects such as small farm purchases by squatters, cottage industries, and workshops.

(*e*) A careful determination should be made of colonized areas that can be wholly or partly turned over to the squatter occupants. Where squatters have moved to rural or suburban plots, the task is easier than in the central cities, where the land that squatters hold is worth fighting for.

(f) Tracts of land should be found in or near the cities where sale of plots to squatters can be made. The preparation of development plans for resettlement areas and for service roads and utilities should follow. Sales contracts with the occupants should be concluded on practical and realistic terms with nominal down payments or a hire-purchase arrangement. The plots should always be allotted before the squatters are moved, and the wishes of squatters to move as a group with their families and neighbors should be respected. Urban land selected for squatter resettlement should not be far from employment and transportation. Furthermore, the resettlement agency should have power to expropriate land for resale to squatters and to develop the sites.

(g) Agricultural colonies should be established for those squatters who have been farmers and are prepared to go back to the land. Plans should include aid in the purchase of implements, construction of feeder roads, clearing of forests, digging of wells and irrigation ditches, establishment of marketing facilities, accessible medical assistance, schools, and all other undertakings necessary for solvent settlements. To relieve population pressures in the cities, a rural resettlement program is one of the most important aspects of a squatter-resettlement policy.[21] Where rural squatting practices and slash-and-burn methods of farming exist (in Latin America, for example), every effort should be made to stabilize tenure by grants of land and continuing agricultural aid and supervision.

(h) Urban squatters should be moved in groups when their new plots are ready. In this way, compact areas can be cleared and restored to their rightful owners or to their intended uses. Individual or piecemeal removal too often leads to the clandestine filling of gaps overnight by new squatters. The cleared areas should be posted and fenced off or put to use, and new violators should be dealt with summarily. Movement of huts and belongings should be aided through provision of essential trucking by the authorities. Technical assistance should be given in the reconstruction of huts on sound foundations. Synchronization of the squatter-clearance program with the new land and housing programs is indispensable.

(i) Aid for core houses, installment building, or land and utility projects should be available for those eligible under the housing pro-

---

[21] A pitiful example of the wrong way of resettling squatters was in the Philippines, where a group of squatters had responded eagerly to a rural-resettlement proposal. The land allotted to them was far from civilization, malaria-infested, and inaccessible even by road. When a representative of the welfare administration visited them, many were ill and unattended but tenaciously hung on to their plots against the most dismal odds. Resettlement of this kind is hardly a model to follow.

gram. In proper cases, a simple self-help program properly supervised may accompany the clearance of squatter settlements. A limited number of apartment houses may be built in the city for workers who prefer such dwellings and can pay for them.

(*j*) In appropriate cases, betterment contributions should be collected from private owners whose lands have been freed of squatters by the government. The clearing of the land means the diminution of slum life for the city, but it also saves the owner the cost of legal proceedings and brings him a substantial gain for which he can often be assessed. The funds obtained might be earmarked to help defray the outlays of the agency in charge of resettlement.[22]

(*k*) A few pilot cooperatives and other voluntary organizations should be encouraged among the squatters for furthering mutual-assistance projects. Squatters are often able and willing to join in a common resettlement program. Where they are willing, their desires should be respected and implemented.

(*l*) The agency dealing with the problem should have its duties, responsibilities, and relationships to other agencies defined by law. Passage of such a law would manifest the public sanction for the program.

Though the policy outlined cannot be applied in all areas, the targets must always be clear, the program completed by a fixed date, and the agency given freedom to adjust policy to experience. Putting a horde of squatters on the pavements is no answer. A humane alternative rehousing or resettlement plan is essential.

One successful clearance weakens the hold of squatters in other areas. It is often best to select an area for the first clearance where the moral case for squatting is minimal, as where speculators or civil servants have bought in. Dealing with a representative committee selected by the squatters will often facilitate negotiations.

11. Prevention of Squatting

Avoidance of squatting is more important than dealing with the problem after the fact. The squatting problem should be viewed as more than simply a contest between law and lawlessness. Inherent in its existence is also a human need for living space. While some squatting is opportunistic, there is more often a dignity beneath the squalor that merits a

---

[22] Conflagrations of squatter houses are a boon to the landowners and in some cases may even be set by the owners themselves. After a large fire in Singapore which would have tripled the value of the squatter sites, a law was enacted authorizing the government to acquire the land at the value before the fire occurred, i.e., a third of the market value of the cleared site after the fire.

recognition of the underlying causes. Frequently squatting is the product of poor land policy or no policy at all.

Squatting can be avoided by anticipating population movements and planning for them in advance. A policy that proclaims "Squatters Welcome" and makes land available in advance of their arrival can often produce more durable and more morally structured communities than the "No Trespass" sign that may stimulate disregard for the law. To men in desperation, property rights are more apt to be respected when there is a lawful alternative to flouting them. Accessible land should be allocated, laid out in plots, supplied with utilities, and designated as the future areas of permissible settlement. If specific areas are designated on which squatters may settle legally, the justification for illegal settlement no longer exists. Those settling elsewhere can then be dealt with more sternly and justifiably.

Quality and upkeep of squatter areas converted to lawful tenure vary with the certainty of the tenure. In Ankara, shacks were improved measurably once title was given, but in Karachi and Kingston the worst types of hovel persisted because tenure was viewed as temporary. In the new city of Ciudad Guayana, Venezuela, I recommended allocation of a specific area to the squatters and aid in building their houses. Help in laying out sites and some loans for building or materials may not produce the best housing at the start, but planned slums are more likely to emerge into better housing than are unplanned slums.[23]

12. Encouragement of Cooperation

Cooperation, which has proved a novel and difficult achievement in countries like the United States and England, is hardly new in the less developed countries. The extended family, the tribe, the clan, and the village with its many interdependent links, all embody cooperative ingredients. Cooperation in these instances has been the product of tradition, mutual benefit, necessity, fear, or self-protection. In-migrants have often carried with them to their new environments self-help and cooperative associations, building and loan societies, and other vehicles for cooperative effort. Out of these institutions have frequently grown firm, if modified, cooperative devices. The benefits of such cooperation can either be salvaged in the urbanizing process and built upon or be lost irrevocably. When the law grants ample inducements to cooperation in the form of low interest rates and tax subventions, it pays to cooperate.

One of the main obstacles to housing cooperation in cities is the fragmentation of personal relationships. Patterns of segmentation exist in every aspect of housing—land, financing, rent, family relationships, etc. To bring cooperation into urban housing requires the offering of some

[23] Provision for reacquisition of the land upon payment of compensation might be reserved, if the area should later be scheduled for renewal or clearance.

special benefit. Then, if proper leadership, expertness, and financial aid can be corralled for the venture, cooperation may succeed.

Despite the many obstacles in cities, housing cooperation has flourished in the cities of Scandinavia and Holland. It has been successful largely because there were competent people to assume leadership and because government encouraged them.

Sweden's HSB (a "mother cooperative") is a large building company with experienced executives and an organization prepared to undertake the complex tasks of building and supervising the "daughter cooperatives" that take over the completed projects. Sweden also has favorable government financing. The most important advantage of cooperative living is its reasonable cost.

If cooperation is to advance in other countries, a strong experienced organization is needed to launch and finance the ventures without being encumbered by the help of disparate groups of amateur factotums. The voice of such groups must be welcomed in defined areas (e.g., at stated meetings to pass on major policies, elect officers, and select a manager), but the amateurs should not meddle with building specifications or the other technical decisions that can best be tackled by the experienced few or by management.

In the United States, until recently, true housing cooperatives had not taken hold. Many foundered because the imaginative power of the cooperators was not matched by their purchasing power. In other cases, financial mechanisms were lacking to make cooperatives attractive. But there is now a growing trend toward cooperative ownership. In 1962 the United Housing Corporation had built close to 15,000 units in New York City; its associate, the FCH (Foundation for Cooperative Housing), has helped establish twenty-two projects in fourteen states for 6500 families; and new projects are being started at an increasing rate. The liberal financing in New York State and New York City has stimulated cooperative growth there, while more liberal federal aid has encouraged it elsewhere. Government insurance of loans, direct 100 per cent financing authorized in 1961, and allowances of income tax deductions for mortgage interest and for local rates have also sparked cooperative efforts.

In the less developed areas, there have been manifestations of cooperation even in the squatter colonies, where the need for concerted resistance to eviction has made joint organization essential. Cooperation among these people is often the legacy of the rural, tribal, or familial environment. Cooperative organization is also found in labor organizations and civil service groups. If cooperation in cities is to be fostered and advanced in the less developed areas, mechanisms must be created for encouraging cooperative effort, for obtaining land, and for easier financing. Ways must also be found for resolving the disputes that inevitably arise among cooperators, and for managing or supervising the enterprise where necessary. The formation of regional as well as national cooperative federations would be helpful.

13. Sensible Rent Controls or Their Repeal

Rent control, the most common form of price control, is usually promised as only an emergency measure. But controls tend to continue even after the housing shortage has eased. When tenants are the dominant group numerically, they tend to be firm in their opposition to rent rises or to the lifting of eviction controls even when release of such controls may be justified. Yet rent control should be viewed as temporary, since ceilings on rents never produce roofs overhead.

Rent control may apply to either old or new buildings and, as in Singapore, may embrace both business and commercial property. Legal rents on new buildings may be fixed at a percentage of capital cost, as in Malta or the Netherlands West Indies; or they may be left to determination by a local rent board that considers cost and other factors, as in Turkey or Ceylon.

Rent control without an accompanying housing program will inevitably face evasion and cause as much mischief as it is designed to check. Chicane and political pressures by tenants increase unless the law is rigidly and impartially enforced, but real enforcement requires special skills and would cost the taxpayers a fortune. Hence, the beleaguered rent agencies often tend to acquiesce in unlawful deals between tenants and landlords.[24]

The least constructive application of rent control is to new buildings. Control tends to discourage the new private construction, which could reduce housing shortage. No one is likely to invest (nor will the mortgagee be inclined to lend) when rents may not cover future operating charges. In most cases, controls on business premises are also inadvisable.

Rent controls should never be instituted unless absolutely essential. The claim that rent control on existing buildings is invariably responsible for the housing shortage, however, often confuses cause with effect. Some aspects of rent control do discourage building, such as inability of owners to rebuild on occupied sites and fear that new investments may be crippled by new controls. But most often, rent control is the consequence of shortage rather than its cause.[25]

Modifying or repealing rent control is a politically sensitive operation,

[24] Undercover rent payments are called "tea money," "pugree" and "salaami" in the Far East and "key money" or "schlüssel-gelt" elsewhere. Payments in Burma have exceeded a year's rental. Frequently tenants have become sublessors profiting from controls or exacting ransoms for possession.

[25] After World War II, New York City, where controls were limited to old buildings, enjoyed the biggest private home-building boom in its history. The fact that for a long time France did not enjoy a similar boom was ascribed to rent control, but was also due to its lack of an effective building-finance mechanism.

but if the aims and principles are stated frankly, the difficulties will be minimized. The justification for controls lies in extreme cases of hardship where it is essential to protect tenants, particularly those with low income who are faced with unconscionable rent rises or with wholesale evictions. One of the results of controls is the encouragement of disrepair and evasions that ultimately tend to break down the protections. Where instituted, policy should not only enforce repairs and improvements but also encourage them by allowing adequate compensation for extraordinary repairs and for improvements. Demolition should be permitted where the replacement will produce more dwelling units than are destroyed. Public demolition should be held to a minimum, and adequate protection and compensation should be provided to the displaced families. The controlling agency must be efficiently and amply staffed so that tenants and landlords can have ready access to it and have their claims adjudicated promptly and fairly. Review of the agency's determinations by an independent body should be afforded. The agency should be staffed for research and surveys. Where indicated, a gradual transition should be effected from the compulsions of law to the contractual relationship. Controls should be removed entirely when the rental market has returned to normal, and every effort should be made to increase the housing supply while controls are in effect.

THE EFFECT OF GOVERNMENT BUILDING PROGRAMS ON FUTURE PATTERNS

The decision to build a city or its suburbs will establish the pattern for future generations. Every city in the developed or developing world is dominated by the decisions of the past. The gridiron pattern of New York City's bustling Manhattan Island was determined by a plan made twenty-two years after the nation's founding, when the tallest structures were church spires. In the most ancient and still-functioning cities, old and new are superimposed as on a palimpsest. Rome, built on the relics of the original city, is an example. The framework of modern Dublin was mainly the work of commissioners appointed in 1757.[26] London's "main street framework of today," say Sir William Holford and C. H. Holden, "was determined by the position of the Roman gates and the roads connecting them," and the rebuilding acts after the fire of 1666 have "governed buildings of solid construction ever since." London's new plan "pays scrupulous attention to those ancient sites and historic structures still remaining which give the city its character."[27]

[26] Patrick Abercrombie, Sydney A. Kelly, and Manning Robertson, *Dublin Sketch Development Plan* (Dublin: The Corporation of Dublin, 1941), p. 7.
[27] C. H. Holden and W. H. Holford, *The City of London* (London: The Corporation of London and the Architectural Press, December 1950), pp. 56, 153, 106, 231.

Old patterns also influence the cities in the less developed areas. Most South American cities, for example, reflect the policies established by Carlos V in the laws of the Indies and were based on the town-planning precepts of Vitruvius. The patterns established between 1500 and 1600 have continued virtually unchanged.[28]

A city built today should therefore take account of the essential expansion tomorrow. Yet cities built under the pressures of industrial fluctuations and population pressures will hardly reflect careful planning. They may have to be rebuilt when occasion permits. Therefore, while the wealthier nations are now engaged in urban renewal, the underdeveloped ones must plan for urban renewability. In that sense, the building of dispensable (low-cost, not temporary) buildings is preferable to lasting mediocrity and blight. Zoning should limit density and height until the area is ripe for renewal. The lot layouts and the placement of utilities and roads are the principal conditioning factors in rebuilding. If the houses are simple, they are improvable or dispensable.

In the more developed countries, planning is concerned mainly with correcting errors of the past. Planners focus on clearing slums and blight, easing traffic snarls, zoning, providing better housing, renewing older areas, and regulating urban and suburban growth. Because these countries were developing when engineering knowledge was less advanced, their buildings usually had from one to four stories and thus can be demolished without great loss.

Today, however, huge, costly apartment dwellings can be built almost anywhere. They cannot be torn down a few decades later without substantial sacrifice. Moreover, contours cannot be changed easily after street patterns and utilities are fixed. The cost of removal is increased by the presence of stores and costly public and private improvements. If poorly built, such dwellings will be the stubborn slums of tomorrow.

The same engineering advances that have transformed Tokyo and New York City are available to the less developed countries. Vertical buildings, for example, entailing heavy investment are rising in Singapore, Hong Kong, San Juan, Nigeria, and Latin America.

While general rules should never be sacred, it would seem wise when possible to widen roads and bring cheap open land into use, retaining some property in public ownership as a reserve. (To prevent squatting, reserved tracts should be farmed or put to public use.) Initially the homes erected on the outskirts should be as cheap as decency permits. Thus core housing, self-help, land and utility projects, or one- and two-story dwellings are appropriate. Wherever practicable, streets and utilities should be soundly planned for future as well as present use. As the

[28] Francis Violich, "Urban Land Policies: Latin America," *Urban Land Problems and Policies, Housing and Town and Country Planning, Bulletin #7* (New York: United Nations, 1953), p. 90.

city grows, the houses can be replaced with taller buildings of higher densities. A recapture clause enabling the government to reacquire the property upon payment of value might be practical in many cases.

Where there is no alternative to costly apartment dwellings in or near the center of cities, they should be built to stand the test of time. When possible, apartments should be planned so that they are easily expandable. The less height and the more open space available, the better. In the long run, the most blighting influence on a city is not the one-story shack, however bad, but the tall crowded tenement with its small cubicles for masses of people. Planners exhort nations to build well and permanently. The nations that can afford to do so should, but in the poorer countries not only is the choice narrow and the time short but the stakes are large and the mistakes enduring. If compromises must be made because of emergency, the planners who make them should weigh both the immediate by-products and the future means of rectifying them.

16

The Role of Aid Programs

THE AID RACE

The ideological contest between the two most powerful nations has ushered in a political competition for aid to the underdeveloped areas. The Soviet Union, besides aiding metallurgical development in India, helping to build the Aswan High Dam on the Nile, providing a technological institute, hotel, and hospital in Burma and stadiums in Indonesia, Guinea, and Mali, has also been giving technical assistance for housing and urban development. Soviet specialists are working out plans for two large residential districts of Accra and Tema in Ghana and making a general plan for Hodeida in Yemen. The U.S.S.R. is also supplying building materials, construction machinery, and engineering equipment to a number of countries. Its visiting specialists emphasize prefabricated elements as the hallmark of Soviet building performance.[1]

Soviet aid, however, is only a small fraction of the aid given by international agencies and by the United States. Its assistance for housing has been relatively recent and only a curtain raiser on the international propaganda stage, but it may well move toward the larger limelight when and if a change in the libretto is indicated.

American aid, although it is far more substantial than the Soviet Union's in all areas of activity, has been small and painfully disorganized in the areas of housing and urban development. By 1961, however, there

[1] United Nations, *Report of the Ad Hoc Group of Experts on Housing and Urban Development,* Economic and Social Council, Social Commission, 14th Session (New York, April 2, 1962), N. N. Smirnoff, Appendix, p. 27.

were signs that politicians were recognizing the urban problems that the aid experts had disdained. Stirred into action following the rise of Castroism and the military fiasco in Cuba, "urban and rural housing programs to provide decent homes for all our people" won esteem in the Alliance for Progress program. Specific objectives also included a fairer system of land tenure, more adequate taxation on real estate, credit facilities at reasonable interest, drinking water and drainage for not less than 70 per cent of the urban population, and construction of inexpensive houses for low-income families. Since there is no Alliance for Progress for the rest of the world, the home-hungry nations of Africa and Asia have to be satisfied mostly with U.N. technical advice, which often means telling officials to do what they are in no position to do.

United States multilateral aid to countries outside Latin America consists of contributions of its share to the United Nations, the International Bank for Reconstruction and Development (World Bank), the International Development Association, and the International Monetary Fund. The main form of U.N. aid is through its technical-assistance programs, to which the United States has contributed for the years 1959, 1960, 1961, 1962, and 1963 only $11.9 million, $14.7 million, $17.8 million, $19.6 million, and $21.8 million, respectively. Only a tiny fraction of this amount (not more than one million dollars annually at best) has gone to the small staff administering the U.N.'s Housing, Building and Planning Branch.

Though minuscule when compared to what it has pledged for Latin America, the U.S. contribution to technical assistance has been substantial when measured against what other nations do, since its share represents 35 per cent of the total from all U.N. sources. The U.S. contribution to the U.N. Special Fund (a maximum of only $31.3 million in 1963) has been 40 per cent of the total. American aid has thus been a pittance that appears generous only by comparison.

THE LACK OF HOUSING AID

The United States cannot be blamed for refusing to finance the whole U.N. international aid show. But the over-all effect has been that U.N. technical assistance of all kinds is small, and what goes for urbanization and housing hardly worth mention. The more developed nations have all but closed their eyes to the more imperative urban needs of the rest of the world.

The International Development Association (IDA), whose funds for world aid of all kinds in 1961 were only a small fraction of what the United States had assigned to Latin America alone, was specifically set up to help with such projects as housing. But IDA has evolved no concrete proposals. One reason is that the same officials who operate the World

Bank run IDA, and the same resistance to urban and housing loans prevails.

At any rate, the IDA has only limited funds, and if it is ever induced to go into housing, it will be only on a pilot basis. The housing catacomb is replete with "one-shot" memorials running the gamut from costly assembly-line techniques to primitive self-help operations. "Pilot housing scheme" has become, in the language of aid, a means of giving a stepchild program mention without attention. Whatever funds are devoted to it can be conveniently nominal.

Experimental schemes should, of course, not be ruled out. But the world's housing shortage will be resolved less by pilot schemes than by the laborious evolution of proper policy within a broad social and economic context, and by the development and integration of skills and materials, transport and land programs, savings and financing techniques, all of which should be supported by outside technical assistance and some financial aid where necessary.

The reasons for the lack of constructive aid to housing and urbanization have been the following:

1. SELF-INTEREST OR SELF-PROTECTION. These attitudes have turned the concern of the aiding nations toward projects supporting their own defenses or those of friendly armies. In other cases, projects have been favored that enhance the donor's prestige or influence with the aided countries. Financial assistance is often given in order to build up alliances, foster trade, or obtain other advantages. Social and political stability are subordinate factors unless a real threat such as communism emerges.

2. FRUSTRATION. The feeling is prevalent among international aid officials that the cost of tackling urbanization and housing would be so astronomical that they would never see its end. Aid, it is felt, should therefore not be given at all.

3. VAGUENESS OF IDEAS ON PRIORITIES. Some policy-making experts are still inclined to subordinate social programs to industrial development. In this view, production of shelter and urban development should be solely the residual outgrowth of industrialization.

4. UNAWARENESS. Those in high command fail to see the conditions under which people live. The increase of housing aid to Latin America followed quick looks by President Eisenhower's brother and President Kennedy at some squatter areas in Caracas. Few high officials have done even as much as that in the rest of the world. Most international aid agencies have taken little interest.

5. INSULATION. Aid officials in national and international field stations, particularly those with specialized training, have been unable to cope with the housing problem and its place in the general framework of urban development. Though having the power to act, they tend to recommend things within their ken, such as roads or dams.

6. INTERNATIONAL COMPETITIVENESS. The two most powerful countries with their differing political systems are tempted to demonstrate superiority in everything from javelin throwing to space ships—instead of determining where they can make the most useful additions to human welfare and community stability. Fear that development might compete with home industries plays a part with the other, less powerful nations.

7. BEADLEDOM. This prevents national and international agencies from assuming responsibility, from deciding whom to put in charge of programs, in what agencies to place responsibilities, and where to start.

8. INEXPERIENCE IN DEALING WITH URBANIZATION PROBLEMS. Because of the lack of information and of knowledgeable people, the tendency is to recommend small experimental projects instead of identifying the many deficiencies that beset urban development and dealing with them as part of cohesive programs. In other cases, a pet program adopted in one country becomes the "model" for others, with little regard for its relevancy.

9. INTERNATIONAL PARSIMONY. This has kept nations—particularly the more developed ones in Europe, including both Great Britain and the U.S.S.R.—from favoring any new or expanded programs in U.N. or other international agencies that call for additional outlays of money by their governments.

A principal obstacle to expanding urban development and housing aid has been the general limitation on funds for all foreign development aid. The head of the U.N. Special Fund has estimated that some $20 billion must be found during the 1960's from new sources to bring about adequate economic development—primarily for essential public facilities and services, which may not produce recoverable revenues. The loans would have to be soft, or nonbankable. But the only housing contemplated even under such an extensive proposal—and one in which housing should have a main role—is "pilot housing."[2]

[2] "Thus projects such as water supply, sanitation, *pilot housing* and the like are eligible for financing." (Italics by the author.) Paul G. Hoffman, *One Hundred Countries, One and One Quarter Billion People* (Washington, D.C.: Albert D. and Mary Lasker Foundation, February 1960), p. 51.

Even if IDA's capital of a billion dollars[3] were substantially augmented, it would still lack the orientation and expertise to launch a housing program, while the United Nations Housing, Building and Planning Branch, which has the orientation, lacks funds to finance any project it might recommend. Despite its "elevation" to a committee of the Economic and Social Council, there is every indication that the United Nations will continue to give mainly technical advice on housing. Even if the major implementing and financing agencies, such as IDA and the World Bank, had more funds available to them and if they were to show a new interest by earmarking a fair portion for housing and urban development, their operations would still be isolated from the U.N. Housing Committee and the recommendations of its U.N. missions.

ORGANIZING INTERNATIONAL AID FOR HOUSING

Ideally, there should be, under U.N. jurisdiction, a specialized agency for urban development, armed with funds and powers to implement its missions' recommendations. Housing and urban transportation and development should be under its aegis. Without spending power, which is the cornerstone of sovereignty and influence, the United States would never have matured into a nation and the United Nations will never become a major influence in the affairs of the world. But what is sensible is not always feasible within the U.N. jungle of national pressures and counterpressures. Thus, in trying to raise up the impoverished world, the U.N. is thwarted daily by impotence and indigence. That it has accomplished as much as it has is a miracle.

Although the funds for housing and urbanization are meager and the machinery is weak, there are still a number of improvements that can be made:

The World Bank, IDA, and the Inter-American Development Bank should be in closer touch with the Committee on Housing, Building and Planning of U.N.'s Economic and Social Council and with the work of its missions, so that these agencies can act more directly on a U.N. mission's recommendation. Joint meetings of staffs would keep both apprised of what the other is doing.

There should be a reexamination of the role of international agencies, such as the regional agencies of Europe, Africa, Southeast Asia, and Latin America, in order to eliminate duplication of work and assure

---

[3] This is payable by seventeen industrialized member countries in gold or freely convertible currencies, while fifty-one less developed member countries will pay 10 per cent of their subscriptions in such currencies and 90 per cent in their national currencies.

greater cooperation with the United Nations. In urban problems like housing, building, and city planning, the ECOSOC Committee on Housing, Building and Planning should be the fountainhead for programming and the pool of growing talent.

Liaison should also be established among the United Nations, the Pan-American Union, and the agencies administering the Alliance for Progress program, as well as the U.S. Housing and Home Finance Agency and the Inter-American Development Bank (IDB). The purpose would be a better exchange of information and a more efficient use of resources.

Simultaneously, the U.N. Special Fund's powers should be expanded and liberalized to permit more comprehensive aid in urbanization problems and building projects that generate production in other industries. More aid should be given also to training and education programs, to development of capital through savings, to research into new sources of multilateral aid, and to other aspects of urban development. If the Special Fund could make direct loans to implement the recommendations of U.N. missions, it would be a gain too. This, of course, will not happen without a better understanding of the problem by U.N. member nations and a willingness to put up more money.

If, on rare occasions, some money is made available for housing under U.N. sponsorship, either it must fall within the Special Fund's limited authority or extraordinary cooperation among several agencies is required. For example, rebuilding of a squatters' area on the fringes of Mexico City in December 1961 received the technical advice of the U.N. Bureau of Social Affairs, the International Labor Organization, and the World Health Organization, while the U.N. Children's Fund allocated $247,000 for construction tools, materials, transport, and advisory teams. Better housing doubtless makes for better children, but this type of cooperation can hardly make for efficiency.[4] In another case, the U.N. Housing Committee may be persuasive enough to get a private group to put up a small amount of money for a self-help project or a study. But an international agency like the United Nations should hardly have to depend on private solicitations to perform its operations.

THE ROLE OF THE UNITED STATES

A true concept of international philanthropy has not yet matured. What is handed out in charity has too often been suspect in motive. President Kennedy declared that the United States is ready to aid "the poorer people of the world, looking for hope and help," and that we are "launching a decade of development on which will depend, substantially,

[4] *New York Times*, December 26, 1961, p. 8.

the kind of world in which we and our children shall live."[5] Under this commitment, hunger, homelessness, and poverty should have no political earmarks. No justification therefore exists for hemispheric concentration of aid or for preferring one poor nation over another poor nation.

The main trouble with the Eisenhower aid program was the similar lack of a realistic philosophy. There was no stated set of objectives. Self-interest was the dominating motivation except when an earthquake or a famine tinctured it with humanitarian impulses. There is nothing wrong with self-interest, but it is wrong to acclaim it as benevolence. Developing nations will welcome technical assistance if those who are sent to help are capable and worthy of respect. But the United States has never really built such a corps of special competency for work abroad. Its aid experts have been more like civil servants, and its most prominent aid symbol has been the money carried in its representatives' sleeves. In contrast, little Israel, which has provided no aid money, developed considerable prestige by offering a pool of competent experts to African and Asian nations. This is not to say that financial aid is unimportant, but instead of being the lead item, it should be incidental to aid proffered in each case on its merits. Aid should be provided without the profit or political motive when benevolence is warranted and at appropriate interest rates and terms when not so warranted.

The United States aid program has also yielded too easily to pressures of special-interest groups in both the United States and the recipient countries. Aid that should have been extended without strings was often conditioned on purchases in dollar currency. When substantial aid for housing was given to Pakistan through the use of "480" funds, there was not even a qualified expert on hand to advise on how it could be spent most usefully. Except for the Peace Corps program, United States aid programs in 1963 still tended to follow easy routines and to lack the spark of imagination and originality. A "Peace Corps of Experts" in fields where experts rather than youngsters are needed would be a useful supplement to prevailing efforts.

A greater respect for existing cultures and a more cooperative attitude among U.S. aid officials toward their counterparts in international agencies would be a blessing for both, and for the underdeveloped countries too. There is no reason for an American expert to regard another American or a Dutch expert on a U.N. mission as a rival in a contest for ingratiation. And if the U.N. representatives have a good idea, the U.S. agency should be eager to support it. This nation's aid program would command more respect and accomplish more if funds were granted solely on considerations of the idea's worth, not its parent-

[5] *New York Times*, March 23, 1961, President Kennedy's Message to Congress on Foreign Aid, March 22, 1961.

hood. A small first step in this direction was taken following my testimony before a Senate subcommittee in 1963.[6]

In multilateral aid, the United States should assume the leadership in asking existing international agencies to include urban problems and housing among their responsibilities. In bilateral aid programs, the failure to make urban development and housing a real part of its foreign aid was one sign of the general weakness of the Eisenhower administration's efforts. While the International Cooperation Administration (predecessor of AID) did set up a special Housing Division in Washington, with a skeletal staff, the top officials deprived the housing staff of authority to make policy for the field. The result was that most ICA field personnel were either hostile to housing aid or so ignorant of what to do that they elected to do nothing. Where local pressures for housing could not be resisted, aid took the form of experimental self-help projects which, whether or not they actually demonstrated something, ended with the demonstration. At the close of the Kennedy administration, the entire Washington staff administering the housing program for the whole world numbered only three people.

The United States Housing and Home Finance Agency's foreign housing division, which in 1963 did have nine people on its Washington staff, has operated mainly as a compiler of technical manuals, an observer at international conferences, and a welcoming committee for foreign housing officials arriving to observe us. The main justification for its existence has been the mistaken notion that those administering American housing know a good deal about housing in other countries. The division's talents have been dissipated on useless routines, and its duties have never been clearly defined within a framework of objectives. Thus it was not surprising that in the Eisenhower days ICA soon breached its contract with HHFA under which HHFA was to select experts for ICA housing missions. The division should either be given a distinct function such as recruiting experts for AID missions, be consolidated into AID's housing

[6] An AID directive dated August 8, 1963, and cabled to forty-six countries, contained the following excerpt from the hearings before the Senate Subcommittee on Housing [*Study of International Housing*, Subcommittee on Housing, Committee on Banking and Currency, United States Senate, 88th Congress, 1st Session, Washington, D.C., March 1963]: "I [Frank Coffin, AID Deputy Administrator] would accept Mr. Abrams' suggestion that when we see a good project which was commenced by the United Nations but which was inadequately funded for the reasons he mentioned, . . . we should not be reluctant to go in and support that project." A closer relationship between AID and the special agency of the United Nations was thereafter viewed as "proper and desirable." AID, in its directive, suggested that in briefing U.N. missions the U.N. experts confer with U.S. AID missions to see if "480" funds could be used in financing housing projects. *AID Circular XA 137*, signed by Secretary of State Dean Rusk.

section, or be abolished. In 1964, there were signs that HHFA personnel would be given a more definite function in AID operations.

THE UNITED STATES AND THE INTERNATIONAL AID AGENCIES

If at least part of the national purpose is to help other countries to develop, we could well make greater use of the United Nations. We should encourage employment of as many American experts on U.N. missions as possible, and also make it easier for them to go to other countries. Similarly, if the United States pressed for larger contributions of U.N. aid for urban improvement and offered to meet its share of the additional cost, the gratitude around the world would outlast the thanks for some of the useless road-building operations, the financier of which is forgotten after the ribbon is cut. There is already an accumulating backlog of U.N. recommendations in the urban field. Many are good recommendations but lack two vital ingredients: money and people who know how to put it to best use.

For both national and international agencies a central question is whether aid should simply be capital to finance housebuilding or whether there is a way to build more houses for less money. The first course is as easy as signing a check, but it will not produce much housing.

The objective of aid is not to translate dollars into equivalent houses but to increase a country's capacity to build by using as much of its own material as possible. Aid should be a priming operation with generative effects. It should be coupled with technical assistance to help develop local skills, savings, and materials for the maximum increase in housing production and neighborhood solvency. The social cement that holds neighborhoods together is as important as the cement that binds the bricks.

SOME PRINCIPLES FOR URBAN AID

From the rude evidence available, some general principles may be drawn. These are outlined in the following paragraphs.

Neither the United States nor the U.S.S.R. nor any other nation can finance the world's housing requirements single-handed. While money will help, money alone is not enough. There are no magic remedies. Housing is a long-term investment and urbanization a continuing development. It requires mobilization of each country's own resources of land, skills, materials, savings, and finance mechanisms. Often it is better to use aid money to establish local materials factories or technical schools than to lavish reserves on one extravagant venture or build a small pilot project leading nowhere.

An underdeveloped country is usually underdeveloped not only in skills and technology but also in fundamental laws and institutions for land use, finance, rational urban growth, and security of tenure. These laws and institutions are the groundwork of programming and the girders upon which the rights of the individual rest. From these rights derive the morality of the state, and the moral state in turn reinforces the rights of the individual.

Devices cannot be universalized and packaged for export. Instead of studying the problems of each country first, the eagerness to produce quick results has tempted AID and IDB to propose universal remedies at the central source of policy and then press for their application on a continental or worldwide basis. For example, cooperative housing, aid to labor unions, or capitalizing savings and loan associations may help in some parts of Latin America, but may be of secondary importance elsewhere.

Sending architects or specialized technicians to a country before its legal and institutional patterns are devised is generally a waste of time and effort. A comprehensive knowledge of the country's needs and priorities is essential before specialists are sent. The laws that are written for the country and the agencies that are set up will have a significant impact on the country's political and institutional character in the years that follow.

Slums, homelessness, and overcrowding are not exclusively capitalist afflictions. While discontent with living conditions can spur communism, communization does not guarantee improved housing conditions. The greater the industrialization, the greater the housing problem, and it matters little what political system ushered in the industrialization.

Increasing income can improve the family's capacity to pay for housing, but unless housing productivity is simultaneously improved, the gap between shelter cost and capacity to pay will continue unbridged for most workers. The housing problem may even be intensified by land speculation and the pressure of increased demand.

The failure of a building industry to function will impede not only housing production but factory building and the general industrial progress of a country. Stimulating its operation, however, will not necessarily mean supplanting private mechanisms; it can also imply encouraging their creation or expansion. There is a particular need for educating native contractors and for capital to help them finance their jobs. Also required is a rationalizing of those aspects of the economy concerned with home building, such as improving planning techniques and land, finance, and savings policies, stimulating materials production, and providing adequate transport and utilities to expand the urban land supply.

Though every effort should be made to salvage and improve central city areas, the slum may have to be accepted as a transitional phase of urban and industrial change. While slum formation may be unavoidable in the face of mass migration, it can be controlled and guided in its locations so that better developments in other parts of a city are not affected. Meanwhile, the cheaper dwellings should be laid out and built so that they can be improved, added to, or replaced in later years. A planned slum is better than an unplanned slum when it consists of separate shelters that are individually owned. Without a program that acknowledges the inevitability of slums, costly, permanent, and unimprovable slum formations will be the product.

Short-term measures must be deliberately related to long-term plans, or both will become inextricably snarled. Thus, the wrong kind of temporary structures (particularly when substantial and costly) can entail almost the same investments for utilities and tend to become permanent.

Aid programs must be measured against a country's skills, materials, land patterns, finances, and administrative competence. It is not only what the aid expert feels is right for the country that counts—what he recommends must also be what the country can manage to do successfully.

Each country has values, culture, customs, and ways of life which, when built upon, can make the difference between a program's success and failure. Tribal relationships and kinships, building traditions, cooperative devices, particular savings habits, and other characteristics must be discovered and, whenever possible, adapted and utilized in the formulation of assistance programs.

IMPROVING EFFICIENCY OF MISSIONS

Since there are so few experts on urbanization and so few city planners with experience in the less developed areas, more people will have to be trained and more brought into the field from related disciplines. The United States, Great Britain, and the U.S.S.R. are not the only sources of expertise. The United Nations as an international agency has an advantage in that it can call upon the talents that do exist from all over the world. But it should pay less attention to the nationalities of its housing personnel and mission members than to their greater ability to do the job.

Experts on urbanization are scarce not because education has stagnated or because there is a lack of people who can become qualified for the work but because education and enterprise have advanced too far along specialized lines and because little or no effort has been made to integrate the disciplines that relate to the urbanization problem.

City planning, which has valiantly tried to fill the gap, is still a fledgling profession and is so hard pressed to supply urban experts at home that it can yield only a few for service abroad. Nor are there more than a few who are trained for such service. Too many young university students are entering the physical sciences and the better-known or more lucrative professions. Even if more could be induced to enter the city-planning field, it would take years of postgraduate experience and training before they would be prepared to render constructive service to the developing nations. One approach is adult education, and drawing people from other professions or from enterprise who have already had experience in kindred fields. Among those recruited for service should be a sufficient number who are willing to give up what they are doing, be prepared to undergo additional training, and go on missions. Some of these people can become the essential pool of expertness, leadership, and teaching required for the longer and more comprehensive efforts.

An international nonprofit agency should be organized to assemble the qualified people needed for missions upon which the United Nations, international agencies, and individual nations could draw. An agency like the Ford Foundation could take the initiative in organizing the project. Special training courses would increase the number of experts. Such a move might successfully offset the effects of firms operating in the field that use their initial retainers to secure lush architectural, materials, or building contracts.

While some missions of experts have helped immeasurably, technical advice has been either too general, too specialized, or too remote from national objectives. Sometimes an expert sent abroad may know about materials in New York but not in Djakarta. A recommended policy may be sound in theory but fail for want of personnel. Despite a roomful of the latest equipment, a building research program may miscarry after the expert has gone home.

At least one member of each mission should remain until the mission's major recommendations are safely launched. Discontinuity has been the bane of some technical missions and aid programs. Too long a span between the exploratory and the implementary missions has too often proved fatal.

The experts should be required to deliver their reports while in the country, or if this is not possible, they should file an interim report containing their more significant recommendations. Tentative commitments to the recommended policies should be sought from the government. Wherever feasible, the program or a portion of it should be announced and launched while the mission is still in the country or while the member who is to remain is still available.

Frequently each team or expert acts in isolation if not at cross-purposes with others. One mission may not even be aware of the presence of another. Where there are concurrent missions on different assignments, they should meet and synthesize their work. An expert's survey of water, electricity, or power should be coordinated with the city-planning process. The city-planning expert must relate his recommendations to those of the specialist on agriculture, migration, economics, finance, health, and kindred matters. Those who have been on missions to a particular country should be periodically brought together for consultation and evaluation of new reports on that country.

Sometimes the newly arrived expert discovers that what the country really wants is beyond the talents of one man. When I went to advise Turkey on its building code, I soon learned that it would take six months to translate the code into English, and hardly anyone obeyed codes in Turkey anyway. The real problem was not the code but the development of a well-rounded building profession, including trained staffs that could read and approve plans, enforce codes, and regulate building operations. Misunderstandings of this kind can be reduced by more exploratory missions. A general expert should be able to identify the main problems before the full team is recruited. On his return, he should help define the ensuing mission's field. This would help make the currently useless "briefing sessions" of experts meaningful.

There should be better cooperation of experts and missions not only among the United Nations and its related agencies but also among other international aid agencies. In one instance, the International Labor Organization submitted a long questionnaire on housing that should have originated with the United Nations. The Pan-American Union, AID, and the IDB have often duplicated one another's efforts without proper coordination of aims and programs. The World Bank's expert reports without knowing of relevant U.N. studies. All agencies should know what the others are doing and work with them, each operating where it can make the best contribution.

Since know-how is the key to successful programs, a realistic science of urban development should replace the existing crude set of pat remedies. An imaginative expert can often come up with fresh approaches that cannot be found in the books. There is room for innovation and new thinking as well as for the rediscovery of what has proved workable for centuries, like good roofs of native material, ventilation devices, uses of lime and other local materials, planned compounds, and small park commons.

The decisions of the Ford Foundation to help plan the Calcutta region and of the M.I.T.-Harvard Joint Center for Urban Studies to help plan the new steel city in Guayana, Venezuela, are examples of pioneering efforts. Diaries should be kept of events and of problems as they occur. These case studies should not only add to the store of information but increase the number of qualified people for work in the field. They may not know all the answers, but by working with others in related fields, they might begin raising the questions.

Lack of sustained, comprehensive training courses in the United States or in the world on the problems of urbanization, housing, and urban land economics in underdeveloped countries will remain a serious default for years to come. In-service training for personnel in the aid agencies would help expand horizons. The present practice of giving foreign students the orientation of the country in which they study is frustrating, for what the students learn is too often irrelevant, and what they take home is inapplicable.

There is not a single textbook (good or bad) on urbanization problems. In fact, the literature on urban development even in some of the more sophisticated countries is an assortment of unassembled and unevaluated data, much of it dated, self-serving, or propagandistic. The data that exist on underdeveloped areas should be available at a central source.

Interfusing of disciplines should be encouraged in a world suffering from overspecialization. In dealing with the newer societies, sound generalizations that can put the many specialized disciplines in their proper place can be of inestimable value, particularly if they can be linked to implementation policies. Important information exists on some aspects of development (notably economics, law, and public administration) in universities of the United States and abroad; but it is specialized and unintegrated, and sometimes there is no communication even among the departments of the same university. Perspectives would become more comprehensive if more views were exchanged with people who have operated in the field and if there were more interdepartmental interuniversity seminars to which government officials were invited.

More instruction in institutional aspects of development such as law, politics, and administration would be particularly helpful to countries whose institutional patterns are still crude and faltering. Draftsmen of legislation are more than technicians—when knowledgeable in public law and government as well as in the problems of urbanization, they can help create the framework for practical programs as well as for democratically oriented policy.

Fostering more graduate as well as undergraduate institutions of learning in foreign lands can be a vital key to training and to the development of democratic leadership. More help from American universities should be solicited. A university, in fact, can be a nation's most effective ambassador. The Bogotá training center of the Organization of American States is a good example of instruction in housing, although its training embraces only a few specialized fields. The training centers for city planning in Indonesia and Ghana are creditable as initial efforts for training some planners, but there are far too few similar operations.

After World War II, every American embassy and consulate throughout the world was required to supply the government with information on housing conditions, laws, and policies in the country in which it was situated. The product, varying greatly in quality, represented at least the first contemporaneous compilation of housing conditions and policies in the world, but it was never publicized or evaluated. To fill this gap, therefore, the U.S. State Department should order new studies. Furthermore, existing studies at the United Nations and elsewhere should be withdrawn from the archives, evaluated, and released.

Foreign business firms and their field executives can be useful to U.N. missions and aid programs. They play an important part in a country's economic development; their executives are trained, remain for long periods, and learn the customs, problems, and language. They are often influential in local business circles and in government. But the services of those who might be willing to help are rarely solicited by the aid agencies or embassies. Most British and American businessmen who would happily donate their services at home to such organizations tend to be indifferent or isolated in the underdeveloped areas. A large British-based international corporation in Ghana thought its obligation for the country's progress was settled when it made a gift of a small playground. It could have contributed much more by helping to organize a thrift association, which it was asked to do and refused.

THE NEED FOR INDIVIDUALIZED PROGRAMS

One temptation in every area in which knowledge and experience are lacking is to standardize remedies. If a program works in one place, it tends to become the sanctioned precedent for other places. Dollar aid to thrift societies might be entirely warranted in one country, but a guarantee of deposits by the aided country might be equally or more effective as a spur to deposits and make IDB or AID financing unnecessary.

There is no "standard housing-aid contract" that can be written for all countries. Apartment house projects may be indicated in some places, terrace housing in others, while urban self-help may work in some cities under favorable circumstances. Aid for a few access roads to the suburbs or improved water transport to outlying areas can frequently do more to speed housing development than a costly housing project in the urban center. Core housing may not be suitable in places like Hong Kong, Singapore, or the dense centers of large cities, but it may be suitable elsewhere.

While homeownership should be encouraged wherever possible, there are places where tenancy is the only alternative. Tenancy may be given roots through a right of purchase or a "condominium" arrangement (i.e., ownership of the individual unit in a multiple-unit venture).

Not only will conditions vary between countries, but they will differ within cities and regions. Ability to identify the differences is one of the main qualifications for experts and may make the difference between success and frustration. In some countries, skilled workers can be quickly trained; elsewhere, training will be a tedious process. A mortgage system exists in some places, while income is so low in others that only self-help and land distribution, supplemented by more substantial foreign aid, will be authorized. Some countries have all the necessary materials for housing; others that require imports can save money by mass purchases of standardized products. In a few, the legal basis for housing policy and legislation already exists, but in most, the legislative and institutional framework must still be formulated. In some countries, the central government is equipped to do the job; in others, local communities may be superior.

Competent people should be sent as a team to each country before any aid commitment is made. Because American aid is handed out before all the facts are known about the country, and before the priorities are determined by those who know how, much of our aid money is destined for the drain.

SOURCES OF CAPITAL

Economic growth necessitates substantial capital outlays, and some economists want all such outlays reserved for industrialization to the exclusion of social welfare programs; others have argued that agricultural production must come first. More recently, most economists have accepted the need for capital to finance the "infrastructure," i.e., roads, ports, health, and social welfare. But housing is still a step-child in the new infrastructure family. Acquisition of land for housing simultaneously with acquisition for roads, ports, and other improvements could make the expenditure do double duty at lower cost. But too often, the outlays for roads and ports are made separately. Housing construction might also inspire materials production, absorb urban unemployment, spur savings, tax revenues, and general industrial development; but these factors too are ignored in development policy.

Because the available capital in most low-income countries is limited, all conditions that constrict its flow into housing should be carefully reviewed. Capital drawn into housing does not necessarily come from the same sources as capital that goes into industrial development. Savings re-lent for home building can often be attracted to thrift associations when they might not be drawn into commercial banks. The incentive to save instead of spend can be stimulated if the incentive is created for home acquisition.

In some countries, a limited quantity of capital can be borrowed on the country's own credit. In others, capital can be accumulated through social security funds, savings and loan associations, lotteries, government savings banks, or other media. In many countries, capital may be accommodating higher-income families. When the worker has to put so much capital into land that not much is left for building his house, land reform may be as vital as capital. So too, improving savings devices, stabilizing currencies, and relaxing price and rent controls on new buildings can all contribute to increasing the capital inflow into home building.

Few countries can boast freedom from waste and from inconsistency in policy. Improvidently used, $100 million might build only 20,000 houses; knowledgeably used, it might provide ten times that number. Where capital is limited, spending it on transportation, water, and other utilities instead of on costly houses will increase the supply of usable city land. Then, with a proper program, families can build cheap houses with their own or hired labor and with indigenous materials.

Although sound policies will help hold down the need for capital, some external capital will still be required. The World Bank, the Development Loan Fund, the Inter-American Development Bank, the Alliance for Progress program, and "480" counterpart funds, can all be utilized if prevailing preconceptions are reexamined.

How much housing capital is needed for the underdeveloped world, or for a particular country, depends on estimates of need, standards, rationalization of building costs and materials production, organization of internal resources, length and types of programs, and numerous other factors.

The United Nations has estimated the number of dwellings that must be built in Asia, Africa, and Latin America over a thirty-year period to house the increased population and provide for current obsolescence.[7] Its conclusion is that 19 to 24 million dwellings would have to be constructed annually throughout the decade 1960–1970.

At conventional cost levels, such a building program would consume investment resources of the nations in the three continents equal to 10 per cent of their gross national product, which in many cases would account for the total investment resources available in these countries.

It is clear, therefore, that more practical devices than now exist must be found for paring down construction costs and standards. The notion that the developing nations can build public housing projects of the American type or new towns with houses of British standard is completely unrealistic.

If we assume that only about 20 per cent of total capital formation can be invested in housing, a far less expensive start must be made. Slum

[7] United Nations, *The United Nations Development Decade,* Proposals for Action, Report of the Secretary-General (New York, 1962), p. 59. See also preliminary memorandum on which the estimate is based, *Housing and Urban Development in the Decade of Development,* Housing, Building and Planning Branch, Bureau of Social Affairs (New York: United Nations, April 1962).

clearance must be curtailed for the present, and increased reliance must be placed on roof-loan schemes, cores, self-help, suburban transport, and land and utilities programs in which the workers put up their own dwellings with the minimum aid that is practicable. Cheap land must be acquired and made available in small plots, local building materials production techniques must be improved, and savings and mortgage mechanisms devised to help finance the operations.

It is clear too that the underdeveloped nations must plan for their development in a two-stage operation in which at first there may have to be dense occupancy of the buildings and permissible subletting in dwellings of low standard. The second stage in the distant future will entail improving the standards of life established in the first stage. If the two stages of development are planned for, a way out of a painful dilemma may be envisioned for the future.

According to the United Nations estimate, even if the resources of the less developed countries could be expanded so that $6 billion to $7 billion could come from the poorer nations themselves for the first stage, from $3 billion to $4 billion a year would still have to come from external sources.[8] No financing mechanism exists, however, to meet even this requirement, and by 1964 none was being contemplated. Yet the allocation of $3 billion to $4 billion a year from external sources is not unrealistic, particularly when compared to expenditures for arms, terrestrial and lunar rockets, and other programs.

INTERNATIONALIZATION OF ROOFS

The roof is usually the most difficult part of the house for a poor family to procure. Many countries have raw materials of one kind or another for roofs but lack the facilities for fabricating them. Roofing industries (shingles, iron, asbestos, cement, etc.) should be developed and financed by international aid. If families are helped with roofs or in other cases with doors and windows on reasonable credit terms, many will somehow manage to use their own or a neighbor's skills to provide the walls and other parts of their shelter. Frequently, however, imported roofs (and doors and windows) may be cheaper or more efficient than indigenous products and the supporting material it may call for. International credits for purchase of roofing, mass production of roofs, doors, and windows according to more or less standard specifications, and quantity purchase

[8] *Housing and Urban Development in the Decade of Development, op. cit.* Under the United Nations estimate, external funds would be needed in the early years of the decade, but it is felt that the initiation of the program would help the countries by 1970 to sustain from their own resources the necessary housing and urban development programs—if both the expansion of resources envisioned in the development decade and a substantial reduction in building cost are assumed.

can hold down costs. If the responsibility for roofs, doors, and windows could be assumed by international agencies, a good start could be made toward meeting the housing problem in many of the low-income countries.

AN INTERNATIONAL BANK FOR URBAN DEVELOPMENT

An international bank with appropriate powers to lend, borrow, or guarantee investment in urban development and housing could help break the capital blockade in most areas. Membership should be open to all countries. Both the more and the less industrialized nations should provide the initial capital, the former in freely convertible currencies and the latter partly in such currencies but mostly in their own national money. Part of the capital might be subscribed by the World Bank or other international agencies. The new bank would also be empowered to borrow on the open market.

The bank would have several purposes. It would assist in urban development and housing programs by providing some of the essential capital for plans and financing of projects. Eventually it should become the financing and implementing arm of the ECOSOC Committee on Housing, Building and Planning of the U.N. and of other international agencies whose functions reach into urban development and housing. Another proposal would be for the bank to make loans for the development of materials industries, including roofs, doors, windows, and utility equipment, either for domestic use or export. The bank would not only promote private foreign investment by loan guarantees or participation in loans and investments made by private investors but also finance the importation of materials. Finally, it would promote the development of thrift associations by assuring them of liquidity, but only where domestic funds or national guarantees were inadequate to spur internal savings for the development of building capital.

Loans would be made directly to member countries, to their political subdivisions, or to private enterprises that further housing development. The bank would require loans to be guaranteed by the aided country. But no loans would be made for land acquisition, though loans for land development would qualify. Nor would loans be made where local politics encourages nonpayment of private obligations.

The bank would solicit individual countries to help finance or supplement the financing of specific projects. Thus while a project would originate in the United Nations and the bank, individual countries would get the credit for helping to implement it. In certain cases, mortgages made by foreign investors could be guaranteed by the housing bank, which in turn would be protected by national guarantees.

Loans would be made by the bank to the underdeveloped countries for materials production not only for domestic use but for export to other underdeveloped countries. Thus standardization of parts would be encouraged. A "common market" for the development of materials might permit underdeveloped countries that manufacture more building products than they need domestically to export their surpluses to other underdeveloped countries. The bank would survey production potentials by regions and advise on the most economic development of production facilities.

In giving technical assistance, the bank should rely primarily on the ECOSOC Committee on Housing, Building and Planning, which should be adequately staffed for the purpose and either be in close contact with the bank or be located in its offices. Teams of trained foremen capable of supervising projects and teaching skills would be attached to the U.N. agency or the bank.

Properly dispensed, loans not only would be self-liquidating but could help generate considerable economic improvement in the countries affected. Housing for low-income families would be stressed, particularly since such housing costs the least and uses a maximum of local materials. Commitments for periodic subsidies to reduce the interest or rents of such families could be secured from the borrowing country as a condition for loans.

By sponsoring such an organization, offering to put up 40 per cent of the capital, and supplementing specific projects through AID, the United States could not only make more practical and more economical use of its aid outlays but move from hemispheric self-interest to fulfilling President Kennedy's pledge to the poorer people of the world "looking for hope and help."

EXAMPLES OF AID TO HOUSING AND URBANIZATION

Before any aid is given, the general preliminary study previously referred to would be made of the country's needs and priorities, and a mission of experts knowledgeable in the main problems outlined in the study would be asked to make the more specific recommendations. A few examples of recommendations that might be made are given in the following paragraphs.

In Jamaica, B.W.I., a few mortgage investments are made by British insurance companies and investors to private developers, although the government is ready to guarantee the mortgages. Because the interest rates are 7 per cent, lower-income families do not benefit. Jamaica desperately needs a housing program, particularly to ease its troublesome squatting problem. Although Jamaica can subsidize some of these families, it cannot finance the initial capital cost of the houses. A loan could therefore be made on Jamaica's guarantee, provided that it agreed to use most of the money for building houses for low-income families. The 7 per cent interest rate on homes would be reduced through an annual interest contribution made from Jamaica's budget. A similar arrangement might be made for Trinidad. Elsewhere the proceeds of a tax might be earmarked for the required subsidies.

Loans to Pakistan might finance utilities and house cores that could be expanded by the owners as their earnings permit. Supplemental loans could also be made later to help expand these cores.

In Chile, loans might be made for self-help housing. Similar loans would be made in other countries where there are towns, villages, or cities in which self-help operations are practical.

Instead of advancing moneys at 2 per cent or less to Peru and seeing them re-lent at 12 per cent, as was the fate of previous housing loans, any loans made to thrift associations should require interest rates on mortgages for lower-income families to be close to the original lending rate.

The squatting problem in a city like Caracas should not be separated from the building and financing of the new city of Ciudad Guayana, hundreds of miles away, since development of employment opportunities in the new city would ease the pressure on the capital.

Where people can build their own houses on outlying sites but inadequate transportation holds back the development, a loan for transportation and utilities will qualify. Land can then be earmarked for minimal housing and utilities and supplemental loans made by the government to the homeowners for basic materials. A bank loan for a water system might provide the key to the development of unused land for urban expansion.

A loan application for Lagos, Nigeria, to complete its slum clearance scheme would be rejected. Instead, financing would be proffered for installing a sewer system as part of an over-all program for easing the Lagos housing shortage. The loan might provide for boat and rail transportation to nearby vacant areas that could be made available for settlement as part of a regional development plan.

Loans might be made for regional centers of design and building research, as well as for developing mass building at the sites.

Company housing can be developed into an important source of supply if some of the practices of the nineteenth century are renounced and the accepted gospel is reexamined. The know-how of the companies should be harnessed into organizing the projects. They can be required to advance some of the initial capital, and after completion of the projects they can be relieved of the ownership and operational functions. Sale of the houses to the workers or rental with an option to buy may be one way of meeting the conventional objection that the company holds the whip hand in being both employer and landlord. International loans could be made to help finance operations if the companies either guaranteed them, supplemented the loans, or participated otherwise.

Sound technical advice can help ease the shelter problem and reduce the need for loans. For example, industrial-location policies embracing the more intelligent use of inducements or tax policy could encourage industry to settle where some housing already exists or where capital outlays are minimal. Unnecessary hoarding of excessive sites by a nation's industrial-development agency often prevents land from being used for housing. The government's agreement to provide additional utilities or access roads could induce considerable industrial settlement on sites where housing already exists.

Building new self-contained towns offers an important means of redistributing population and industry. But as new towns can be costly for poorer countries, the expansion of existing cities will often prove cheaper and less risky. Not every city has expanded to its limit. Even in India there are scores of cities with populations of 100,000 or less that can be made more practical bases for increases in population, jobs, and homes. Expert advice along these lines could minimize the need for larger capital outlays. Location of industries near agriculture may not only cut down the need for investment in home building but help provide a means for weathering slumps for workers. Identifying attractions in existing cities and making them more interesting for tourists as well as for the residents might elevate underutilized or defunct towns from their dullness and stagnation.

The strategy of power, minerals, or transport may justify a new town in some cases. When built, it should not be a one-company town where the slackening of the particular industry would leave no choice of other jobs and spell loss of homes. Ample room for development of other industries, small trade, and markets is a must.

There are many reforms that seem trivial but lie at the root of capital shortage for building. The institution of title registration systems is one. The improvement of foreclosure laws is another. This reform is needed because the failure to give mortgagees reasonable rights upon default may be the main block to mortgage lending. And the home buyer pays the penalty. Revision of rent controls is another imperative. A private entrepreneur will not build an apartment house, nor will a bank finance it, if the allowable rent is inadequate or is likely to become so because of currency inflation. When rent controls are taken off new buildings, initial rents may be high for a time, but the supply of dwellings will be increased and will ultimately help ease the shortage. Rent controls on existing buildings should simultaneously be revised to allow owners adequate returns on investment and reasonable compensation for repairs and improvements. Controls on industrial and commercial properties that impede industrial settlement should be relaxed. Regulations should be clear and independent of the *ad hoc* decisions of administrators. Quick reviews of determinations should be provided, and the myriad loopholes that now permit the practice of chicane by landlord and tenant should be plugged. Here foreign specialists can be of inestimable value in helping to clear the way for international loans. Their recommendations not only can point the way for action but, when publicized, can ease the political pressures that keep officials from recommending what they know is the right policy.

AID AND LAND POLICIES

Unless a constructive land policy is adopted by underdeveloped countries, aid money for urban development will be wasted. The solution of the land cost problem can be achieved more practically by national policy than by international monetary aid. Thus international aid for urban development and housing should be conditioned upon urban land reform.

A direct loan to the Philippines for a housing program, for example, would see most of its proceeds going into the hands of land speculators. Since loans used to fatten their purses would serve no national or international purpose, a major revision of Philippine land policy would have to be a condition of any aid given for home building or utility development. This should not, however, preclude loans for land improvements, the development of the country's materials industries, or for housing in localities where the cost of undeveloped land is, say, 10 to 20 per cent of total home cost.

A proper land policy should aim to bring more land into use at reasonable prices and to permit public purchase when essential, particularly for lower-income housing.

Lack of a land policy is due partly to the fact that industrially less developed countries are also politically underdeveloped. Relationships between government and enterprise have not yet matured, and eminent domain, realistic taxation, and even reasonable regulation are still viewed in some quarters as invasions of property rights.

An ad valorem tax on land (such as that levied on all land by cities in the United States) would discourage withholding land and put more on the market. It would not only reduce prices and check a powerful inflationary force but also encourage subdivisions for moderate- and lower-income families, help relieve the squatter problem, and provide important revenue.

Simultaneously, legislation should authorize special assessments for streets, utilities, roads, and other public improvements from which benefits accrue to owners. As much as 50 per cent of the cost of a road or sewer improvement might be paid by the beneficiaries in installments over a period of years.

It is advisable to buy more land than is needed for roads alone so that the increase in land value from improved transportation will inure to the public instead of to the private owners. Part of the land can be sold at the higher value or used for public purposes after the road is completed.

Some of the less developed countries that were once under British rule are likely to deal less firmly with land problems. They have inherited the policies of a country whose landowners had held a specially privileged position and paid no tax on undeveloped land. Pakistan is an example. While there is land shortage in East Pakistan, there is no acute shortage of land in the Western region. Speculators, however, do hold undeveloped tracts in urban areas, waiting for price rises propelled by population increase and by public improvements.[9] The absence of a land tax makes it painless for owners to hold their land out of use.

The U.N. mission to Pakistan proposed three devices for curbing speculation and accelerating land use. One was zoning, including regulations for use, height, coverage, open space, density, and setbacks. Another recommendation was betterment charges for new roads, streets, sewers, and other improvements that would be payable by the owners in installments over a ten-year period. Both of these recommendations were adopted and can be employed in other countries where unreasonable speculation retards urban development.[10] (Compelling dedication of some land for schools, utilities, and open spaces can also be made a condition for approval of subdivisions.)

The key recommendation adopted by the government of Pakistan was the designation of a "use area," which was "any area of land in private ownership which the authority declares is ripe for development but which has remained unimproved for a period of two years from the date of the declaration." The Karachi Development and Housing Authority, created by the statute drawn up by the U.N. team, was empowered to designate a "use area" upon notice to the owner and after a hearing. If the owner failed to use the property adequately, it would be valued by the authority and taxed at 3 per cent of value per annum.

This device not only enforces land use but also provides an opening wedge for a general land tax—which many underdeveloped areas lack.

[9] In contrast to the sky-high prices in the Philippines, West Pakistan in 1957 was buying land for satellite towns at average prices ranging from $157 to $453 an acre. Ten houses could be placed on an acre, and a proper balance between construction costs and land costs maintained. Considerable land, however, continues to be held for the speculative increase.

[10] Charles Abrams and Otto Koenigsberger, *Report on Housing in Pakistan* (New York: United Nations, 1957), pp. 34, 35.

If properly employed in connection with a master plan, it could also be a useful tool for harmonizing and timing private improvements with a city's development plan. Thus those sections would be specified as use areas which the plan designated as ripe for early development.[11]

Often a sensible statute or a timely suggestion may do more than millions in cash pumped into the country. The talent for discovering fresh and relevant formulas will come only from a new type of expert who possesses a sense of the diversities, a feeling of curiosity, and an ability to employ his special skills in a broader context. He must be willing to talk not only to the officials but to the people, who are an important repository of information on home building. Core housing, roof-loan schemes, installment construction, "planned inevitability" to attract industries, and "use area" concepts to stimulate land use are only a few of the interesting recommendations that have issued from missions in which both the people and the officials were consulted. They are only a small beginning, for urbanization is not solely a problem—it is also a frontier.

[11] The "use area" concept and many other provisions, after incorporation by the U.N. team into a "Karachi Order," became law for West Pakistan. Subsequently a similar order was adopted for East Pakistan. Other recommendations made by the U.N. report included a modification of existing Improvement Trust procedures. The Karachi Improvement Trust had been subdividing land, and after providing the public improvements, it resold the subdivided plots to the former private owners. These owners often saw their profits double from the replanning and improvements, while the Trust often paid the administrative costs. The U.N. report recommended that after the land was developed, it be sold at public auction to the highest bidder. In any event, if the former owners were to retain the option to buy back their property, they should be required to contribute the value of the increment.

17

Land Ideologies and Land Policies

The policies made for land, land development, and housing not only shape cities but highlight the differences between the two great ideologies now bidding for commitments from the "uncommitted" nations. Both ideologies have pledged the government to the general welfare; under both, housing and urban land use have become part of the welfare purpose.[1] But neither has yet come up with a quick cure for the problems of housing and land use, despite the vast differences in their approaches.

The democratic ideology is trying to meet new problems by increasing the responsibilities of the state while maintaining the political devices for protecting the individual built up during his struggle against the state ever since Magna Carta. "Public use," "just compensation," "reasonableness" in the exercise of the "police power," "precedent," and "judicial review" are more than lawyers' jargon; they survive as the checkreins against arbitrary power in dealing with the individual's rights to urban as well as rural land. The right to buy and own property exists as does the right to rent, to move from farm to city or to stay put, to trade, to be protected against forfeiture of what one has acquired, and to be reasonably certain in one's property rights under established precedents and under constitutional and judicial safeguards.

[1] The welfare power in the United States was not sanctioned until 1936, after which the right of the federal government to undertake activities in the "general welfare" was judicially approved. For a history of the development, see Charles Abrams, "The Legal Basis for Reorganizing Metropolitan Areas in a Free Society," *Proceedings of the American Philosophical Society*, Vol. 106, No. 3 (June 1962).

Under the Communist ideology of general welfare, the state determines the rules of the game, and the people are expected to conform. There are no ancient traditions to stay its hand, no higher law to act as a restraining force against the state rule. Ownership of land has been socialized. The right to move is conditioned by rigid state planning and controls. Moreover, there are no effective constitutional, traditional, or judicial protections supported by rules or precedents that generally guarantee one's rights of tenure against the central will. The subordination of the state to the individual is not a contemporaneous but an ultimate objective. That the state will "wither away," however, is far from assured.

As the urban revolution sweeps through the world, both systems have been forced by political pressures to vary their original concepts. The Western nations and the United States still recognize the private profit system but have modified private rights in order to improve housing conditions and environment. They have enlarged the spending and public acquisition powers to provide houses for those whom the profit system ignores, and they are allotting a growing portion of government revenues and credit to this purpose. The individual in the home he owns or rents continues to retain the dominant choice in his way of life and his home. Poor as the choice often is, he is at least legally free to seek whatever better opportunity may be available, while the state is trying to cope with existing deficiencies. If he is a farmer, he can till his own land and keep the proceeds. If he is a city dweller, he can buy his own building land and may either occupy it himself or rent it to another. He may rent or buy land on which to conduct a business. His options in relation to land, though they may sometimes be narrow in fact, are still protected in law. He may build on the land he buys and add to it with his own labor or with the hired labor of another. He can sell it with few restrictions or leave it to his heirs. The system of tenure and the emerging state policy are both geared to preserving and respecting the system of family organization, parental sovereignty, and the privacy of the home.

The Communist system, which eliminated private landownership, still exercises central authority over individual decision. Movement from farm to city is restricted; land cannot be bought and sold; and the state controls industrialization, housing, and a good part of the pattern of life. But the underlying urges of individuals for greater freedom to deal with their lives and environments have not been altogether repressed. The state has been compelled grudgingly to acknowledge some of the rights implicit in house (as distinguished from land) ownership, and there has been increasing pressure for a larger degree of individual choice and more local autonomy. Because of the nature of the society, however, protest has been viewed more as rebellion than right. Though in 1963 officials were showing somewhat more tolerance of public discontent than during the Stalin era, public policy has been recently veering toward a subordination of parental sovereignty, and the housing problems as well as the official housing programs are playing an important part in bringing about the change.

The less developed nations are undergoing sudden changes in environment, social groupings, and political organization. Those outside the Communist orbit, while emphasizing industrialization, have recognized the need for more state intervention to improve housing and living conditions. But so far they have generally followed the example of Europe and the United States in not communizing land or trade. Though they have not always guaranteed freedom of speech, assembly, and franchise, they usually recognize the right to individual ownership of land, house, or shop as well as the right to move. The recognition of the family as the main social unit conditions housing policy.

EMERGENCE OF A NORM IN THE NON-COMMUNIST COUNTRIES

Conditions and backgrounds, of course, vary so much among the non-Communist countries that claim to a universal pattern in urban land policies must leave room for deviations within each country. Some regulate or spend more than others, and in most, policies are still in flux. In the two great citadels of private property—England and the United States—however, old restraints upon the state have fallen away as the demands of health and decency have asserted themselves regarding real property. The old argument in the capitalist-oriented United States, that the power to tax is the power to destroy, is now a historical legend. In both countries, the rights of the few have given way to the needs of the many, but still within a framework of respect for private rights, compensation for property acquired by the state, and its reasonable regulation in the interests of health, welfare, or safety.

Almost any program for the "public benefit" now authorizes compulsory purchase. Even the old ethic—not so long ago perhaps the only identifiable ethic with a claim to universality—that land may not be taken from one owner to be transferred to another has been seeing its interpretations so liberalized under urban renewal programs that some may indeed say that the liberalizing has gone too far. If transfer to another owner is an incident of a public benefit such as slum clearance, a better city, or aesthetic planning, the public agency can purchase an owner's property for resale and redevelopment with little check by the courts.[2]

[2] In some of the embryonic political systems leaning toward the democratic formula, however, eminent domain for slum clearance or low-cost housing is still exercised

Although devices and procedures differ among countries, particularly between the more and the less developed, fundamental attitudes conditioning them seem to be steadily moving toward a norm. The powers in the governmental sphere—regulation, tax (and spending), and eminent domain—are all being extended, though not always effectively, wherever their exercise is essential to meet a social or economic contingency. Socialization of housing for the low-income groups is accepted. Socialization of mortgage lending or of the risk in mortgage lending (i.e., by guarantee of private loans) no longer arouses consternation even among old-line capitalist theorists. It will be called "aid to private enterprise" in the United States or "socialism" where the term is politically respectable.

Historically, political systems of many states have often tended to reach beyond national borders to infect neighboring states.[3] The surviving influence of former colonial powers has influenced national policy for the freed nations. Rationalized judgments in legal cases made under given sets of facts are weighed by courts elsewhere as a guide to their own decisions. Greater ease of travel, exchanges of experts, seminars, training of foreign students in British and American schools, and technical-assistance programs are all having their effect in leveling the differences in the political and social approaches to housing and urban-planning problems. The material or political success of a nation may be the reason for its practices being adopted elsewhere, even when some of those practices may not be perfect.

The universal spread of urbanization and slum life is speeding the process of policy contagion, as exemplified by the popularity of urban renewal programs in the more developed countries. The tendency toward emulation is manifested in the adoption by the United States of Britain's public housing program and in Europe's adoption of the American pattern of urban renewal. While Canada was propagating its example of regional

---

very cautiously, though the pressures to exert power more liberally are manifesting themselves. Even in more advanced Norway, industrialists, tradesmen, and retailers cry out against any attempt to reduce the usable portion of their own land, but they now accept the intervention of government to ease the flow of traffic that threatens their operations. Fear of regimentation is still one of the obstacles to broader planning in Austria, but Vienna has nevertheless authorized expropriation when an owner refuses to sell or develop land ripe for use. In Japan, power to exercise eminent domain for public uses is being extended, though slowly and laboriously.

[3] The spread of a universal norm in law or tradition is not new in history. It was evident in the whole process of Europeanization. So too, Roman and canon law once tended to impose a wide uniformity on the civil law, while the Napoleonic Code and the laws of Norway, Sweden, and Denmark have tended to spread uniformity between states and regions. The rise of a common sea law also exemplifies the tendency.

planning between cities, it was embracing the American form of government mortgage insurance; the Philippines, Jamaica, and Trinidad have also copied the American insurance formula. Sweden took a look at American housing cooperation in the ill-fated 1920's (before they had become ill-fated) and made it succeed in Sweden. Now the United States is seriously examining Scandinavia's cooperative formula. The less developed countries are also drawing upon many of the statutory and policy formulas of the more developed nations and incorporating them into their own systems.

While forecasting ultimate patterns is precarious, a way is being sought, both in the democratic nations and in the developing countries with less-than-democratic systems, to allow for some areas of individual choice in land, land tenure, and housing. Property rights in land may be viewed as a basis for the extension of some of the other freedoms in the future, since land and housing involve root programs, from which other human yearnings and political rights may spring. In this respect, time is a positive and vital factor in the ultimate evolution not only of housing and urban policy but of the political systems that produce them or may be conditioned by them.

In respecting the rights of tenure while moving to speed provision of shelter, both developed and developing nations are responding to the pressures of the urban masses for freedom from seizure if not from search, freedom of movement, and freedom to own a plot in the urban complex with some measure of security. Because there is as yet little tendency toward the wholesale land confiscation that prevailed in the U.S.S.R., and because private building and dealing in materials and trade are being permitted in the developing world, there is hope for the gradual emergence of other vital safeguards.

With numerous exceptions that may condition policy in each country, the following may be ventured as emerging trends in both the more developed and the developing areas of the non-Communist world:

1. Housing and land for houses are deemed essentials of life. When access for the "general welfare" is blocked, it is considered to be the state's duty to intervene in order to free the obstructions.

2. The concept of "general welfare," while not uniformly defined, is held to be ever-broadening. It embraces many public activities formerly viewed as outside of the state's scope.

3. The right of a few to hold land while most others are landless, or of the many to hold land that retards development and growth, is no longer absolute. When there is excessive concentration of land or frustrating segmentation, the state is gradually beginning to limit the size of the

holdings, to purchase the land for redistribution,[4] or to allocate publicly owned land for needed development.

4. Taxation is considered reasonable when imposed on property income or, in a number of countries, on its value. A 2 to 3 per cent tax on assessed value is not viewed as unreasonable in the United States[5] or Ireland. A 3 per cent tax on increment in value has been levied in Denmark, while some nations in which taxation on land was once nonexistent are now moving toward land tax levies.[6] Singapore levies a tax of 46 per cent on gross rents.

5. Ownership of land is subject to regulation of its use, provided the regulation is "reasonable." Regulation by zoning, by building laws, and by insistence on proper maintenance is regarded as a state duty.

6. Although rights of owners have been drastically curtailed in Europe and the United States by restrictive exercises, there has been no widespread tendency to expropriate property except for public purposes and then only with compensation. Reasonable restriction of rights to property left under private control is not compensated. Compensation must be paid only when the property is taken for public use, and it must be paid in money in the United States, though it may be payable in other property elsewhere. With few exceptions,[7] compensation is based on current market value.[8]

7. The rights of tenure (including sale, lease, and bequest) are recognized in trade as in homes, and the trader or entrepreneur may enjoy the protections of law in his possession and in the contract that guarantees it.

8. Emergency or crisis may authorize certain regulations that would normally be considered unreasonable. Rent controls, for example, though drastically curtailing the rights of property owners, have been imposed to stay wholesale evictions and curb rent rises, but rent control is re-

---

[4] See, for example, *People of Puerto Rico* v. *Eastern Sugar Associates*, 156 F (2nd) 316.

[5] It is in fact 11 per cent of value in troubled Boston, Massachusetts. Elsewhere 4 per cent is not unusual.

[6] Jamaica, B.W.I., has recently substituted a tax on land for one on land and buildings, a form of levy also employed in New Zealand.

[7] In Ireland slum property constitutes an exception, and value is measured on the basis of a "cleared site less the cost of clearing and levelling." See Charles Abrams, *Urban Renewal Project in Ireland (Dublin)* (New York: United Nations, 1961), pp. 39, 77.

[8] Charles Abrams, *Urban Land Problems and Policies, Housing and Town and Country Planning, Bulletin #7* (New York: United Nations, 1953), p. 57, para. 25. Payment of solatiums of 15 per cent is authorized in India. In Britain, acquisition by railroads carried an extra 10 per cent to owners.

garded as an emergency measure, though political pressures may delay its modification for long periods.

9. While the right of private ownership of land carries no obligation to use the land in some countries, there is an emerging trend in others to induce its use or force its use through taxation, regulation, or compulsory purchase.[9] Not only land use and nonuse but its abuse, misuse, and reuse have moved within the zone of public concern.[10]

10. Compulsory purchase exists in all countries as an inherent power of sovereignty, although it is direct authorization by statute or order that usually calls it into play.[11] While there is opposition to its exercise, particularly in countries with less mobile populations, it is generally no longer held to be confiscation or an arbitrary treatment of individual property. The definition of "public use" is widening. "Public purpose" and "public benefit" are interchangeable and not only embrace roads, parks, schools, and bridges but in a growing number of countries may include housing for the poor and sometimes for the middle classes. Where slums are cleared, the sites may even be relinquished for private uses, but there is an increasing obligation to rehouse the displaced occupants and in some cases to compensate them for their losses. Property may often be acquired for planning and replanning in the interests of neighborhood charm as well as public safety. Parking, airports, rehousing of squatters, markets, industrial uses, and a variety of purposes formerly private have moved or are moving within the ever-widening range of public activities. A charge for rent following acquisition or improvement does not render the use private,[12] nor need the facility be available to everybody.[13]

[9] One of the earliest devices was a law enacted by the New Amsterdam Council requiring owners of vacant lots within the stockade to improve them, pay a tax on them if held unimproved, or surrender them to the city for public sale.

[10] For examples of each, see Abrams, "Urban Land Problems and Policies," *op. cit.*, p. 34.

[11] The right was acknowledged by Pufendorf in the seventeenth century and by Grotius in the eighteenth (*De jure belli ac pacis, Liber* II, Ch. 4, sec. 7). The French Declaration of Rights recognized it in 1791, and it was widely accepted as a government prerogative long before the First World War. As an intrinsic power of sovereignty, it is held to be superior to private property rights. It is sometimes considered to be an exercise by the people of their inherent power to take back the land originally vested in them and appears to antedate constitutions or laws conferring the power. As a prerogative of sovereignty, it can also generally be denied or restricted only by fundamental law. Put another way, it remains quiescent until some statute points up the necessity for its exercise and indicates how and for what purposes it should be invoked.

[12] *New York City Housing Authority* v. *Muller,* 270 NY 233. *Moore* v. *Sanford,* 151 Mass 285.

[13] *Mt. Vernon-Woodberry Cotton Duck Co.* v. *Alabama Interstate Power Co.,* 240

11. In some systems recognizing private enterprise the state may not undertake land operations simply to engage in the real estate business, but the restriction has been steadily qualified so even the semblance of a welfare motive is apt to authorize it. In countries once under British influence, improvement trusts buy large tracts and subdivide and sell them for private development.

12. Land reserves may be accumulated by government for future use or may be sold for private or public redevelopment, and land in excess of public requirements may be acquired and held for subsequent sale.[14] The more sensitive a nation is to employing the compulsory-purchase power, the more it will tend to rely on acquiring land reserves for future development.

13. A privately owned public utility may be granted the right to acquire land compulsorily if it benefits the public. The range of such public utilities is ever-widening so that it embraces not only private railroads and electric companies but limited-profit housing corporations and other regulated development companies.[15] The creation of autonomous public bodies to spur improvement has been accelerated.

14. The need for regional planning has expanded central authority over the autonomous rights of local jurisdictions, except in countries where states' rights or local or regional autonomy is a force (the United States, for example).

15. Housing shortage and urban distortions are increasing the range of beneficiaries formerly outside the public prerogative. Various countries have authorized activities such as insurance of mortgage risks and of

---

US 30. This is generally becoming the rule in Europe, with the spread of public housing, new towns, and urban renewal laws.

[14] Expropriation of extra land is not a new device, its use having been reported in the United States as far back as 1699; but owing to later adverse court decisions on its constitutionality, it remained virtually unused until early in the twentieth century. The practice has been validated by constitutional amendments in a number of states. The power has been exercised in France in connection with public works, especially in laying out streets. Large areas nearby may be acquired and the expropriated zone divided into plots for resale to builders. Excess condemnation has been authorized in Belgium, Italy, the Netherlands, Sweden, and Britain. A number of countries, however, expressly confine compulsory acquisition to the land actually needed for their schemes.

[15] In the United States, where private enterprise has long been the main force in development, early cases even empowered private irrigation and drainage districts to employ eminent domain as well as taxation to facilitate the improvement of large areas of the West.

deposits in savings and loan societies, granting of loans and subsidies for home building, discount of private mortgages, lending on junior mortgage securities, investment in private lending agencies, aid to the low-income groups and the elderly, cooperatives, loans for student housing and for civil servants.

16. The curbing of land speculation is generally within the range of government power and has been attempted in various countries not only by taxation but by price regulation on sale of houses, zoning and subdivision regulations, control of development rights, compulsory purchase, government approval to build, reparceling of plots, building of new towns, and withholding of financial aid to check rocketing land prices.[16]

17. The right to enjoy security in one's own dwelling is being accepted, more often, and as a nation's economy improves, a stronger trend toward ownership is manifesting itself among its rank and file. The shift from tribe to family has been accompanied by increased protections of the freedom to bequeath property. Inheritance through the family is acknowledged, and such protections exist even in the U.S.S.R., although the restrictions on property accumulation sharply limit the scope of inheritance.

18. Ownership by aliens and minorities is being increasingly permitted in countries favorable to private investment, though the less developed countries have not yet fully accepted fee ownership by aliens in the case of real estate. An incipient trend is the greater protection of minorities in housing.[17]

*   *   *

In sum, state power and policy have embraced land and land operations almost universally. In some cases, governments are being forced to underwrite risks and make substantial public investment to keep the spark of private initiative in housing alive. But there is also the firm uni-

---

[16] Abrams, *Urban Land Problems and Policies, op. cit.,* pp. 34 *et seq.*

[17] Equal rights in landownership by minority groups remain an unsettled issue in a number of countries. In the United States, the trend has been to curb racial discrimination in publicly aided housing (and to some extent in private housing). In 1962, the federal government banned discrimination practices in federally assisted housing. By November 1, 1962, seventeen states, the Virgin Islands, and fifty-five cities had enacted antidiscrimination laws of some sort or passed resolutions against discrimination in the housing field. In South Africa the push is for isolation and subordination of the rights of the political minority by the political majority. A number of countries with political or social minorities are establishing one-class housing developments. Caste distinctions persist in India's new towns. The bloody massacres between Hindus and Muslims in India and Pakistan make the minority conflicts experienced in the United States and England insignificant by comparison.

versal acknowledgment that housing, slums, house financing, foreclosure, homeownership, building activity, and many other aspects of the housing economy are now public concerns. The entry of governments into the housing field is new, and the ultimate shape of programs is not yet determinable. There are some perversions and misuses of the new powers, and occasionally the interests of the many are subordinated to those of the few in the interplay of pressures. But there is no longer even the pretense that the state must stand aside as people rot in their hovels or sleep on the streets. Above all, there is a recognition, in both the democratic and the undemocratic non-Communist world, that private ownership of homes and farms must be respected.

THE POSITION OF THE U.S.S.R. COMPARED

When land was collectivized as an essential feature of the U.S.S.R.'s state-controlled economy after the revolution, the inclusion of urban with rural land was accepted as part of the system. Under its constitution, land belonged "to the whole people," and whatever rights in possession, use, or disposition were granted would thereafter emanate from the state. Solving the housing problem was a function of state planning and administration.

To Marx, the housing problem had been a by-product of capitalist exploitation. "The more rapidly capital accumulates in an industrial or commercial town," he wrote, "the more rapidly flows the stream of exploitable human material and the more miserable are the improvised dwellings of the laborers."[18] To Engels, public housing for the poorer worker seemed to aid industry more than the masses. Communism and Communist planning were the real answers to the housing problem and to other capitalist cancers.

Yet as industrialization proceeded, the housing problem cast its shadow on the Communist state as it was doing in the capitalist societies. Confiscation of all urban land and buildings and strong central planning had proved no easy answer.

> Although we have already resolved to provide every family with a separate flat of two or three rooms [said the Deputy Chairman of the State Planning Commission], the situation for the time being is such that entire families are often assigned to each of the rooms in the new houses, so that the new flats once more turn into overcrowded dormitories with all the joyless consequences which could sooner frighten people away from rather than attract them to the idea of communization of life.[19]

[18] Karl Marx, *Capital*, Modern Library Edition (New York: Random House, 1906), p. 726.
[19] S. Strumilin, "Family and Community in the Society of the Future," *Soviet Review*, Vol. 2, No. 2. (February 1961), p. 19.

Although Mr. Khrushchev has not refrained from attacking American slums,[20] the Soviet Union is not free of the same afflictions that are besetting the rest of the urbanizing world. Though the Soviet building rate has risen substantially since 1929, the importance of filling the gap in shelter was emphasized again and again in the 1961 Communist program, the first restatement of Communist doctrine since 1919.

According to a report by a U.N. economic mission to the Uzbek Soviet Socialist Republic in 1961:

> The most serious problem affecting the level of living is, without question, the housing situation. The testimony of factory directors, republic and municipal authorities is unanimous on this point. The floor space per inhabitant in the capital is lower than in other capital cities of the Soviet Union and just as insufficient as it was thirty years ago. Most families in the towns are fortunate if they have two rooms (excluding kitchens and sanitary facilities, which are often communal). About 25 per cent of the residents of Tashkent are estimated to be still living in mud housing.[21]

The destruction or damage of 1700 towns and settlements and more than 10,000 villages and hamlets that reportedly occurred during World War II and the concentration on heavy industry and producer goods have aggravated the Soviet Union's problem. But had there been no destruction, the problem still would have existed. The main cause of continuing shortage in the U.S.S.R. as elsewhere is industrialization and urbanization. However, some 976 towns and 1941 urban-type settlements are said to have come into being between 1926 and 1961, and the Twenty-second Congress of the Communist party hopefully promises an end to the housing shortage by 1970.[22] The U.S.S.R. has made great advances in prefabricated construction of apartment dwellings and has not only increased its housing investment in recent years but attained a higher rate of new housing construction than any other country for

---

[20] "Do you know that according to the latest survey, in December 1956, 13 million families [in the United States] were living in houses not conforming to the accepted standards. Thirteen million families! And the census showed that these figures had remained practically unchanged since 1950." Khrushchev, quoting George Meany's address at a trade conference, March 11, 1958, in the Premier's speech at Meeting of Electors of Kalinin Electoral Area of Moscow, March 14, 1958. See *Speeches by N. S. Khrushchev* (Canada: The Press Office, The U.S.S.R. Embassy in Canada, 1958), p. 18.

[21] United Nations, "Planning for Balanced Social and Economic Development in the Uzbec Soviet Socialist Republic," *Report on the World Social Situation*, Economic and Social Council (New York, April 20, 1961), Annex, pp. 12, 13.

[22] After ending the shortage by 1970, "families that are still housed in substandard dwellings will get new flats. . . . By 1980, every family, including newlyweds, will have a comfortable flat conforming to the requirements of hygiene and cultural living." N. N. Smirnoff, in *Report of the Ad Hoc Group of Experts on Housing and Urban Development* (New York: United Nations, April 2, 1962), Appendix, p. 17.

which statistics are available; this rate has risen from 7 per 1000 inhabitants in 1954 to 10.8 in 1957 and 14.4 in 1959.[23] The assumption of responsibility for housing workers is no longer questioned, and the U.S.S.R. is trying to seal the housing breach with brick and mortar.

Political systems, however, have a way of putting their imprint on the building product as well as on the way of life. "Seventy-one per cent of all housing erected in 1957 was built according to standard blueprints, while in 1959, the percentage rose to 90."[24] Space provided for living is almost uniformly small. Most urban residents live in one room of a communal apartment with a common kitchen. Average occupancy per room in 1961 was still about 2.7 persons.

Central control is maintained over planning and housing as over other forms of production. In 1962, at a meeting of officials of ten nations called to review the role of the United Nations in housing and urbanization, achievements of the Soviet Union in national economic development and housing were described by its representative as:

. . . the direct outcome of the State social, political, and economic structure of the country, the absence of private ownership of the land or the means of production, the State system of national economic planning, the industrialization of the country and the collectivization of agriculture.

Since land is public property in the USSR, the allocation of sites for building is the obligation and responsibility of State organizations.

Plans for the development of towns, residential districts, micro-districts and individual buildings are worked out by the State planning institutes.

The building trusts which erect the housing, the factories which produce building components, fixtures and materials, and the transport organizations are also State undertakings.[25]

There is no doubt that planning by the state, whether such state be monocratic, fascist, or communist, can sometimes work miracles. The building of the Moscow subway was not obstructed by landowner resistance or the fine restrictions of eminent domain. With state planning there is more accuracy in the forecast and in the product. The state decides what is good and what is needed, and somehow everything and everyone is expected to fall into line as projected. Because the whole economy is planned and because land, industrial undertakings, power plants, and transport are public property, industry can be located where

[23] United Nations, *Report on the World Social Situation, op. cit.*, p. 7.

[24] From an official survey cited by B. Svetlichnyi, in "Soviet Town Planning Today," *Voprosy Ekonomiki*, No. 7 (July 1960), translated in *Problems of Economics*, Vol. III, No. 8 (December 1960), p. 35. Cited and discussed in Jack C. Fisher, "Planning the City of Socialist Man," *Journal of the American Institute of Planners*, Vol. XXVIII, No. 4 (November 1962), p. 262.

[25] See N. N. Smirnoff, *Report of the Ad Hoc Group of Experts on Housing and Urban Development, op. cit.*, Appendix, p. 15.

the state decrees, and population is thereby distributed and redistributed according to plan. The difference between planning in the West and in the U.S.S.R., a Soviet representative said, is that in the former the general town plan is merely "a forecast of the directions in which the town may develop."[26] In the U.S.S.R., the town is built as the state's blueprint proposes.[27]

Despite its planned economy, however, the U.S.S.R. has been wincing under some of the same urbanization problems as are other countries. Though Soviet leaders have urged planning for limitation of growth and industrial dispersal, industries and people stubbornly tend to move toward the larger city centers, to the dismay of the planning hierarchy.

Private houses, which compose about 30 per cent of all urban living space, seem contrary to the Communist ideal; but they have had to be tolerated not only because of the housing shortage but because of the pressures exerted by the small section of private householders. Soviet city planners had been urged to provide for some private housing, but have been reluctant to supply them with services or make a permanent place for them.[28]

However, a decree published in *Pravda* on August 7, 1962, sharply restricted private home building and cut off allocations of building plots to private home builders in the capitals of fifteen Soviet Republics, and local councils of ministers elsewhere were vested with discretion to do likewise. Since all land in the Soviet Union belongs to the state, a strict application of the decree could bring private housing construction in major cities to a halt.

Under the new decrees, the Council of Ministers may refuse credit to individual builders and may investigate the sources of funds used by citizens to build private homes and *dachas*. Local courts are empowered to seize properties if evidence of unearned income is found. While the

---

[26] *Ibid.*, p. 20.

[27] "Population figures are computed by the labour balance-sheet method, which can be used to predict the population of every town or district in the country from population growth, manpower requirements, the growth of production, the volume of capital investment in construction of all kinds, the growth of labour productivity and the increase in the population employed in services." Thus, says the writer, the general town plan is not merely a forecast but a practical program for the town builders. "Using this method of computation it is possible to take into account, in addition to natural population growth, migration from one part of the country to another or from the country to the towns." *Ibid.*, p. 20.

[28] Robert J. Osborn and Thomas A. Reiner, "Soviet City Planning: Current Issues and Future Perspectives," *Journal of the American Institute of Planners*, Vol. XXVIII, No. 4 (November 1962), p. 240. Hot water, gas, and a bathtub are rarities in these quarters. See Timothy Sosnovy, "The Soviet City," *Dimensions of Soviet Economic Power*, Hearings, Joint Economic Committee, Congress of the United States, 87th Congress, 2nd Session, December 10 and 11, 1962 (Washington: U.S. Government Printing Office, 1962), p. 336.

measures are directed at reducing profiteering and checking the so-called antisocial activities of individual citizens by restricting the earlier trend toward private building and ownership, the measures seem intended to bring the life and behavior of the Soviet population closer to the classic ideals of the "Communist society."[29]

Confusion exists in the competition between economic councils and local governments, and the Soviet press still reechoes complaints about the shortages of housing, illegal subletting, and the frequency of delays. Shortage of building materials plagues the U.S.S.R. as it does other countries. There is also resentment about priorities given to stadiums over housing and other elementary facilities. The competition for skills is keen; in 1960, less than one quarter of the cities had a chief city architect; where there is one, he is often unqualified. Cities are criticized for holding land without developing it[30]—a complaint heard in many other parts of the world—and there are recriminations about violations of plans by cities holding land.

Misallocation of land, its excessive use by industry, pollution problems, and the flouting of regulations are other headaches.[31] Moreover, hutments and squatters' shanties have cropped up to impede planned expansion. Tearing down occupied buildings is proving as troublesome and as costly as in capitalist countries.

In short, since Communist planning in an urbanized society is not free of the problems encountered in the less planned economies, compromises are being enforced in the Soviet Union as elsewhere. Beadledom is a universal obstruction that rises with bureaucracy in whatever form or system. Recent efforts, in fact, have sought to cope with it by greater decentralization of authority.

Despite the relaxation of controls following the Stalin era, the controls of the Communist state over individual movement and choice are still implicit in the system and its Communist imperatives. The Soviet passport restrains the hinterlander from moving to the city, although the restrictions are not always successful. Officials boast about the marked progress in housing by citing the number of square meters built, but the country seems committed to constructing small standardized apartments as an economical means of meeting need. Occupancy is still mainly one family to a room (often more), and though housing is being built in quantity, overcrowding continues. Neither technical progress nor the Communist ideology has resolved the social vexations of urbanization.

[29] Sosnovy, "The Soviet City," *Dimensions of Soviet Economic Power, op. cit.*, p. 334.

[30] *Izvestia*, September 1, 1961, p. 4. See also Osborn and Reiner, "Soviet City Planning: Current Issues and Future Perspectives," *op. cit.*, p. 243.

[31] Svetlichnyli, "Soviet Town Planning Today," *op. cit.*, pp. 30, 32.

HOUSING AND THE FAMILY IN THE U.S.S.R.

Though freedom to criticize is limited in the Communist society, the problems and theories of housing and education play a prominent part in Communist literature. It is obvious that the housing issue has been complicating the U.S.S.R.'s main efforts. Thus state policy in this area will have an important impact on life in the emerging Communist society.

Not the least important of the possible changes is the shift toward greater control of child rearing by the state. Under the heading "The Public Upbringing of Children of School and Pre-school Age," the Communist draft program of 1961 provides as follows:

> The Communist system of public education is based on the public upbringing of children. The educational influence which the family exerts on children must be brought into ever greater harmony with their public upbringing.[32]

There is no simple explanation for this pronouncement. It is probably the product of many complications within the Communist structure. Employment of both parents has made child rearing difficult. The unorthodox moods and attitudes of Communist youth may be another reason. The need for welding the educational system into an instrument that will more efficiently achieve technological objectives is another factor. The importance of more effective training in the Communist ideology is still another reason. This need was indicated by Premier Khrushchev when, five years before the framing of the Communist party platform, he urged the establishment of more boarding schools in order to rear the "builders of a new society, individuals of great spirit and lofty ideals, wholeheartedly serving their people who are marching in the vanguard of all progressive mankind."[33]

An article "On the New System of Social Upbringing," published in *Soviet Pedagogy,* an official organ of the U.S.S.R. Academy of Pedagogical Sciences, following Khrushchev's statement in June 1956, said:

> Day by day it becomes more and more evident that the existing system of upbringing [by parents and in regular schools] cannot fully cope with the [task] of creating broadly developed builders of the communist society among the new generation.

The author emphasized that it is not

---

[32] "Final Text of the Program of the Communist Party of the Soviet Union," reprinted in *The New Soviet Society,* with annotations and an introduction by Herbert Ritvo (New York: New Leader paperback, 1962), p. 217.

[33] Quoted in Alexander G. Korol, *Soviet Education for Science and Technology* (Cambridge and New York: Technology Press and John Wiley, 1957), p. 33.

. . . enough to add a dormitory to a regular school of general education or to change the "Home for Children" sign to a sign reading "Boarding School" in order to solve the problem.

Many other articles appeared then and later on the same subject. *Pravda*, on June 28, 1956, claimed that "the educational influence of teachers embraces the entire life of children from early childhood, when they no longer need direct maternal care, until maturity." Although some years were expected to pass before the ideal could be achieved, it said, "Soviet authorities looked to the extension of the boarding school principle to the entire school system."

S. Strumilin, the Deputy Chairman of the State Planning Commission, put it this way:

> Complete responsibility for the new member of society, and particularly for his upbringing as a human being and a citizen, can be assumed by society itself, leaving only those functions to the family in which it can be trusted to do no harm to the children.[34]

The need for shaping the child within the Communist ideology without too much interference by the parent is justified in almost Platolike fashion as follows:

> The advantages of public upbringing are so great and evident that they justify any public expense, on any scale, for *all* the children in the country.
> . . . .
>   The children's collective, particularly if not under pressure and guided by the experienced hand of an educator, can do more to inculcate the best social habits than the most sympathetic and loving mother. Prompt and effective reactions on the part of such a collective to all anti-social manifestations prompted by the egoistic disposition of the child are sure to nip them in the bud. On the other hand, all the inborn social instincts and sympathies of the child come to life and are developed by means of the new conditioned reflexes created through comradely relationships, reflexes strengthened by the daily routine of our labor schools and pre-school establishments.
>   Such features of the children's institutions are now being developed in the interests of Communist upbringing. In giving precedence to the public forms of upbringing, it is our task to extend them in the next few years at a tempo that would make them accessible to all—from the cradle to the graduation certification—within fifteen or twenty years. Emerging from a hospital, every Soviet citizen would be assigned to a nursery, then to a

[34] S. Strumilin, "Family and Community in the Society of the Future," *op. cit.*, p. 9. The explanation is as follows: "It is not everyone who is equal to the task of upbringing. Special inclinations and pedagogical training are imperative for this; and it goes without saying that by no means every family has such gifted educators and teachers. Apart from this, the great majority of parents spend much of their time at work and cannot devote very much of it to the upbringing of their children." *Ibid.*, pp. 9, 10.

kindergarten maintained day and night, then to a boarding school, from which he would enter independent life—taking a job in production or continuing his studies in his chosen profession.[35]

"The question might arise," says the author, "whether such an early separation of the child from the family would not be too difficult for the parents and their children, so sensitive to motherly affection." Offering some function to the parents during the child's early years, he answers his question as follows:

> The public organization of upbringing is not aimed at the complete separation of children from their parents. Even now the mothers of infants are able to feed their offspring at the breast during working hours. And it is highly improbable that anyone will prevent them from visiting their children after working hours, when they will be able to visit the children's premises in their own dwelling house as often as the rules permit.[36]

Despite the efforts of a militant minority during the first five-year plan to eliminate the family from Soviet life on the claim that the family was the social and jural upholder of private property[37] the family has survived as an important force. But now the housing problem, coupled with the problems of child rearing, is insinuating a counter force. Thus it may be no coincidence that simultaneously with the emphasis on public upbringing of children has come a strong move toward holding the size of dwellings to a minimum. Deputy Chairman Strumilin gave a clear indication of the link between the new thinking on housing and public upbringing of children when he said that "such institutions of communism as public dining rooms and the public rearing of children will enter fully into the lives of the workers only as elements in the construction of communism itself. The rudiments of these elements already exist and there can be no doubt that they will grow."[38]

Until recently, larger apartments, occupied by two or three families, were being built. The average construction cost of an apartment in 1956 ranged from 55,000 to 60,000 rubles. But if 15 million apartments were to be built under the seven-year plan, that cost had to be cut drastically. If each family is to get a small apartment rather than a room, and if the two or three families presently sharing a dwelling are to be given more space, the apartments simply cannot allow for kitchens or for space to raise a family.

The new "microdistrict" project urged by Soviet planners would har-

---

[35] *Ibid.*, pp. 10, 11.

[36] *Ibid.*, p. 11.

[37] Ruth Nanda Anshen, ed., *The Family: Its Function and Destiny*, revised edition (New York: Harper, 1959), Philip E. Mosely, "The Russian Family: Old Style and New," p. 111.

[38] S. Strumilin, "Family and Community in the Society of the Future," *op. cit.*, p. 8.

monize substantially with the new Communist program. It is described as follows by two Soviet writers:

> To many people in the West the ideal of a comfortable dwelling is a private house with many rooms. "My home is my castle," says the Englishman. This is an eloquent expression of private-property psychology, of goals in bourgeois society.
> . . . the question arises whether there is any need for such an abundance of rooms in an apartment. After all, not many rooms are required for sleeping, rest and some kind of home occupation during one's free time. And is there any need to preserve in the future all the household functions which we now have? We do not think so.

"How is the problem of future living conditions to be solved?" the writers ask. The answer is "only by a consistent development of public catering, of cultural and educational services." Thus

> Large catering establishments, model dining rooms and cafeterias with better food than can be provided at home, various kinds of shops, universal service agencies—all this will replace the home kitchen and do away with petty household chores. Boarding schools, kindergartens and crèches will make our life easier in many ways. Thus there will be no need for individual kitchens, storage rooms, servants' quarters and so on. . . . The new trend toward organization of services not only leads to the liberation of women from the drudgery of unproductively spent labor; it also greatly helps to improve the conditions for raising our new generation. . . . Who will want to cook dinner at home when a rich assortment of dishes to everybody's taste will be obtainable in the dining rooms?[39]

The writings of Soviet planners and officials may not always be the final word in policy, nor is Communist policy static. Widening public pressures may force a change toward a more cohesive family life than projected. But the inference is not too far afield that Soviet policy regarding the housing problem is today heading toward a diminution in the housing options of the individual, in the forms of tenure, in the essential space for family independence, in the greater dependency on

[39] A. Zhuravlev and M. Fyodorov, "The Microdistrict and New Living Conditions," *The Soviet Review*, Vol. II, No. 4 (April 1961), pp. 38–40. The purpose of such building is suggested by the Deputy Chairman of the State Planning Commission: "Formed in the children's nurseries, the ties of the young Communards with surrounding nature and the elements of science and labor, and finally with the whole of the working Communist society, steadily branch out, growing stronger and wider. When they are transferred from the dwelling commune to the boarding school, the Octoberite groups will join the ranks of the Young Pioneers, then of the Komsomol, learning the principles of communist behavior. Joining the maturer labor collectives later on, they will be united in their general tasks and strivings: to work, study and live in the communist manner." S. Strumilin, "Family and Community in the Society of the Future," *op. cit.*, pp. 22, 23.

the state for child rearing, and in the greater standardization of living patterns in general. The indications are of a well-defined shift in the life pattern from one in which the home is the central focus of living to one in which it is not much more than a dormitory. Whether all this will produce the new "Soviet man," to which Russian leaders have so often referred, remains to be seen. As of 1963, there seemed to be a determination to take children from their parental homes at the age of seven and to raise them in boarding schools. "The fact that the new boarding schools are springing up all over the country makes it clear that this is no starry-eyed dream but a present reality."[40]

LESSONS FOR THE MORE DEVELOPED NATIONS

It is not only in the Soviet Union but in every part of the world that the urban revolution is bringing new challenges to the patterns of society. Land and home, which have been the decentralized units for achieving human privacy, have tended during recent centuries to support the foundation of a new individualism, which De Tocqueville had identified as being of democratic origin. He described it as

> . . . a mature and calm feeling, which disposes each member of the community to sever himself from the mass of his fellow-creatures: and to draw apart with his family and friends: so that after he has formed a little circle of his own, he willingly leaves society at large to itself.[41]

In the breakup of tribal organization resulting from the transition to city life, the people from the hinterlands are similarly being forced to act for themselves and to determine their own interests and their own controls over their children.

Yet the formative social and political patterns and processes of the emerging society are becoming increasingly involved with housing and urban land policy. In some cases, state ownership of housing is growing, although other forms of tenure are allowed. In others, the state socializes housing and urban land and then desocializes it to create and retain a greater variety of choices. In still others, the state subsidizes the private builders to enable them to provide a variety of choices. In the centralized or totalitarian order, however, the state housing and land policy tends to be monolithic, the choices are narrowed, and the shelter is becoming another instrument for shaping people's lives and making them conform to the central will and design. The house here is part of the rigid process

---

[40] David and Vera Mace, *The Soviet Family* (Garden City, New York: Doubleday & Co., 1963), p. 315.

[41] Alexis de Tocqueville, *Democracy in America* (New York: The Century Co. 1898), Vol. II, p. 119.

fashioned by the state to subordinate the individual's privacy and his choices.

The democratic norm in housing and urban land today involves principles not fundamentally different from one described by John Stuart Mill as "that of pursuing our own good in our own way, so long as we do not deprive others of theirs or impede their efforts to obtain it." Although millions of people in the world may not be interested in the right to speak when their voices are faint with hunger, or in the freedom of assembly when they are immobilized by fatigue, they can still understand the meaning of the right to their own land and to their own homes, and they are carrying with them to the cities the yearnings for property that they knew in the hinterlands. It may be highly optimistic to expect that democratic societies will inevitably emerge just because rights to property may be given a broader base in the turbulent cities. But if there is to be any real hope of freedom in the evolving societies, there must be at least the right to a home free from state domination, security in one's tenure, the right to move where opportunity beckons, and the existence of the family not simply as a biological cell in which the child is the pawn of the state but as the keystone of the social organization, one of the main influences in the formation of personalities, affections, values, and identities, and the continuing force in educating mankind for participation in the national community.

The rights to move from farm to city or from city to farm, to be free to choose from a multiplicity of landlords who are without access to a dossier of one's past or one's views, to raise one's children, to buy a home or shop, improve or sell it and secure another with the proceeds are not only the expressions of a fundamental human demand but the vital fibers out of which some of the great freedoms have been woven in the rural society of the past. As in Western Europe and the United States, they may yet prove strong enough to produce similar freedoms in the societies that are now in dynamic flux.

18

Communism, *Lebensraum*, Housing, and Cities

THE CHALLENGE TO THE CITY

There is no more fertile ground for revolutionary propaganda than the beleaguered cities of the underdeveloped nations. Misery, bitterness, and resentment in the teeming slums and squatter colonies, low wages and long hours in the new factories, competition for jobs, and child labor, all recall the scene that made the *Communist Manifesto* an alluring document in nineteenth-century Europe.

In Western Europe, communism bowed to reform. Europe weathered the shift to industrialization because there were frontiers to absorb some of the surplus people; institutional roots were more settled; conservative churches counseled prayer, not rebellion; and there was a strong shop-keeper-handicraft economy willing to tolerate change but not revolution.

These buffers are missing in industrializing Asia, Africa, and Latin America. Street sleeping, homelessness, and overcrowding are incomparably worse than anything Marx described in London's East End. Immigration to the more prosperous nations is closed. In the developing areas the middle class is hardly in embryo. Industrialization is cutting adrift the once-settled tribal, family, and village groupings. Institutional roots are frail, and a military *coup d'état* is often viewed with apathy, an assassination with cynicism, a sally by Communist troublemakers as a game to watch or even applaud.[1] To call the industrializing period in these areas

[1] I witnessed, for example, the three-day effort by Communists in 1961 to take over Caracas. Many policemen as well as soldiers were killed. In Europe or the United States, the popular feeling that would follow the killing of even a single

a "revolution of rising expectations" is to deny that it is also a "revolution of rising discontents."

If the spread of communism depends on popular indifference or on the breakdown of order, as it did in Russia in 1918, housing famine can contribute significantly to its ascendancy. And if communism fails, the alternative will probably not be democracy.

Most people in the developing areas nevertheless come from societies in which private property and personal or group ownership are part of the established way of life. Consequently, the Russian strain of communism does not lure them. But discontent, disorganization, and cynicism are everywhere challenging economic and institutional patterns before they have matured. To many among these uneducated, homeless, and hungry people, the revolutionary theme strikes a more hopeful note. Thus one postwar democracy after another either has given way to a new "Communist democracy" or has been replaced by a dictator or junta determined to rule with a strong hand to prevent popular revolt or Communist seizure.

The most important question confronting the democratic world is whether political stability can be maintained while productivity is developed and the painful shift to industrialization is effected. Most of the underdeveloped countries have no alternative but to encourage private capital to help expand industrial output. Officials can make the pretense of regulating industry in the public interest. They can set up social security systems, try to cushion the shock of unemployment, or attempt, as Europe did, to allay unrest with social reforms including some token housing. They can also talk about democracy and freedom of opportunity. But if these countries are to develop industrially, they must truckle to new capital investment. Levies upon such investment must be mild, and a climate must be created to attract venture capital. Far from regulating the capitalist, the state must more often be prepared to favor him with offers of free land, tax immunities, and other incentives. If he seems to exploit labor while establishing a textile mill, he may not otherwise be able to enter his goods competitively in the world markets. If he wants to see his investment back in a year or two, it is part of his price for the hazards that hang over his investment.

With all its callousness, private industry is still more constructive, judged by its total impact, than Tawney's "orgy of soulless cupidity"; it cannot be completely discredited as the simple exploitation of the Asian

---

policeman would be one of sharp resentment against the troublemakers. The public attitude of those to whom I spoke in Caracas was mostly one of unconcern. The battle was viewed more as a private skirmish between the forces of law and their antagonists. The heavy turnout of citizens in the 1963 election may hopefully presage a new public responsibility in this respect.

and African masses that the Communists charge. But the appearance of exploitation and the contrasts between wealth and poverty cannot be hidden. Thus in the new theater of ideological warfare, capitalism makes a convenient villain in the intricate international play in which factual distortion and duress are useful props.

What has been overlooked is that while the democratic process provides greater freedom for protest, its tolerance of opposition and freedom also provides greater opportunity for rebellion. In the urban environment, insurgence can no longer be repressed by a few retainers or concealed behind a manor wall. When there is widespread deprivation or a patent contrast between the well-being of some and the destitution of others, a small well-organized group can manipulate the masses more efficiently than in former eras. The fanatic, the dogmatist, and the opportunist can find a wider audience, and one more willing to listen, in the unsettled cities. Here, as in Marx's day, the contradictions are most obvious and striking; the unemployed, the unsheltered, the students, workers, and squatters can be more easily organized.

The forcible ousting in Delhi of four thousand squatter families from their hovels with no alternative but to let life go on in the rubble calls up Marx's bitter words: "The owner of land, of houses, the business man, when expropriated by improvements . . . not only receives full indemnity . . . but a thumping profit," while "the labourer, with his wife and child and chattels is thrown out into the street."[2]

As Marx effectively argues, the underpaid worker accepts an inadequate diet because he does not fathom the complex reasons for the difference in the menus of the rich and the poor. But the contrast between the slum and the mansion is more evident and thus easier to resent:

> The intimate connection between the pangs of hunger of the most industrious layers of the working class, and the extravagant consumption, coarse or refined, of the rich, for which capitalist accumulation is the basis, reveals itself only when the economic laws are known. It is otherwise with the "housing of the poor." Every unprejudiced observer sees that the greater the centralization of the means of production, the greater is the corresponding heaping together of the labourers, within a given space; that therefore the swifter capitalistic accumulation, the more miserable are the dwellings of the working people.[3]

While the distortions of the land problem in the rural areas are more obvious today than in the past, it is toward the cities that the major flow of revolutionary propaganda is being directed. Castro's land confiscations have served him well by bringing into sharp relief the imperative need

---

[2] Karl Marx, *Capital*, Modern Library edition (New York: Random House, 1906), p. 725.

[3] *Ibid.*, pp. 721, 722.

for initiating and accelerating genuine land reform throughout rural and urban Latin America. Some countries, like Mexico, have broken up the old haciendas and either turned them into cooperatives or distributed the land to small farmers. Puerto Rico took similar steps many years ago. Bolivia virtually confiscated land, but is trying to redistribute it to its rank and file in both rural and urban areas. Marked pressure for comprehensive reforms has been felt in other parts of Latin America too.

But real land reform and land redistribution are still far from general or comprehensive, and parts of the old latifundia stubbornly persist. Though 60 per cent of all Latin Americans are in agriculture, almost 80 per cent of the cultivatable soil is still in the hands of 5.5 per cent of the landowners.[4] The land problem in the cities is no closer to solution and is, in fact, being almost wholly ignored not only in Latin America but in Asia and Africa as well. In the absence of a program that holds out hope to the masses in the cities as well as in the rural areas, the confused but emotionally charged Castro blueprint will continue to compete for mass support. The *progress* of the Alliance for Progress will always be threatened. A program that promises land distribution for the masses and individual ownership in the cities could strike a revolutionary note politically more vital than communism. It is the denial of this promise that is the greatest weakness of the Soviet Communist prospectus.

In this encounter of forces, the United States is trying to operate primarily at two levels: by emphasizing the virtues of its own system and by giving financial and technical aid in selected areas to speed the process of change or alleviate hunger and disease. To meet the Communist revolutionary onslaught, President Kennedy suggested a revolution born of "the most powerful forces of the modern age—the search for the freedom and self-fulfillment of man."[5] Such liberal sentiments had contagious qualities in 1789 and were even able to spark revolutions in eighteenth- and nineteenth-century Europe. They are still, perhaps, meaningful to people who have had access to Jefferson in the paperbacks. But the trouble is that in the developing countries many of America's best friends (including those prime ministers who have read Jefferson) are not yet prepared to give their own people all or most of the freedoms. Indeed, some friendly administrators are disquieted by the democratic example of free elections and liberal patterns of political conduct. Besides, people's stomachs must be filled and shelter secured before the higher aspirations become especially significant. In this respect, Russia's example of productivity under communism—despite the price in freedom it exacts and the dubious promises it offers the little man—cannot be dis-

---

[4] Tad Szulc, "Now It Is Up to Latin America," *New York Times Magazine,* August 13, 1961, p. 89.

[5] President Kennedy's Message to Inter-American Economic and Social Conference, *New York Times,* August 6, 1961, p. 29.

missed as irrelevant. Its greatest attraction is not in what it offers but in its assault on what the non-Communist societies have not yet fulfilled.

A REVOLUTION RECALLED

The pivotal place of widespread property ownership in the evolution of democracy is evident from history. Toward the close of the eighteenth century, two political theories divided the world, as is the case today. One was founded on the advantage of the state and the policy of expedience, the other on "the immutable principles of morals." In an era when status and wealth went together and when the great mass of humanity had neither, the one founded on morals struck a universal note among the world's people.

In his *History of the United States,* George Bancroft sums up the impact of the American Revolution as follows:

> The new republic, as it took its place among the powers of the world, proclaimed its faith in the truth and reality and unchangeableness of freedom, virtue, and right. The heart of Jefferson in writing the Declaration, and of congress in adopting it, beat for all humanity; the assertion of right was made for the entire world of mankind and all coming generations, without any exception whatever; for the proposition which admits of exceptions can never be self-evident. As it was put forth in the name of the ascendant people of that time, it was sure to make the circuit of the world, passing everywhere through the despotic countries of Europe; and the astonished nations, as they read that all men are created equal, started out of their lethargy, like those who have been exiles from childhood, when they suddenly hear the dimly remembered accents of their mother tongue.[6]

Though the Declaration of Independence emphasized only human rights as inalienable, one of the most appealing aspects of the new republic and its system was that life, liberty, *and property* were welded into a unit. The new system not only guaranteed protection to property[7] but soon also made property available to those who came. The English system of great landholdings could never survive in a country settled by the yeomen of England who saw in land the liberty they had once experienced at home and which the enclosures had taken away.

The United States and the U.S.S.R. based their revolutions on two

[6] George Bancroft, *History of the United States of America* (New York: D. Appleton & Co., 1886), Vol. 4, p. 450.

[7] The Fifth Amendment guaranteed individuals against deprivation of "life, liberty or property." The Virginia Constitution declared: "All men are by nature equally free, and have inherent rights, of which, when they enter into a state of society, they cannot by any compact, deprive or divest their posterity; namely the enjoyment of life and liberty, with the means of acquiring and possessing property, and pursuing and obtaining happiness and safety."

divergent theories. The former desocialized land acquired by the state; the latter socialized what was already in private hands. From the beginning, America accepted the family as the unit in which the individual was nourished and grew; the property a family acquired was its own, receiving all the protections that law and government could provide. Extensive landownership became a more important force for building democracy than the Constitution. As Jefferson wrote: ". . . as few as possible shall be without a little portion of land. The small land holders are the most precious part of a state."[8]

When industrialization transformed much of the rural land into urban land, the United States retained the pattern of individual ownership and decision. The U.S.S.R., on the other hand, extended its hold on the individual into the urban sphere. As industrial capitalism grew, the United States expanded the controls for evening out some of the inequalities, but it did so within the framework of the democratic institutional structure established during the agricultural period. While stimulating enterprise to make it function more effectively, it acknowledged individual ownership or the access to it. Private farm ownership continued, and when both farm and home ownership were threatened, they were reinforced by public credits. Small trade was respected too, even as large-scale corporate ownership grew. The essential freedoms—of movement, franchise, speech, prayer, assembly, and protest, and the right to be judged within a framework of law and under the guidance of precedent —managed to survive both the transition from a rural to an industrial economy and the crises that periodically intervened. With some variations, Western Europe moved along similar lines.

Though the broad view of earth and sky has shrunk to a world of pavements and huddled shelters on narrow streets and byways, the move to the cities is accompanied by certain aspirations—not the least of which is a small plot, or its equivalent, in which a man can raise his own family.[9] Here the land problem has begun to resemble in some respects the age-old struggle for the soil.

URBAN LAND AND LEBENSRAUM

Though the Soviet system confiscated land, forbade petty trade, and turned independent farmers into wage workers of the state, it is not improbable that popular pressures may force it ultimately to concede a greater measure of individual rights in tenure. The U.S.S.R.'s rural land

[8] Paul L. Ford, ed., *The Writings of Thomas Jefferson* (New York and London: Putnam, 1893), Vol. VII, pp. 33–36.

[9] Its "equivalent" can include: ownership of an apartment (condominium) in the very dense areas where real land shortage exists; cooperative ownership; or rental with the right of purchase.

policy has been a failure in contrast with the progress made even among its satellites. It has in the past been grudgingly compelled to countenance some ownership of small buildings outside the large city centers (though not yet of the land), and it may again be forced to relax its recent restrictions on private building. It has promised cooperative ownership in the cities and protection against the seizure of property without compensation. It has tolerated ownership of some personal property as well as a "free market" in which the collective farmers come by truck to sell some of their homegrown produce. Restrictions on the right to move may eventually be relaxed. Despite the Communist blueprint of 1961, the Soviet Union may even shift or modify both its housing policy and its latest party line on the state raising the child.[10] The post-Stalin blueprint, though still unfavorable to individualism, may prove less ironclad when failure or mounting pressures threaten. If the picture behind the iron curtain is not bright, it may not be completely hopeless.

The real challenge to man's freedoms under worldwide industrialization—both to the U.S.S.R. and to the United States—may in the long run lie less in the contest between the two great ideologies than in the ever-recurring rumble of the *Lebensraum* concept, from which there has been no surcease since man first lumbered out of his cave.

The drive for *Lebensraum* defined by Hitler for Nazi Germany is far from an original or an exclusive concept. It has spurred ambitious nations to conquest since early times. Philosophers like Malthus sought the answer to man's land hunger in the disciplining of his sex impulse. National leaders looked to empire or war. Hitler voiced nakedly only what others before him dressed up as patriotism or justice when he claimed "the right to a greater living space than other peoples. . . . Germany's future was therefore wholly conditional upon the solving of the need for space."[11] He declared: "The increasing number of [German] people required a larger *Lebensraum*. My goal was to create a rational relation between the number of people and the space for them to live in. The fight must start here. No nation can evade the solution of this problem."[12]

The drive for space may be held down by fear of annihilation, but eventually the growing victory against disease may again spur the battle.

---

[10] Khrushchev, who often referred to capitalism as a "worn-out mare" and a system in which "the strong swallow the weak," has not hesitated more recently to chide his own bureaucrats on their failure to take advantage of some of capitalism's methods of production and organization. He has cited Lenin's instruction "to be able, if necessary, to learn from the capitalists, to imitate whatever of theirs is sensible and advantageous." See "Khrushchev and Capitalism," *Wall Street Journal*, March 4, 1963, p. 16.

[11] Quoted in William L. Shirer, *The Rise and Fall of the Third Reich* (New York: Fawcett World Library, Crest Books, 1962), p. 419.

[12] *Ibid.*, p. 869.

Just as the pressures of dense populations in Italy, Germany, and Japan played their sinister role in past wars, they may someday play a similar part in China and wherever the problem exists.

Yet in one respect the industrializing and urbanizing patterns of our time are providing a safety valve. Man is small, and his needs for work space and homes in cities are relatively insignificant. In a world of cities, the shortage of space should no longer be a factor in the struggle for survival. But its misuse and its lack of rationalization are.

Space shortage nevertheless appears more serious than ever because of the intense competition for sites within the small urban cores and the areas forming around them. If the urban radius within each country can be stretched by proper land policy and by the addition of transportation and utilities, the accommodation for homes and workplaces will be ample by the year 1980 and even by the year 2000. If industrialization can be managed intelligently and hunger appeased, a rational urbanization can redirect man's drives from the *extensive* emphasis of the agricultural world to an *intensive* expansion within the borders of each nation. Western Europe, Japan, and the United States have already demonstrated this approach. In the highly industrialized United States, for example, urbanized land occupies less than 2 per cent of the entire land supply—a situation not very different in many other industrialized countries. The solution to the problems of urbanization may be the key to an international rapprochement—and even to a more lasting peace.

The main obstacle is of course the dearth of talent and knowledge for meeting the challenges of urbanization. What should be one of the most vital sciences is as yet not even a minor discipline.[13] In Africa, Asia, and Latin America, more than a billion people are forced to live under conditions unfit for beasts. Though more than 20 million homes are needed each year in those continents, there are no prospects, little knowledge, no real programs to meet even a tiny fraction of the need. In the last twenty years, when technology has made unprecedented strides, housing conditions have grown steadily worse.[14]

In their failure up to 1964 to deal with the problem of urban space and housing famine, the aid programs of the more developed nations and international agencies have overlooked man's craving for a home, for privacy, and for the opportunity to raise his family in a free and

[13] To cite only one example, the most imperative device for cities is one for the simple disposal of man's wastes. The world's engineers could make a greater contribution to society by inventing a chemical or other simple means for disposing of human excrement on the earth than by making contact with the moon.

[14] Despite all of India's housing efforts, for example, her housing shortage had doubled over that of ten years ago. See C. P. Malik in United Nations, Social Commission, 14th Session, *Report of the Ad Hoc Group of Experts on Housing and Urban Development* (New York, April 2, 1962), Appendix, p. 2.

decent environment. Nevertheless, these are among the most potent aspirations in the evolution of democratic political systems in the pre-industrial world and now among the most potent in the urbanizing world.

THE CITY—THREAT AND HOPE

Thirty-five years from now, the world's population will have increased by some 3 billion, and the day when the earth must hold 7 billion is no further away than World War I is from today. The impact will be felt most in the cities of the less developed world. Although total population in these regions will grow by 40 per cent in fifteen years, urban population will double. The urban population of Africa will probably grow from 58 million in 1960 to 294 million by the year 2000; that of Asia from 559 million to 3444 million; and that of Latin America from 144 million to 650 million.[15]

The embattled city, toward which this contest for space is fast moving, has witnessed both freedom and revolt during its periods of transition and crisis. Despite its more complex environment, the city has somehow been able to proffer the hope of progress to the world's underprivileged people. The availability of training in a city has brought man greater opportunity to equip himself with a skill to fit an aspiration and more jobs from which to make the choice. It is in the city that he can best acquire the knowledge essential to identify more electives and strive for their attainment through a greater number of avenues. With all its distortions, the city remains the man-made means of facilitating escape from the bush into the world of mortals and mortar, newspapers and books, recreation and promise. It continues its ancient role as the haven of the censured and the misfits of the fields; of the inspired and the uninspired in search of animation; of the tired soul in quest of solitude, privacy, or seclusion; of those who seek fame and of the dishonored who seek anonymity; of the black and the brown looking for betterment among the white; of the beggar, the halt, the deviate, the lonely, and the old as well as the young and the enterprising.

Because the city is still where men and women assemble in market-places to sell and buy goods, they tend to tolerate each other's peculiarities if for no other reason than that a sale can be made, a bargain reaped, a cheaper hand hired. While they press for the freedom to buy and sell, they tend to support courts of justice that can enforce the contract and redress their wrongs. The marketplace and the widespread ownership of

---

[15] Estimate by Homer Hoyt, *Study of International Housing*, Subcommittee on Housing, Committee on Banking and Currency, United States Senate, 88th Congress, 1st Session, March 1963, p. 17.

land and shelter are still the seeds from which larger freedoms have grown and can continue to grow in the world's new societies.

Because people are nearer to one another in the city and because there are universities, streets, telephones, lawyers, publicans, friends, and newspapers, the molestation of an individual is harder to conceal. Today's city is nearer than ever before to the outside world and its examples, and there are more group organizations that serve as buffers between state and individual and through which protest can be made with greater immunity against reprisals. For all these reasons, the city that cradled freedom in the older industrial areas may yet cradle it in the new.

But the city with its privations, its poverty, homelessness, and overcrowding also offers more dangers today than in the past. Time is essential if the institutions that the city reinforces are not to weaken and if today's masses are not to become tomorrow's mob. In this sense, the failure to settle the problems of land distribution and housing in the world's cities threatens not only the industrialization programs of the developing world—it also threatens world stability.

Shelter and land play a vital role in the destiny of the city and in the reaffirmation of its values. But also at stake are the fate of the emerging societies, the freedoms they might help nourish and sustain, and the peaceful progress of nations within their own borders.

Index

THE M.I.T. PAPERBACK SERIES

K-73